KILL SHAKESPEARE

CREATED AND WRITTEN BY
Conor McCreery
and
Anthony Del Col

ART BY
Andy Belanger

COLORS BY
Ian Herring

LETTERING BY
Chris Mowry, Robbie Robbins, and Neil Uyetake

ORIGINAL SERIES EDITS BY
Tom Waltz

COLLECTION COVER BY
Kagan McLeod

COLLECTION DESIGN BY
Chris Mowry

COLLECTION EDITS BY
Justin Eisinger

www.IDWPUBLISHING.com

ISBN: 978-1-60010-781-8 13 12 11 10 1 2 3 4

IDW™

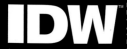

IDW Publishing is: Operations: Ted Adams, CEO & Publisher • Greg Goldstein, Chief Operating Officer • Matthew Ruzicka, CPA, Chief Financial Officer • Alan Payne, VP of Sales • Lorelei Bunjes, Director of Digital Services • Jeff Webber, Director of ePublishing • AnnaMaria White, Dir., Marketing and Public Relations • Dirk Wood, Dir., Retail Marketing • Marci Hubbard, Executive Assistant • Alonzo Simon, Shipping Manager • Angela Loggins, Staff Accountant • Cherrie Go, Assistant Web Designer • Editorial: Chris Ryall, Chief Creative Officer, Editor-In-Chief • Scott Dunbier, Senior Editor, Special Projects • Andy Schmidt, Senior Editor • Bob Schreck, Senior Editor • Justin Eisinger, Senior Editor, Books • Kris Oprisko, Editor/Foreign Lic. • Denton J. Tipton, Editor • Tom Waltz, Editor • Mariah Huehner, Editor • Carlos Guzman, Assistant Editor • Bobby Curnow, Assistant Editor • Design: Robbie Robbins, EVP/Sr. Graphic Artist • Neil Uyetake, Senior Art Director • Chris Mowry, Senior Graphic Artist • Amauri Osorio, Graphic Artist • Gilberto Lazcano, Production Assistant • Shawn Lee, Graphic Artist

Originally published as KILL SHAKESPEARE Issues #1–6.

I suppose we'll start this with my rather sketchy credentials: There is no love lost between myself and the Bard in question. As a matter of fact, in high school if someone had yelled "Kill Shakespeare" I'd have zealously seconded. My memories of high school Shakespeare are not unlike my memories of French language class: vague and irritating, like there was a different word for everything. Three pages into that muckety-muck and I'd gloss over and reach for a Ross MacDonald novel or a Detective Comic. Class discussion often amounted to the teacher reading the play a line at a time with a crushingly thorough translation of each word and phrase and cunning inference. For my story-starved teenage brain it was like being beaten to death with a dictionary in slow motion. My inability to fall into the old man's pentameters and rhythms kept me from enjoying his work on any level other than plot construction and basic character interplay.

That being said, here we are.

So let's look at this shiny new collection and see if we can figure out how these guys kept me from glossing over and reaching for the aforementioned MacDonald novel.

Comic creator and pundit Frank Santoro is a wise and passionate advocate of comics. He recently wrote:

> The market can now support multiple perspectives. It is not a monolithic community. There is no official definition of Comics now. It's too big. Finally 'comics' doesn't just mean American mainstream super-hero action adventure stories. (Well, comics never meant just that genre, but y'know what I'm saying: Marvel and DC have lorded over the form for almost 50 years.) In 2009 you can walk into a comics store like Copacetic Comics in Pittsburgh and see no superhero comics on display at all. There are enough "alternative" or "literary" comics/graphic novels out in the world to fill a whole (small) store. And there are "alternative" publishers who don't use (or are shut out from) the Direct Market and who use book trade distributors to get the work out to stores.
>
> So we got what you might call a bifurcated market. The two traditions, once folded together in the same market, have split. There are two sandboxes now. What that means is that if you grew up reading comics from, say, 1999 to now you didn't necessarily have to read superhero comics to get your comics fix or even go to a store that sold both. This is a good thing. It's a new audience, and a broader one than maybe any of us old school dinosaurs could have anticipated.

I couldn't agree more with Santoro's assessment. With such a broad area of opportunity available, is it possible to create entertaining comics that will attract an audience outside the superhero and artcomix demos? The more immediate question is: will it sell well enough to feed and clothe you? With a market this large and undefined, how can you be sure you're not going to fade into the sea of work on the shelves? I sense that this was top of mind for Anthony and Conor when they built this project, much as it was on my mind when I began looking at my first book outside the big two. The answer is, if you're worried that no one at the party will recognize you, bring a famous friend along. For myself, that was an amoral thief named Parker and his Grand Master, Donald Westlake. These guys... well, let's just say they started at the top.

The title alone is a work of genius. *Kill Shakespeare*. I could spend a lifetime in a climate-controlled room full of monkeys with a monolithic story title matrix running 24-7 and it would never produce a better, more provocative title.

Then we have a premise that lives up to the title. All of Shakespeare's "creations" live in a kingdom ruled by their deity: the Bard himself. The good and evil forces within this kingdom are in a race to possess the Bard's mythical quill—the source of all power and life.

Here is the point in most independent projects where after a promising launch and another spotty issue or two everything fades away. To mount a project of this size, you need more than a catchy title and an evocative premise to drive your passion to create. You need to be entrepreneur as well as artist. You need the vision and

...oresight to construct a solid long-term plan and then find a way to finance that plan through to its conclusion. ...o you hear that? *Really* hear that? Because it's a lot tougher than it sounds. Weeks and perhaps months of ...haping your premise into an entertaining story that lasts 12 issues. Endless rounds of potentially humiliating ...meetings with potentially helpful investors, using your charm and passion to convince them to put their money where your mouth is. The horrifying work of attracting and auditing a publisher that you trust to give your efforts the best leg up in the market. Then there's the actual creation of the work, the damned endless stream of pages needed to fuel serial fiction of a periodic nature. Once you're actually in the shit, say, working on issue four or five, you're juggling three issues through various stages of creation/production, you're coordinating with your publisher, editor, and printer, you're tracking sales and evaluating what's working and what isn't, you're doing all the press you can. Signings. Misprints. Paying people in a timely fashion.

If the above paragraph was an old EC Horror comic, the shock ending would be "And now, do it all in your spare time because you need to stay at your day job if you want to keep yourself in Ramen and cut-rate California wine! Ha ha ha ha!"

What I'm saying is it takes gigantic, Vegas-sized gambler balls and a work ethic to match to pour this kind of effort into something with no guaranteed outcome. So before I even opened the first issue, they had my professional admiration.

From a storytelling standpoint, I was impressed. Deft handling of dozens of known characters and a quest-driven plot that keeps the story rolling forward. Classically retarded individuals such as myself with only a passing knowledge of these characters are given everything we need to enjoy the story without having to read dense thickets of expository narrative. For example, I remembered that Othello had a "brother," but not his name or personality. In *KS* this all comes out organically, through dialogue and action. I never feel I need to research to enjoy the current chapter. Visually, Belanger has had the sense to commit an ocean of time to design so the reader is immersed in a convincing "world" where these characters live and breathe. There's no cheating on backgrounds here or vague scumbling—I have no idea if the details are authentic but they're executed with a clarity and confidence that convinces.

My only problem with *KS* is that I always thought Hamlet was a bit of an emo douche. Am I right? He's like the hole in the donut of life. Always whining. I suspect that the boys have a long-term character arc that will make a man out of him.

So my hat is off to these young men.* They're pragmatic enough to create something with obvious market potential and universal recognition and passionate enough to actually follow through and produce quality work.

Imagine fifty such tight creative teams at work today. That is where the mass market will "discover" us. Again. It probably won't even be in print form. It certainly won't be through four-dollar "super-jock" floppies or artfully crafted lit-comics. It will come through entertainment with broad appeal and creative execution.

Darwyn Cooke
2010
Just East of Burnham Wood

*I'd like to note that my hat is also off to me for sparing you, dear reader, the obvious comparisons to the LOEG template and for not using an actual quote from Shakespeare during this entire introduction. Y'know something horrible like, "Read on, MacDuff!"

Darwyn Cooke is an Eisner and Harvey Award-winning comics creator whose major works include DC: The New Frontier, Selina's Big Score, The Spirit, and adaptations of Richard Stark's Parker novels, including The Hunter...

WE CAN NO OTHER ANSWER MAKE BUT THANKS, AND THANKS...

What an incredible journey this has been thus far... We have so many supporting players we wish to credit in this adventure...

Owen and Elizabeth McCreery, Brian McCreery, Anna Del Col, Jim and Marianne Del Col, Jennifer Heath, Crystal Luxmore, Trina Mendoza, Mom and Pop Belanger, The Belanger Brothers, Vanessa King, Anthony Iantomo, Jeremy Boxen, Sir Tom Stoppard, Arvid Nelson, Dave Elliott, Becka Kinzie, Arwen Savage, Darwyn Cooke, J. Bone, Ty Templeton, Ramon Perez, Kalman Andrasofszky, Scott Hepburn, Willow Dawson, Cameron Stewart, Stuart and Kathryn Immonen, Mike Cho, Kwanza Johnson, Ben Abernathy, Ron Perazza, Kody Peters, George Zotti, Chris Butcher, Doug Simpson, Kevin Boyd, Gina Gagliano, Martha Cornog, Simon Dimuantes, Kuo-Yu Liang, Calvin Reid, Rich Johnston, Mark Askwith, Sarah Hashem, CYBF, Josh Howard, Chris Smith, Sharon Fleming, Ted Fleming, Frank Galea, Andrew Apangu, Al Bugeja, Rob Chiasson, Steve Lawlor, Sarah Stevens, Debby de Groot, Lonnie McCullough, Dan Smith, Jason Chan, Spencer Rysdale, Tony Kramreither, Michael Ball, Danielle Restivo, Marla Boltman, Jethro Bushenbaum, Clement Wan, Samir Jain.

Every single person at IDW and Diamond — they have been a pleasure to work with — but especially Chris Mowry for all his hard work.

Every writer, blogger, podcaster, reader, and fan who has talked to us — or others — about our series.

And, of course, the big man himself... William Shakespeare (or Sir Francis Bacon, Christopher Marlowe, or Edward De Vere...)!

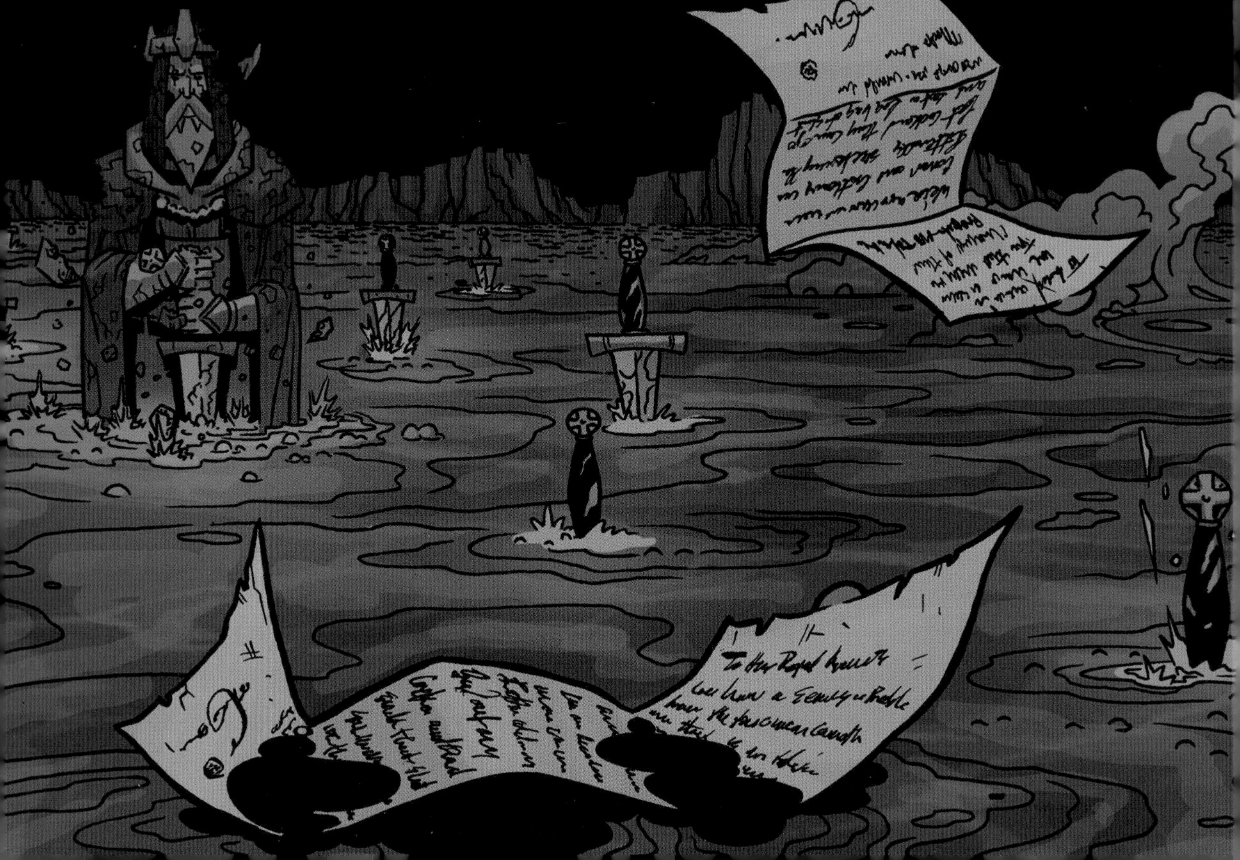

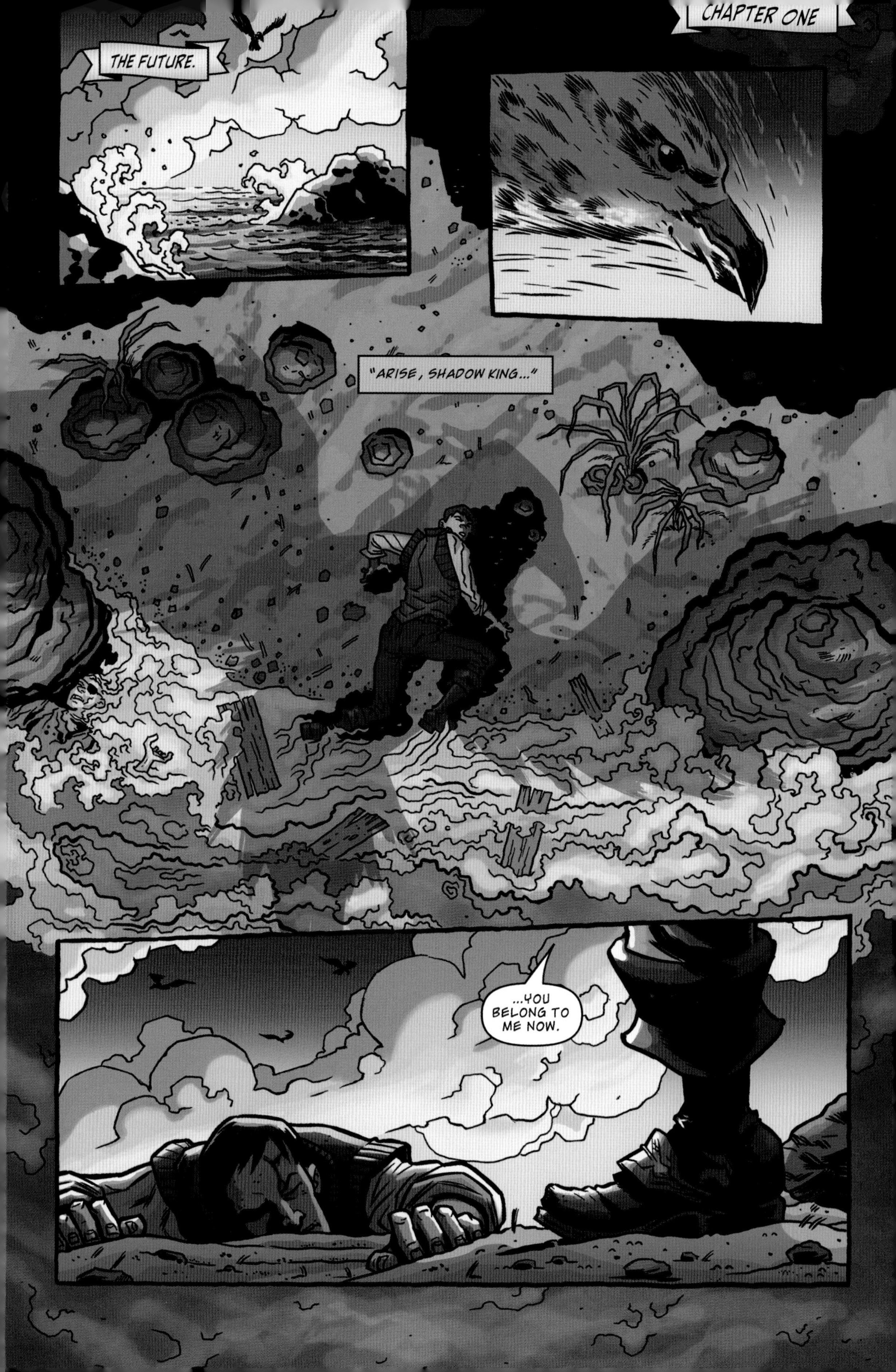
CHAPTER ONE
THE FUTURE.
"ARISE, SHADOW KING..."
...YOU BELONG TO ME NOW.

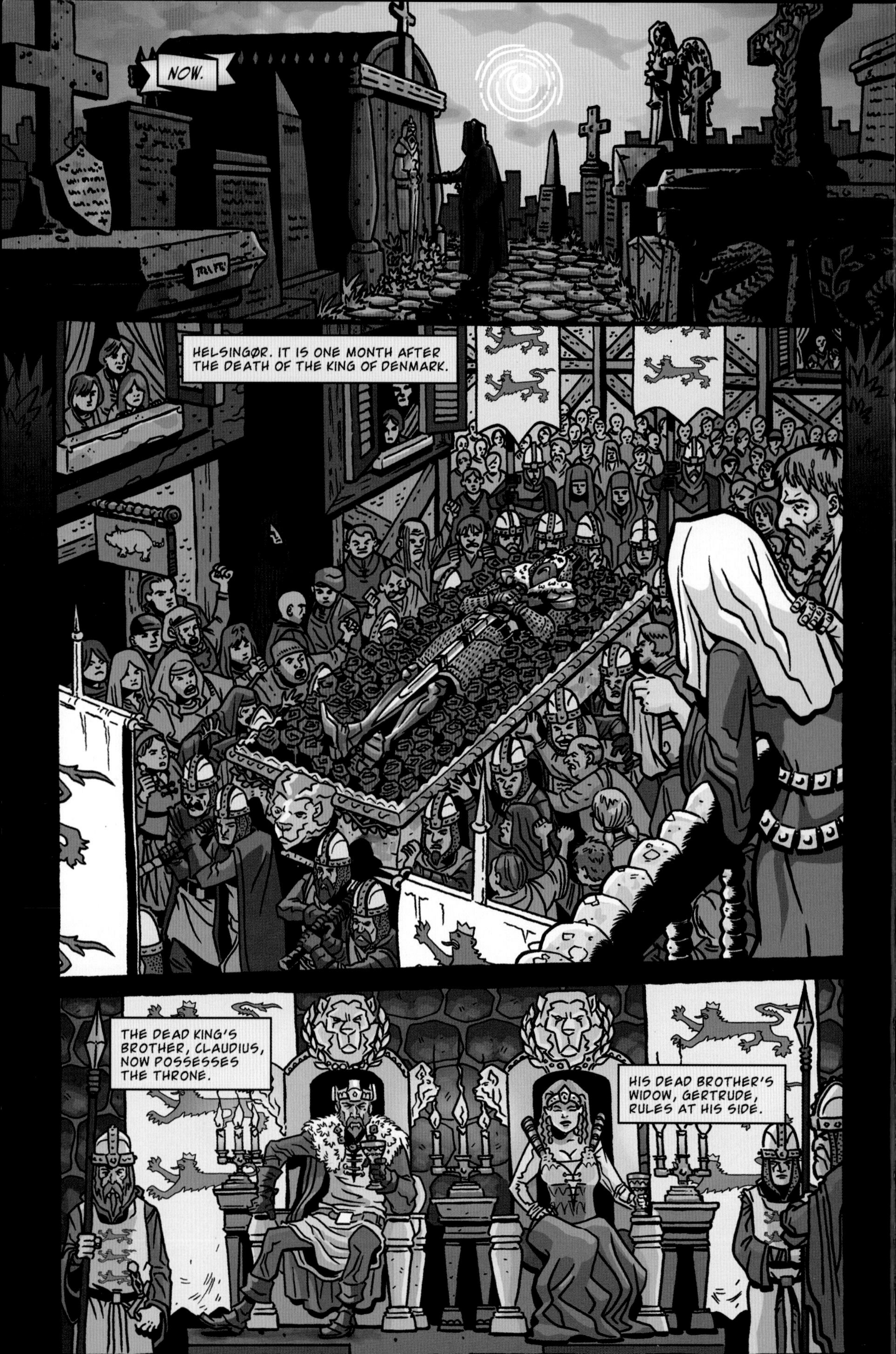
NOW.
HELSINGØR. IT IS ONE MONTH AFTER THE DEATH OF THE KING OF DENMARK.
THE DEAD KING'S BROTHER, CLAUDIUS, NOW POSSESSES THE THRONE.
HIS DEAD BROTHER'S WIDOW, GERTRUDE, RULES AT HIS SIDE.

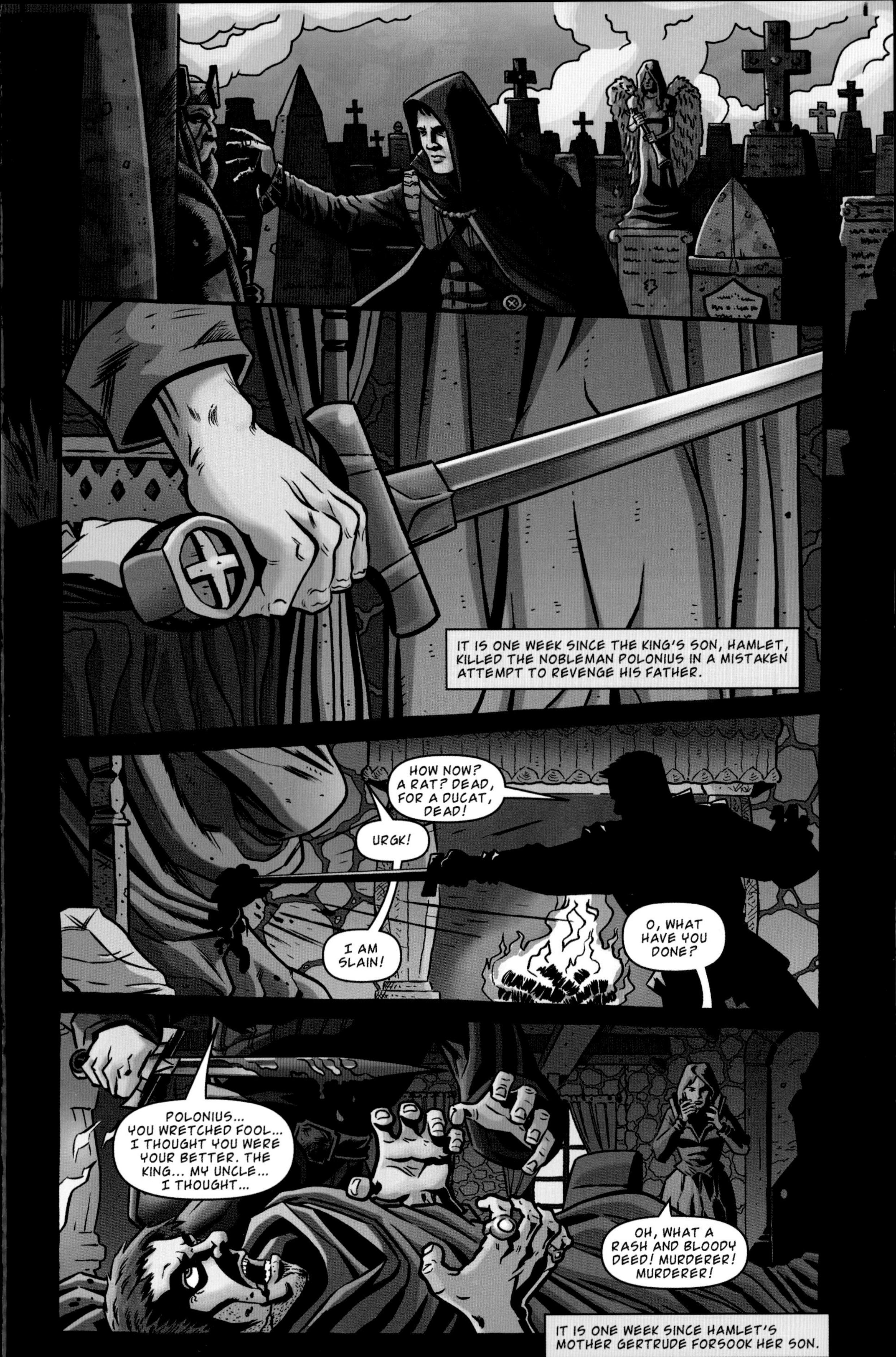
IT IS ONE WEEK SINCE THE KING'S SON, HAMLET, KILLED THE NOBLEMAN POLONIUS IN A MISTAKEN ATTEMPT TO REVENGE HIS FATHER.
HOW NOW? A RAT? DEAD, FOR A DUCAT, DEAD!
URGK!
I AM SLAIN!
O, WHAT HAVE YOU DONE?
POLONIUS... YOU WRETCHED FOOL... I THOUGHT YOU WERE YOUR BETTER. THE KING... MY UNCLE... I THOUGHT...
OH, WHAT A RASH AND BLOODY DEED! MURDERER! MURDERER!
IT IS ONE WEEK SINCE HAMLET'S MOTHER GERTRUDE FORSOOK HER SON.

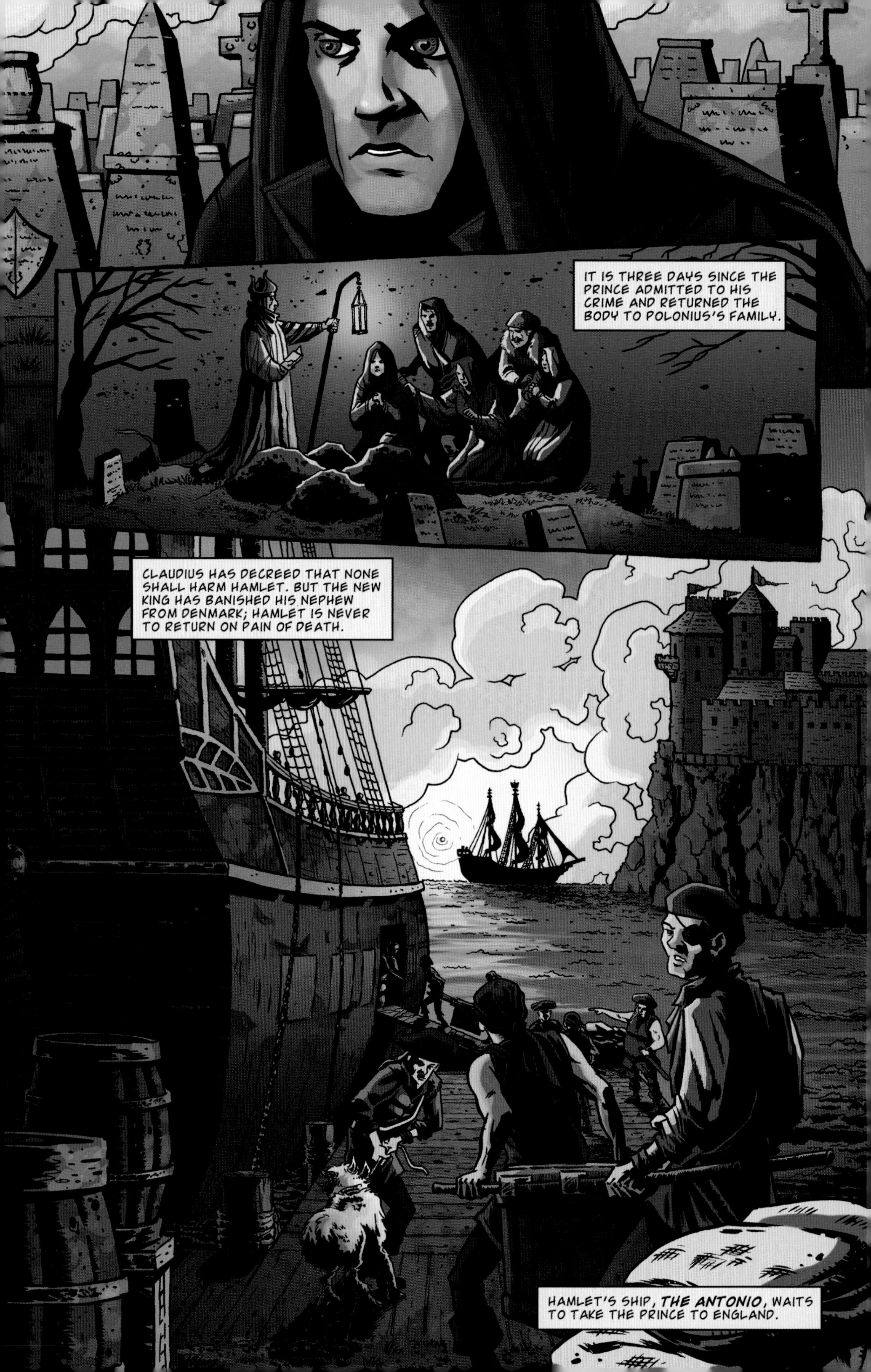
IT IS THREE DAYS SINCE THE PRINCE ADMITTED TO HIS CRIME AND RETURNED THE BODY TO POLONIUS'S FAMILY.
CLAUDIUS HAS DECREED THAT NONE SHALL HARM HAMLET. BUT THE NEW KING HAS BANISHED HIS NEPHEW FROM DENMARK; HAMLET IS NEVER TO RETURN ON PAIN OF DEATH.
HAMLET'S SHIP, *THE ANTONIO*, WAITS TO TAKE THE PRINCE TO ENGLAND.

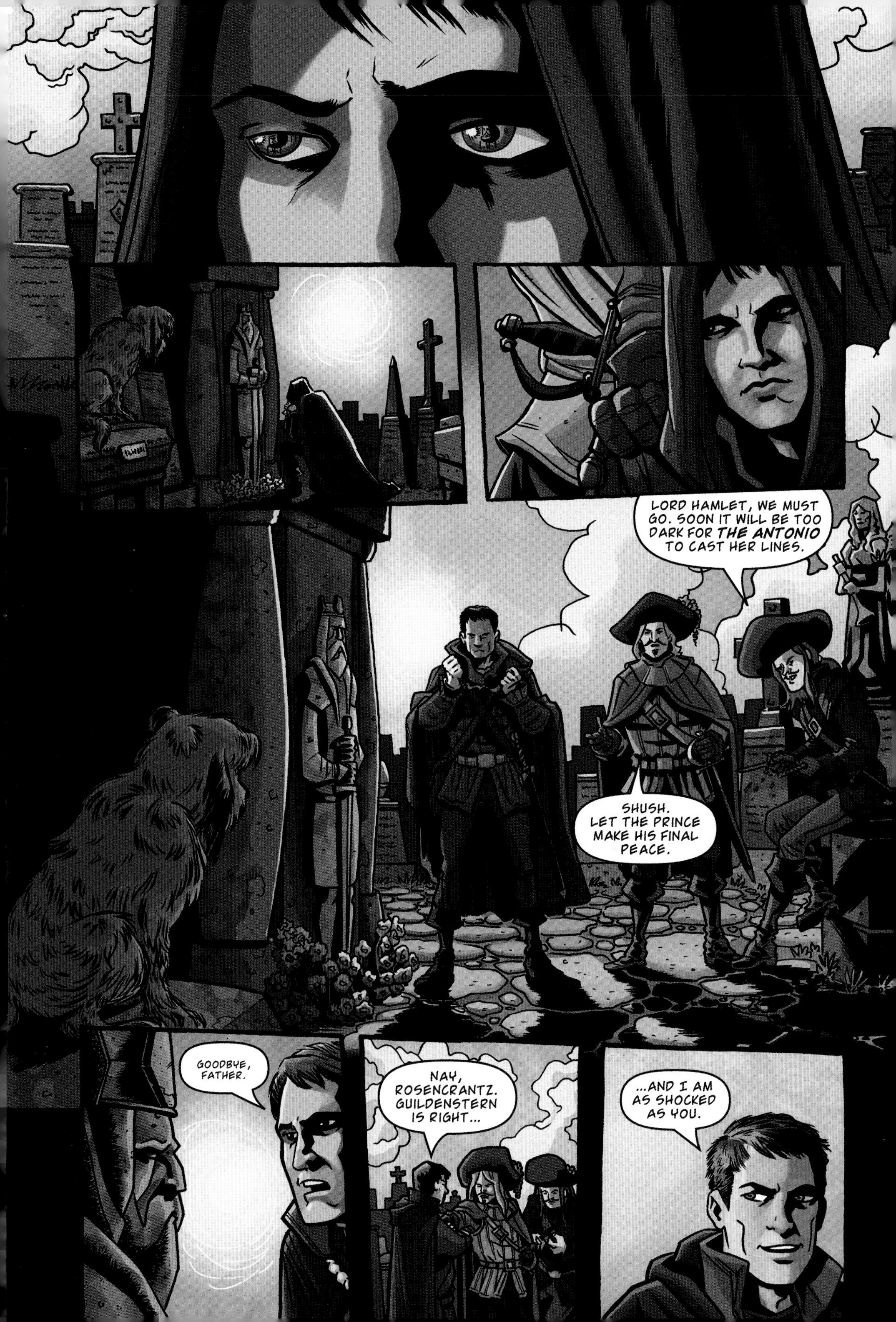
LORD HAMLET, WE MUST GO. SOON IT WILL BE TOO DARK FOR *THE ANTONIO* TO CAST HER LINES.
SHUSH. LET THE PRINCE MAKE HIS FINAL PEACE.
GOODBYE, FATHER.
NAY, ROSENCRANTZ. GUILDENSTERN IS RIGHT...
...AND I AM AS SHOCKED AS YOU.

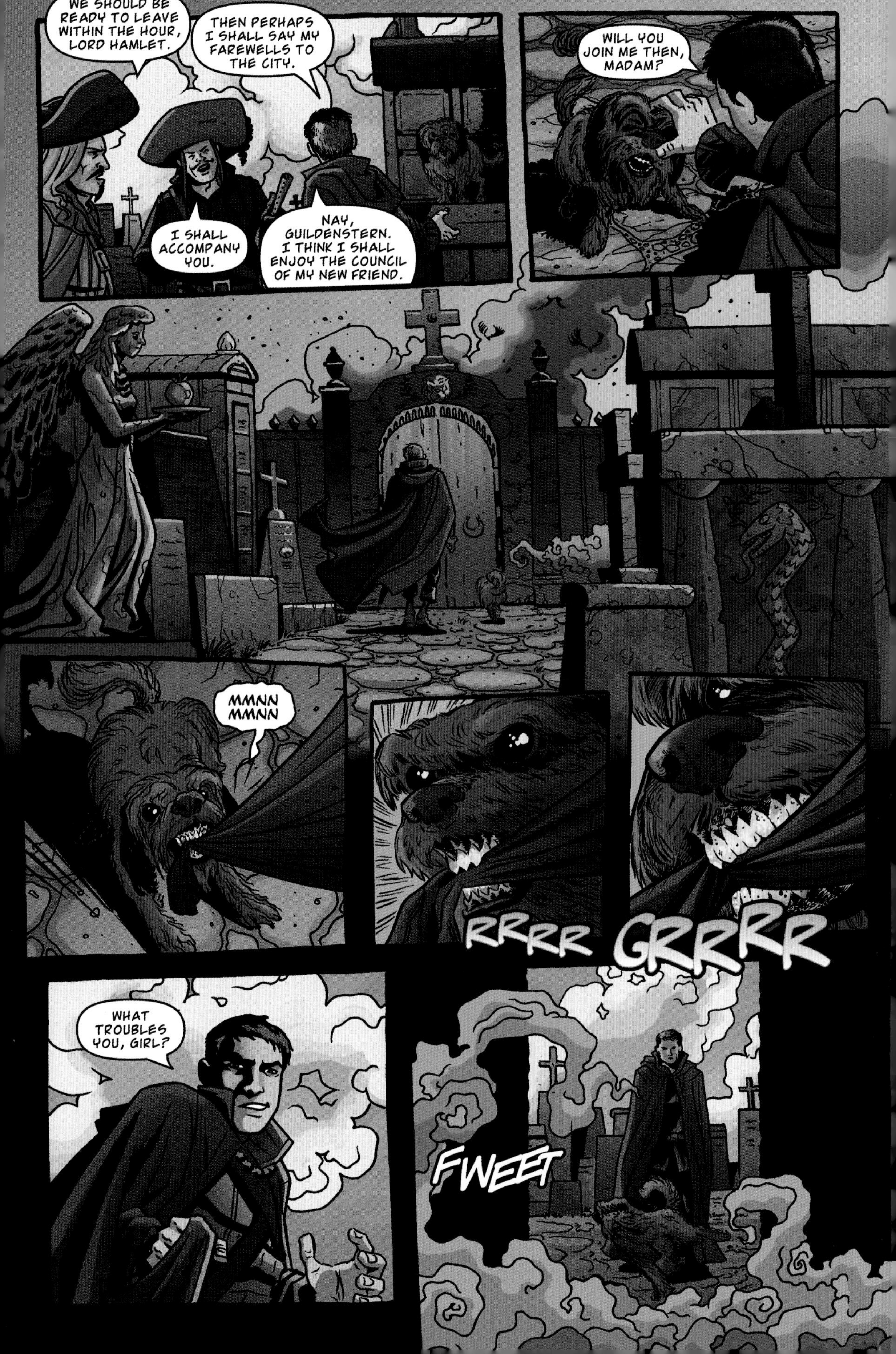
WE SHOULD BE READY TO LEAVE WITHIN THE HOUR, LORD HAMLET.
THEN PERHAPS I SHALL SAY MY FAREWELLS TO THE CITY.
I SHALL ACCOMPANY YOU.
NAY, GUILDENSTERN. I THINK I SHALL ENJOY THE COUNCIL OF MY NEW FRIEND.
WILL YOU JOIN ME THEN, MADAM?
MMNN MMNN
RRRR GRRRR
WHAT TROUBLES YOU, GIRL?
FWEET

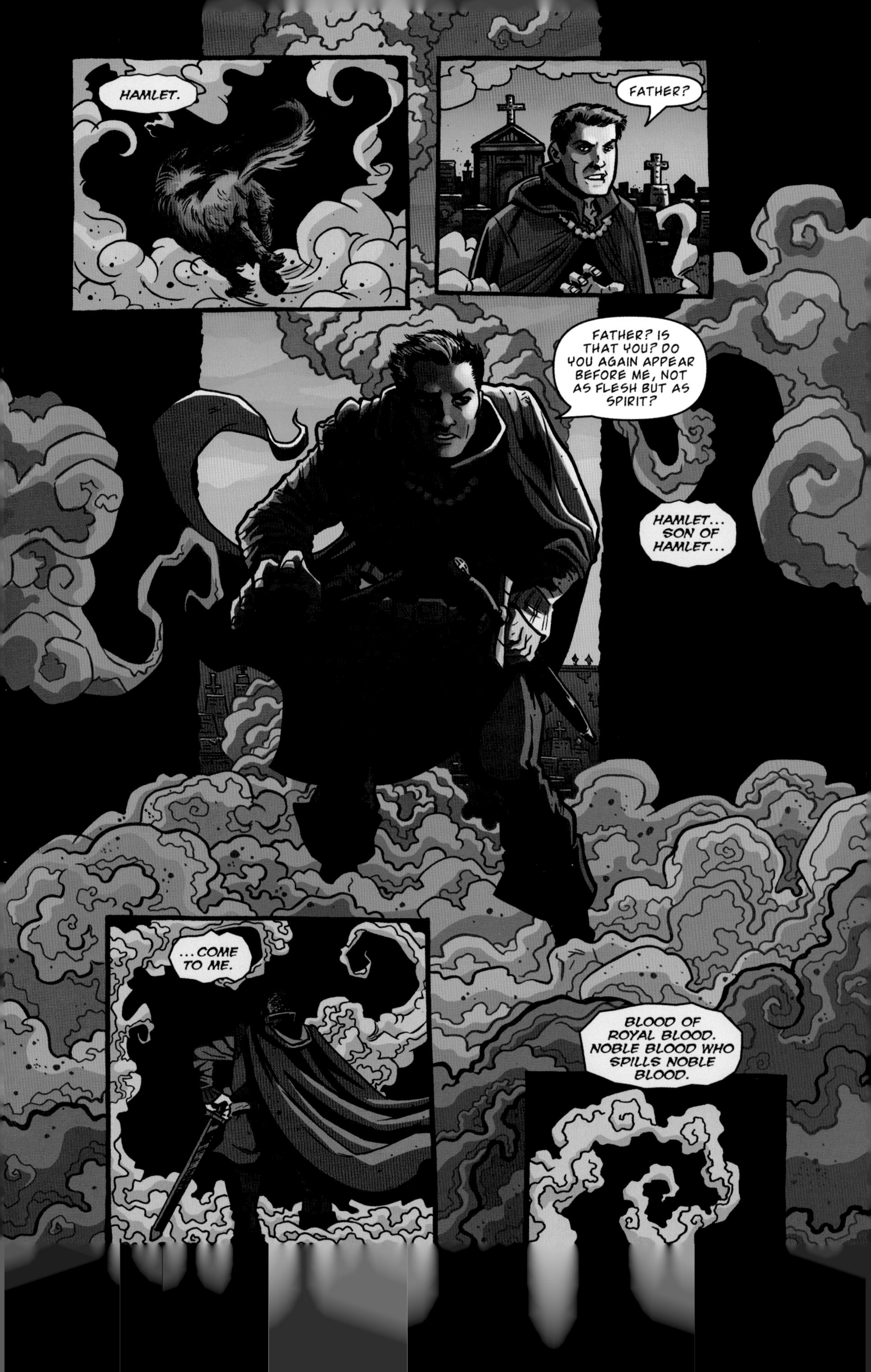
HAMLET.
FATHER?
FATHER? IS THAT YOU? DO YOU AGAIN APPEAR BEFORE ME, NOT AS FLESH BUT AS SPIRIT?
HAMLET... SON OF HAMLET...
...COME TO ME.
BLOOD OF ROYAL BLOOD. NOBLE BLOOD WHO SPILLS NOBLE BLOOD.

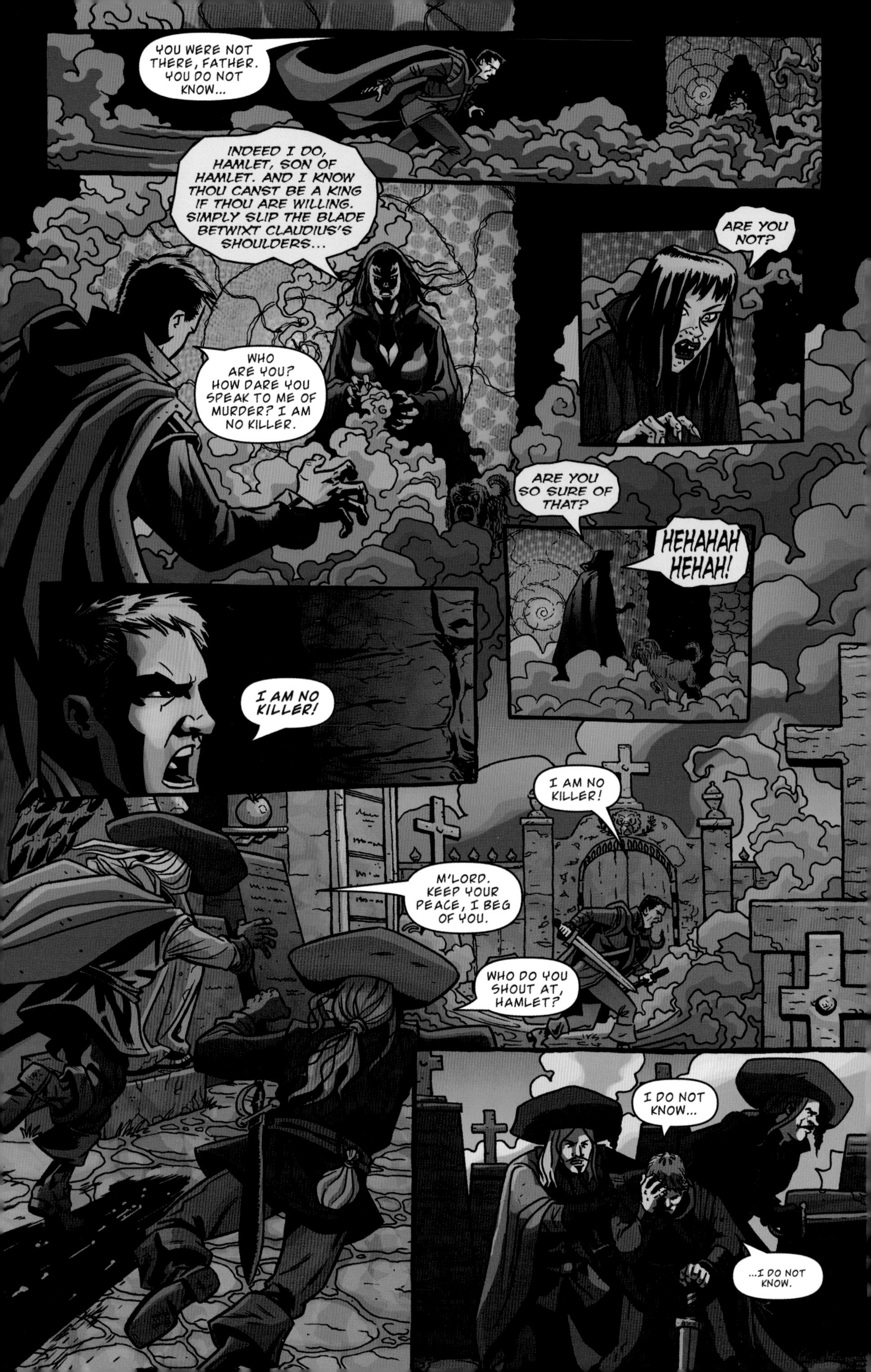
YOU WERE NOT THERE, FATHER. YOU DO NOT KNOW...
INDEED I DO, HAMLET, SON OF HAMLET. AND I KNOW THOU CANST BE A KING IF THOU ARE WILLING. SIMPLY SLIP THE BLADE BETWIXT CLAUDIUS'S SHOULDERS...
WHO ARE YOU? HOW DARE YOU SPEAK TO ME OF MURDER? I AM NO KILLER.
ARE YOU NOT?
ARE YOU SO SURE OF THAT?
HEHAHAH HEHAH!
I AM NO KILLER!
I AM NO KILLER!
M'LORD. KEEP YOUR PEACE, I BEG OF YOU.
WHO DO YOU SHOUT AT, HAMLET?
I DO NOT KNOW...
...I DO NOT KNOW.

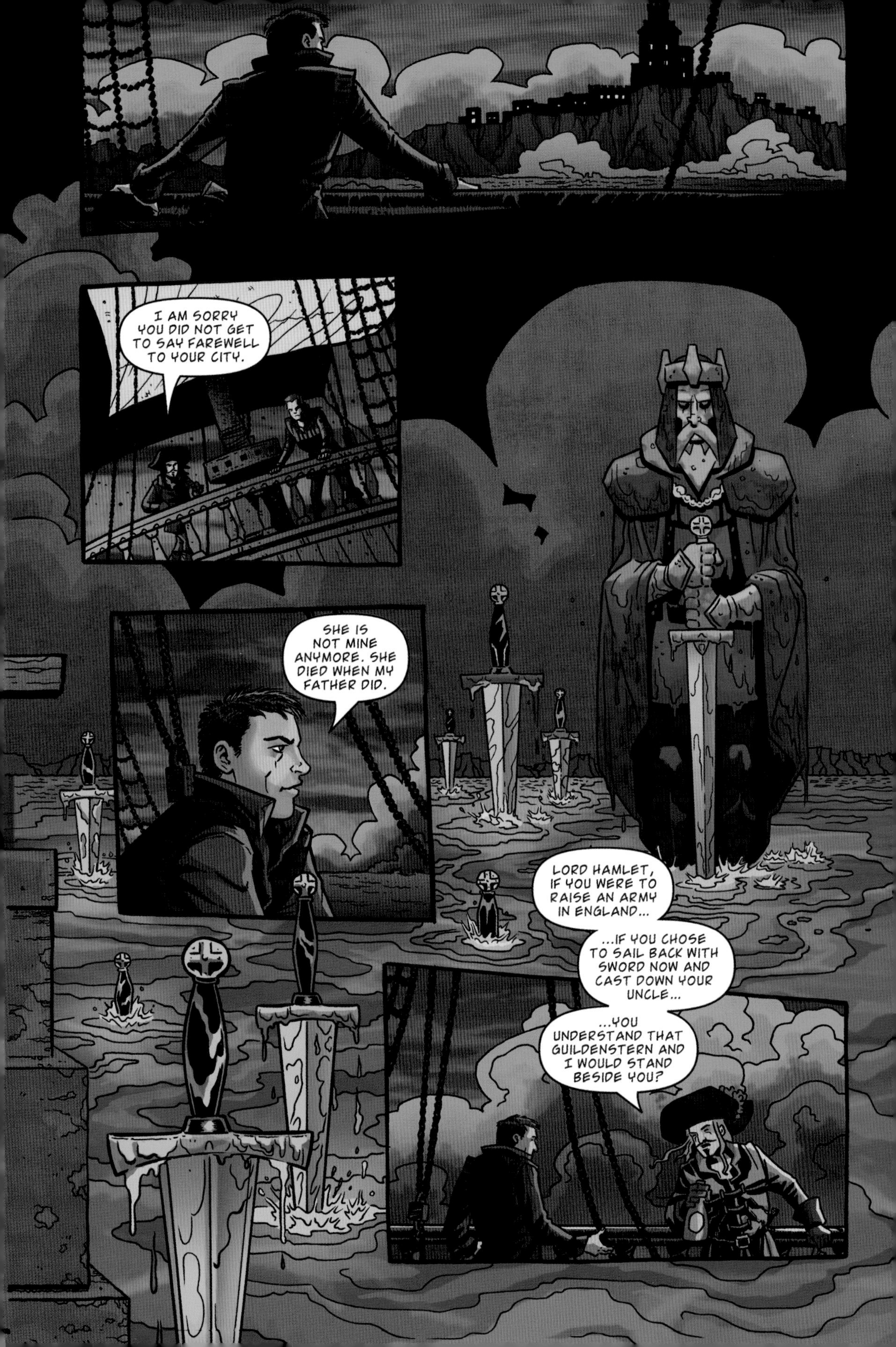
I AM SORRY YOU DID NOT GET TO SAY FAREWELL TO YOUR CITY.
SHE IS NOT MINE ANYMORE. SHE DIED WHEN MY FATHER DID.
LORD HAMLET, IF YOU WERE TO RAISE AN ARMY IN ENGLAND...
...IF YOU CHOSE TO SAIL BACK WITH SWORD NOW AND CAST DOWN YOUR UNCLE...
...YOU UNDERSTAND THAT GUILDENSTERN AND I WOULD STAND BESIDE YOU?

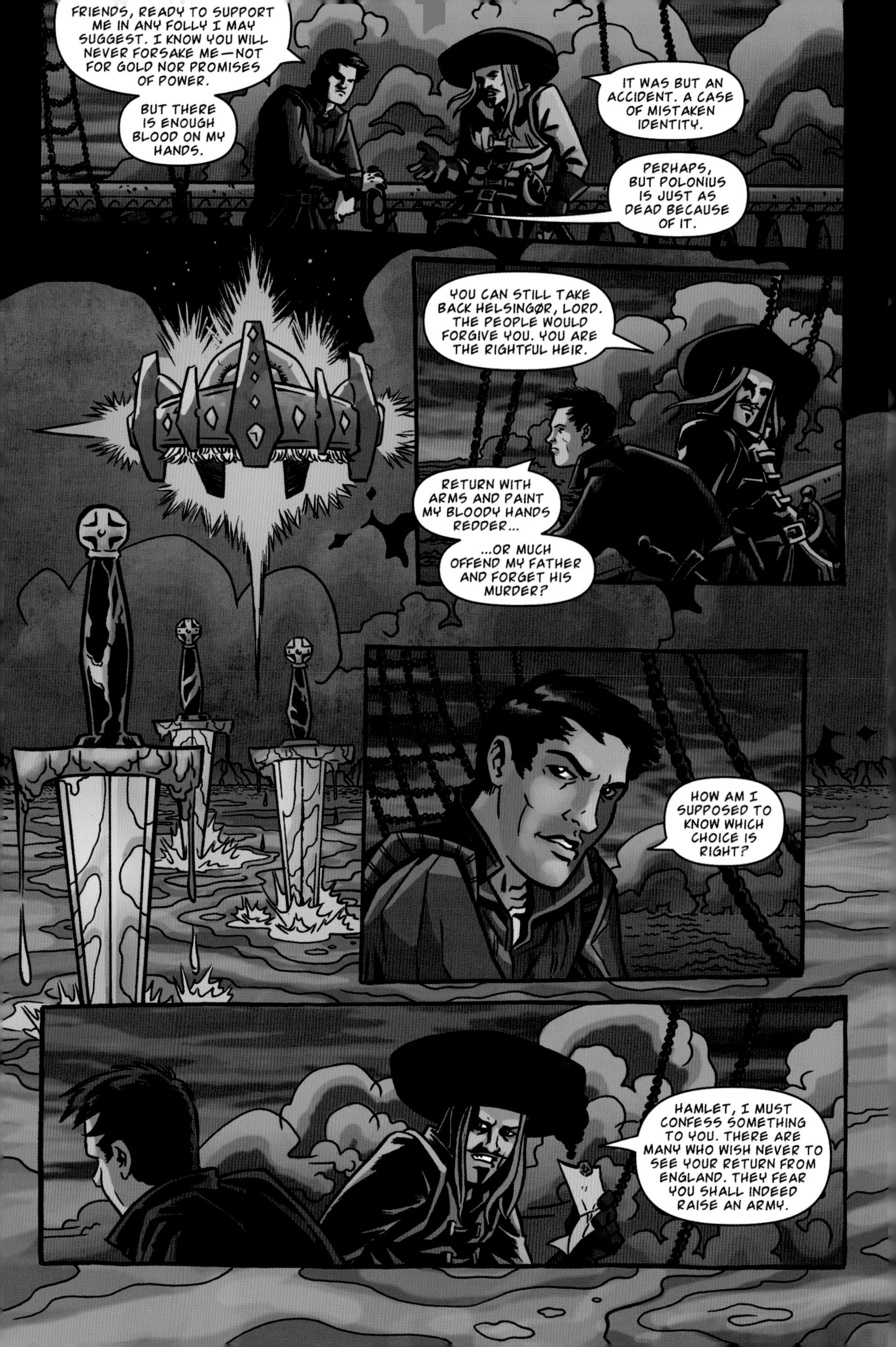
FRIENDS, READY TO SUPPORT ME IN ANY FOLLY I MAY SUGGEST. I KNOW YOU WILL NEVER FORSAKE ME—NOT FOR GOLD NOR PROMISES OF POWER.
BUT THERE IS ENOUGH BLOOD ON MY HANDS.
IT WAS BUT AN ACCIDENT. A CASE OF MISTAKEN IDENTITY.
PERHAPS, BUT POLONIUS IS JUST AS DEAD BECAUSE OF IT.
YOU CAN STILL TAKE BACK HELSINGØR, LORD. THE PEOPLE WOULD FORGIVE YOU. YOU ARE THE RIGHTFUL HEIR.
RETURN WITH ARMS AND PAINT MY BLOODY HANDS REDDER...
...OR MUCH OFFEND MY FATHER AND FORGET HIS MURDER?
HOW AM I SUPPOSED TO KNOW WHICH CHOICE IS RIGHT?
HAMLET, I MUST CONFESS SOMETHING TO YOU. THERE ARE MANY WHO WISH NEVER TO SEE YOUR RETURN FROM ENGLAND. THEY FEAR YOU SHALL INDEED RAISE AN ARMY.

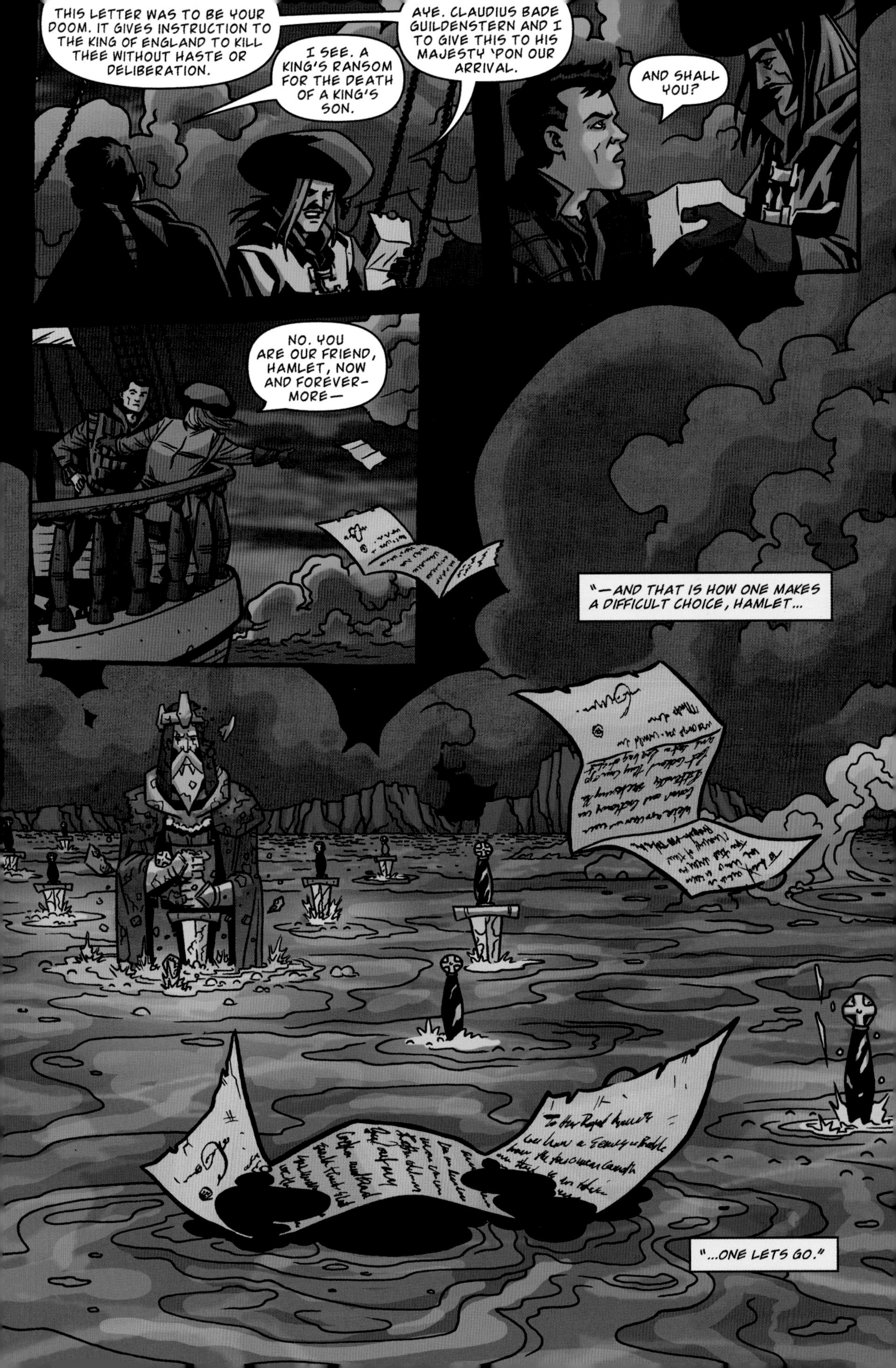
THIS LETTER WAS TO BE YOUR DOOM. IT GIVES INSTRUCTION TO THE KING OF ENGLAND TO KILL THEE WITHOUT HASTE OR DELIBERATION.
I SEE. A KING'S RANSOM FOR THE DEATH OF A KING'S SON.
AYE. CLAUDIUS BADE GUILDENSTERN AND I TO GIVE THIS TO HIS MAJESTY 'PON OUR ARRIVAL.
AND SHALL YOU?
NO. YOU ARE OUR FRIEND, HAMLET, NOW AND FOREVER-MORE—
"—AND THAT IS HOW ONE MAKES A DIFFICULT CHOICE, HAMLET...
"...ONE LETS GO."

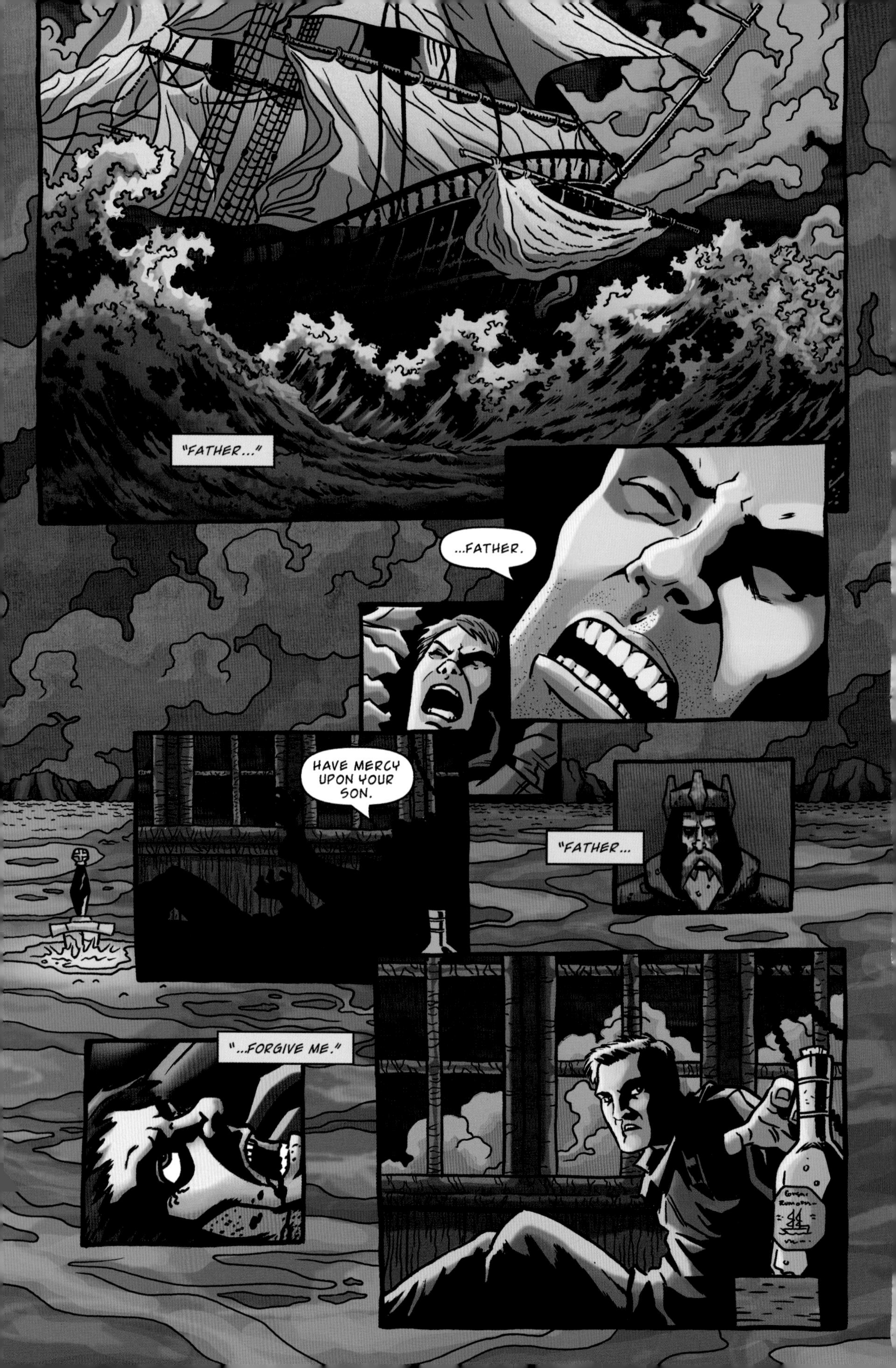
"FATHER..."
...FATHER.
HAVE MERCY UPON YOUR SON.
"FATHER...
"...FORGIVE ME."

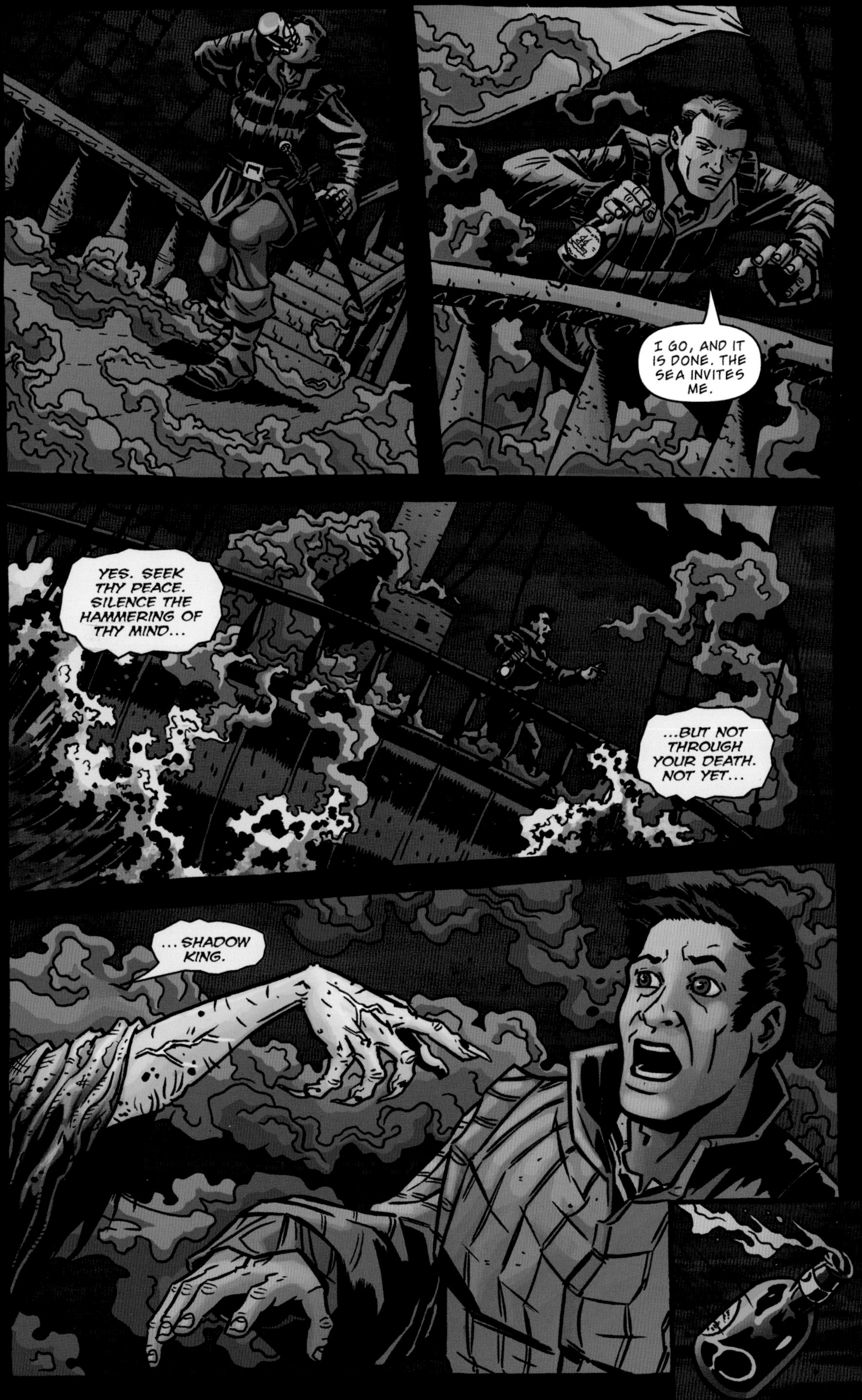
I GO, AND IT IS DONE. THE SEA INVITES ME.
YES. SEEK THY PEACE. SILENCE THE HAMMERING OF THY MIND...
...BUT NOT THROUGH YOUR DEATH. NOT YET...
...SHADOW KING.

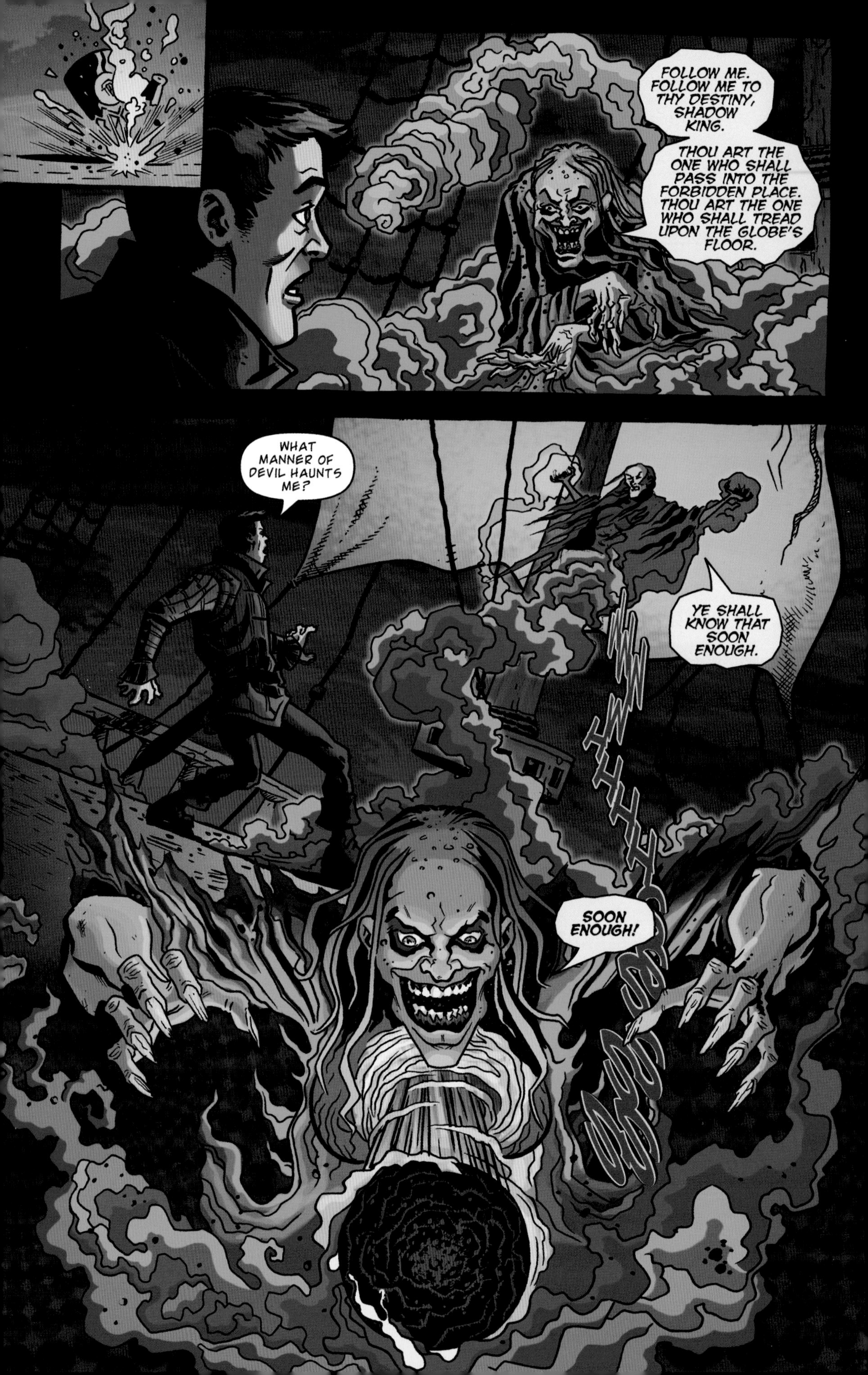
FOLLOW ME. FOLLOW ME TO THY DESTINY, SHADOW KING.
THOU ART THE ONE WHO SHALL PASS INTO THE FORBIDDEN PLACE. THOU ART THE ONE WHO SHALL TREAD UPON THE GLOBE'S FLOOR.
WHAT MANNER OF DEVIL HAUNTS ME?
YE SHALL KNOW THAT SOON ENOUGH.
SOON ENOUGH!

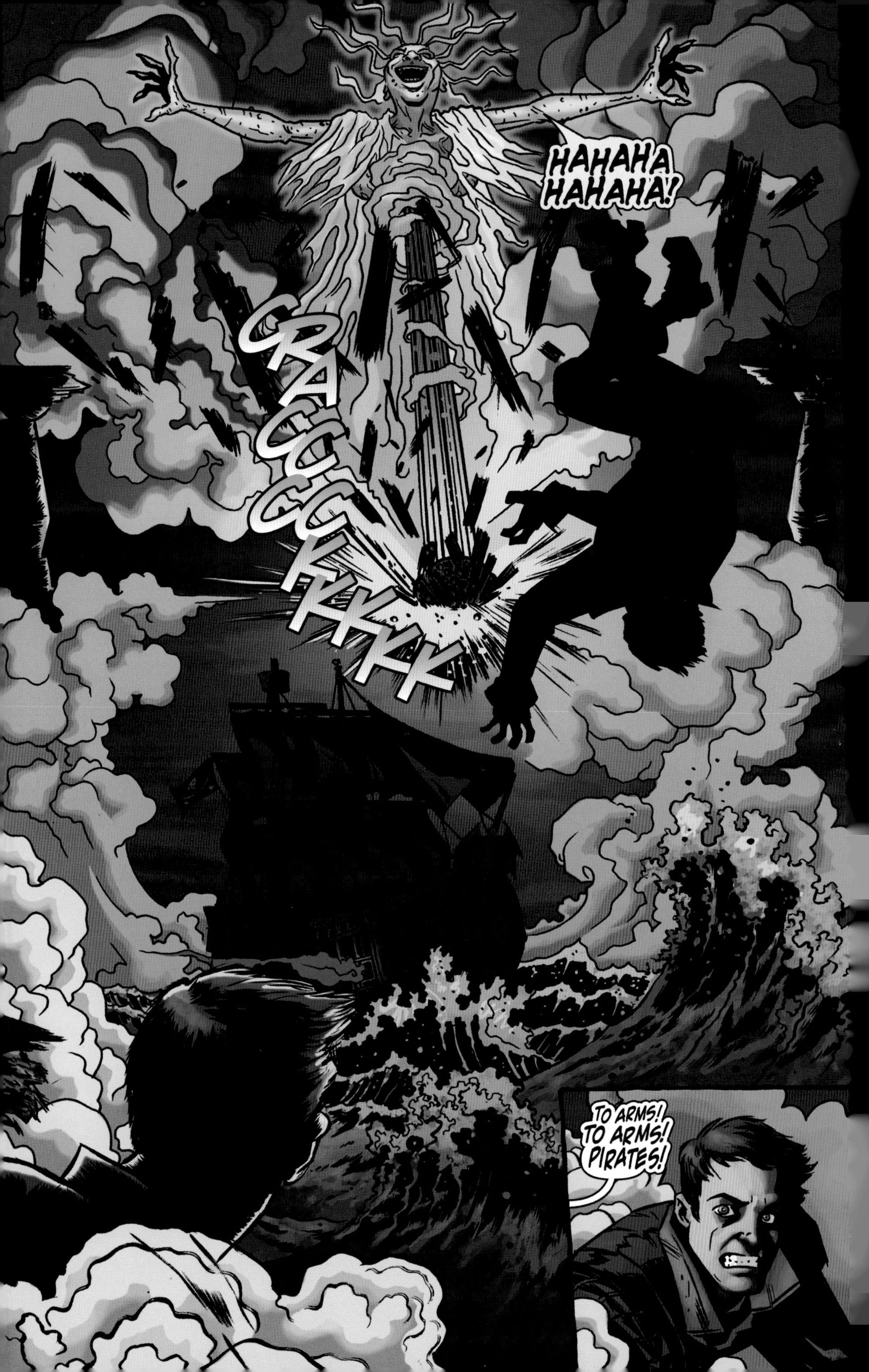
HAHAHA HAHAHA!
CRACCCKKKK
TO ARMS! TO ARMS! PIRATES!

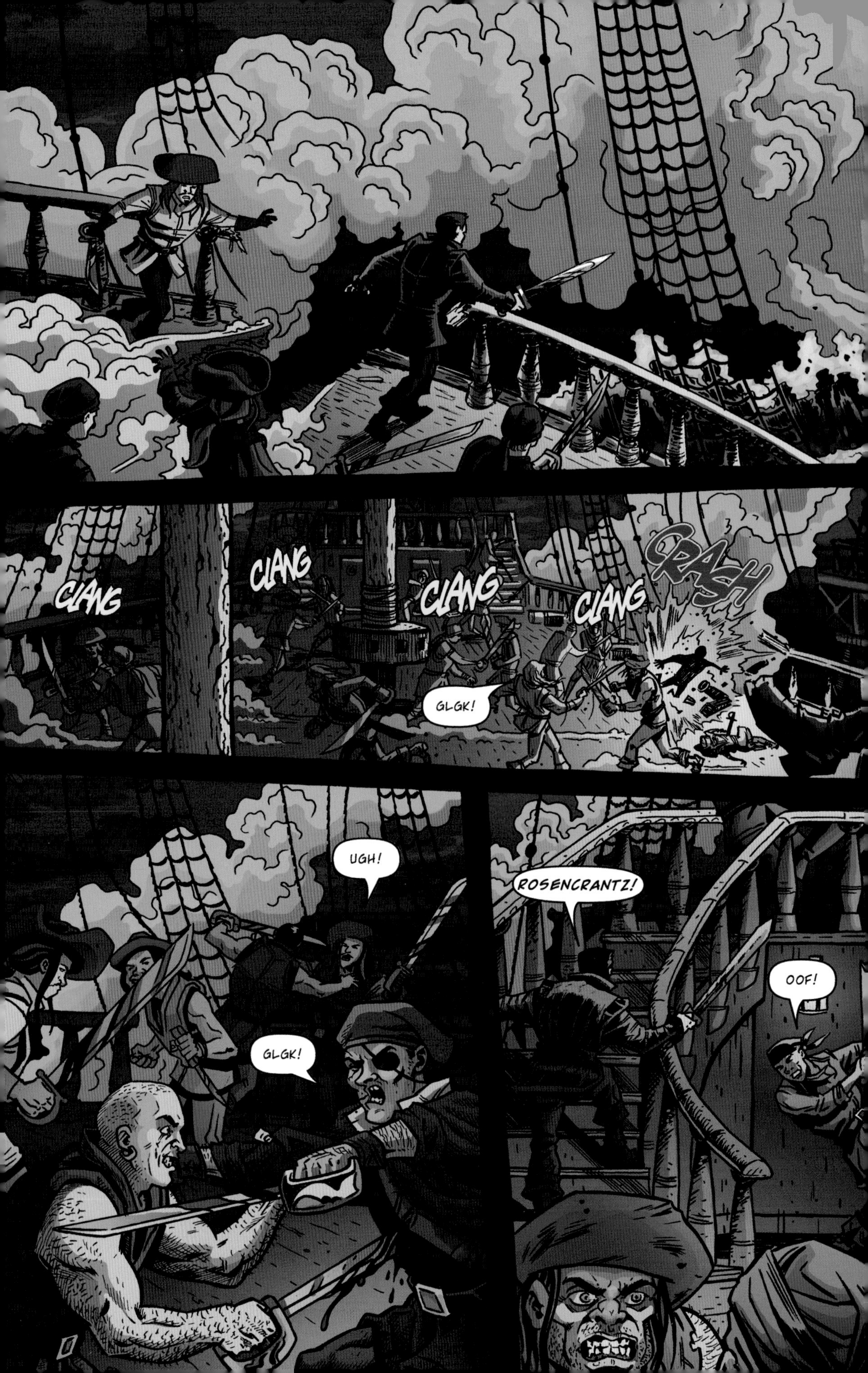
CLANG
CLANG
CLANG
CLANG
CRASH
GLGK!
UGH!
GLGK!
ROSENCRANTZ!
OOF!

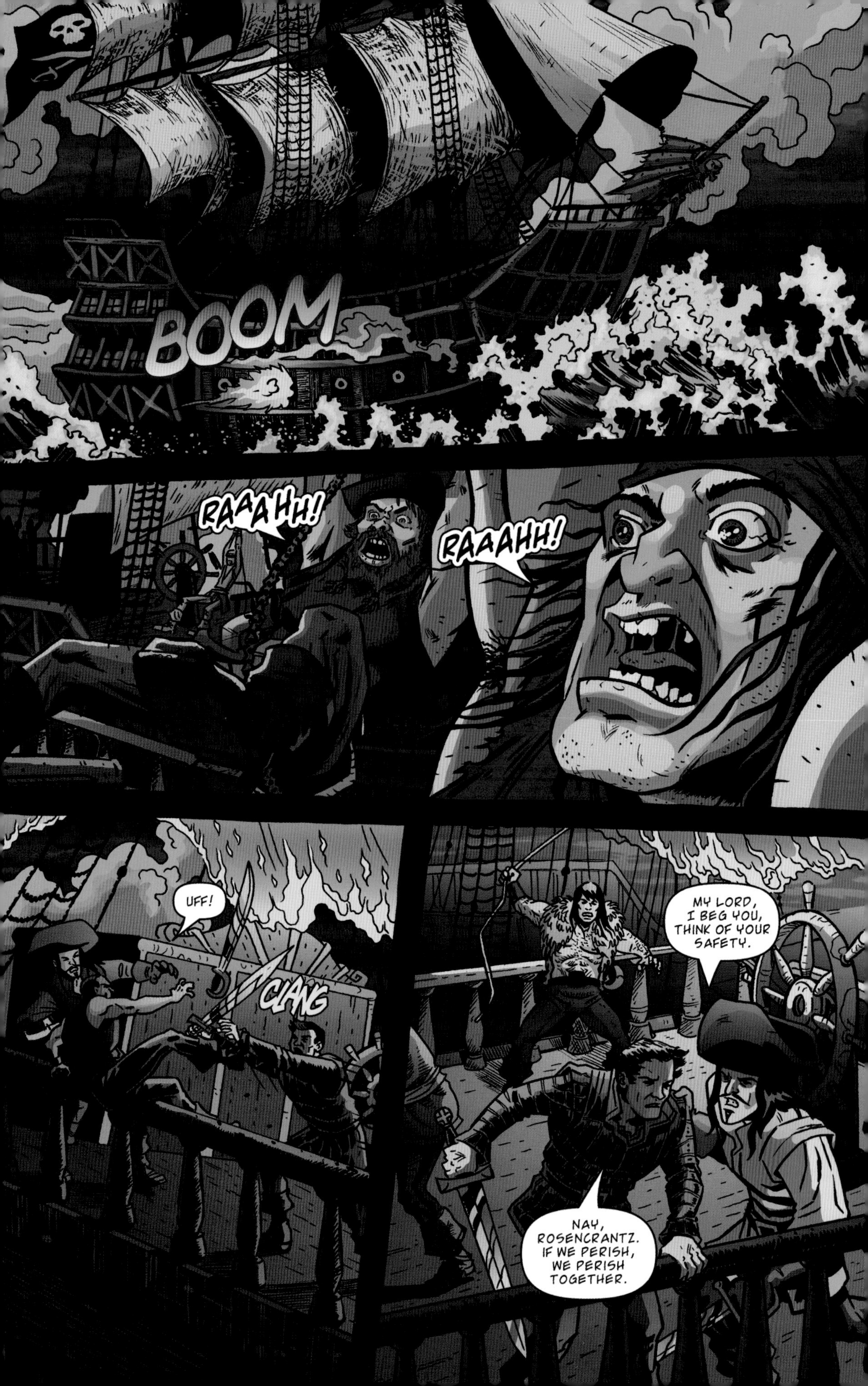
BOOM
RAAAHH!
RAAAHH!
UFF!
CLANG
MY LORD, I BEG YOU, THINK OF YOUR SAFETY.
NAY, ROSENCRANTZ. IF WE PERISH, WE PERISH TOGETHER.

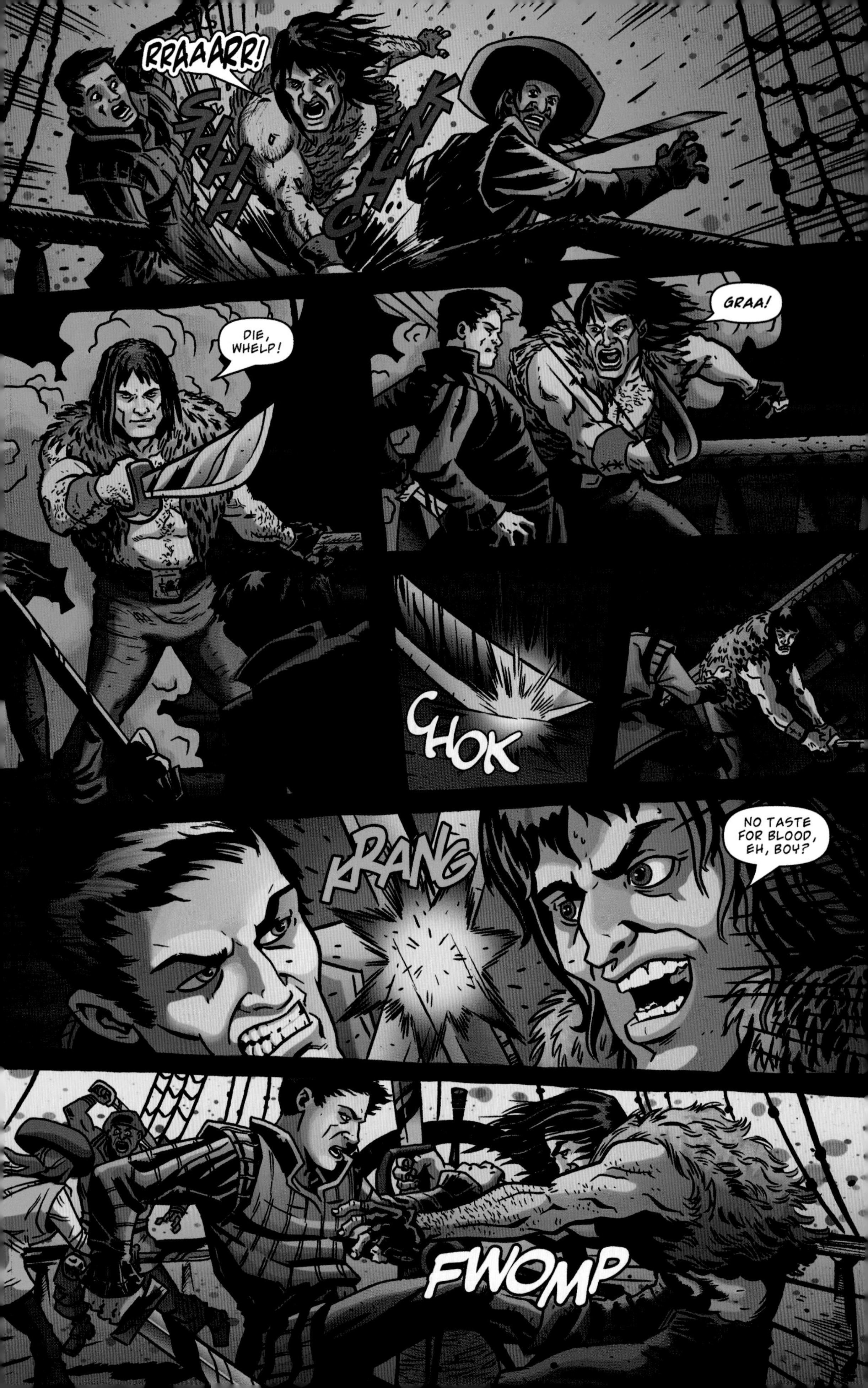

RRAAARR!
SHHH
CHUNK
DIE, WHELP!
GRAA!
CHOK
KRANG
NO TASTE FOR BLOOD, EH, BOY?
FWOMP

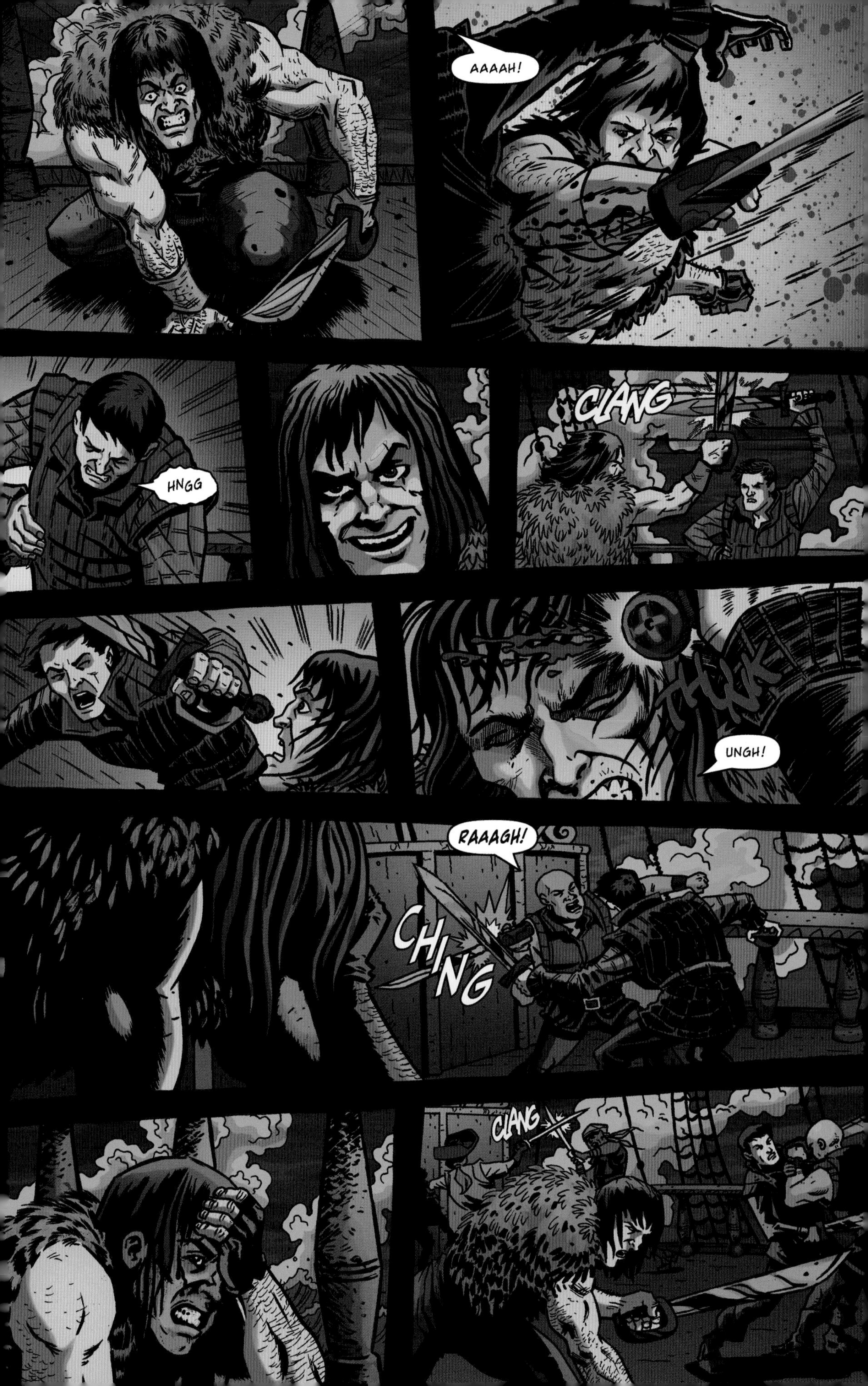
AAAAH!
HNGG
CLANG
THUK
UNGH!
RAAAGH!
CHING
CLANG

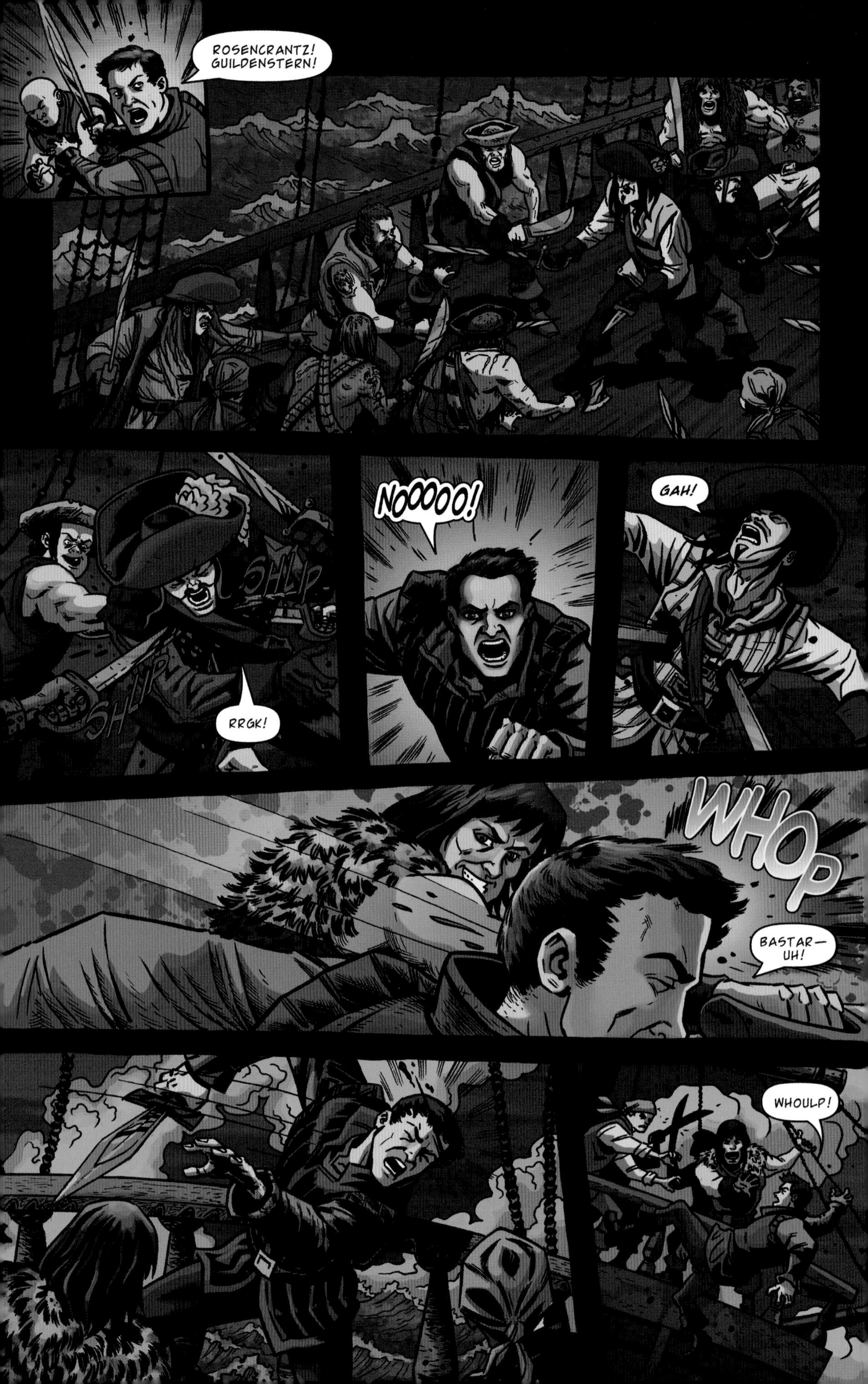
ROSENCRANTZ! GUILDENSTERN!
SHUP
SHUP
RRGK!
NOOOOO!
GAH!
WHOP
BASTAR— UH!
WHOULP!

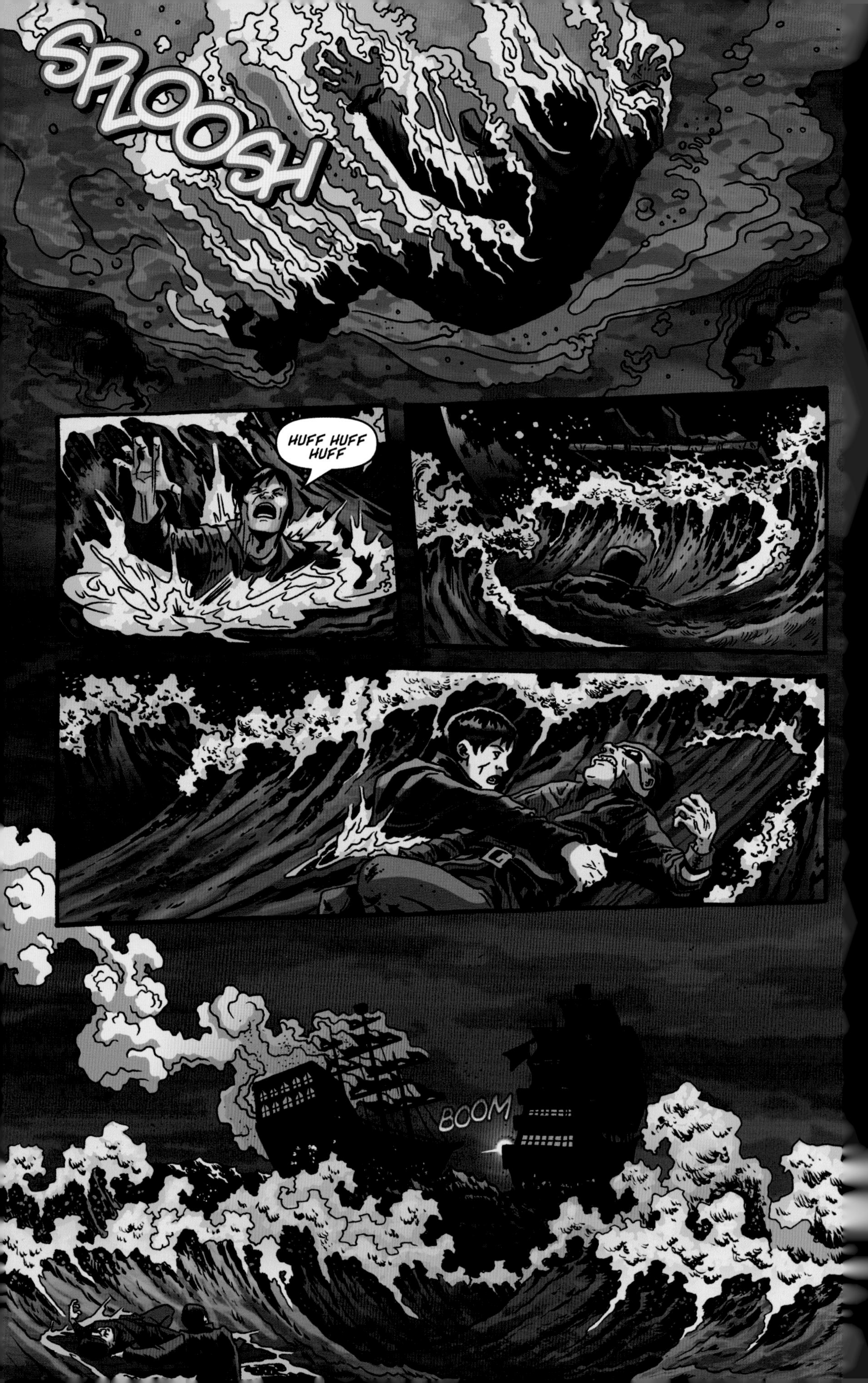
SPLOOSH
HUFF HUFF HUFF
BOOM

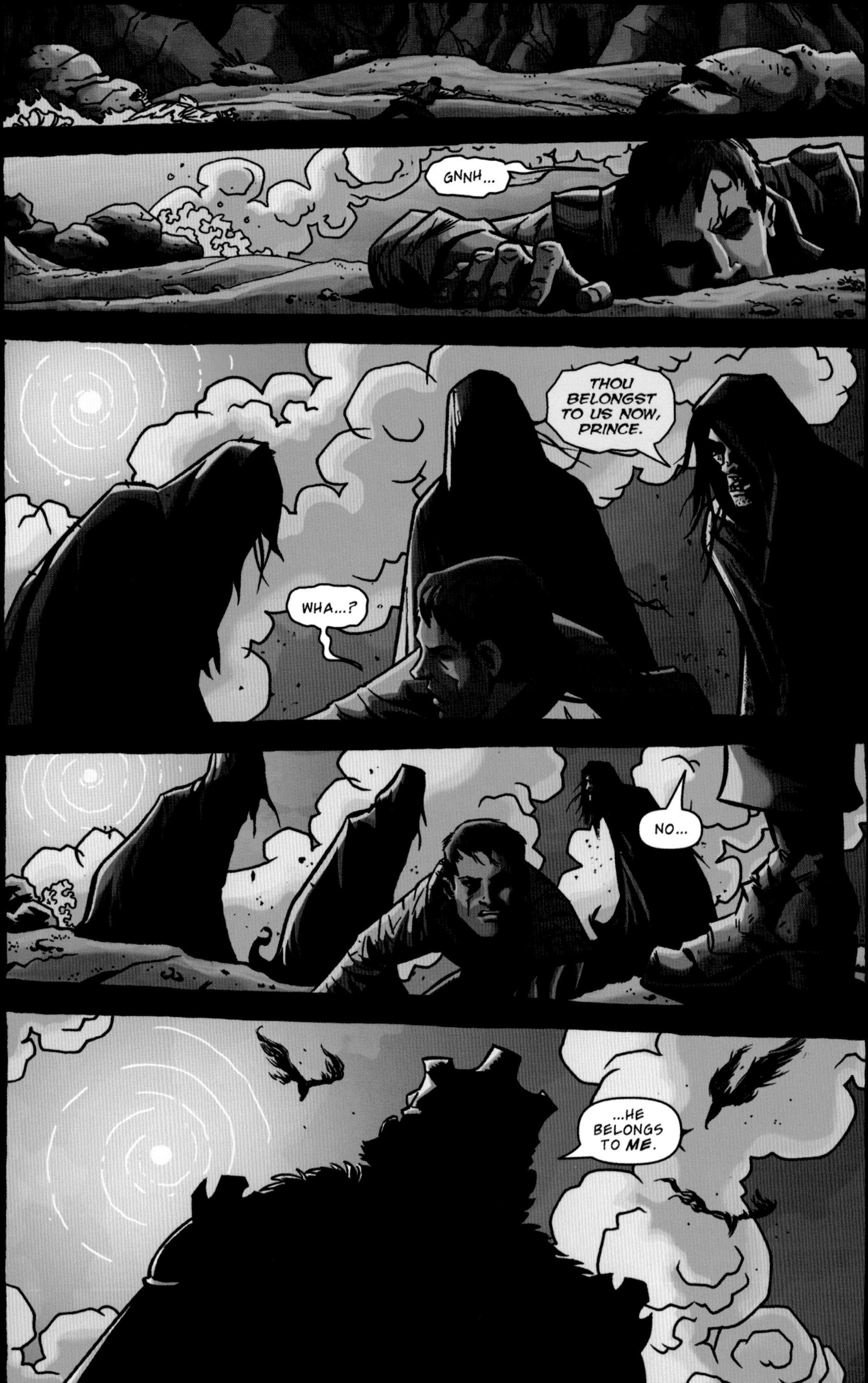
GNNH...
THOU BELONGST TO US NOW, PRINCE.
WHA...?
NO...
...HE BELONGS TO *ME*.

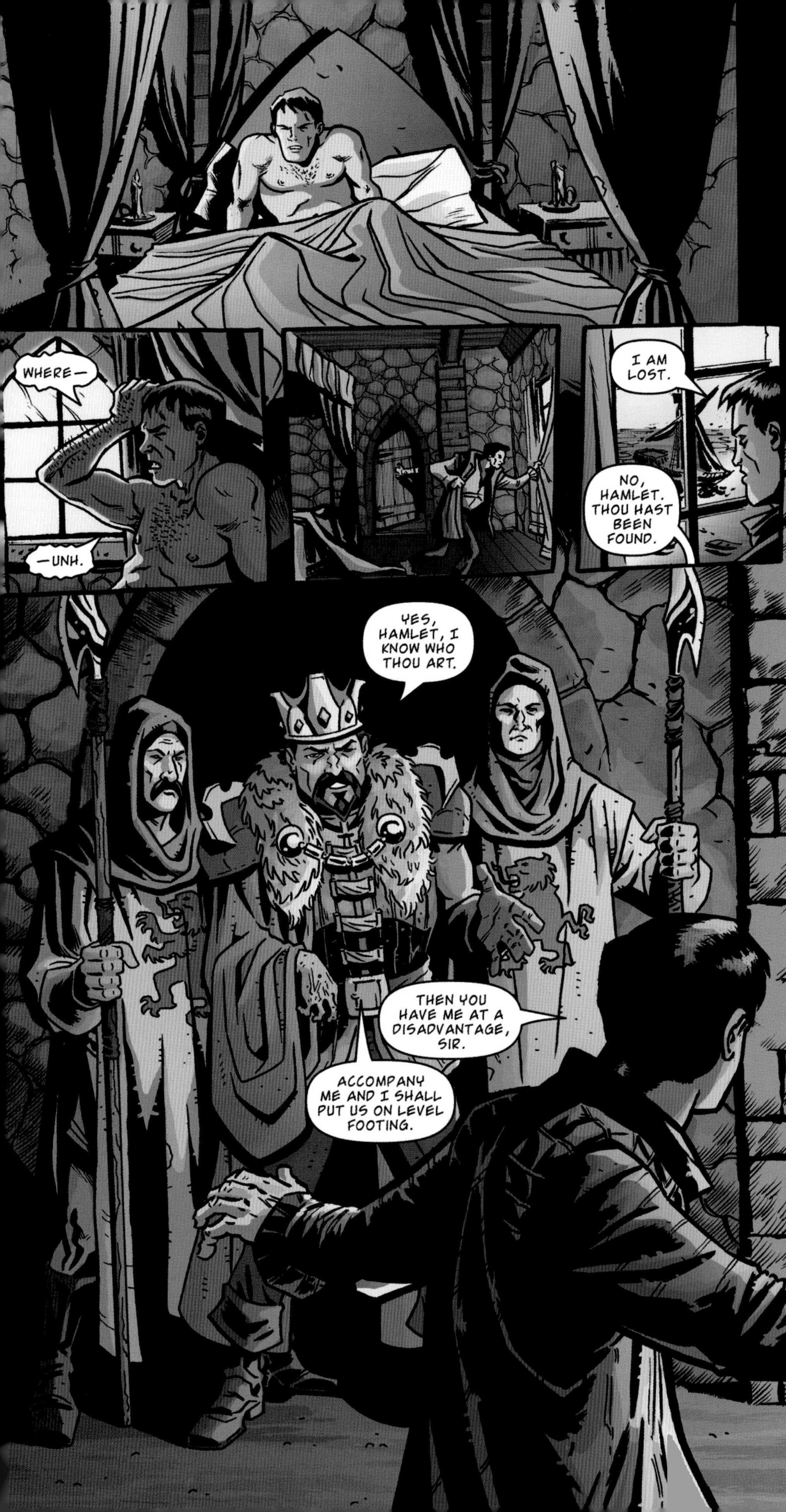
WHERE—
—UNH.
I AM LOST.
NO, HAMLET. THOU HAST BEEN FOUND.
YES, HAMLET, I KNOW WHO THOU ART.
THEN YOU HAVE ME AT A DISADVANTAGE, SIR.
ACCOMPANY ME AND I SHALL PUT US ON LEVEL FOOTING.

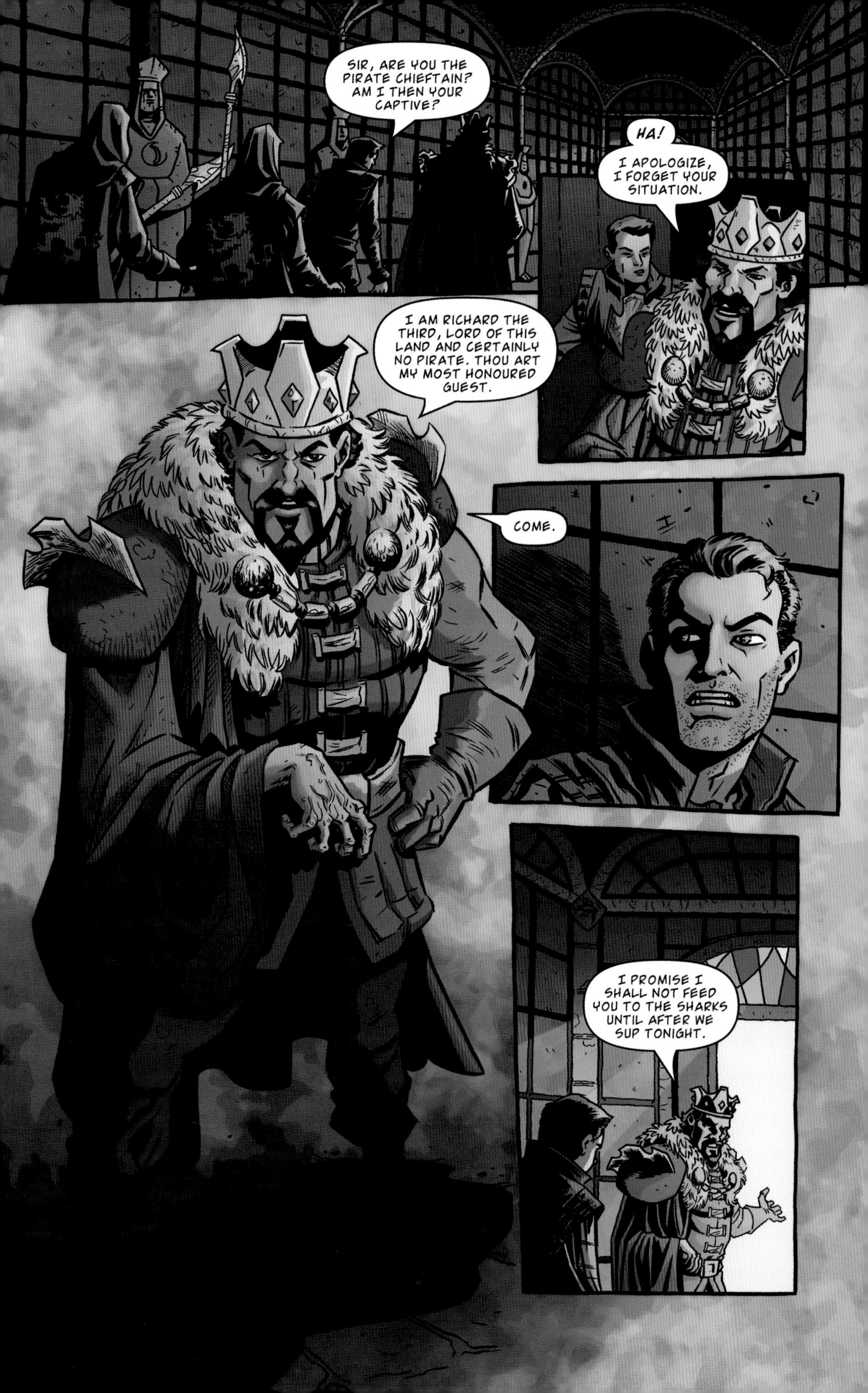
SIR, ARE YOU THE PIRATE CHIEFTAIN? AM I THEN YOUR CAPTIVE?
HA!
I APOLOGIZE, I FORGET YOUR SITUATION.
I AM RICHARD THE THIRD, LORD OF THIS LAND AND CERTAINLY NO PIRATE. THOU ART MY MOST HONOURED GUEST.
COME.
I PROMISE I SHALL NOT FEED YOU TO THE SHARKS UNTIL AFTER WE SUP TONIGHT.

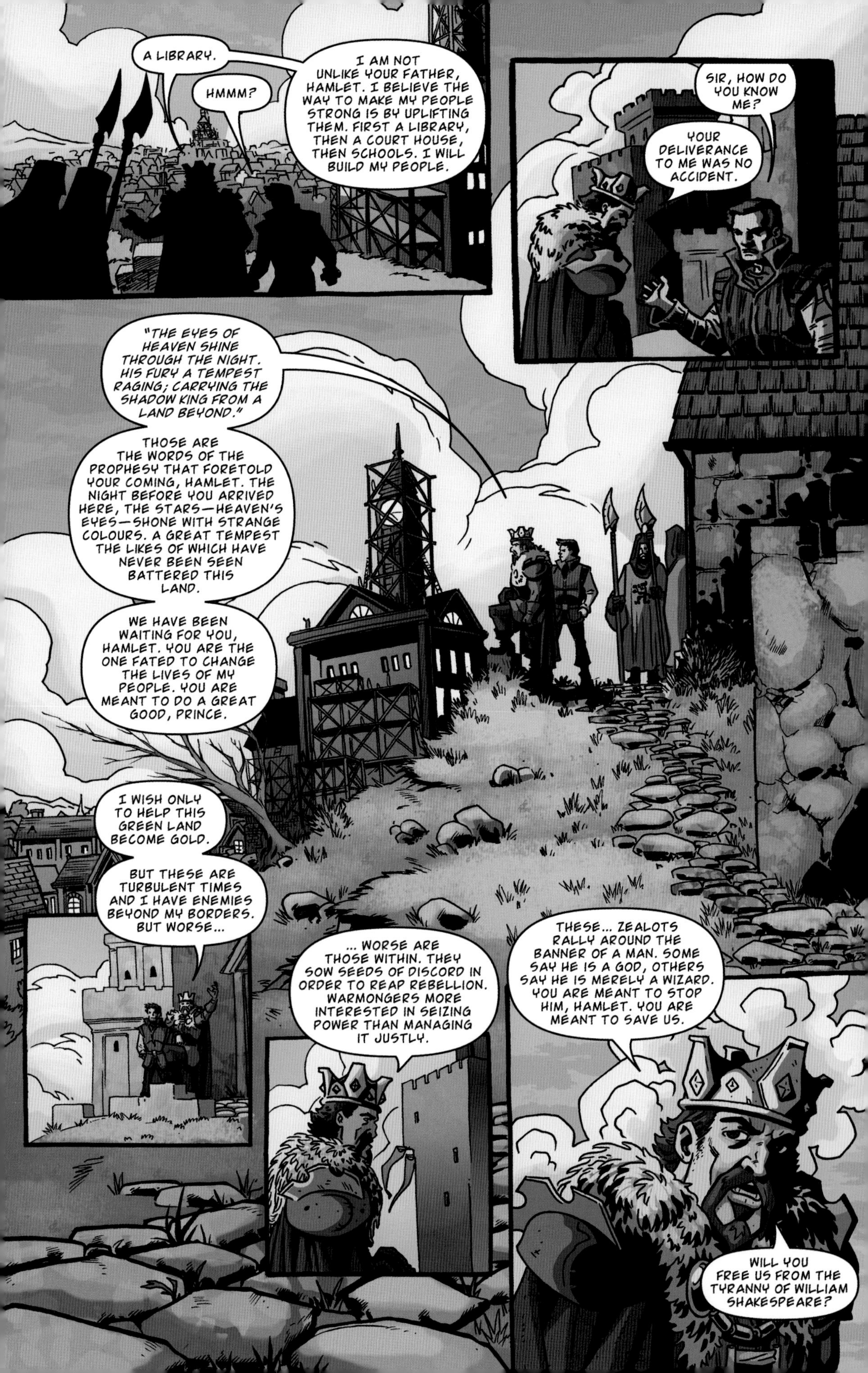
A LIBRARY.
HMMM?
I AM NOT UNLIKE YOUR FATHER, HAMLET. I BELIEVE THE WAY TO MAKE MY PEOPLE STRONG IS BY UPLIFTING THEM. FIRST A LIBRARY, THEN A COURT HOUSE, THEN SCHOOLS. I WILL BUILD MY PEOPLE.
SIR, HOW DO YOU KNOW ME?
YOUR DELIVERANCE TO ME WAS NO ACCIDENT.
"THE EYES OF HEAVEN SHINE THROUGH THE NIGHT. HIS FURY A TEMPEST RAGING; CARRYING THE SHADOW KING FROM A LAND BEYOND."
THOSE ARE THE WORDS OF THE PROPHESY THAT FORETOLD YOUR COMING, HAMLET. THE NIGHT BEFORE YOU ARRIVED HERE, THE STARS—HEAVEN'S EYES—SHONE WITH STRANGE COLOURS. A GREAT TEMPEST THE LIKES OF WHICH HAVE NEVER BEEN SEEN BATTERED THIS LAND.
WE HAVE BEEN WAITING FOR YOU, HAMLET. YOU ARE THE ONE FATED TO CHANGE THE LIVES OF MY PEOPLE. YOU ARE MEANT TO DO A GREAT GOOD, PRINCE.
I WISH ONLY TO HELP THIS GREEN LAND BECOME GOLD.
BUT THESE ARE TURBULENT TIMES AND I HAVE ENEMIES BEYOND MY BORDERS. BUT WORSE...
... WORSE ARE THOSE WITHIN. THEY SOW SEEDS OF DISCORD IN ORDER TO REAP REBELLION. WARMONGERS MORE INTERESTED IN SEIZING POWER THAN MANAGING IT JUSTLY.
THESE... ZEALOTS RALLY AROUND THE BANNER OF A MAN. SOME SAY HE IS A GOD, OTHERS SAY HE IS MERELY A WIZARD. YOU ARE MEANT TO STOP HIM, HAMLET. YOU ARE MEANT TO SAVE US.
WILL YOU FREE US FROM THE TYRANNY OF WILLIAM SHAKESPEARE?

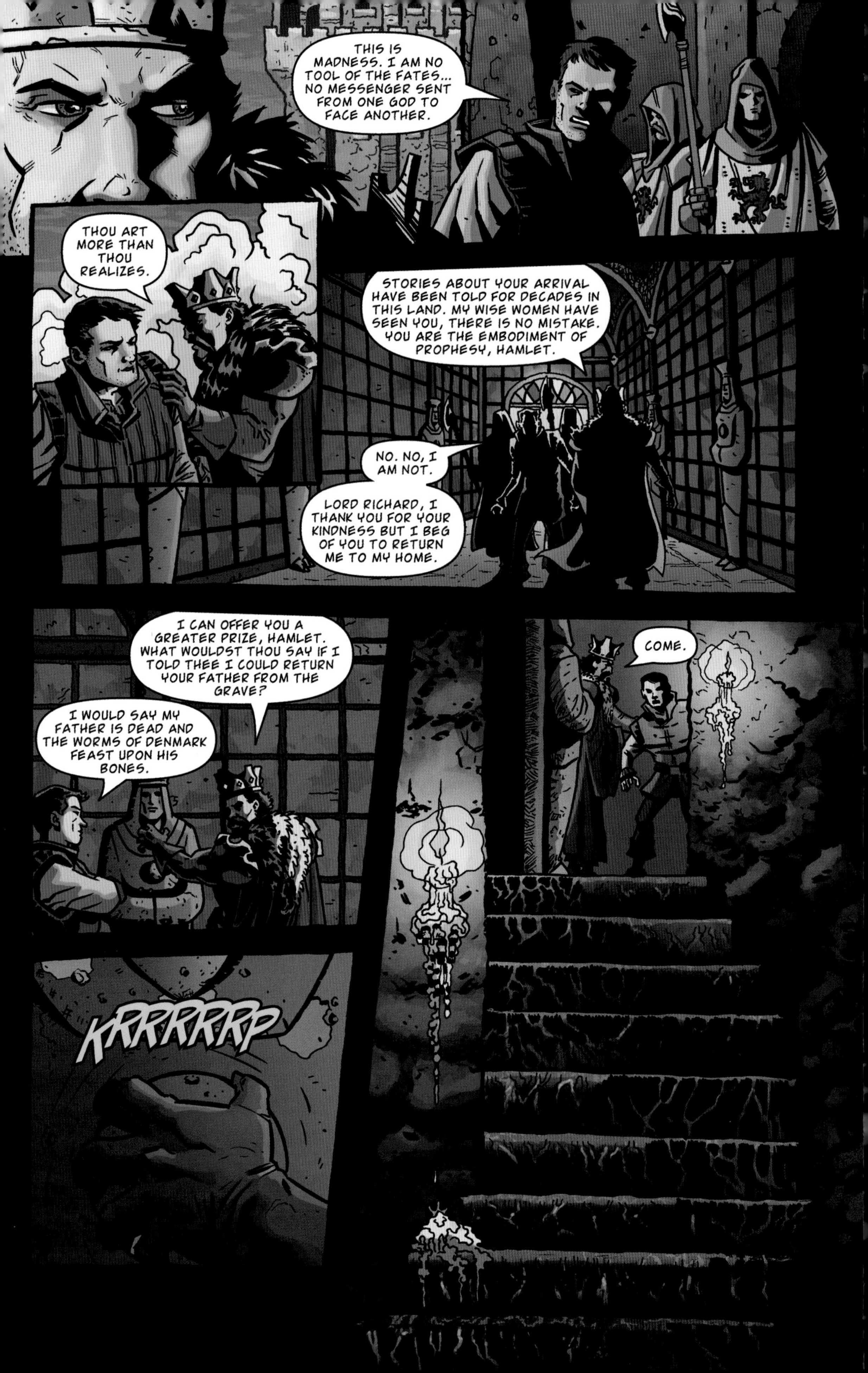
THIS IS MADNESS. I AM NO TOOL OF THE FATES... NO MESSENGER SENT FROM ONE GOD TO FACE ANOTHER.
THOU ART MORE THAN THOU REALIZES.
STORIES ABOUT YOUR ARRIVAL HAVE BEEN TOLD FOR DECADES IN THIS LAND. MY WISE WOMEN HAVE SEEN YOU, THERE IS NO MISTAKE. YOU ARE THE EMBODIMENT OF PROPHESY, HAMLET.
NO. NO, I AM NOT.
LORD RICHARD, I THANK YOU FOR YOUR KINDNESS BUT I BEG OF YOU TO RETURN ME TO MY HOME.
I CAN OFFER YOU A GREATER PRIZE, HAMLET. WHAT WOULDST THOU SAY IF I TOLD THEE I COULD RETURN YOUR FATHER FROM THE GRAVE?
I WOULD SAY MY FATHER IS DEAD AND THE WORMS OF DENMARK FEAST UPON HIS BONES.
KRRRRRRP
COME.

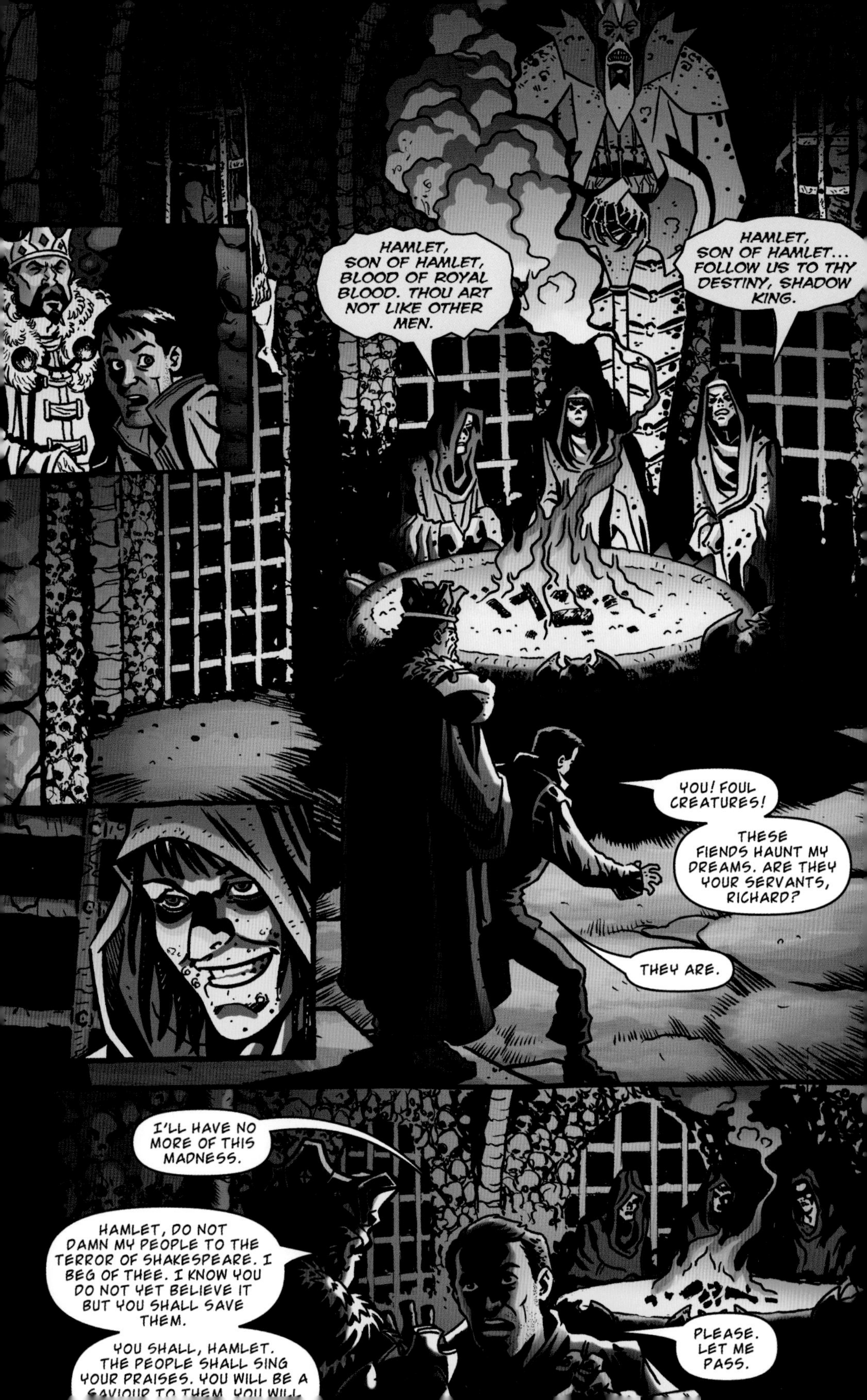
HAMLET, SON OF HAMLET, BLOOD OF ROYAL BLOOD. THOU ART NOT LIKE OTHER MEN.
HAMLET, SON OF HAMLET... FOLLOW US TO THY DESTINY, SHADOW KING.
YOU! FOUL CREATURES!
THESE FIENDS HAUNT MY DREAMS. ARE THEY YOUR SERVANTS, RICHARD?
THEY ARE.
I'LL HAVE NO MORE OF THIS MADNESS.
HAMLET, DO NOT DAMN MY PEOPLE TO THE TERROR OF SHAKESPEARE. I BEG OF THEE. I KNOW YOU DO NOT YET BELIEVE IT BUT YOU SHALL SAVE THEM.
YOU SHALL, HAMLET. THE PEOPLE SHALL SING YOUR PRAISES. YOU WILL BE A
PLEASE. LET ME PASS.

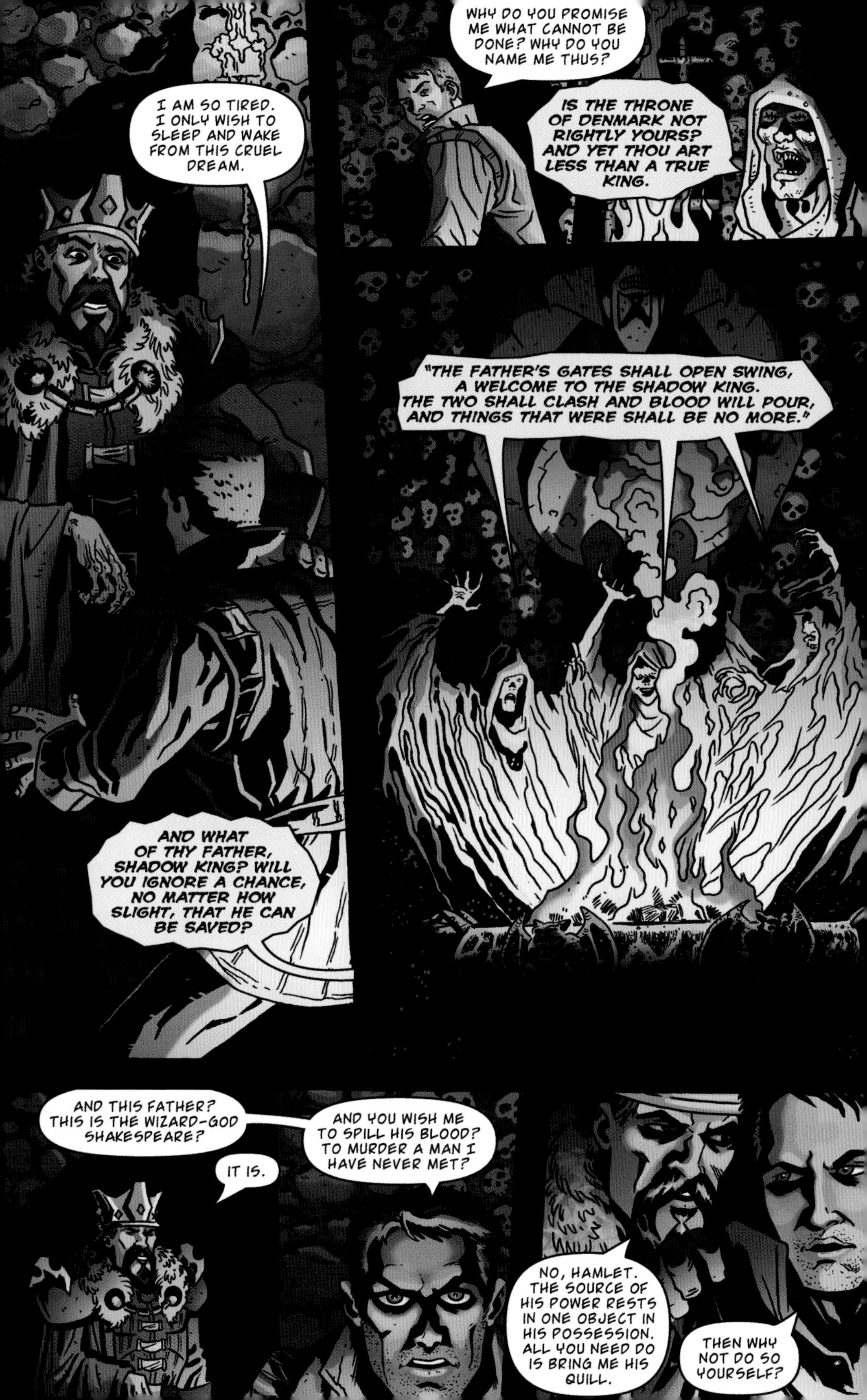
I AM SO TIRED. I ONLY WISH TO SLEEP AND WAKE FROM THIS CRUEL DREAM.
WHY DO YOU PROMISE ME WHAT CANNOT BE DONE? WHY DO YOU NAME ME THUS?
IS THE THRONE OF DENMARK NOT RIGHTLY YOURS? AND YET THOU ART LESS THAN A TRUE KING.
"THE FATHER'S GATES SHALL OPEN SWING, A WELCOME TO THE SHADOW KING. THE TWO SHALL CLASH AND BLOOD WILL POUR, AND THINGS THAT WERE SHALL BE NO MORE."
AND WHAT OF THY FATHER, SHADOW KING? WILL YOU IGNORE A CHANCE, NO MATTER HOW SLIGHT, THAT HE CAN BE SAVED?
AND THIS FATHER? THIS IS THE WIZARD-GOD SHAKESPEARE?
IT IS.
AND YOU WISH ME TO SPILL HIS BLOOD? TO MURDER A MAN I HAVE NEVER MET?
NO, HAMLET. THE SOURCE OF HIS POWER RESTS IN ONE OBJECT IN HIS POSSESSION. ALL YOU NEED DO IS BRING ME HIS QUILL.
THEN WHY NOT DO SO YOURSELF?

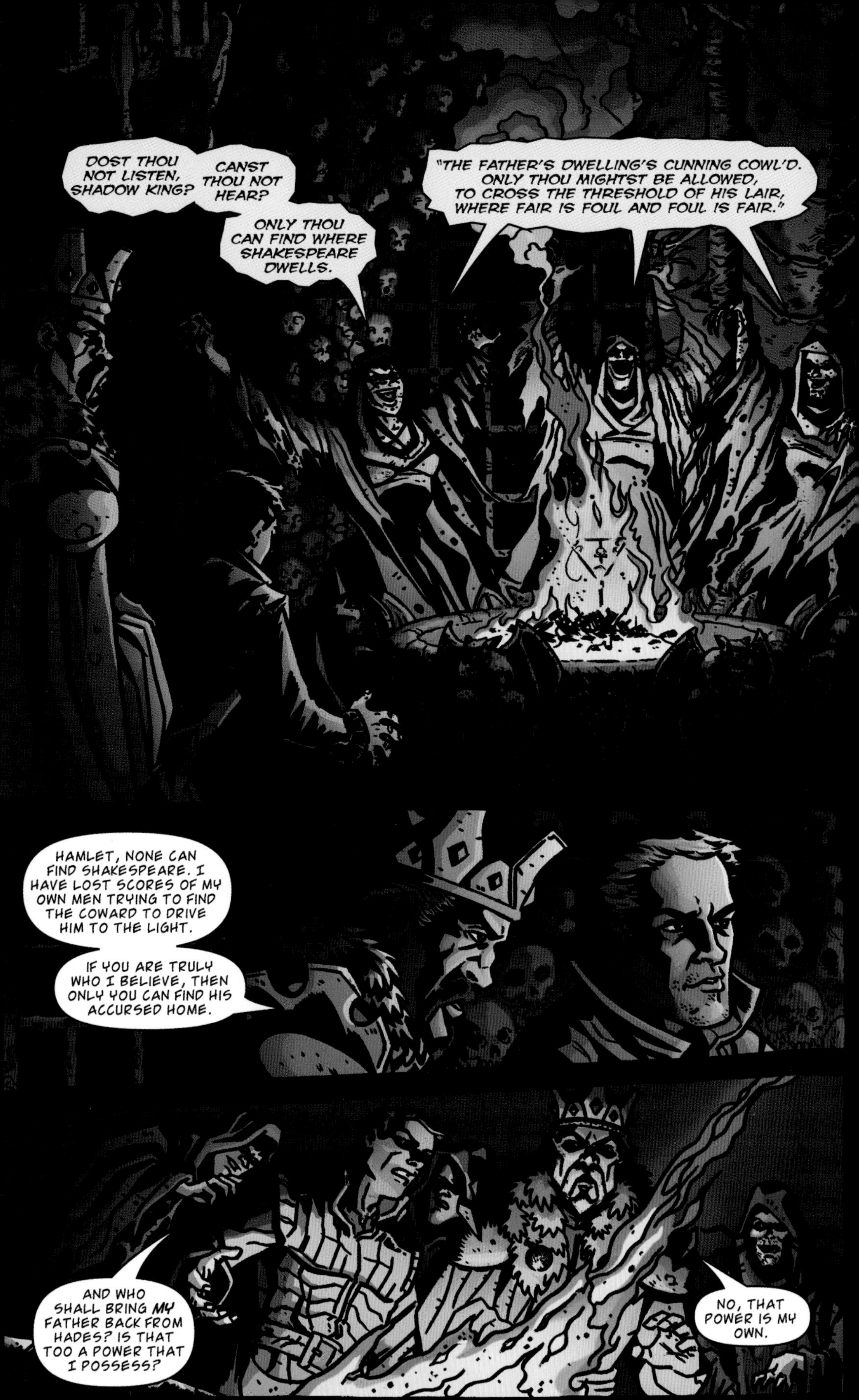
DOST THOU NOT LISTEN, SHADOW KING?
CANST THOU NOT HEAR?
ONLY THOU CAN FIND WHERE SHAKESPEARE DWELLS.
"THE FATHER'S DWELLING'S CUNNING COWL'D. ONLY THOU MIGHTST BE ALLOWED, TO CROSS THE THRESHOLD OF HIS LAIR, WHERE FAIR IS FOUL AND FOUL IS FAIR."
HAMLET, NONE CAN FIND SHAKESPEARE. I HAVE LOST SCORES OF MY OWN MEN TRYING TO FIND THE COWARD TO DRIVE HIM TO THE LIGHT.
IF YOU ARE TRULY WHO I BELIEVE, THEN ONLY YOU CAN FIND HIS ACCURSED HOME.
AND WHO SHALL BRING *MY* FATHER BACK FROM HADES? IS THAT TOO A POWER THAT I POSSESS?
NO, THAT POWER IS MY OWN.

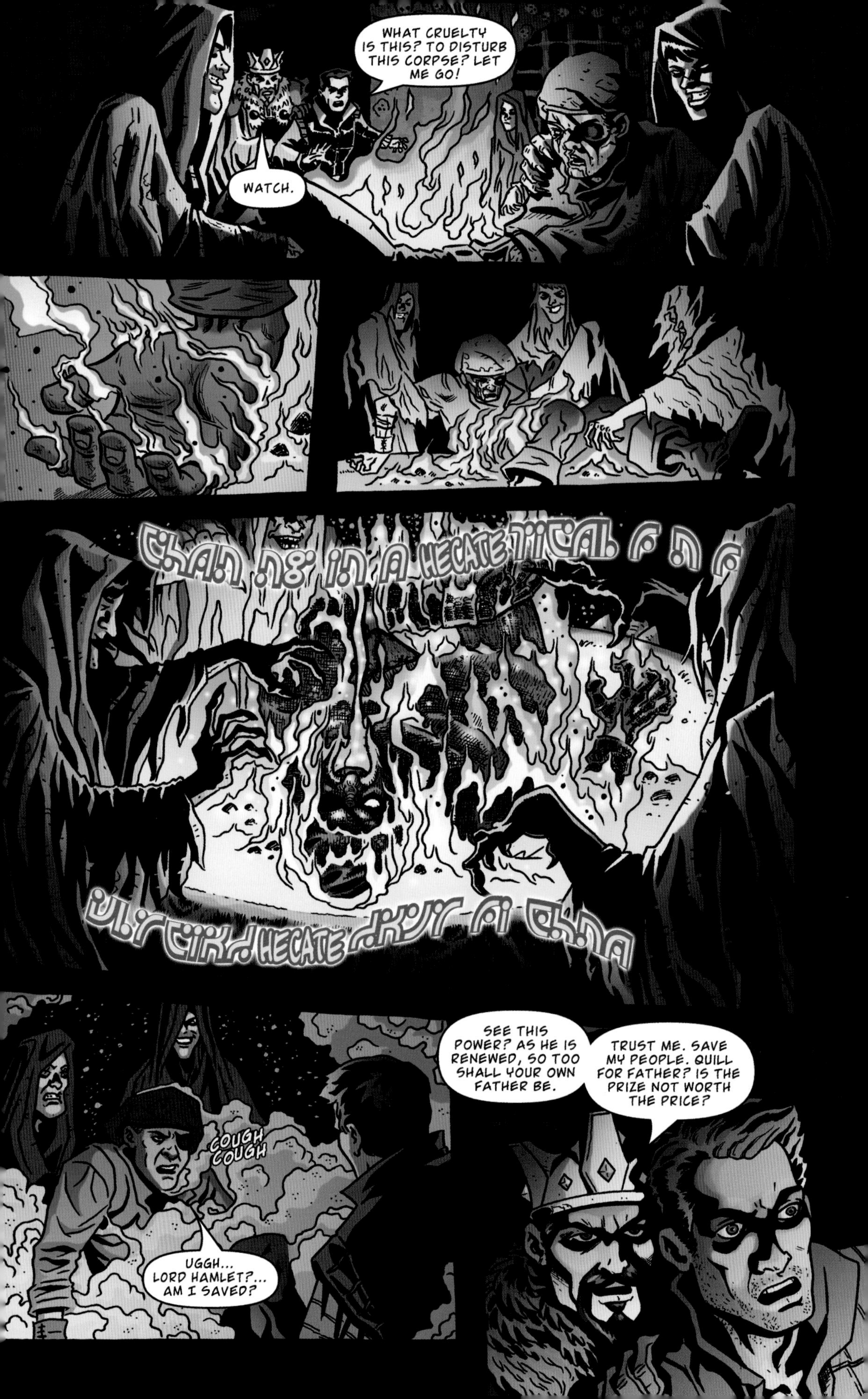
WHAT CRUELTY IS THIS? TO DISTURB THIS CORPSE? LET ME GO!
WATCH.
HECATE
HECATE
COUGH COUGH
UGGH... LORD HAMLET?... AM I SAVED?
SEE THIS POWER? AS HE IS RENEWED, SO TOO SHALL YOUR OWN FATHER BE.
TRUST ME. SAVE MY PEOPLE. QUILL FOR FATHER? IS THE PRIZE NOT WORTH THE PRICE?

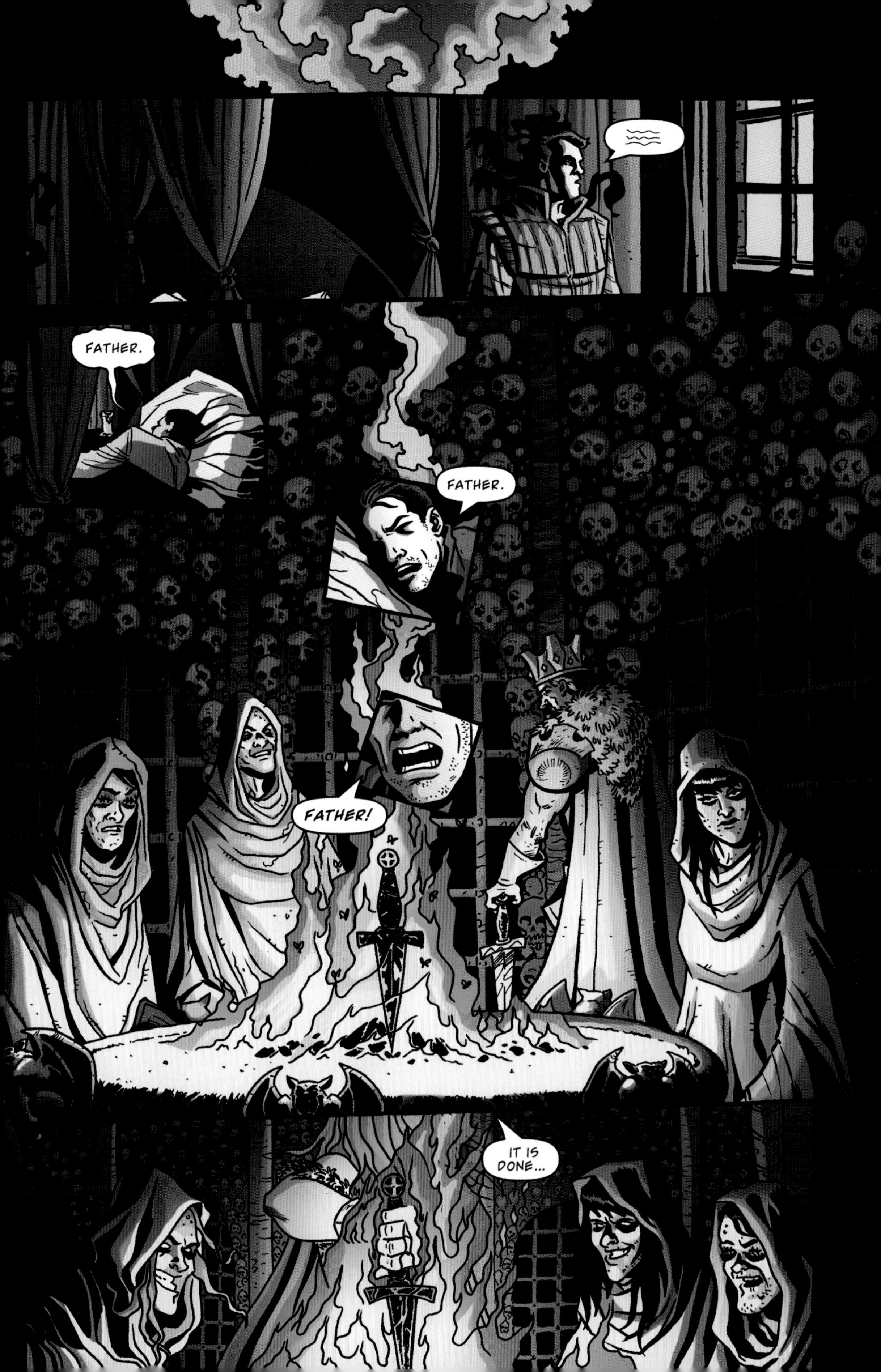

FATHER.
FATHER.
FATHER!
IT IS DONE...

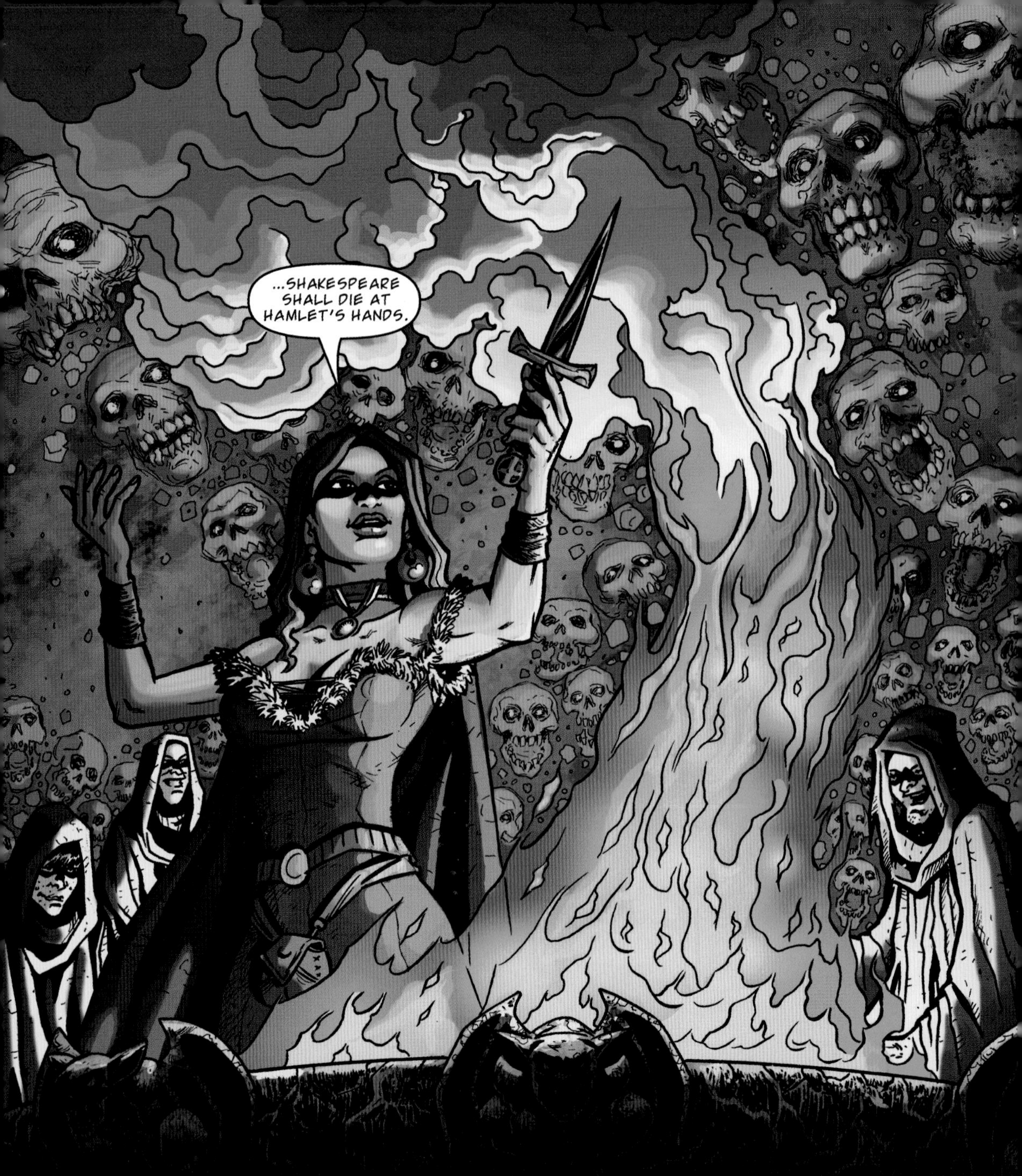
...SHAKESPEARE SHALL DIE AT HAMLET'S HANDS.

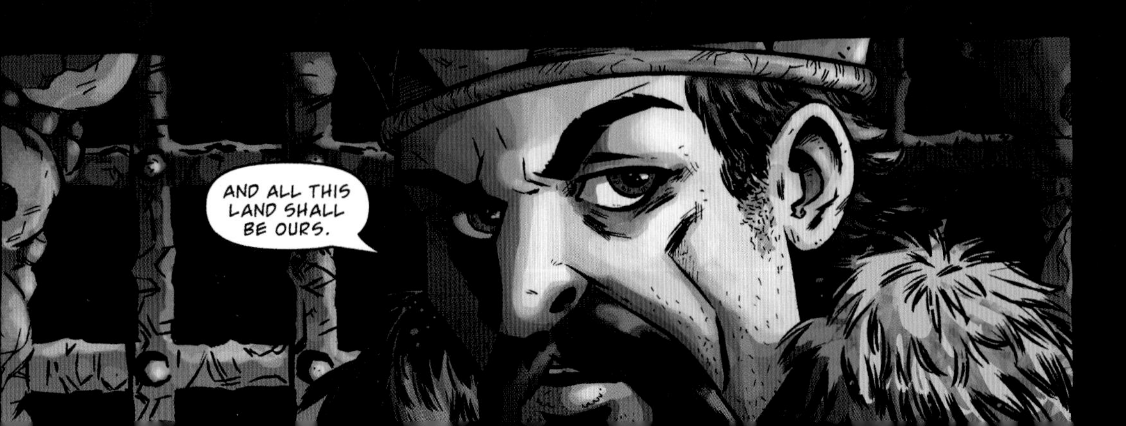
AND ALL THIS LAND SHALL BE OURS.

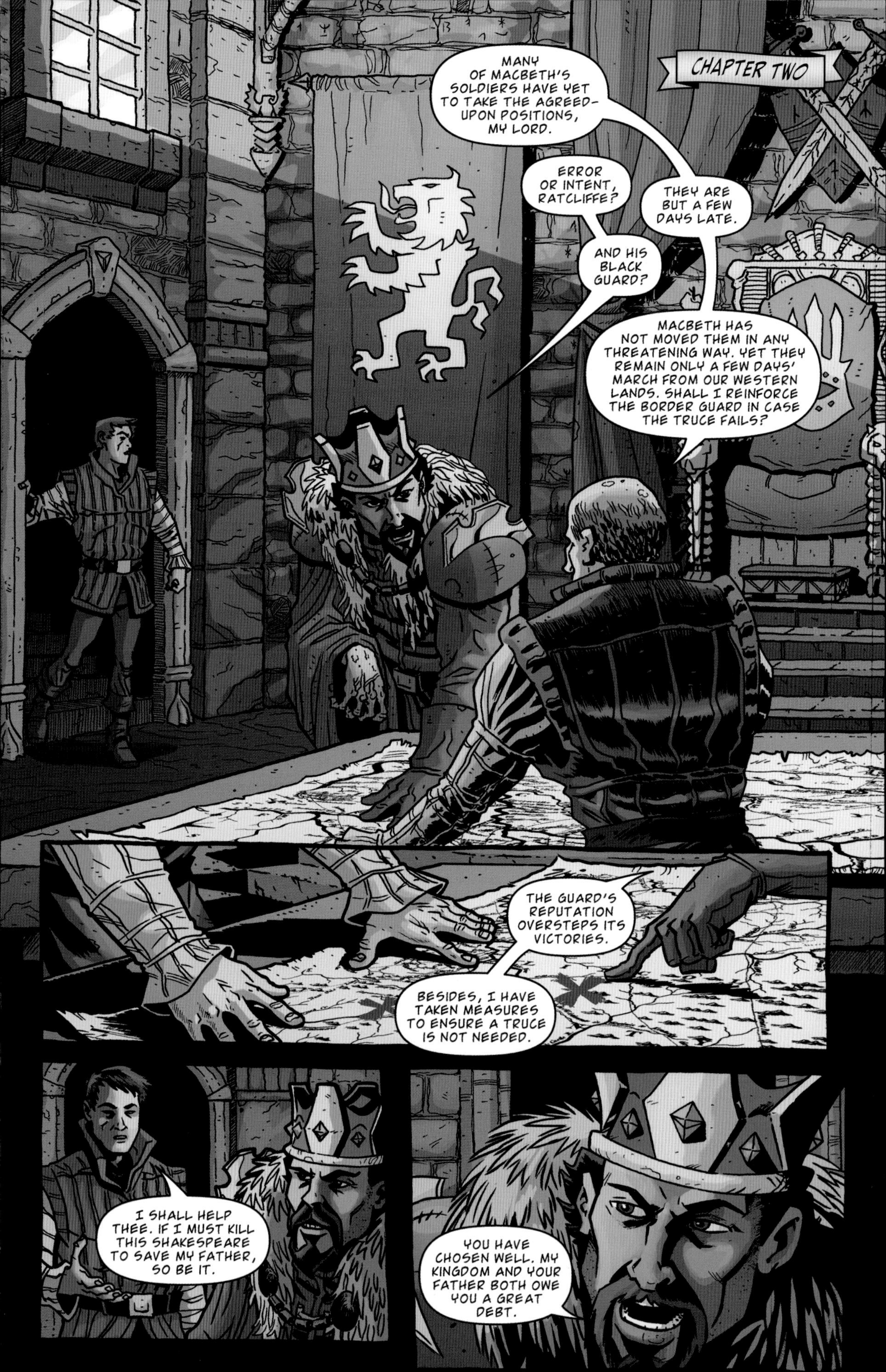
CHAPTER TWO
MANY OF MACBETH'S SOLDIERS HAVE YET TO TAKE THE AGREED-UPON POSITIONS, MY LORD.
ERROR OR INTENT, RATCLIFFE?
THEY ARE BUT A FEW DAYS LATE.
AND HIS BLACK GUARD?
MACBETH HAS NOT MOVED THEM IN ANY THREATENING WAY. YET THEY REMAIN ONLY A FEW DAYS' MARCH FROM OUR WESTERN LANDS. SHALL I REINFORCE THE BORDER GUARD IN CASE THE TRUCE FAILS?
THE GUARD'S REPUTATION OVERSTEPS ITS VICTORIES.
BESIDES, I HAVE TAKEN MEASURES TO ENSURE A TRUCE IS NOT NEEDED.
I SHALL HELP THEE. IF I MUST KILL THIS SHAKESPEARE TO SAVE MY FATHER, SO BE IT.
YOU HAVE CHOSEN WELL. MY KINGDOM AND YOUR FATHER BOTH OWE YOU A GREAT DEBT.

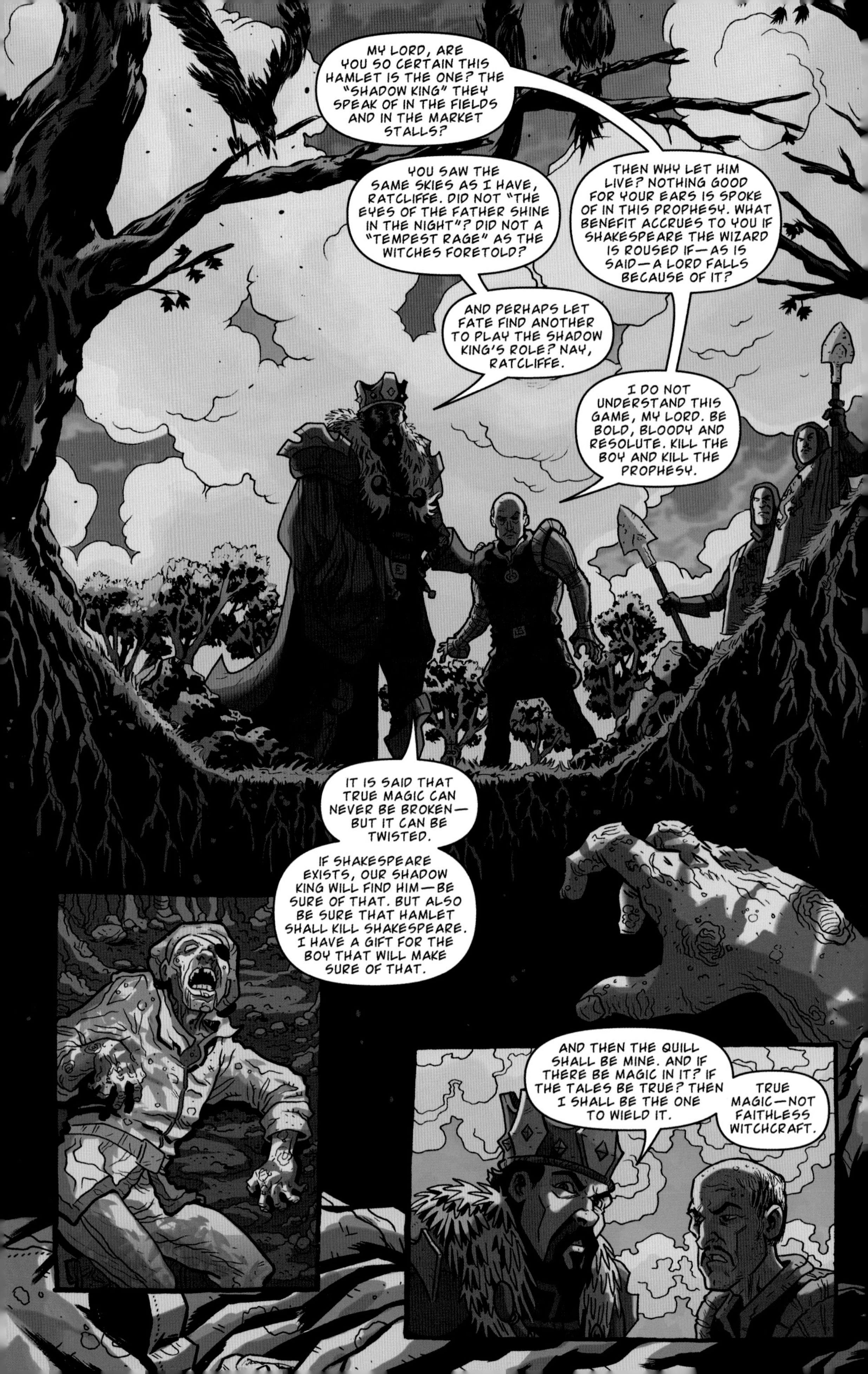
MY LORD, ARE YOU SO CERTAIN THIS HAMLET IS THE ONE? THE "SHADOW KING" THEY SPEAK OF IN THE FIELDS AND IN THE MARKET STALLS?
YOU SAW THE SAME SKIES AS I HAVE, RATCLIFFE. DID NOT "THE EYES OF THE FATHER SHINE IN THE NIGHT"? DID NOT A "TEMPEST RAGE" AS THE WITCHES FORETOLD?
THEN WHY LET HIM LIVE? NOTHING GOOD FOR YOUR EARS IS SPOKE OF IN THIS PROPHESY. WHAT BENEFIT ACCRUES TO YOU IF SHAKESPEARE THE WIZARD IS ROUSED IF—AS IS SAID—A LORD FALLS BECAUSE OF IT?
AND PERHAPS LET FATE FIND ANOTHER TO PLAY THE SHADOW KING'S ROLE? NAY, RATCLIFFE.
I DO NOT UNDERSTAND THIS GAME, MY LORD. BE BOLD, BLOODY AND RESOLUTE. KILL THE BOY AND KILL THE PROPHESY.
IT IS SAID THAT TRUE MAGIC CAN NEVER BE BROKEN—BUT IT CAN BE TWISTED.
IF SHAKESPEARE EXISTS, OUR SHADOW KING WILL FIND HIM—BE SURE OF THAT. BUT ALSO BE SURE THAT HAMLET SHALL KILL SHAKESPEARE. I HAVE A GIFT FOR THE BOY THAT WILL MAKE SURE OF THAT.
AND THEN THE QUILL SHALL BE MINE. AND IF THERE BE MAGIC IN IT? IF THE TALES BE TRUE? THEN I SHALL BE THE ONE TO WIELD IT.
TRUE MAGIC—NOT FAITHLESS WITCHCRAFT.

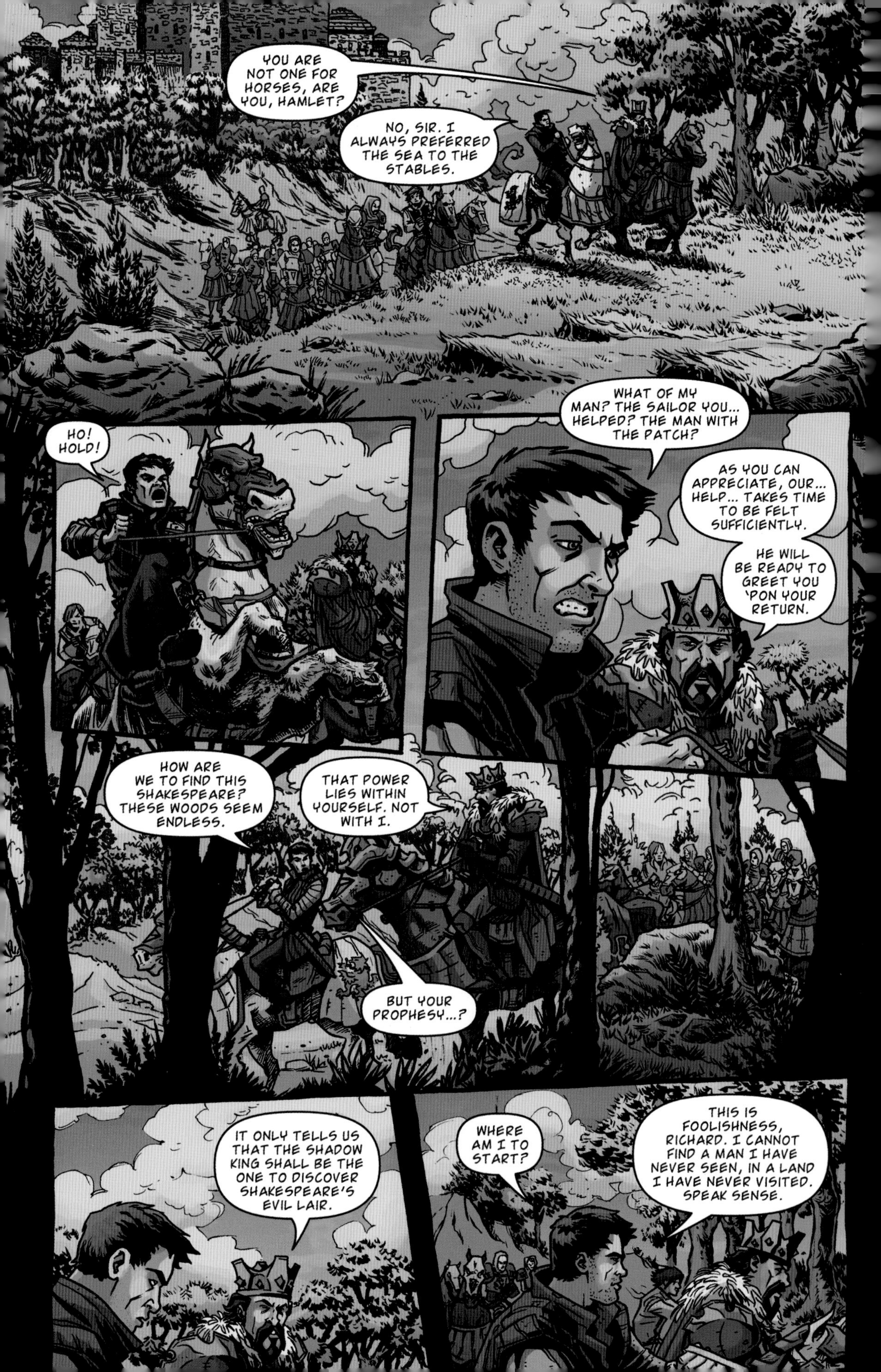
YOU ARE NOT ONE FOR HORSES, ARE YOU, HAMLET?
NO, SIR. I ALWAYS PREFERRED THE SEA TO THE STABLES.
HO! HOLD!
WHAT OF MY MAN? THE SAILOR YOU... HELPED? THE MAN WITH THE PATCH?
AS YOU CAN APPRECIATE, OUR... HELP... TAKES TIME TO BE FELT SUFFICIENTLY.
HE WILL BE READY TO GREET YOU 'PON YOUR RETURN.
HOW ARE WE TO FIND THIS SHAKESPEARE? THESE WOODS SEEM ENDLESS.
THAT POWER LIES WITHIN YOURSELF. NOT WITH I.
BUT YOUR PROPHESY...?
IT ONLY TELLS US THAT THE SHADOW KING SHALL BE THE ONE TO DISCOVER SHAKESPEARE'S EVIL LAIR.
WHERE AM I TO START?
THIS IS FOOLISHNESS, RICHARD. I CANNOT FIND A MAN I HAVE NEVER SEEN, IN A LAND I HAVE NEVER VISITED. SPEAK SENSE.

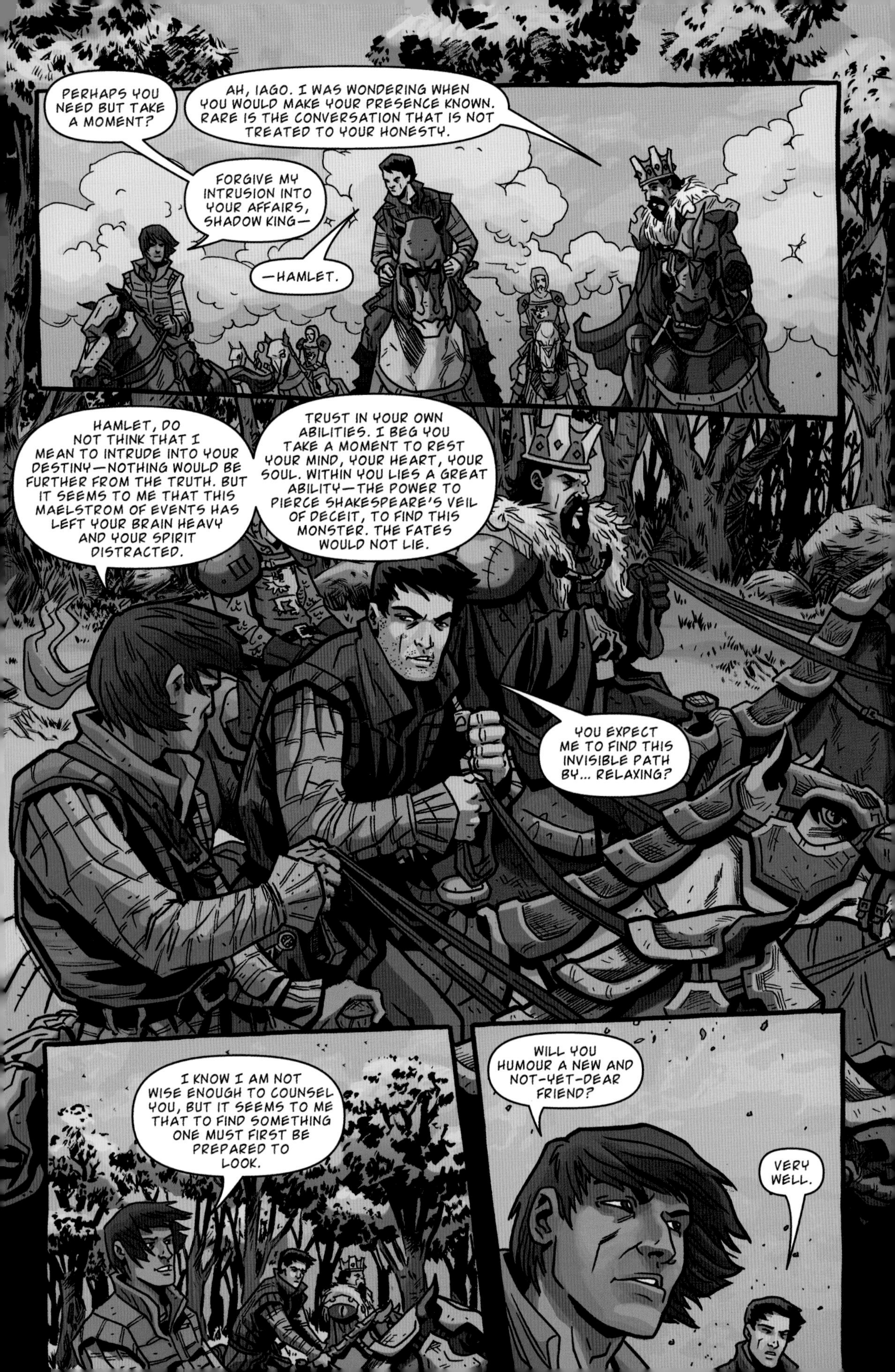
PERHAPS YOU NEED BUT TAKE A MOMENT?
AH, IAGO. I WAS WONDERING WHEN YOU WOULD MAKE YOUR PRESENCE KNOWN. RARE IS THE CONVERSATION THAT IS NOT TREATED TO YOUR HONESTY.
FORGIVE MY INTRUSION INTO YOUR AFFAIRS, SHADOW KING—
—HAMLET.
HAMLET, DO NOT THINK THAT I MEAN TO INTRUDE INTO YOUR DESTINY—NOTHING WOULD BE FURTHER FROM THE TRUTH. BUT IT SEEMS TO ME THAT THIS MAELSTROM OF EVENTS HAS LEFT YOUR BRAIN HEAVY AND YOUR SPIRIT DISTRACTED.
TRUST IN YOUR OWN ABILITIES. I BEG YOU TAKE A MOMENT TO REST YOUR MIND, YOUR HEART, YOUR SOUL. WITHIN YOU LIES A GREAT ABILITY—THE POWER TO PIERCE SHAKESPEARE'S VEIL OF DECEIT, TO FIND THIS MONSTER. THE FATES WOULD NOT LIE.
YOU EXPECT ME TO FIND THIS INVISIBLE PATH BY... RELAXING?
I KNOW I AM NOT WISE ENOUGH TO COUNSEL YOU, BUT IT SEEMS TO ME THAT TO FIND SOMETHING ONE MUST FIRST BE PREPARED TO LOOK.
WILL YOU HUMOUR A NEW AND NOT-YET-DEAR FRIEND?
VERY WELL.

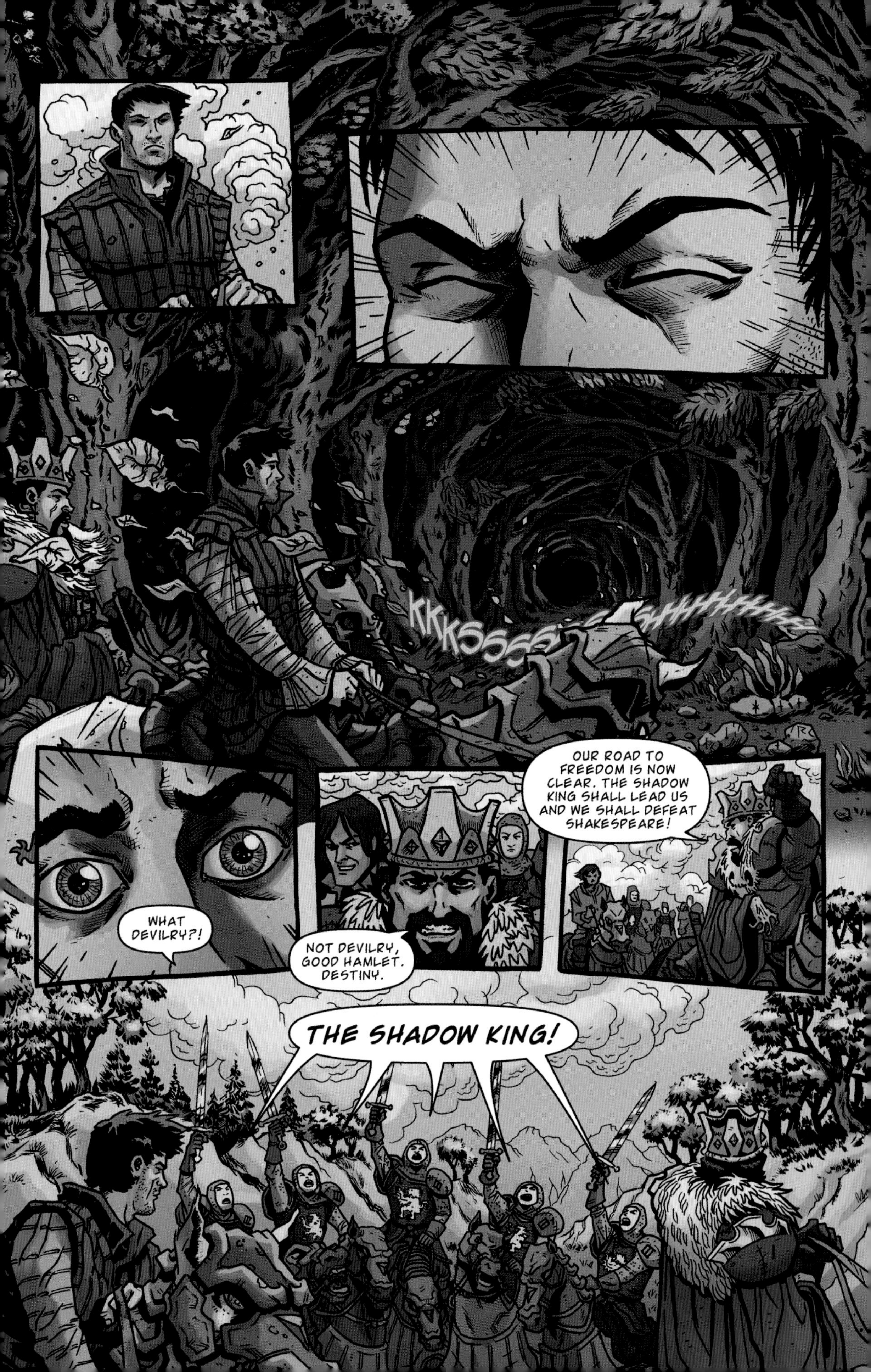
KKKSSSSSHHHHHHHH
WHAT DEVILRY?!
NOT DEVILRY, GOOD HAMLET. DESTINY.
OUR ROAD TO FREEDOM IS NOW CLEAR. THE SHADOW KING SHALL LEAD US AND WE SHALL DEFEAT SHAKESPEARE!
THE SHADOW KING!

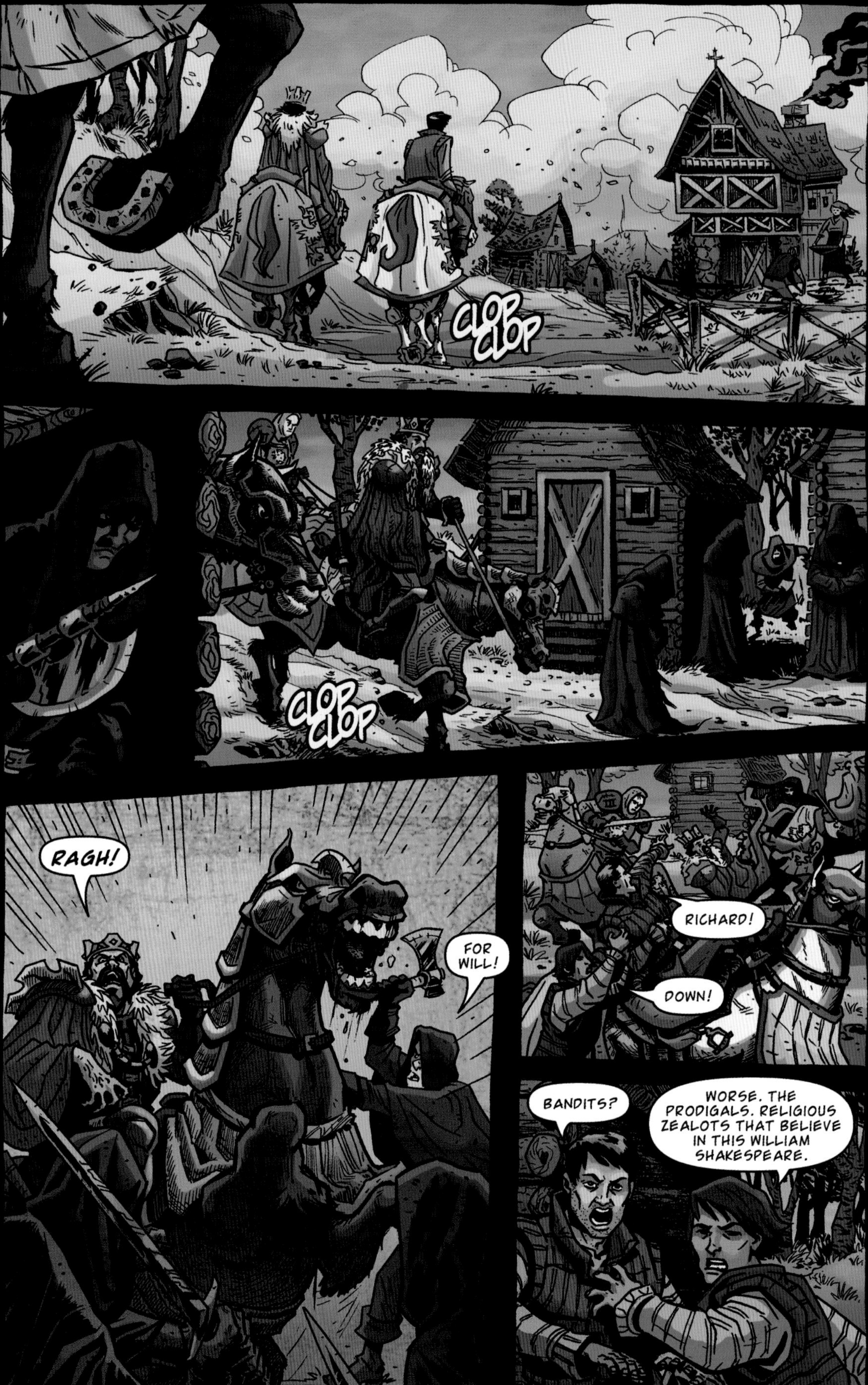
CLOP CLOP
CLOP CLOP
RAGH!
FOR WILL!
RICHARD!
DOWN!
BANDITS?
WORSE. THE PRODIGALS. RELIGIOUS ZEALOTS THAT BELIEVE IN THIS WILLIAM SHAKESPEARE.

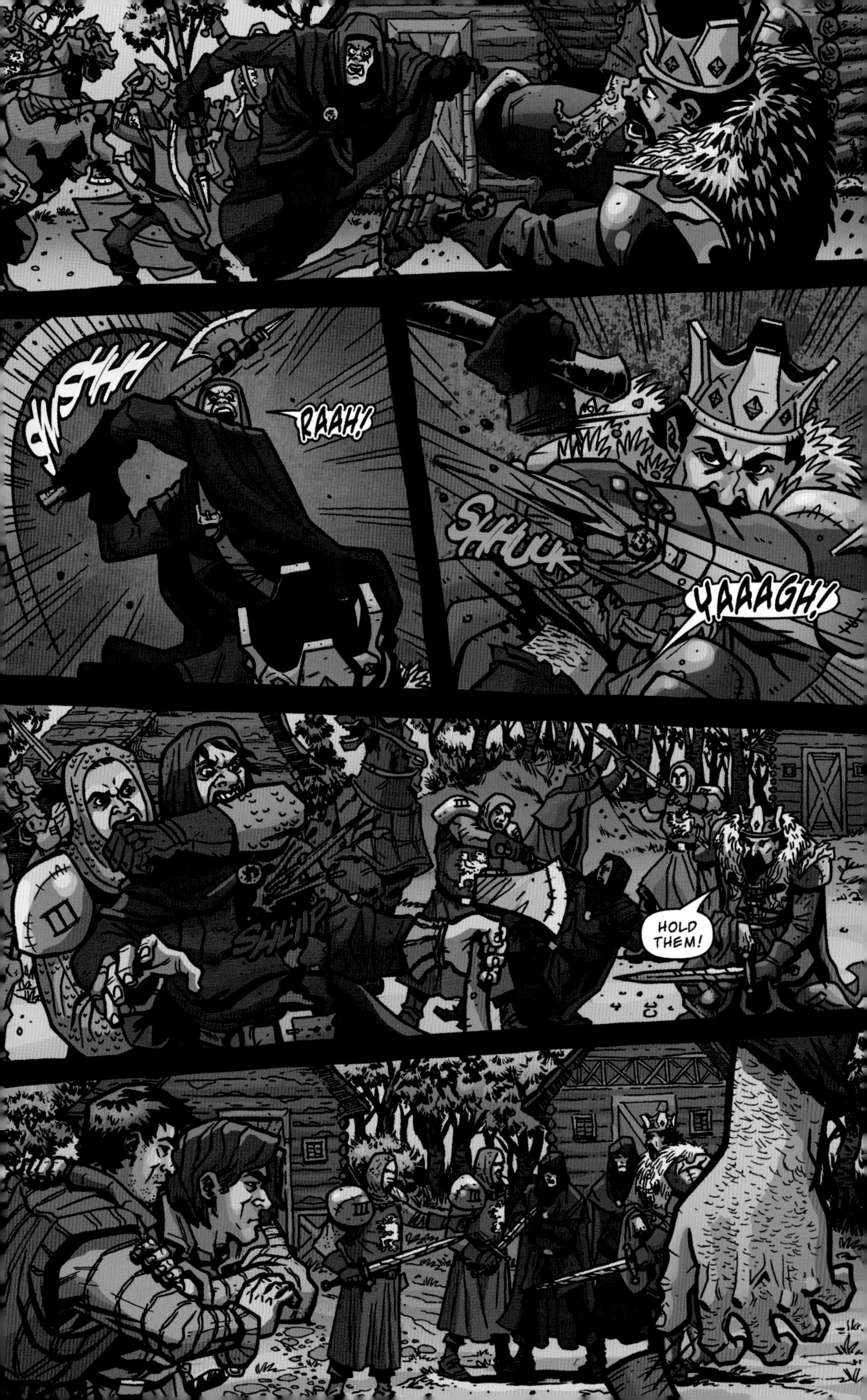
RAAH!
SHUUK
YAAAGH!
HOLD THEM!

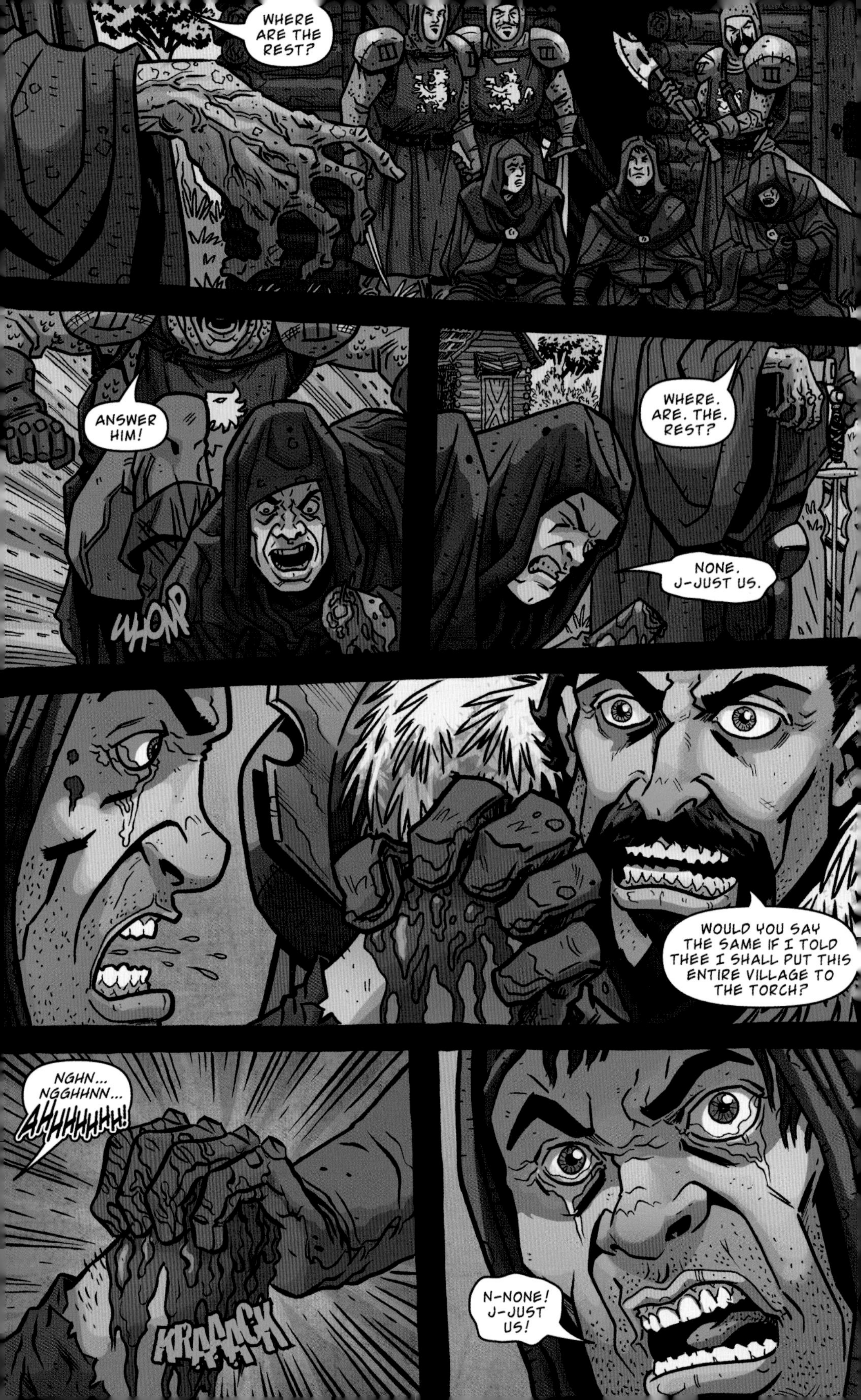
WHERE ARE THE REST?
ANSWER HIM!
WHOMP
WHERE. ARE. THE. REST?
NONE. J-JUST US.
WOULD YOU SAY THE SAME IF I TOLD THEE I SHALL PUT THIS ENTIRE VILLAGE TO THE TORCH?
NGHN... NGGHHNN... AHHHHHHH!
KRAAACK
N-NONE! J-JUST US!

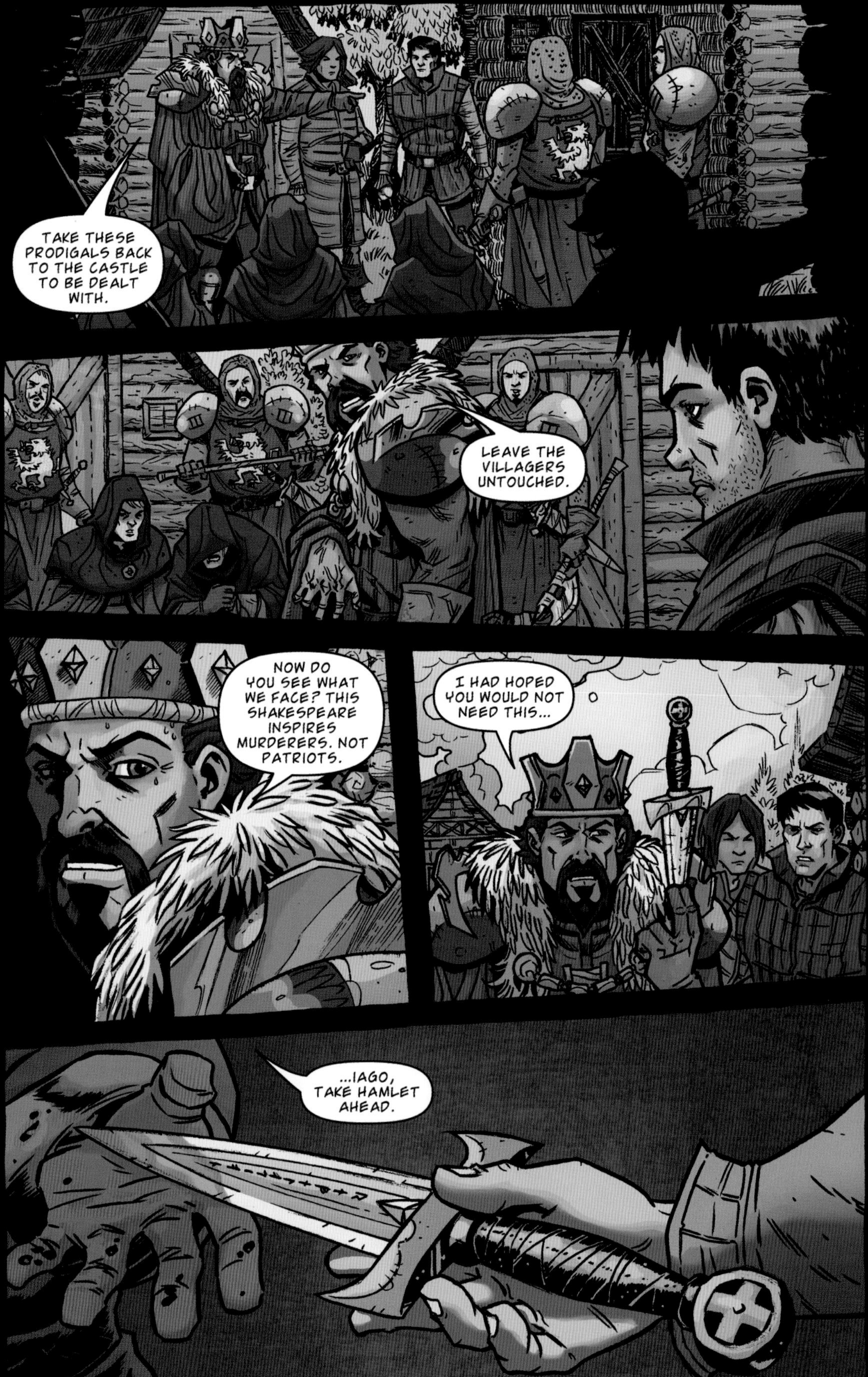
TAKE THESE PRODIGALS BACK TO THE CASTLE TO BE DEALT WITH.
LEAVE THE VILLAGERS UNTOUCHED.
NOW DO YOU SEE WHAT WE FACE? THIS SHAKESPEARE INSPIRES MURDERERS. NOT PATRIOTS.
I HAD HOPED YOU WOULD NOT NEED THIS...
...IAGO, TAKE HAMLET AHEAD.

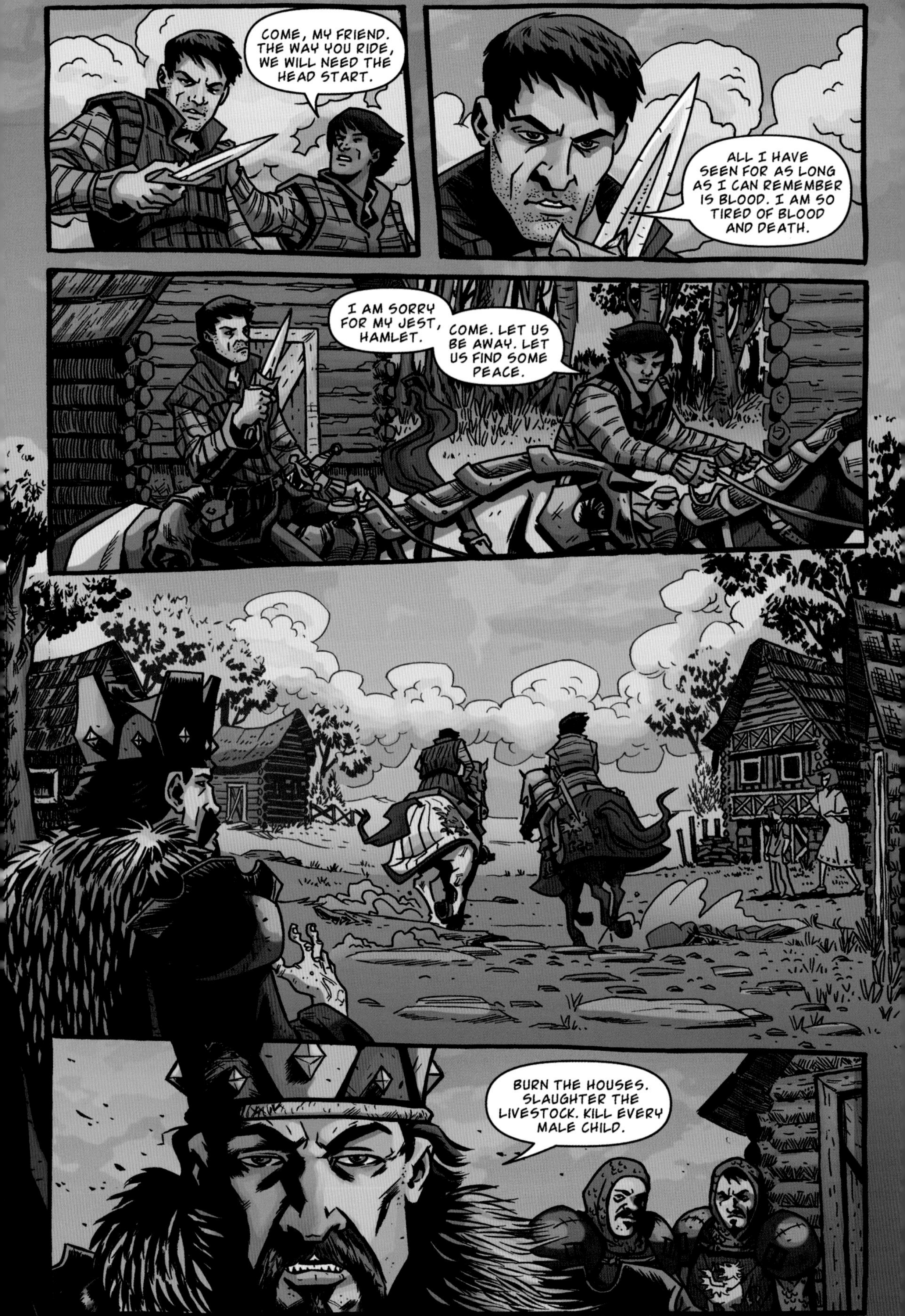
COME, MY FRIEND. THE WAY YOU RIDE, WE WILL NEED THE HEAD START.
ALL I HAVE SEEN FOR AS LONG AS I CAN REMEMBER IS BLOOD. I AM SO TIRED OF BLOOD AND DEATH.
I AM SORRY FOR MY JEST, HAMLET.
COME. LET US BE AWAY. LET US FIND SOME PEACE.
BURN THE HOUSES. SLAUGHTER THE LIVESTOCK. KILL EVERY MALE CHILD.

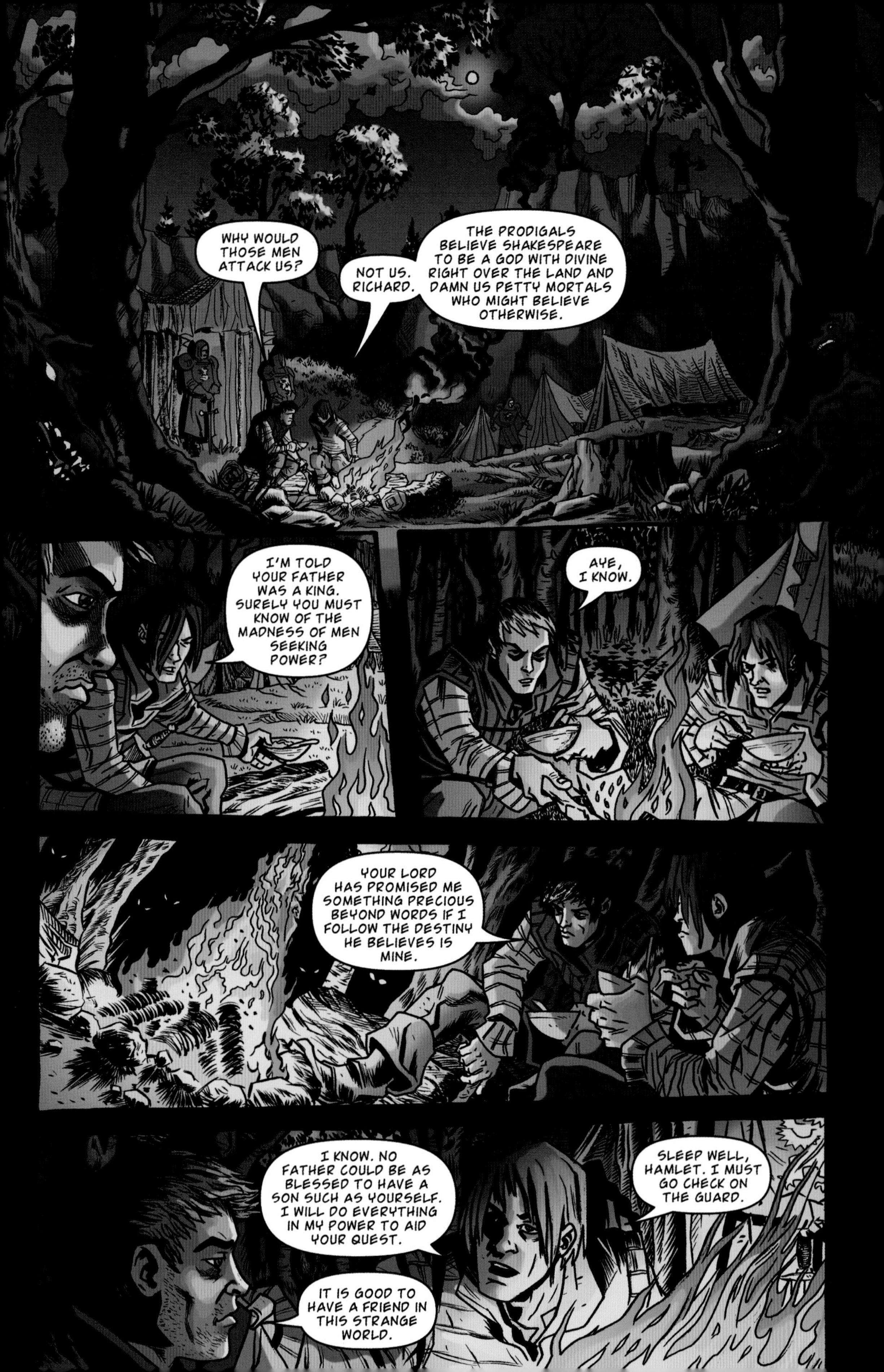
WHY WOULD THOSE MEN ATTACK US?
NOT US. RICHARD.
THE PRODIGALS BELIEVE SHAKESPEARE TO BE A GOD WITH DIVINE RIGHT OVER THE LAND AND DAMN US PETTY MORTALS WHO MIGHT BELIEVE OTHERWISE.
I'M TOLD YOUR FATHER WAS A KING. SURELY YOU MUST KNOW OF THE MADNESS OF MEN SEEKING POWER?
AYE, I KNOW.
YOUR LORD HAS PROMISED ME SOMETHING PRECIOUS BEYOND WORDS IF I FOLLOW THE DESTINY HE BELIEVES IS MINE.
I KNOW. NO FATHER COULD BE AS BLESSED TO HAVE A SON SUCH AS YOURSELF. I WILL DO EVERYTHING IN MY POWER TO AID YOUR QUEST.
IT IS GOOD TO HAVE A FRIEND IN THIS STRANGE WORLD.
SLEEP WELL, HAMLET. I MUST GO CHECK ON THE GUARD.

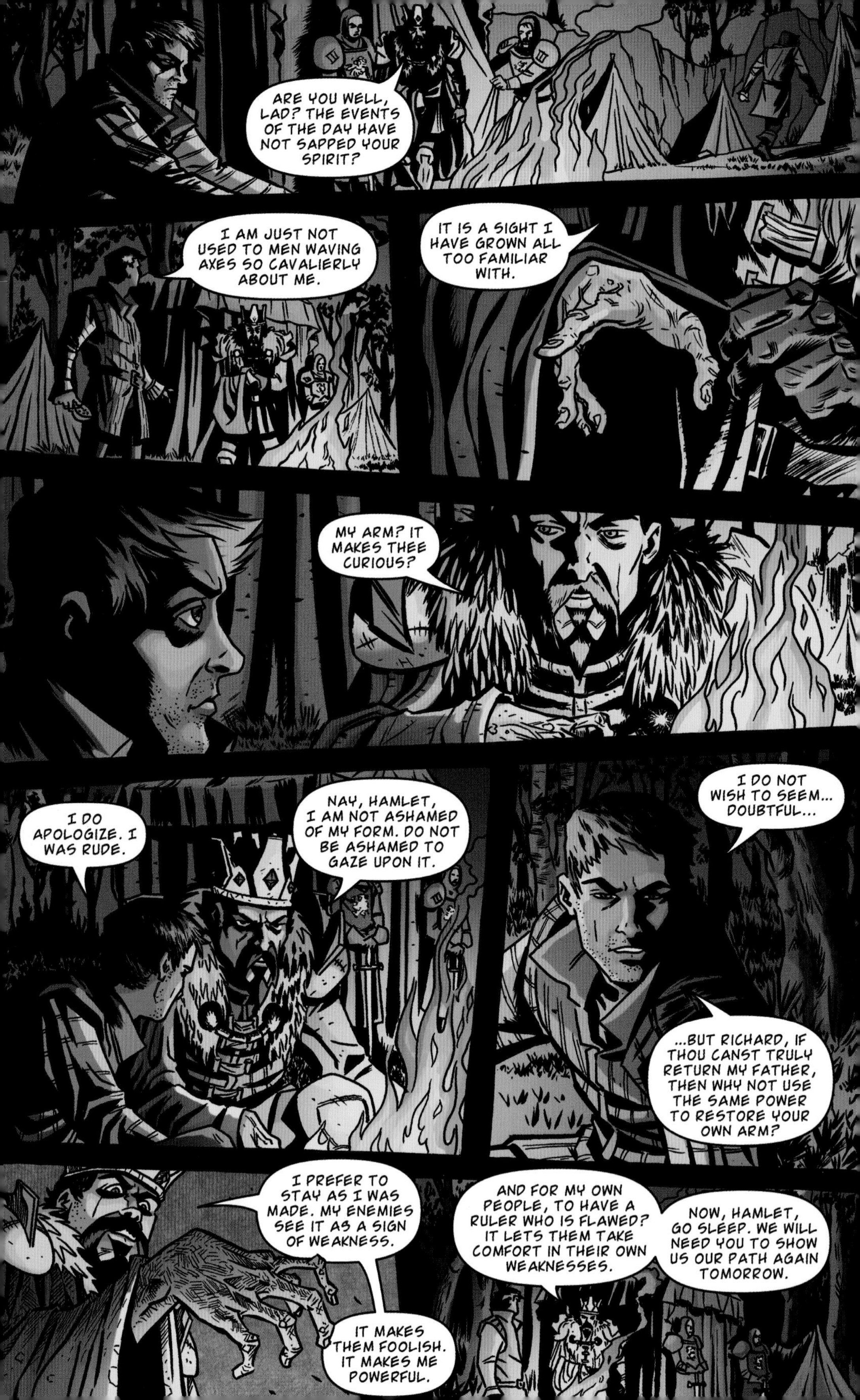
ARE YOU WELL, LAD? THE EVENTS OF THE DAY HAVE NOT SAPPED YOUR SPIRIT?
I AM JUST NOT USED TO MEN WAVING AXES SO CAVALIERLY ABOUT ME.
IT IS A SIGHT I HAVE GROWN ALL TOO FAMILIAR WITH.
MY ARM? IT MAKES THEE CURIOUS?
I DO APOLOGIZE. I WAS RUDE.
NAY, HAMLET, I AM NOT ASHAMED OF MY FORM. DO NOT BE ASHAMED TO GAZE UPON IT.
I DO NOT WISH TO SEEM... DOUBTFUL...
...BUT RICHARD, IF THOU CANST TRULY RETURN MY FATHER, THEN WHY NOT USE THE SAME POWER TO RESTORE YOUR OWN ARM?
I PREFER TO STAY AS I WAS MADE. MY ENEMIES SEE IT AS A SIGN OF WEAKNESS.
IT MAKES THEM FOOLISH. IT MAKES ME POWERFUL.
AND FOR MY OWN PEOPLE, TO HAVE A RULER WHO IS FLAWED? IT LETS THEM TAKE COMFORT IN THEIR OWN WEAKNESSES.
NOW, HAMLET, GO SLEEP. WE WILL NEED YOU TO SHOW US OUR PATH AGAIN TOMORROW.

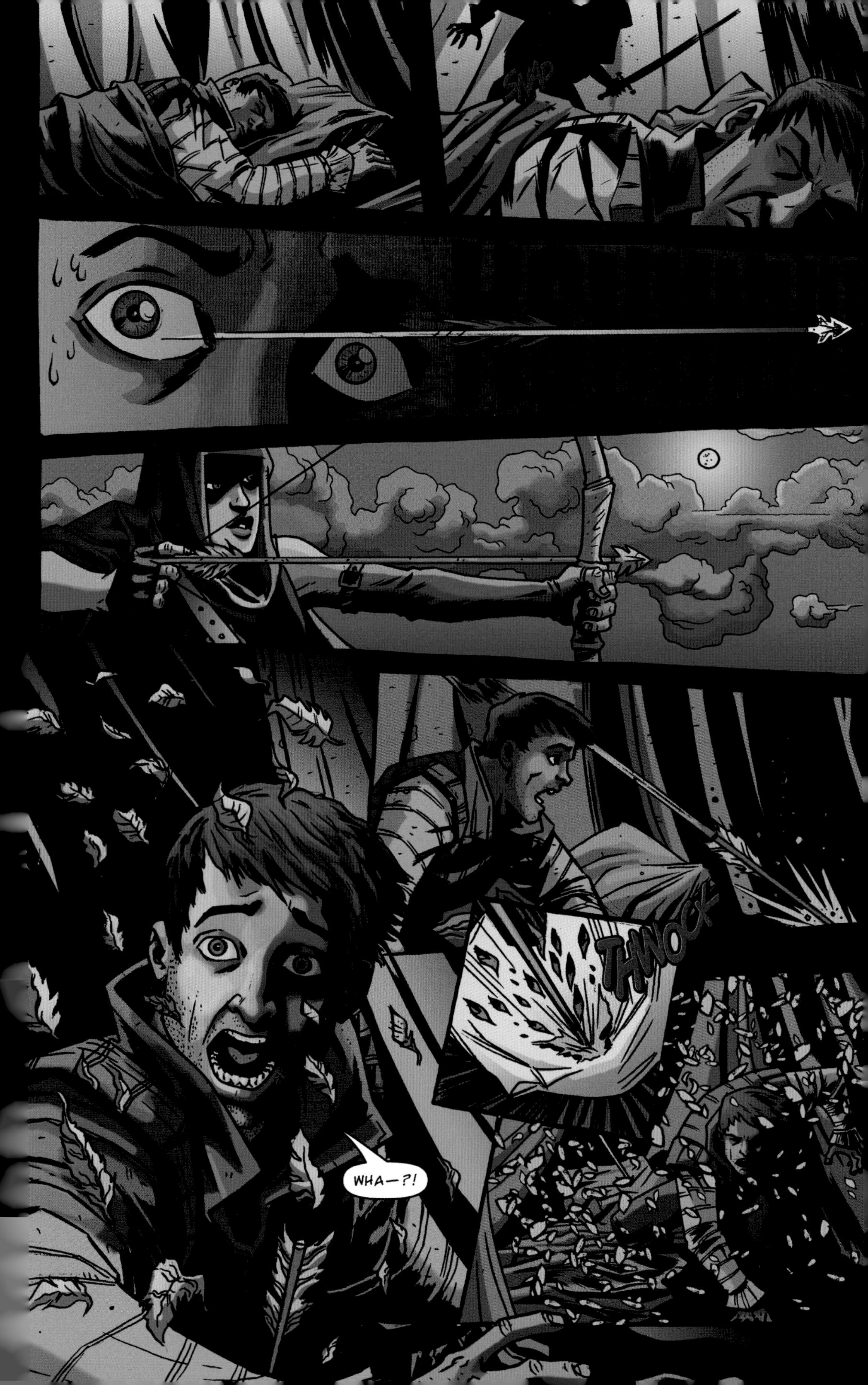
SNAP
THWOCK
WHA—?!

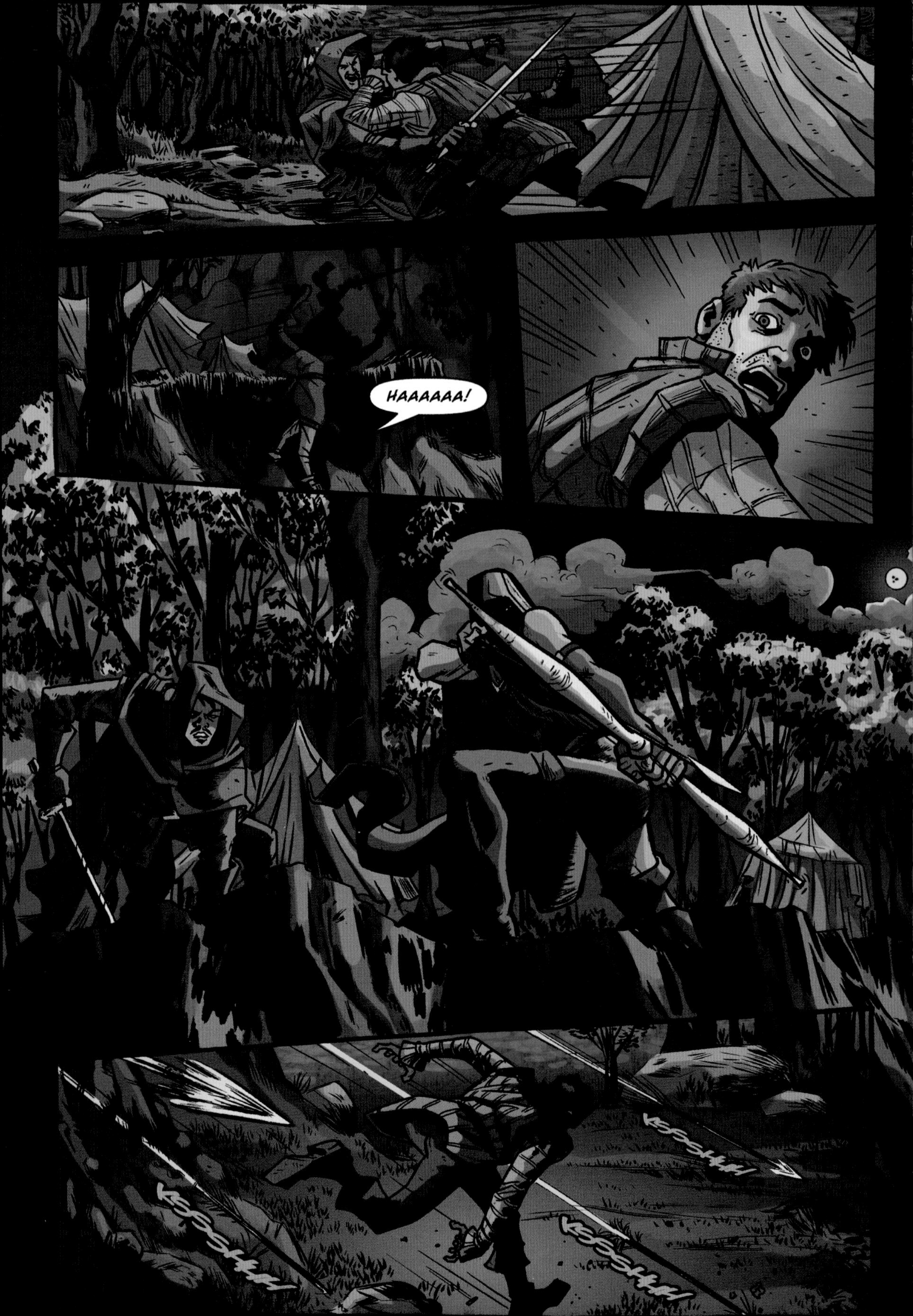
HAAAAAA!
KSSSHHH
KSSSHHH
KSSSHHH

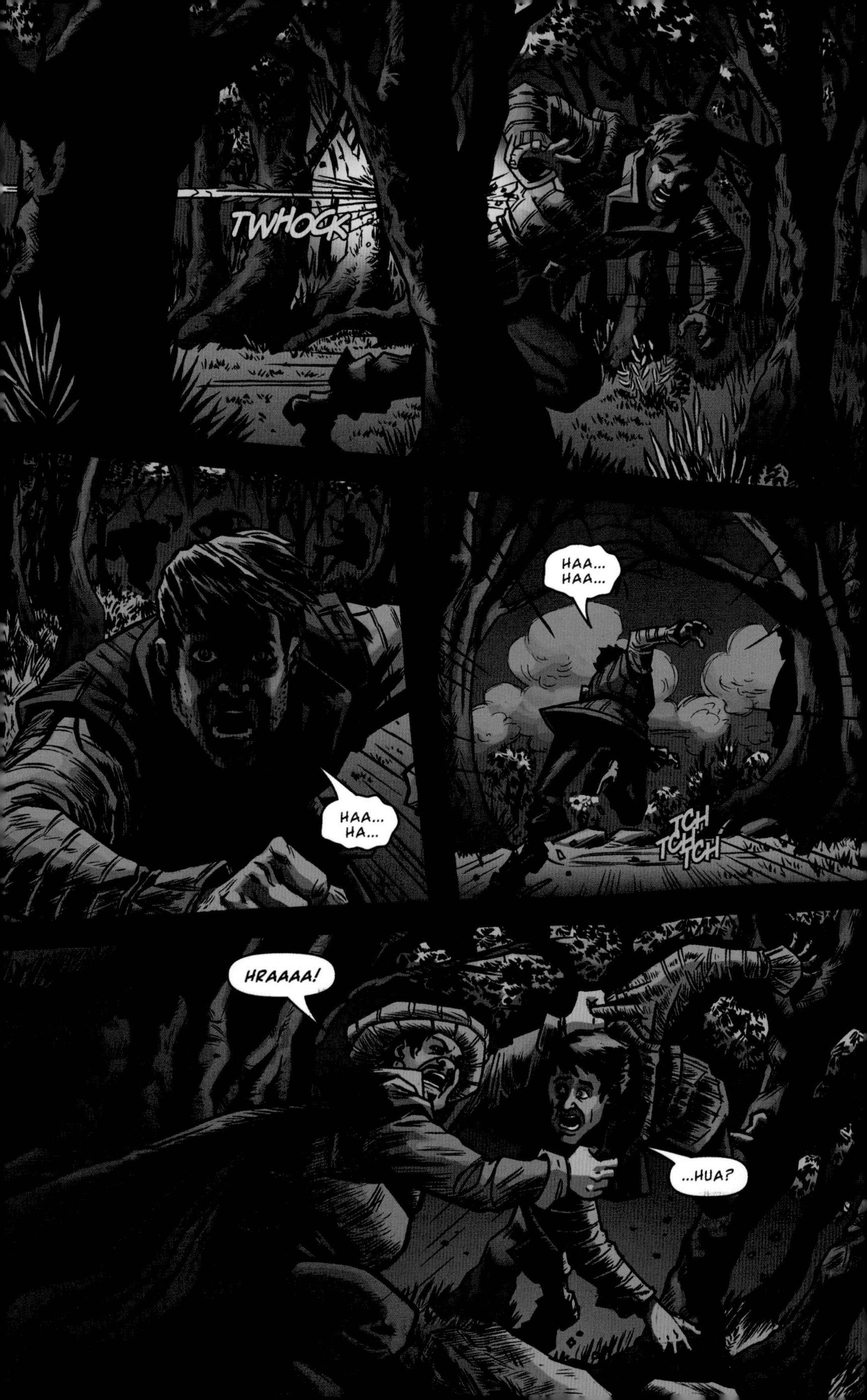
TWHOCK
HAA... HA...
HAA... HAA...
TCH TCH TCH
HRAAAA!
...HUA?

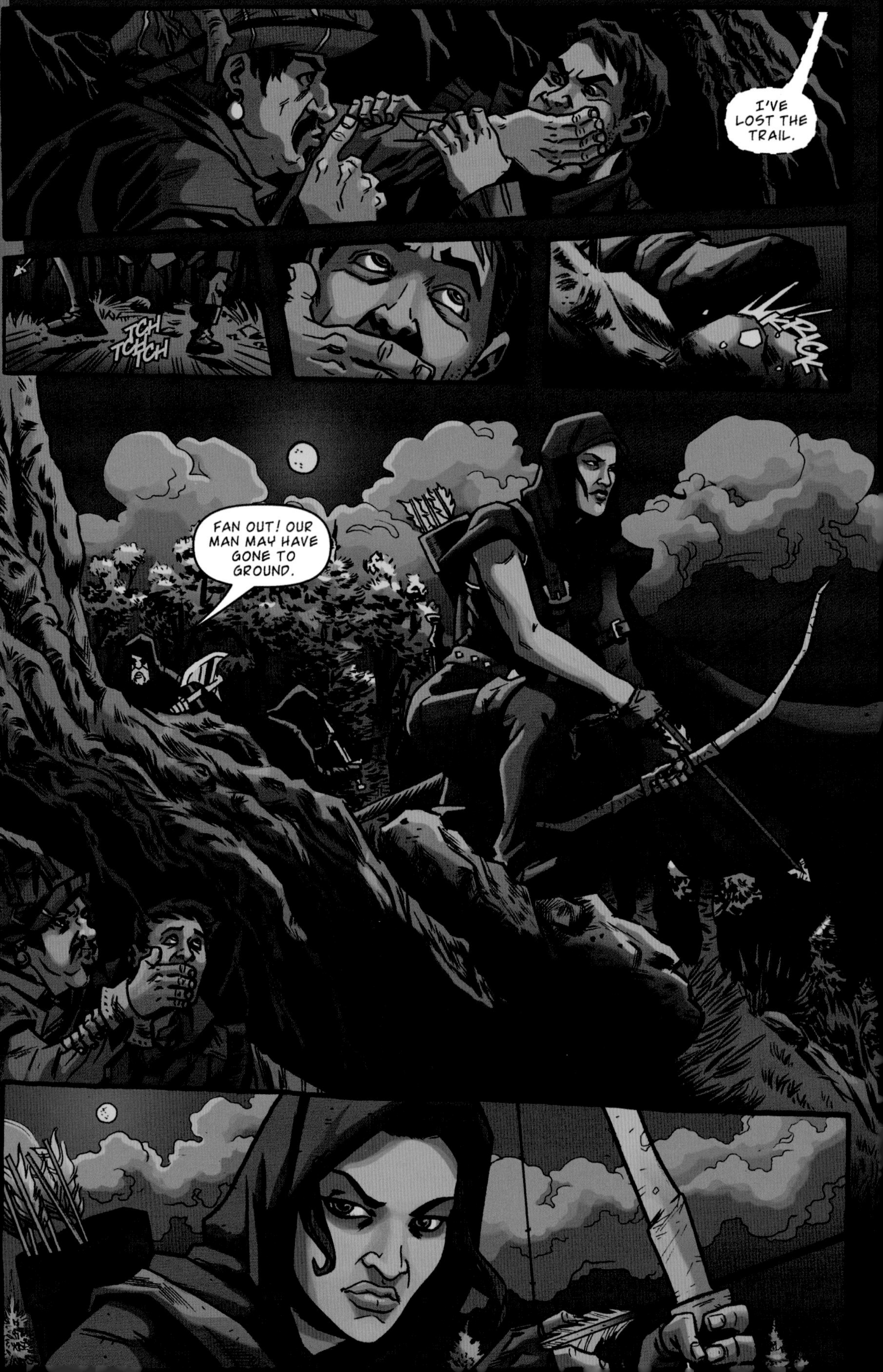
I'VE LOST THE TRAIL.
TCH TCH TCH
FAN OUT! OUR MAN MAY HAVE GONE TO GROUND.

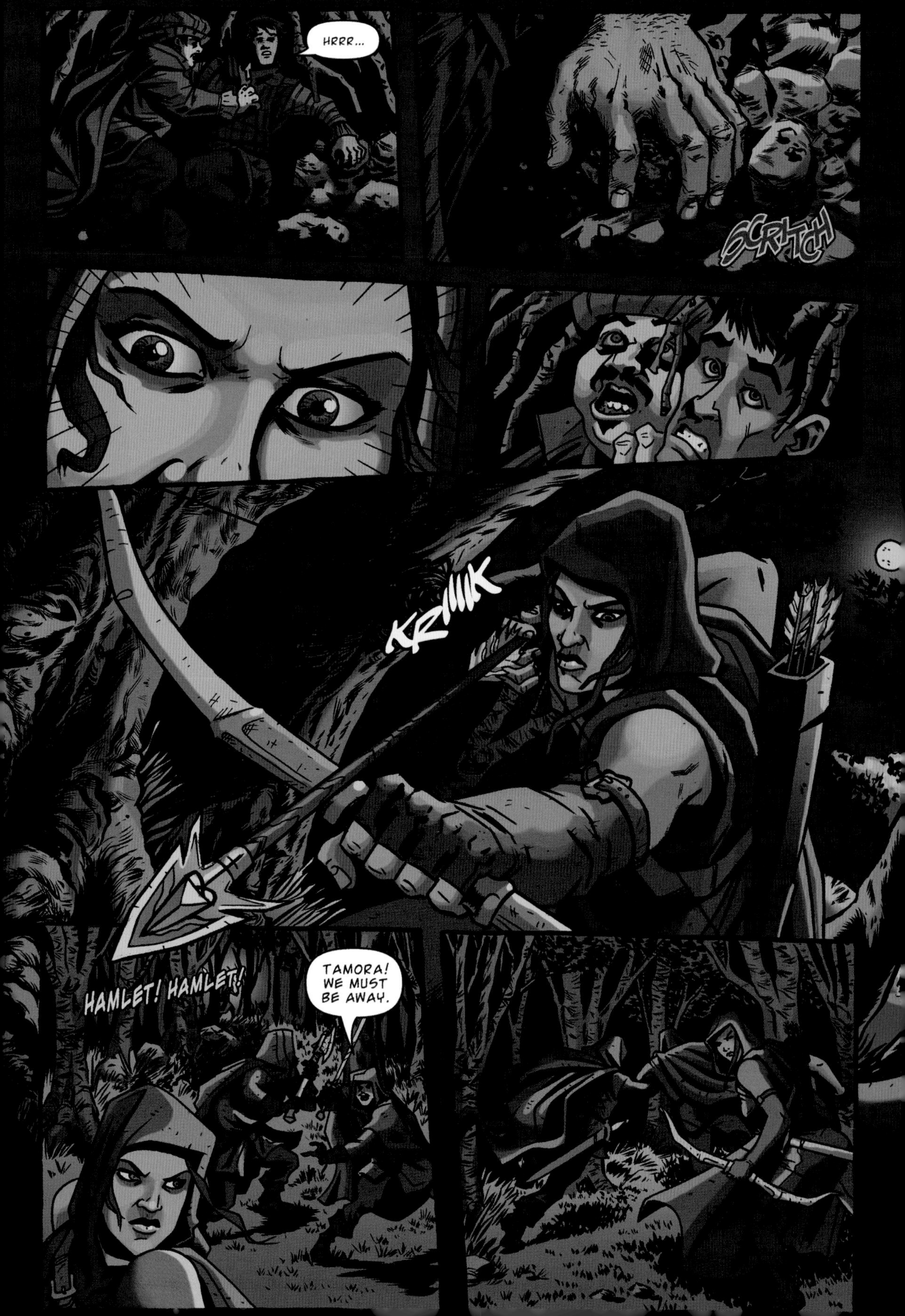
HRRR...
SCRITCH
KRIIIIK
HAMLET! HAMLET!
TAMORA! WE MUST BE AWAY.

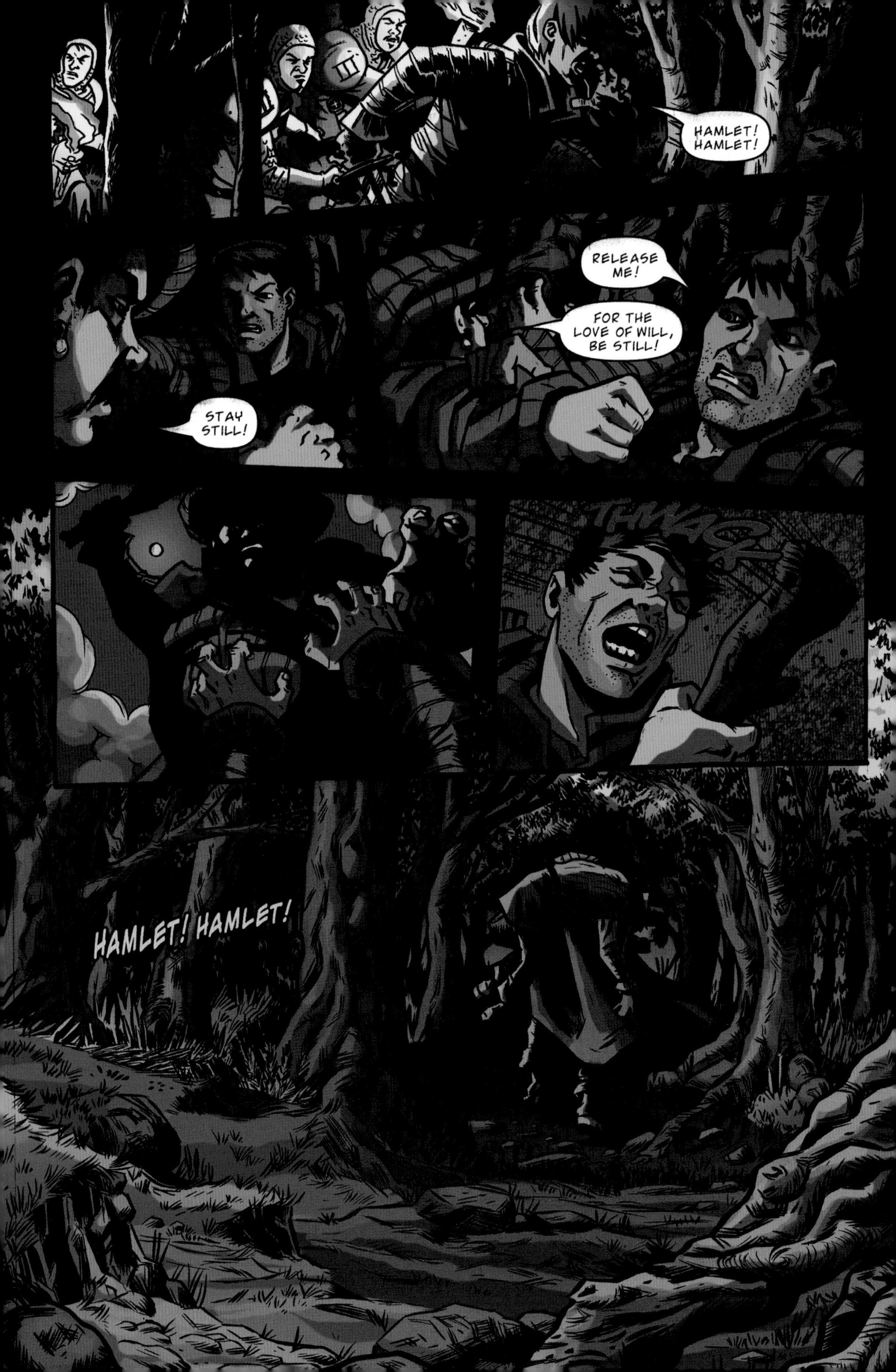
HAMLET! HAMLET!
RELEASE ME!
FOR THE LOVE OF WILL, BE STILL!
STAY STILL!
THWACK!
HAMLET! HAMLET!

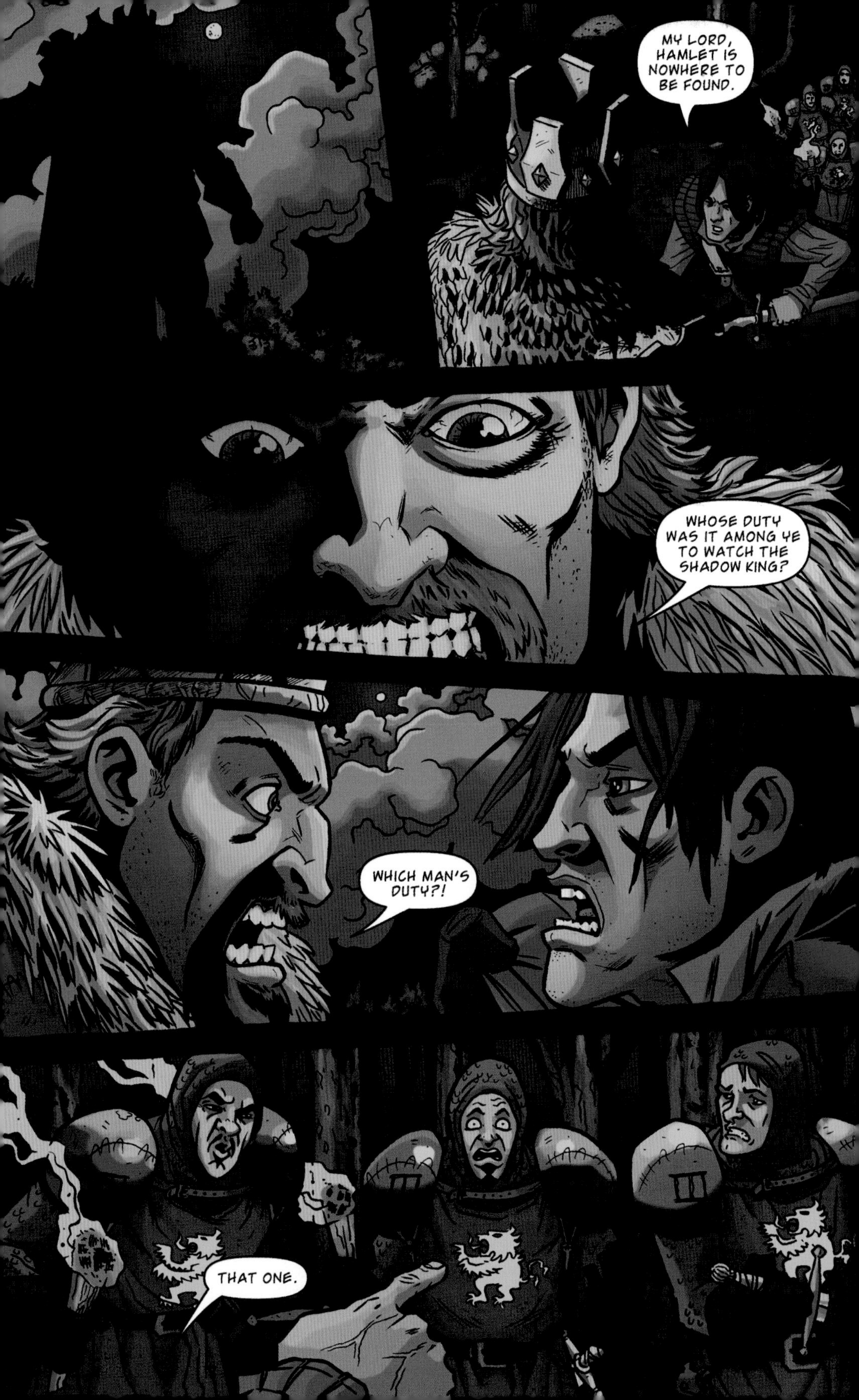
MY LORD, HAMLET IS NOWHERE TO BE FOUND.
WHOSE DUTY WAS IT AMONG YE TO WATCH THE SHADOW KING?
WHICH MAN'S DUTY?!
THAT ONE.

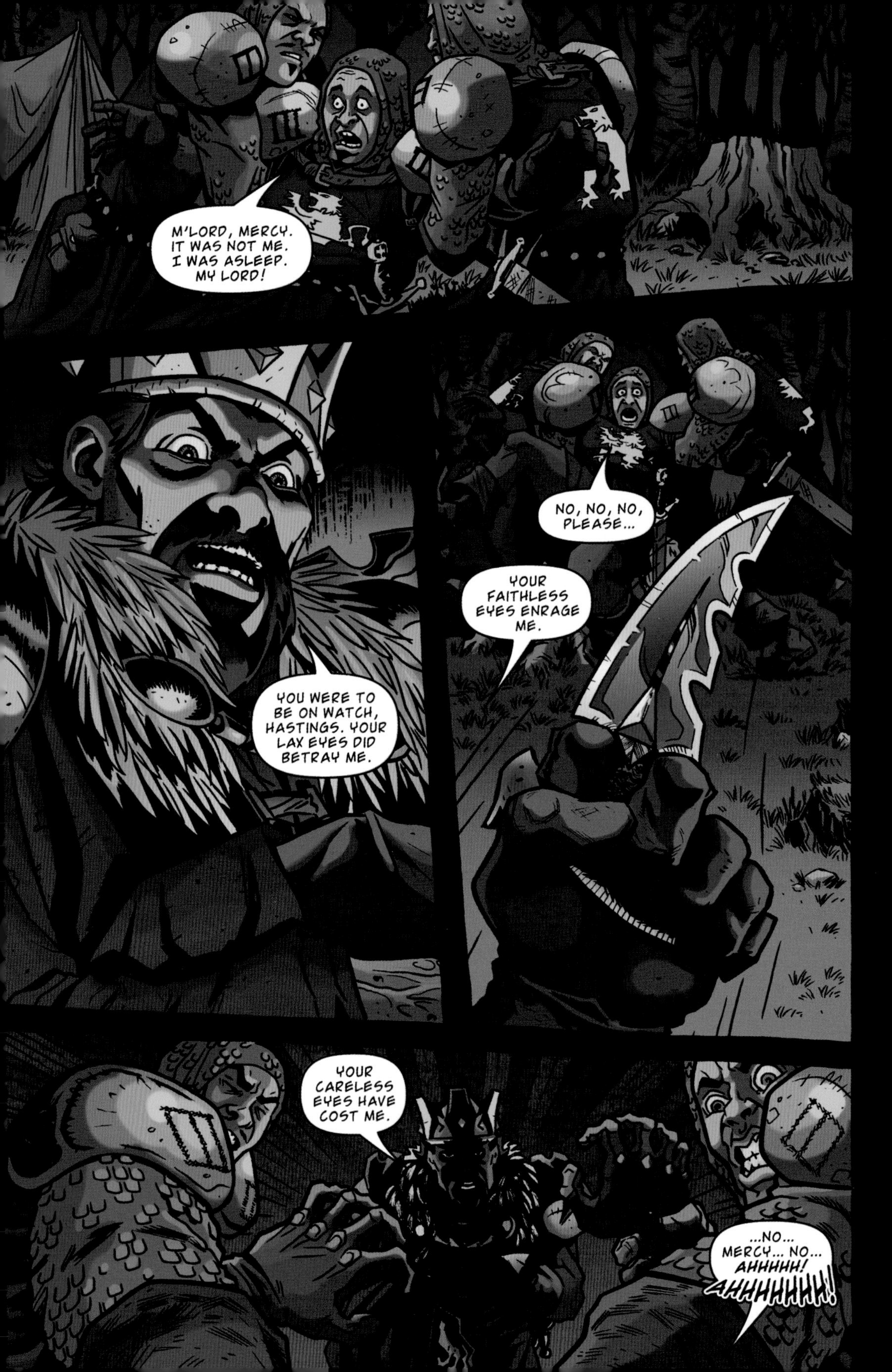
M'LORD, MERCY. IT WAS NOT ME. I WAS ASLEEP. MY LORD!
YOU WERE TO BE ON WATCH, HASTINGS. YOUR LAX EYES DID BETRAY ME.
NO, NO, NO, PLEASE...
YOUR FAITHLESS EYES ENRAGE ME.
YOUR CARELESS EYES HAVE COST ME.
...NO... MERCY... NO... AHHHHH! AHHHHHHH!

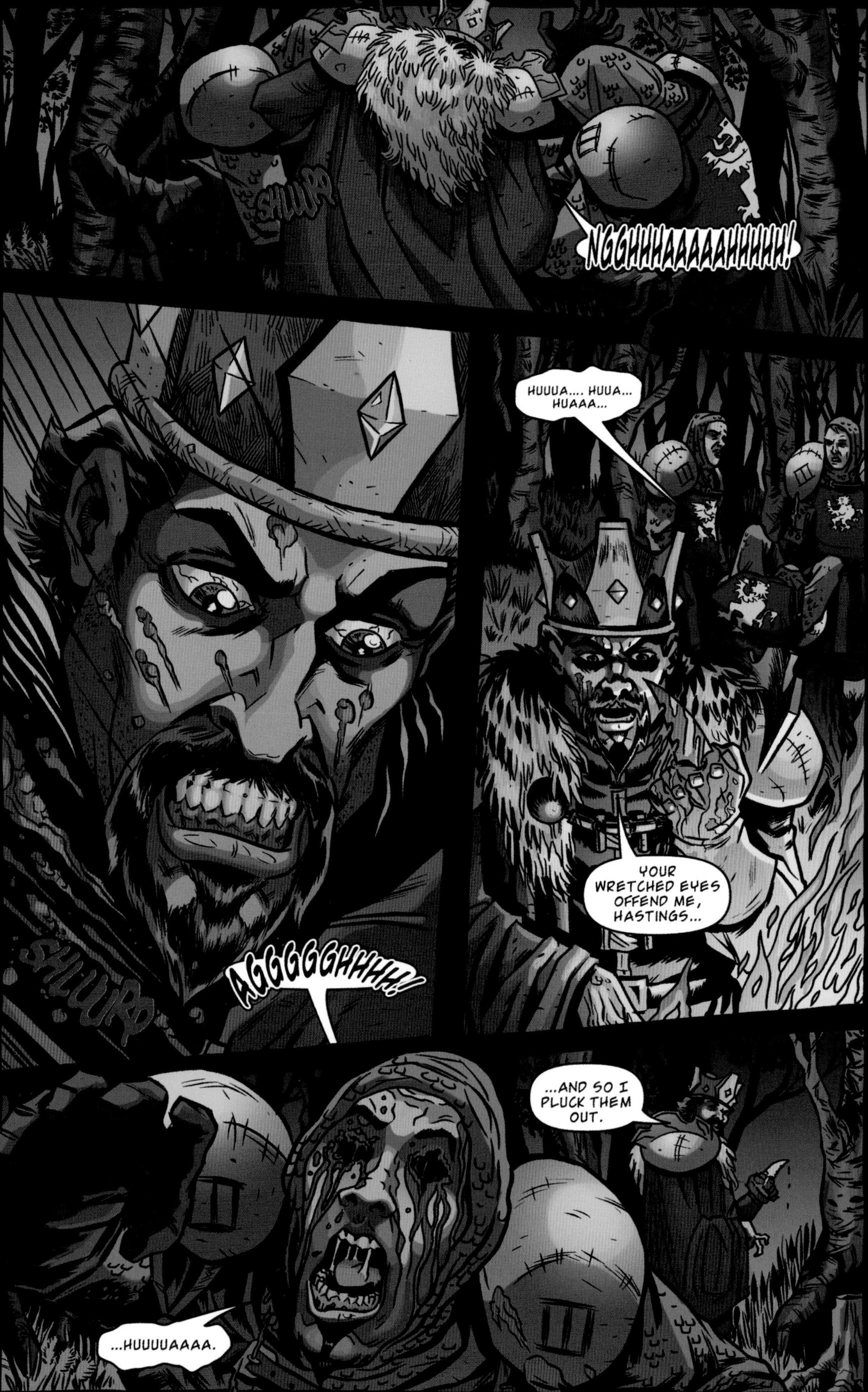
SHLURP
NGGHHHAAAAAHHHHH!
HUUUA.... HUUA... HUAAA...
YOUR WRETCHED EYES OFFEND ME, HASTINGS...
SHLURP
AGGGGGHHHH!
...AND SO I PLUCK THEM OUT.
...HUUUUAAAA.

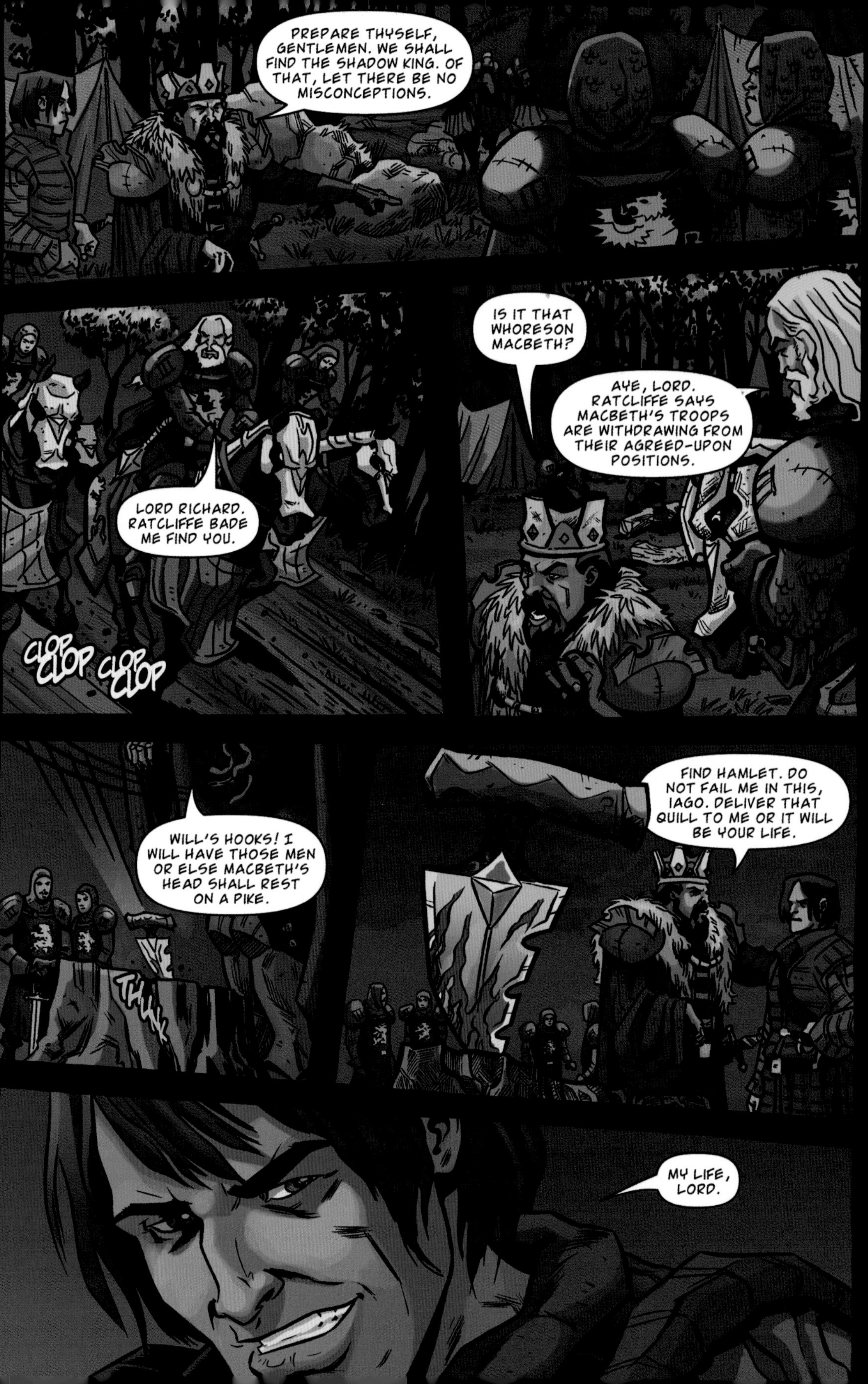
PREPARE THYSELF, GENTLEMEN. WE SHALL FIND THE SHADOW KING. OF THAT, LET THERE BE NO MISCONCEPTIONS.
LORD RICHARD. RATCLIFFE BADE ME FIND YOU.
CLOP CLOP CLOP CLOP
IS IT THAT WHORESON MACBETH?
AYE, LORD. RATCLIFFE SAYS MACBETH'S TROOPS ARE WITHDRAWING FROM THEIR AGREED-UPON POSITIONS.
WILL'S HOOKS! I WILL HAVE THOSE MEN OR ELSE MACBETH'S HEAD SHALL REST ON A PIKE.
THUNK
FIND HAMLET. DO NOT FAIL ME IN THIS, IAGO. DELIVER THAT QUILL TO ME OR IT WILL BE YOUR LIFE.
MY LIFE, LORD.

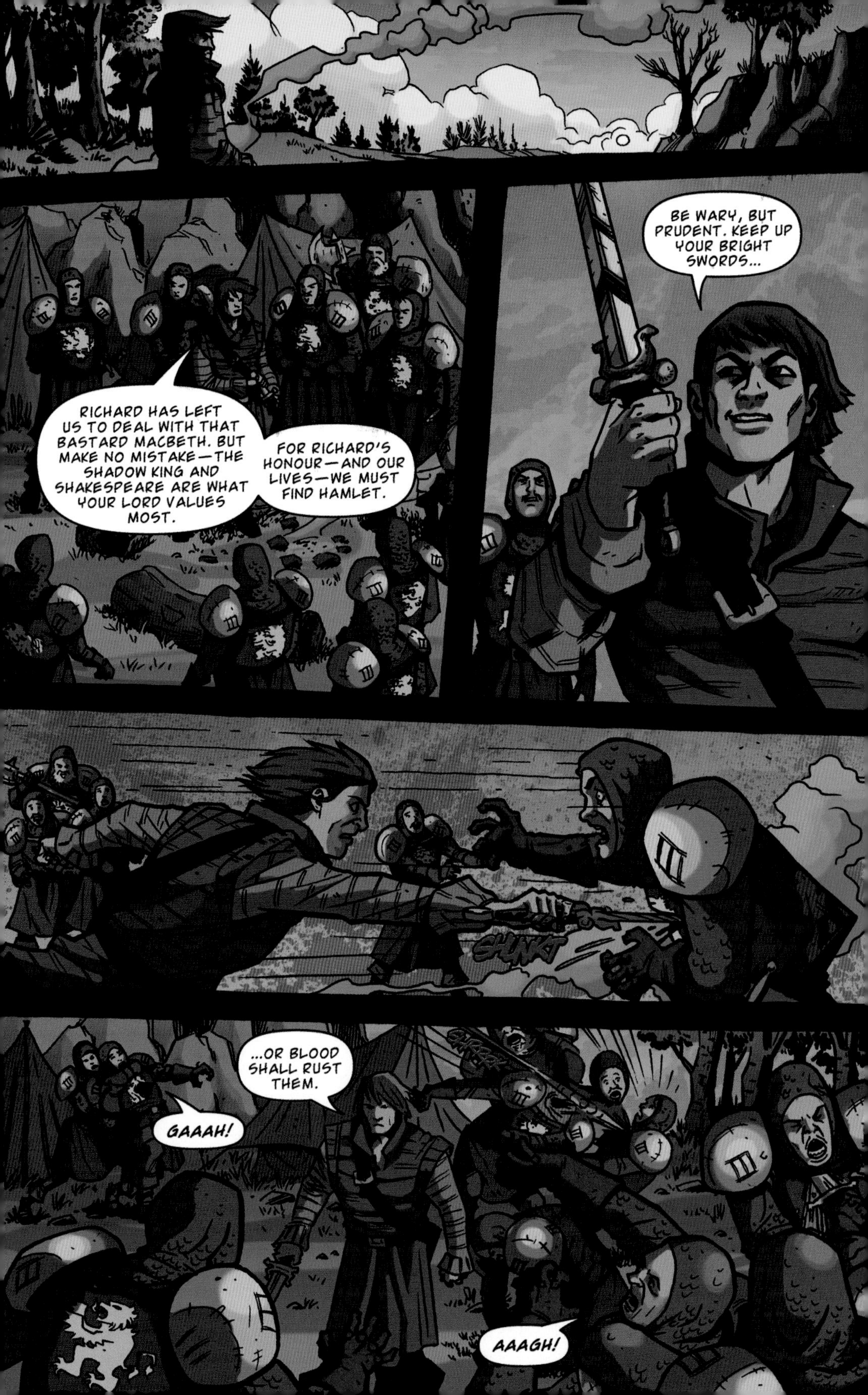
RICHARD HAS LEFT US TO DEAL WITH THAT BASTARD MACBETH. BUT MAKE NO MISTAKE—THE SHADOW KING AND SHAKESPEARE ARE WHAT YOUR LORD VALUES MOST.
FOR RICHARD'S HONOUR—AND OUR LIVES—WE MUST FIND HAMLET.
BE WARY, BUT PRUDENT. KEEP UP YOUR BRIGHT SWORDS...
SHUNKT
...OR BLOOD SHALL RUST THEM.
GAAAH!
AAAGH!

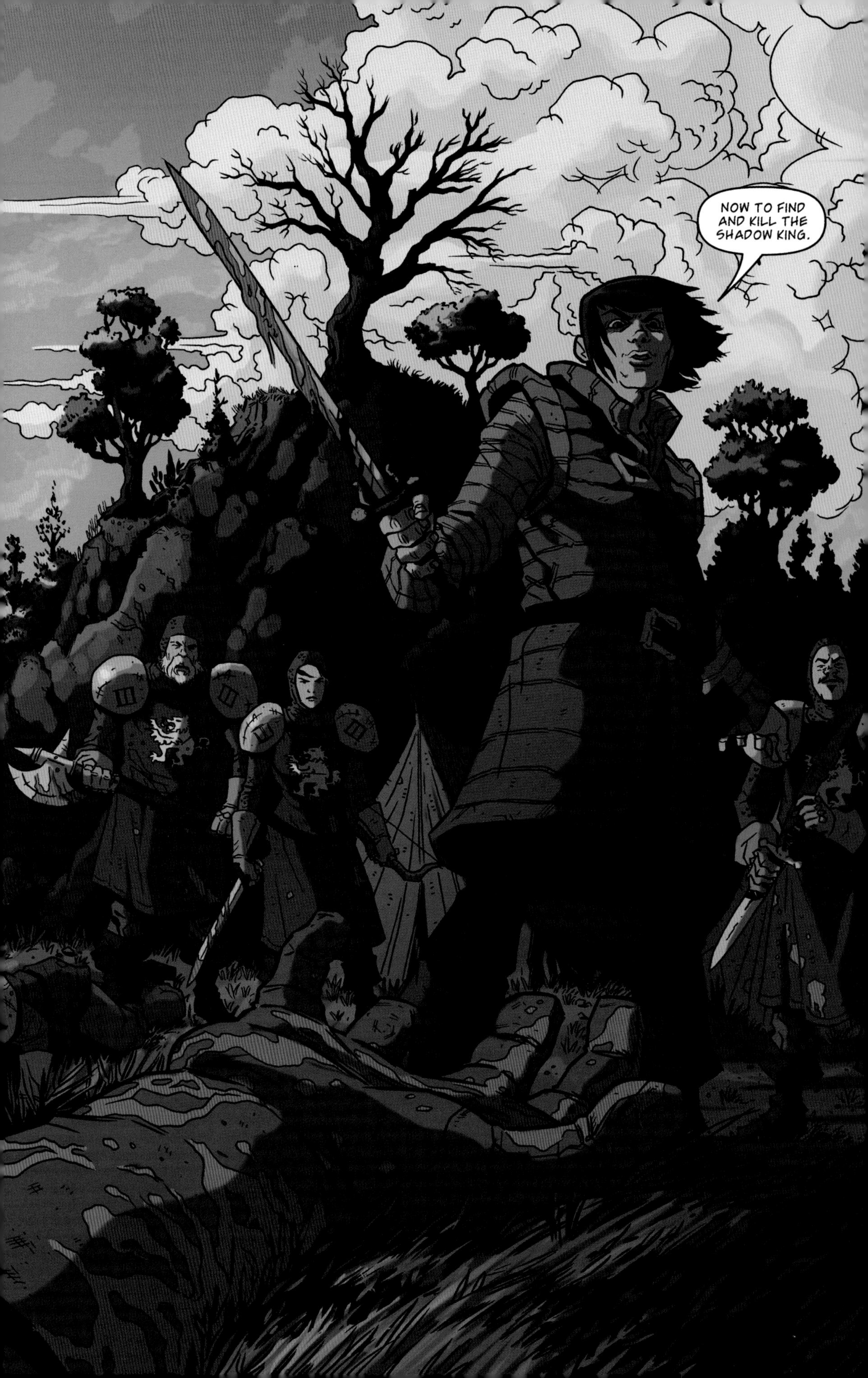
NOW TO FIND AND KILL THE SHADOW KING.

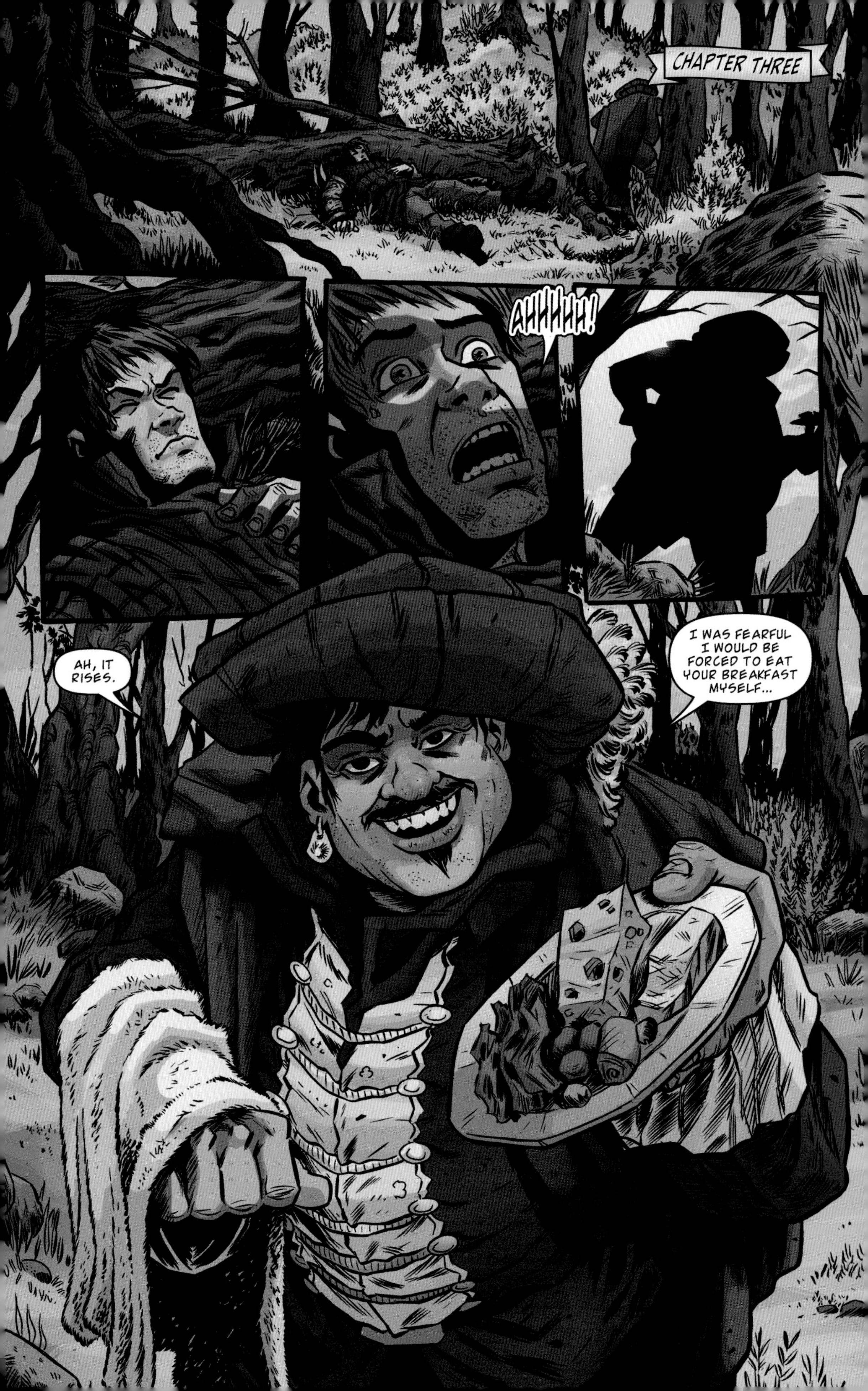
CHAPTER THREE
AHHHHH!
AH, IT RISES.
I WAS FEARFUL I WOULD BE FORCED TO EAT YOUR BREAKFAST MYSELF...

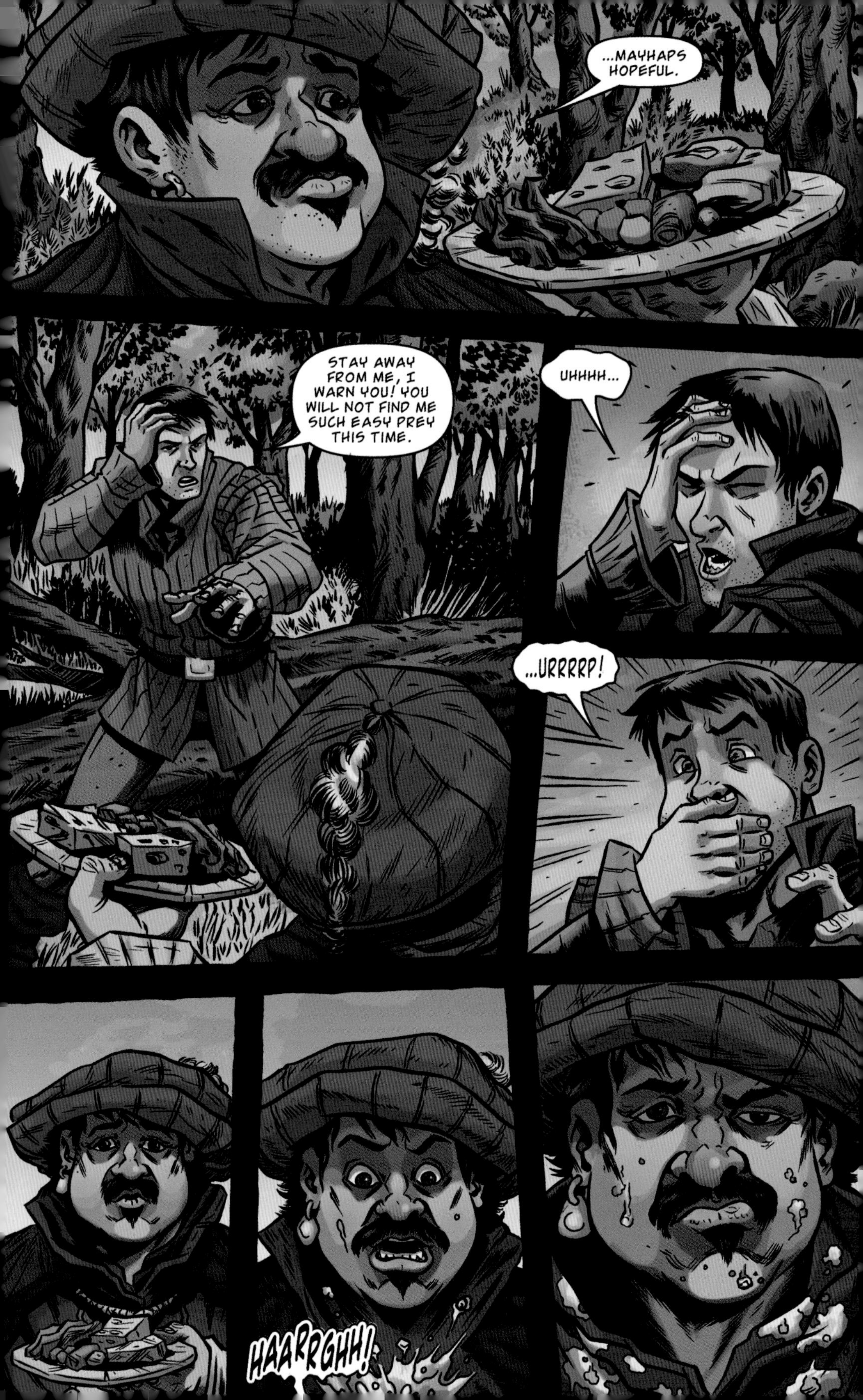
...MAYHAPS HOPEFUL.
STAY AWAY FROM ME, I WARN YOU! YOU WILL NOT FIND ME SUCH EASY PREY THIS TIME.
UHHHH...
...URRRRP!
HAARRGHH!

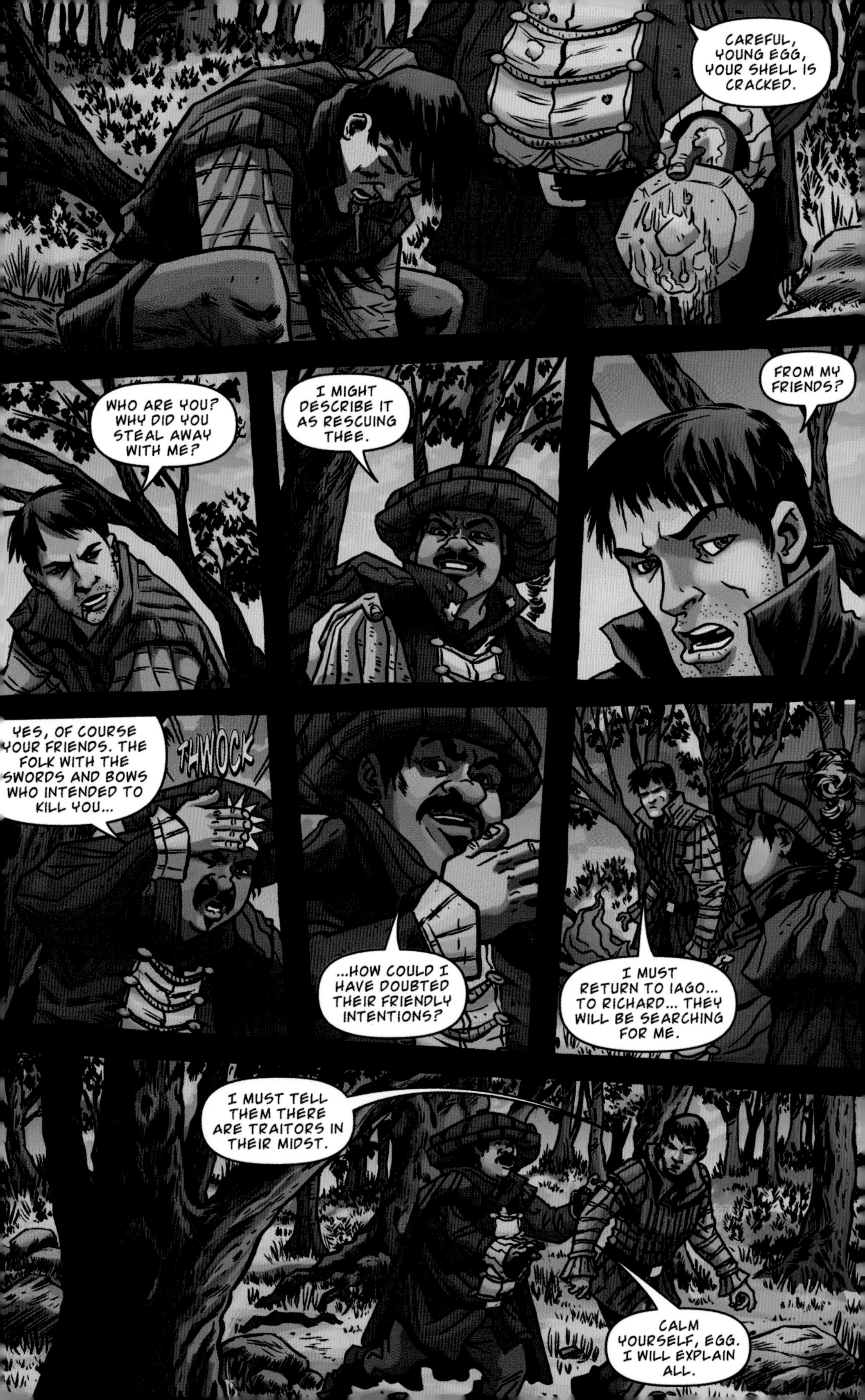
CAREFUL, YOUNG EGG, YOUR SHELL IS CRACKED.
WHO ARE YOU? WHY DID YOU STEAL AWAY WITH ME?
I MIGHT DESCRIBE IT AS RESCUING THEE.
FROM MY FRIENDS?
YES, OF COURSE YOUR FRIENDS. THE FOLK WITH THE SWORDS AND BOWS WHO INTENDED TO KILL YOU...
THWOCK
...HOW COULD I HAVE DOUBTED THEIR FRIENDLY INTENTIONS?
I MUST RETURN TO IAGO... TO RICHARD... THEY WILL BE SEARCHING FOR ME.
I MUST TELL THEM THERE ARE TRAITORS IN THEIR MIDST.
CALM YOURSELF, EGG. I WILL EXPLAIN ALL.

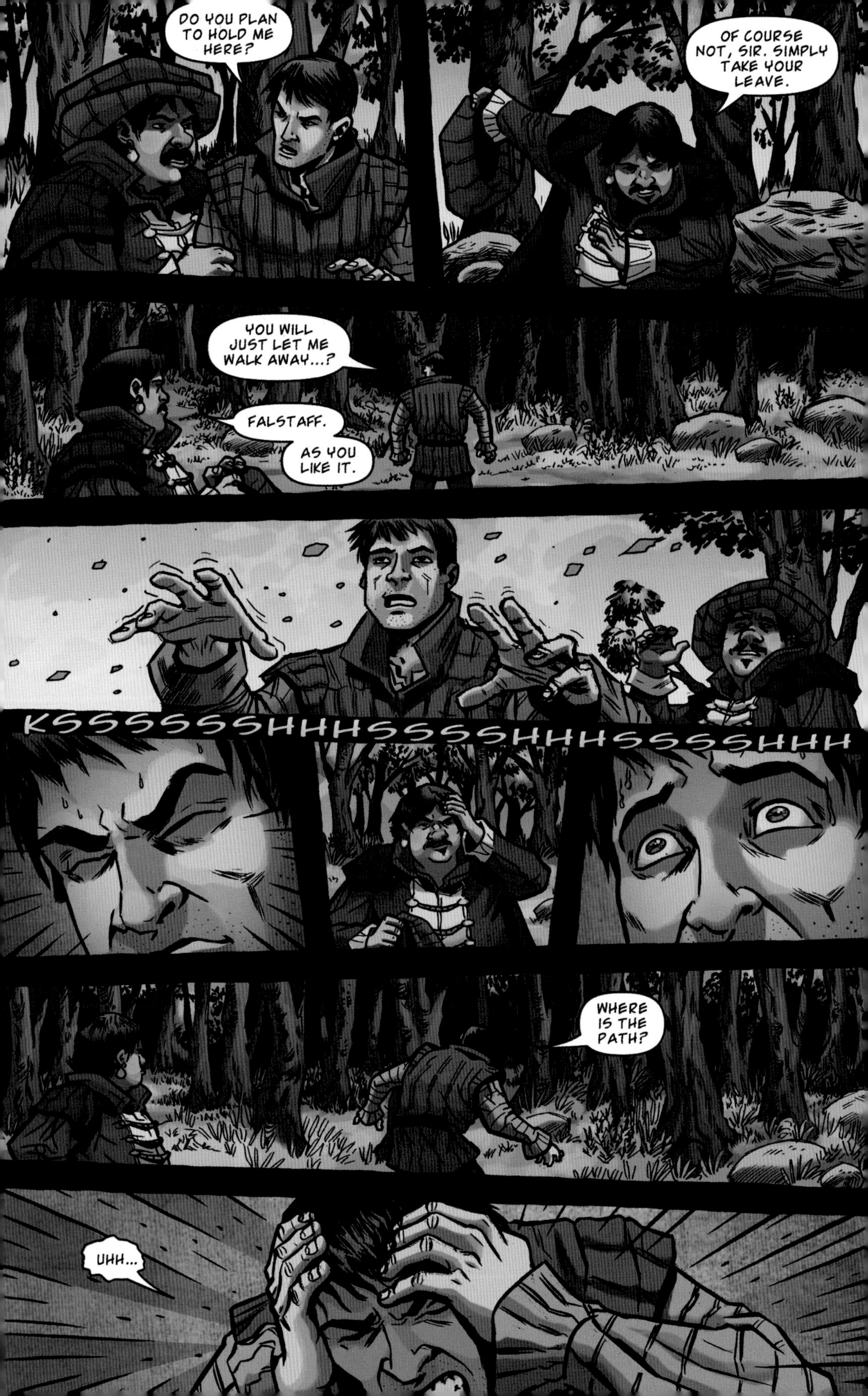
DO YOU PLAN TO HOLD ME HERE?
OF COURSE NOT, SIR. SIMPLY TAKE YOUR LEAVE.
YOU WILL JUST LET ME WALK AWAY...?
FALSTAFF.
AS YOU LIKE IT.
KSSSSSSSHHHHSSSSSSHHHHSSSSSSHHH
WHERE IS THE PATH?
UHH...

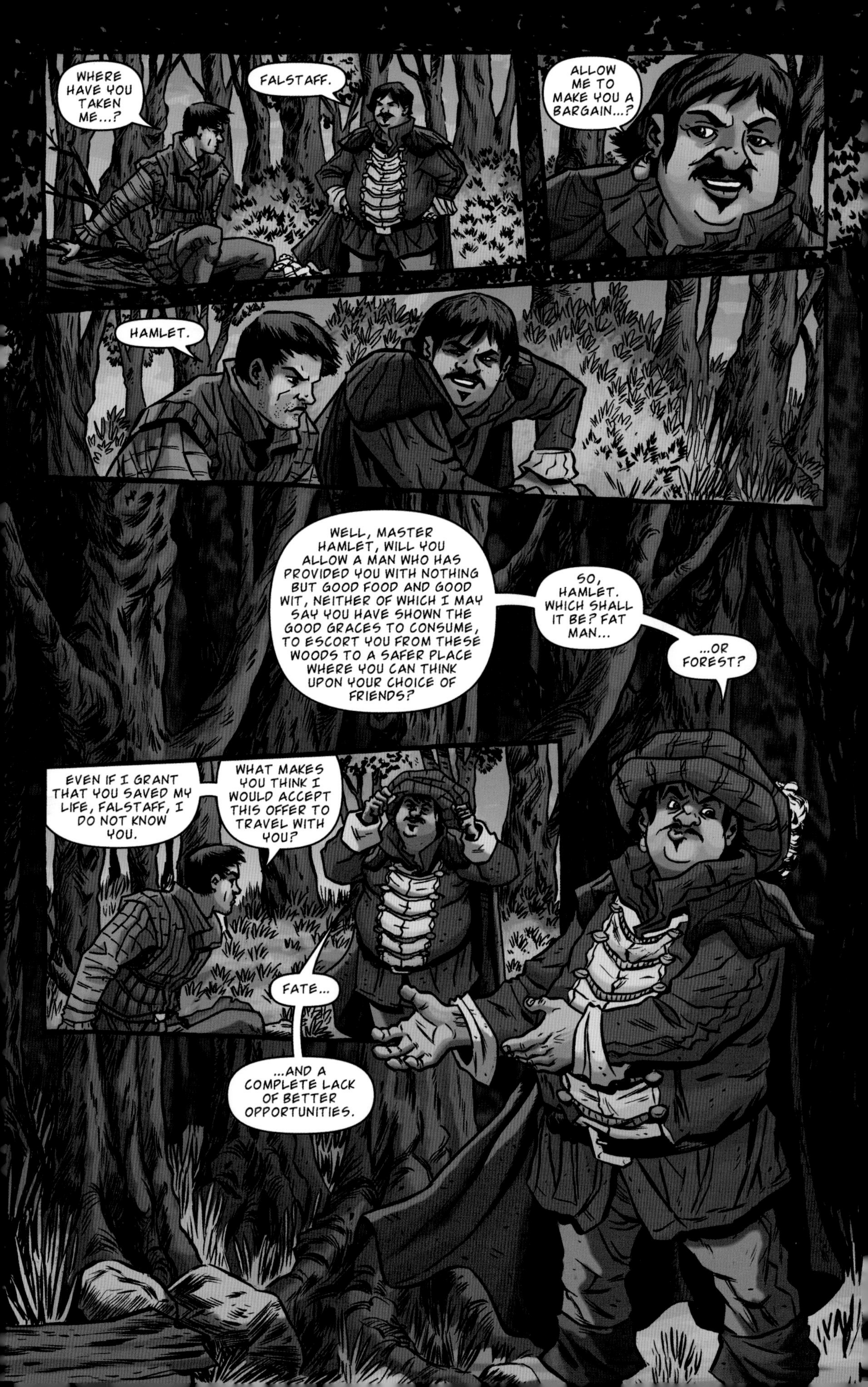
WHERE HAVE YOU TAKEN ME...?
FALSTAFF.
ALLOW ME TO MAKE YOU A BARGAIN...?
HAMLET.
WELL, MASTER HAMLET, WILL YOU ALLOW A MAN WHO HAS PROVIDED YOU WITH NOTHING BUT GOOD FOOD AND GOOD WIT, NEITHER OF WHICH I MAY SAY YOU HAVE SHOWN THE GOOD GRACES TO CONSUME, TO ESCORT YOU FROM THESE WOODS TO A SAFER PLACE WHERE YOU CAN THINK UPON YOUR CHOICE OF FRIENDS?
SO, HAMLET. WHICH SHALL IT BE? FAT MAN...
...OR FOREST?
EVEN IF I GRANT THAT YOU SAVED MY LIFE, FALSTAFF, I DO NOT KNOW YOU.
WHAT MAKES YOU THINK I WOULD ACCEPT THIS OFFER TO TRAVEL WITH YOU?
FATE...
...AND A COMPLETE LACK OF BETTER OPPORTUNITIES.

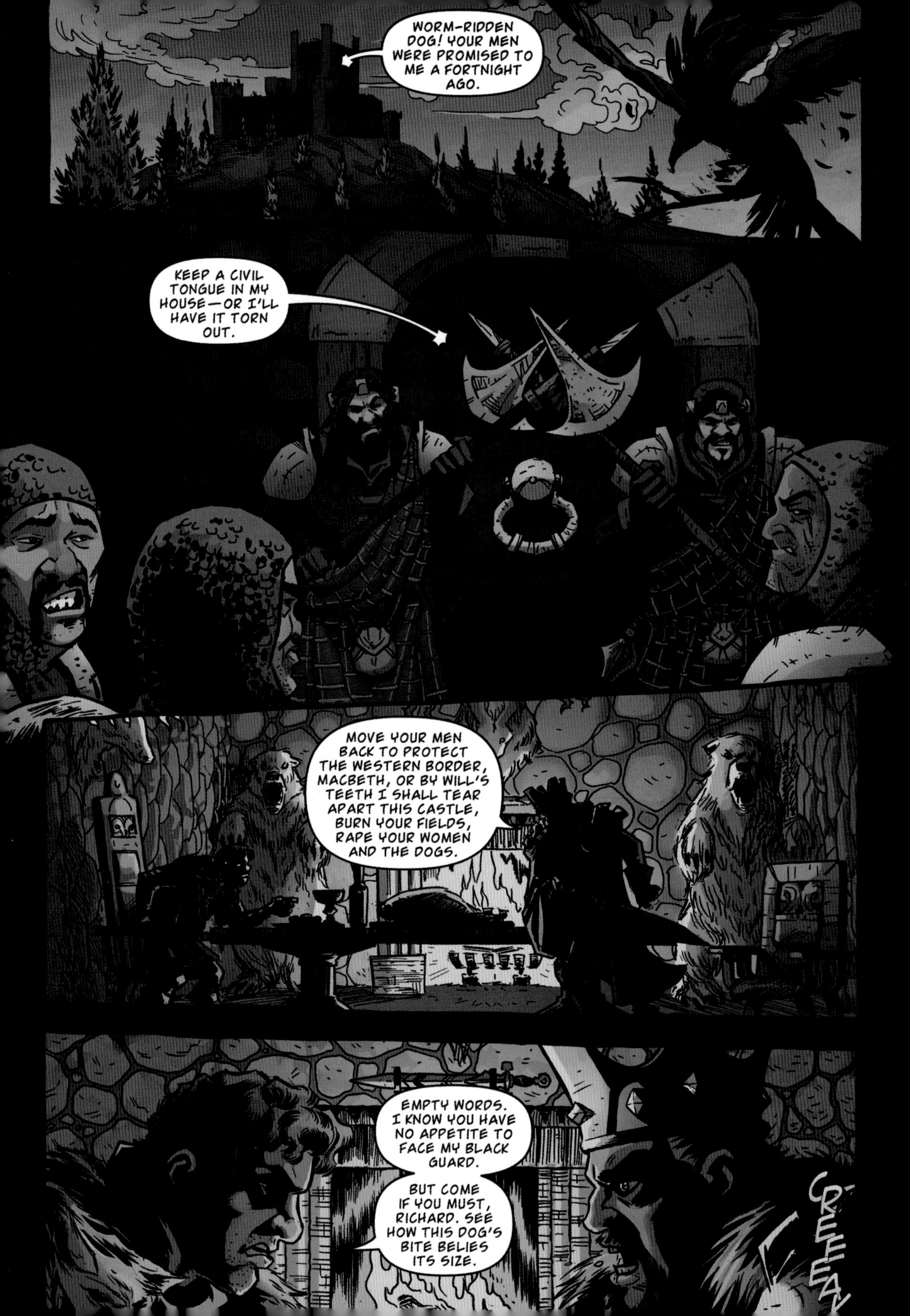
WORM-RIDDEN DOG! YOUR MEN WERE PROMISED TO ME A FORTNIGHT AGO.
KEEP A CIVIL TONGUE IN MY HOUSE—OR I'LL HAVE IT TORN OUT.
MOVE YOUR MEN BACK TO PROTECT THE WESTERN BORDER, MACBETH, OR BY WILL'S TEETH I SHALL TEAR APART THIS CASTLE, BURN YOUR FIELDS, RAPE YOUR WOMEN AND THE DOGS.
EMPTY WORDS. I KNOW YOU HAVE NO APPETITE TO FACE MY BLACK GUARD.
BUT COME IF YOU MUST, RICHARD. SEE HOW THIS DOG'S BITE BELIES ITS SIZE.
CREEEAK

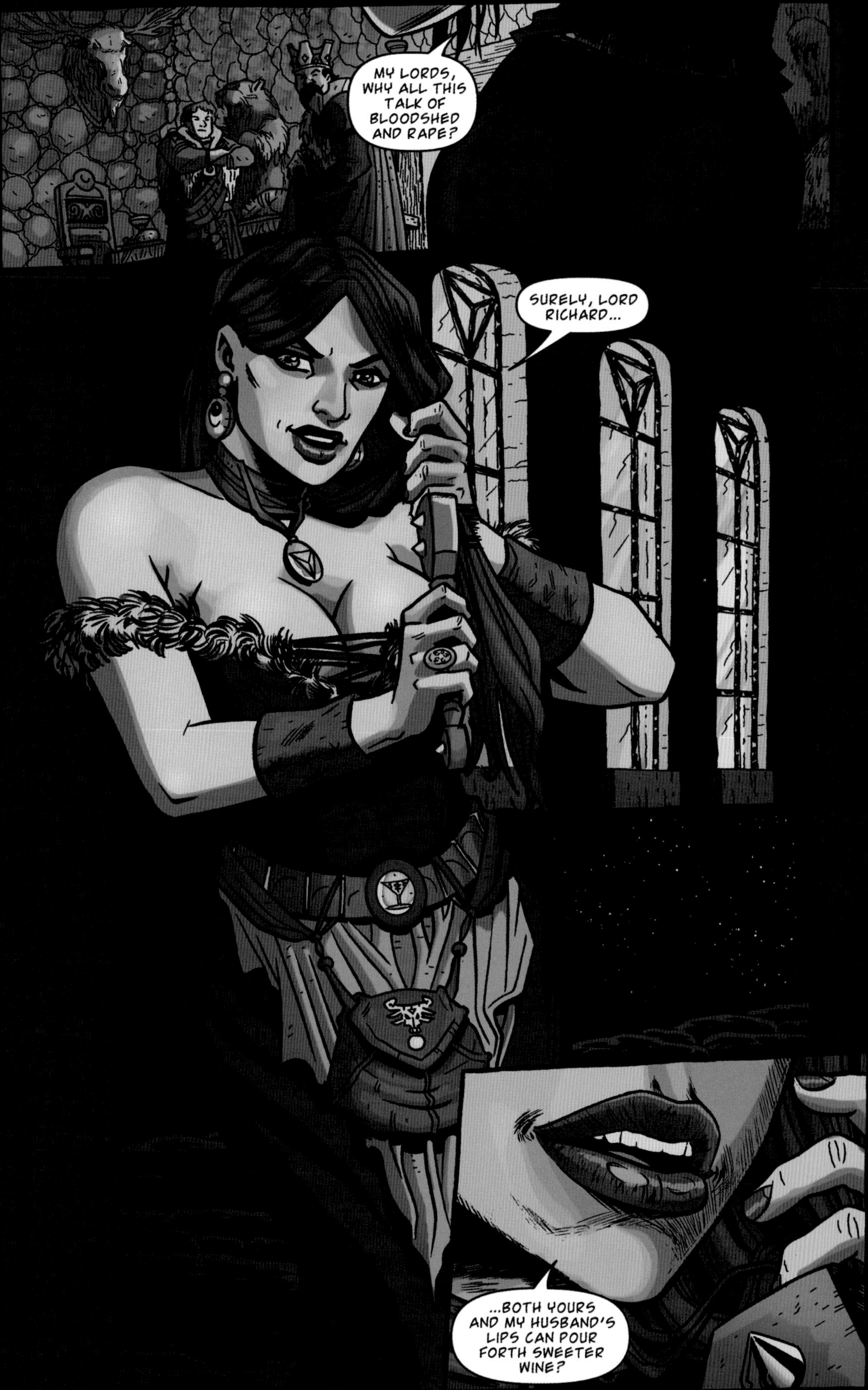
MY LORDS, WHY ALL THIS TALK OF BLOODSHED AND RAPE?
SURELY, LORD RICHARD...
...BOTH YOURS AND MY HUSBAND'S LIPS CAN POUR FORTH SWEETER WINE?

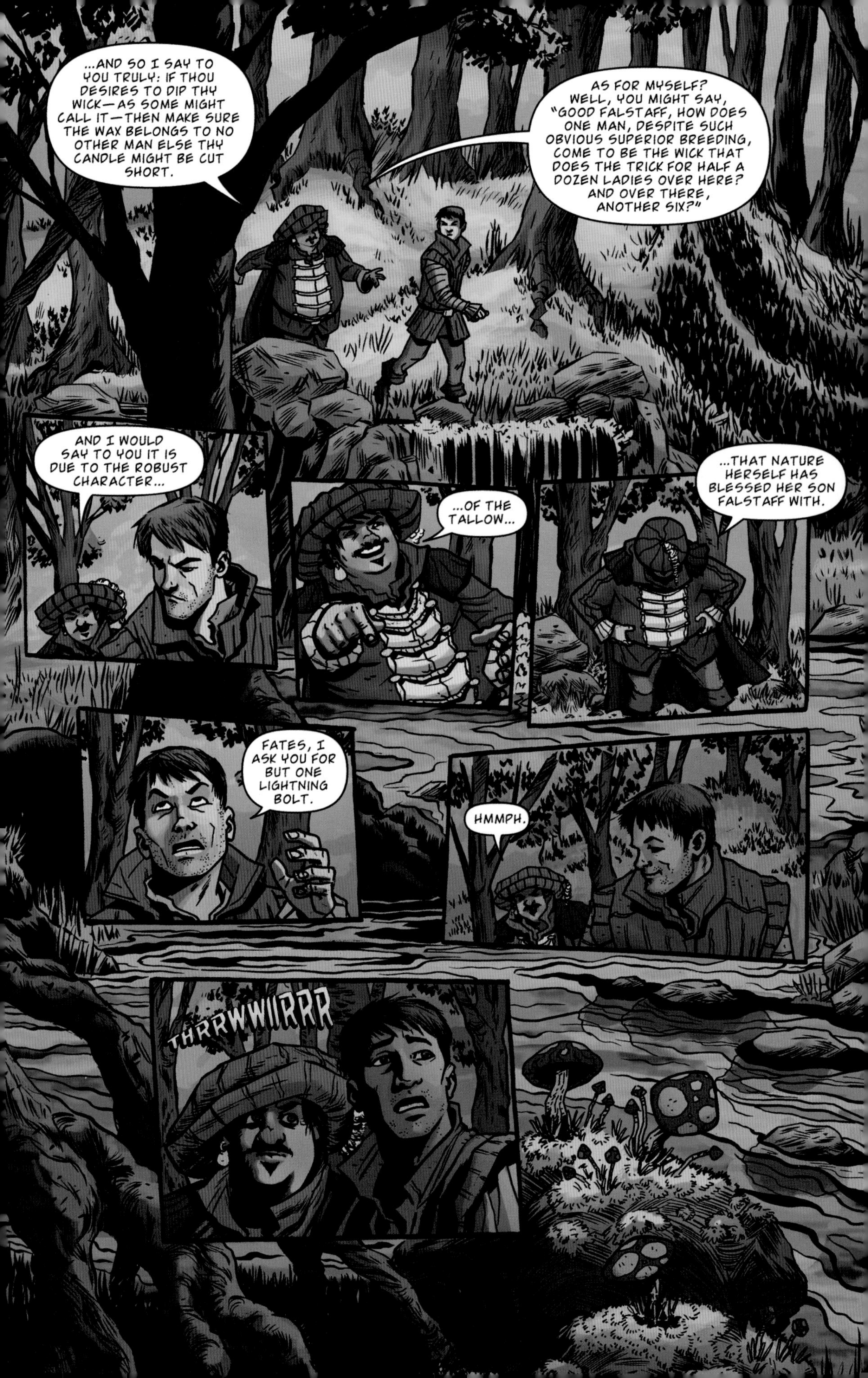
...AND SO I SAY TO YOU TRULY: IF THOU DESIRES TO DIP THY WICK—AS SOME MIGHT CALL IT—THEN MAKE SURE THE WAX BELONGS TO NO OTHER MAN ELSE THY CANDLE MIGHT BE CUT SHORT.
AS FOR MYSELF? WELL, YOU MIGHT SAY, "GOOD FALSTAFF, HOW DOES ONE MAN, DESPITE SUCH OBVIOUS SUPERIOR BREEDING, COME TO BE THE WICK THAT DOES THE TRICK FOR HALF A DOZEN LADIES OVER HERE? AND OVER THERE, ANOTHER SIX?"
AND I WOULD SAY TO YOU IT IS DUE TO THE ROBUST CHARACTER...
...OF THE TALLOW...
...THAT NATURE HERSELF HAS BLESSED HER SON FALSTAFF WITH.
FATES, I ASK YOU FOR BUT ONE LIGHTNING BOLT.
HMMPH.
THRRWWIIRRR

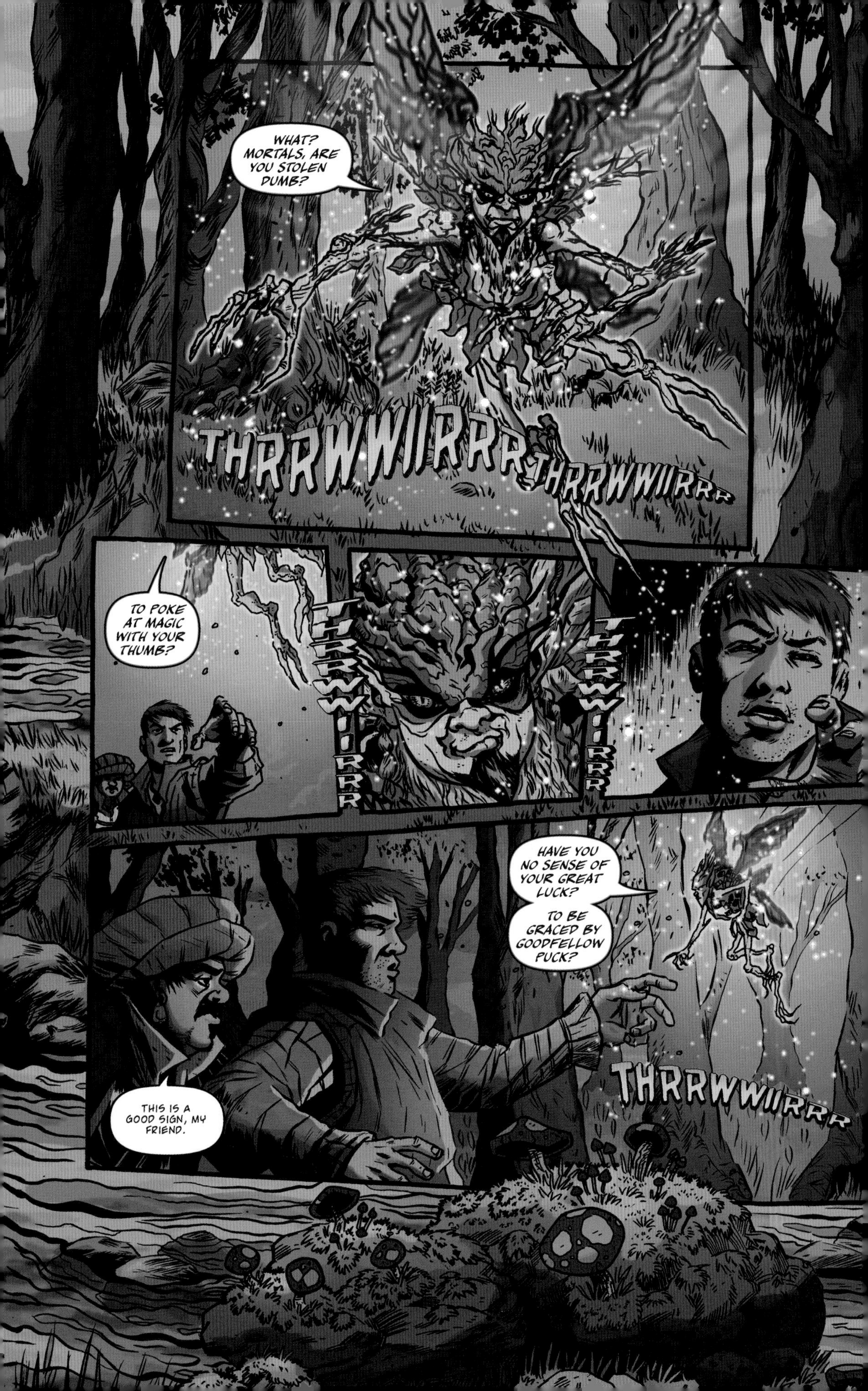
WHAT? MORTALS, ARE YOU STOLEN DUMB?
THRRWWIIRRRR THRRWWIIRRRR
TO POKE AT MAGIC WITH YOUR THUMB?
THRRWWIIRRR
THRRWWIIRRR
HAVE YOU NO SENSE OF YOUR GREAT LUCK?
TO BE GRACED BY GOODFELLOW PUCK?
THIS IS A GOOD SIGN, MY FRIEND.
THRRWWIIRRRR

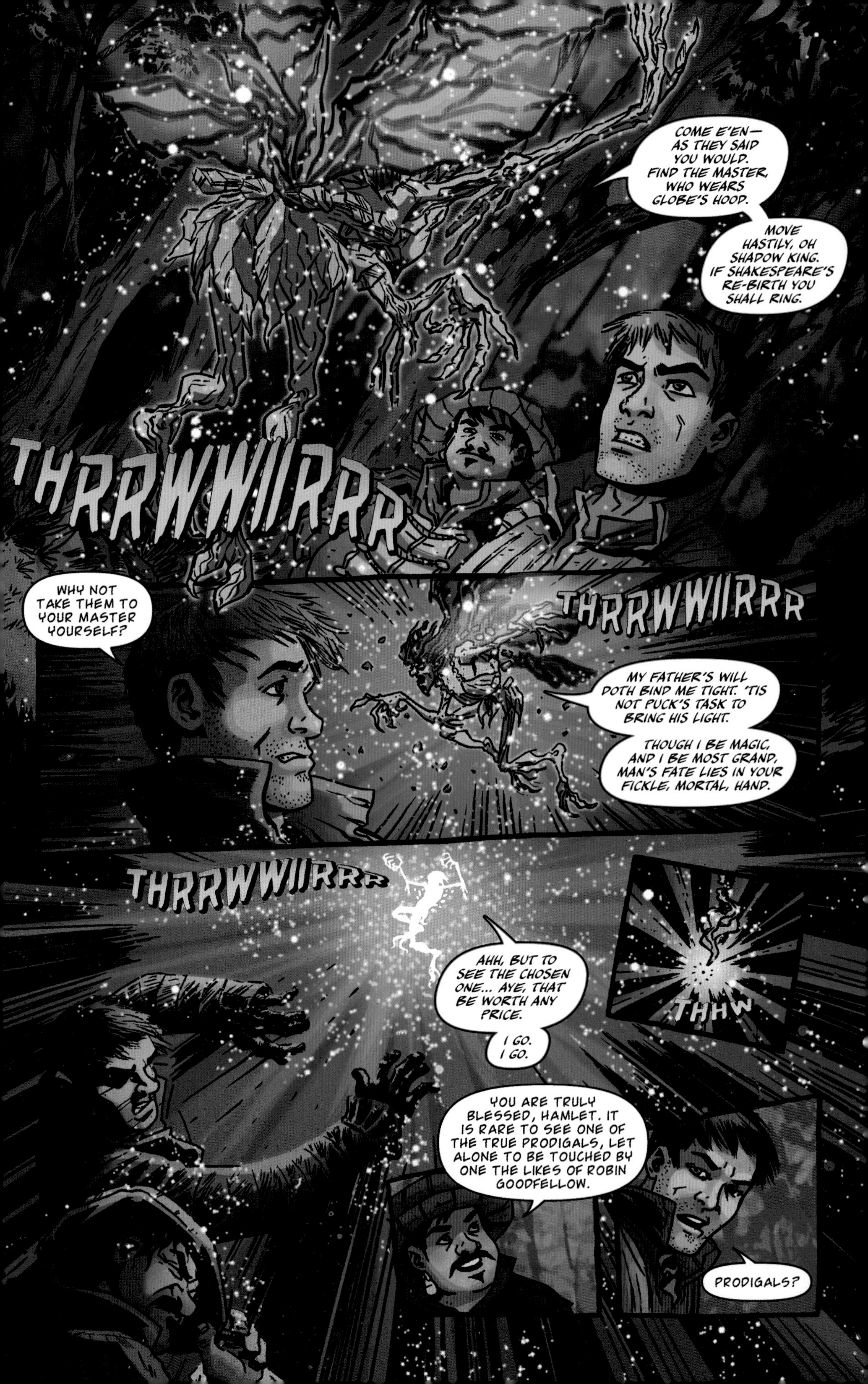
COME E'EN— AS THEY SAID YOU WOULD. FIND THE MASTER, WHO WEARS GLOBE'S HOOD.
MOVE HASTILY, OH SHADOW KING. IF SHAKESPEARE'S RE-BIRTH YOU SHALL RING.
THRRWWIIRRR
WHY NOT TAKE THEM TO YOUR MASTER YOURSELF?
THRRWWIIRRR
MY FATHER'S WILL DOTH BIND ME TIGHT. 'TIS NOT PUCK'S TASK TO BRING HIS LIGHT.
THOUGH I BE MAGIC, AND I BE MOST GRAND, MAN'S FATE LIES IN YOUR FICKLE, MORTAL, HAND.
THRRWWIIRRR
AHH, BUT TO SEE THE CHOSEN ONE... AYE, THAT BE WORTH ANY PRICE.
I GO. I GO.
THHW
YOU ARE TRULY BLESSED, HAMLET. IT IS RARE TO SEE ONE OF THE TRUE PRODIGALS, LET ALONE TO BE TOUCHED BY ONE THE LIKES OF ROBIN GOODFELLOW.
PRODIGALS?

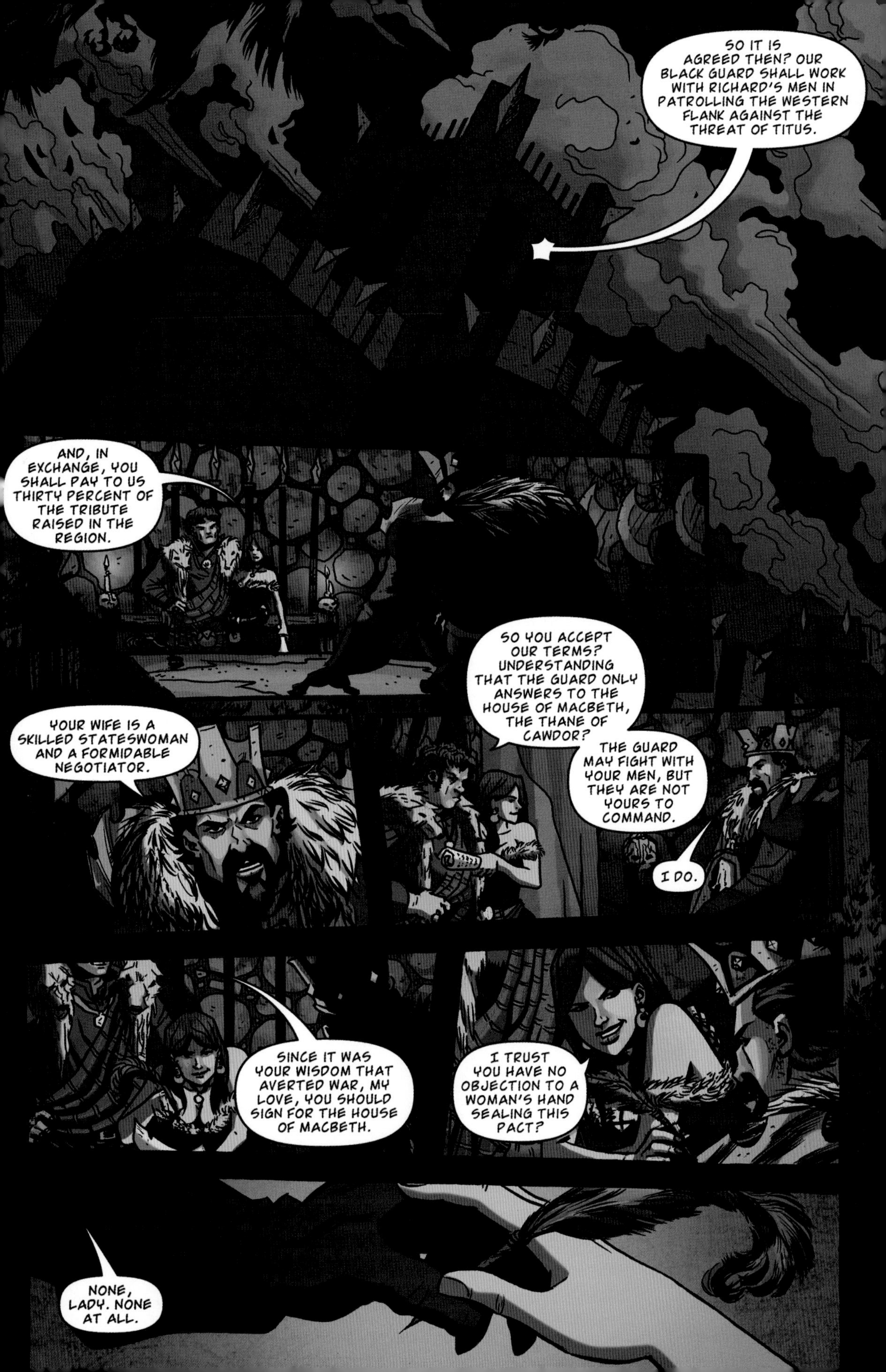
SO IT IS AGREED THEN? OUR BLACK GUARD SHALL WORK WITH RICHARD'S MEN IN PATROLLING THE WESTERN FLANK AGAINST THE THREAT OF TITUS.
AND, IN EXCHANGE, YOU SHALL PAY TO US THIRTY PERCENT OF THE TRIBUTE RAISED IN THE REGION.
YOUR WIFE IS A SKILLED STATESWOMAN AND A FORMIDABLE NEGOTIATOR.
SO YOU ACCEPT OUR TERMS? UNDERSTANDING THAT THE GUARD ONLY ANSWERS TO THE HOUSE OF MACBETH, THE THANE OF CAWDOR?
THE GUARD MAY FIGHT WITH YOUR MEN, BUT THEY ARE NOT YOURS TO COMMAND.
I DO.
SINCE IT WAS YOUR WISDOM THAT AVERTED WAR, MY LOVE, YOU SHOULD SIGN FOR THE HOUSE OF MACBETH.
I TRUST YOU HAVE NO OBJECTION TO A WOMAN'S HAND SEALING THIS PACT?
NONE, LADY. NONE AT ALL.

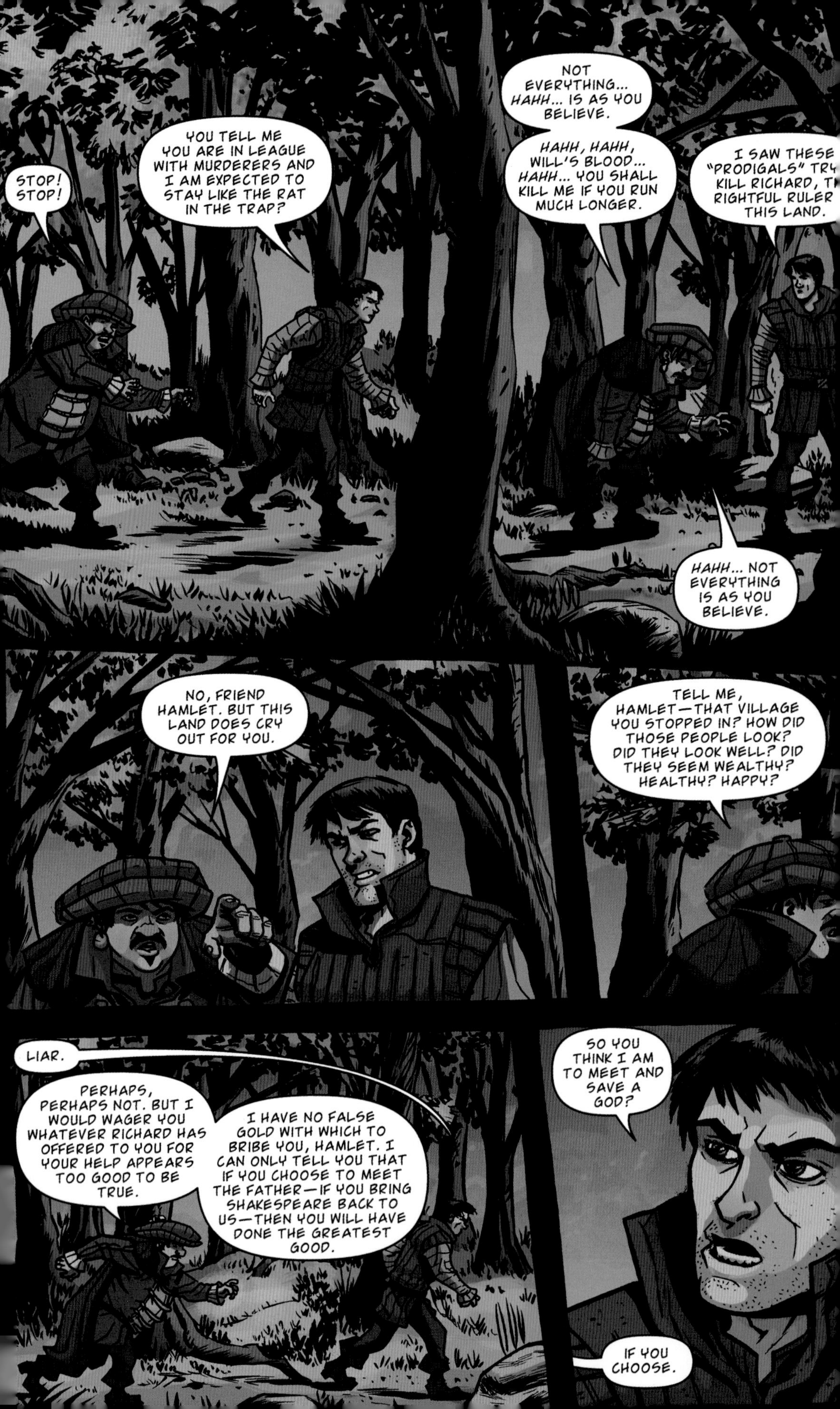
STOP! STOP!
YOU TELL ME YOU ARE IN LEAGUE WITH MURDERERS AND I AM EXPECTED TO STAY LIKE THE RAT IN THE TRAP?
NOT EVERYTHING... HAHH... IS AS YOU BELIEVE.
HAHH, HAHH, WILL'S BLOOD... HAHH... YOU SHALL KILL ME IF YOU RUN MUCH LONGER.
I SAW THESE "PRODIGALS" TRY KILL RICHARD, TH RIGHTFUL RULER THIS LAND.
HAHH... NOT EVERYTHING IS AS YOU BELIEVE.
NO, FRIEND HAMLET. BUT THIS LAND DOES CRY OUT FOR YOU.
TELL ME, HAMLET—THAT VILLAGE YOU STOPPED IN? HOW DID THOSE PEOPLE LOOK? DID THEY LOOK WELL? DID THEY SEEM WEALTHY? HEALTHY? HAPPY?
LIAR.
PERHAPS, PERHAPS NOT. BUT I WOULD WAGER YOU WHATEVER RICHARD HAS OFFERED TO YOU FOR YOUR HELP APPEARS TOO GOOD TO BE TRUE.
I HAVE NO FALSE GOLD WITH WHICH TO BRIBE YOU, HAMLET. I CAN ONLY TELL YOU THAT IF YOU CHOOSE TO MEET THE FATHER—IF YOU BRING SHAKESPEARE BACK TO US—THEN YOU WILL HAVE DONE THE GREATEST GOOD.
SO YOU THINK I AM TO MEET AND SAVE A GOD?
IF YOU CHOOSE.

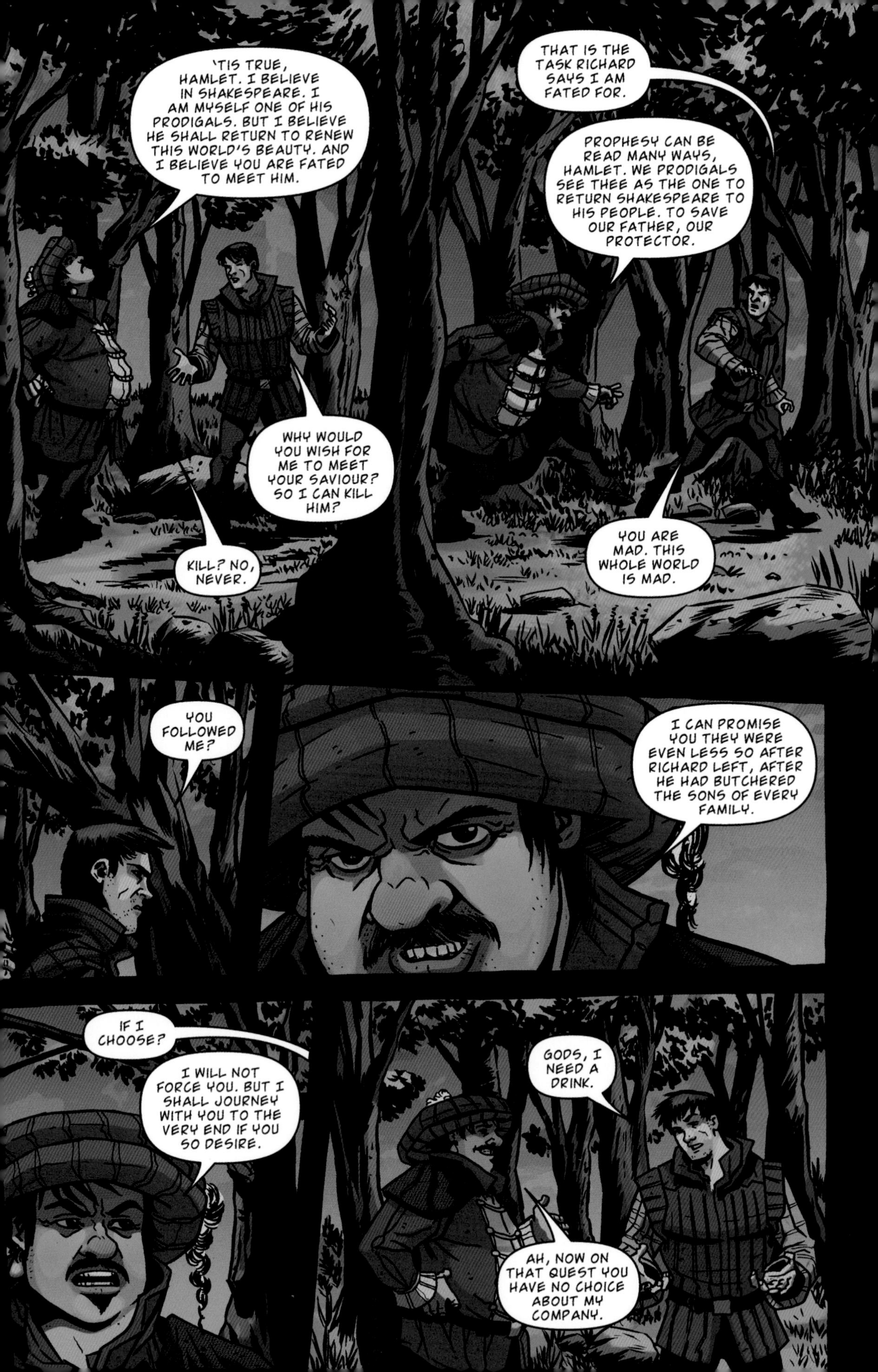
'TIS TRUE, HAMLET. I BELIEVE IN SHAKESPEARE. I AM MYSELF ONE OF HIS PRODIGALS. BUT I BELIEVE HE SHALL RETURN TO RENEW THIS WORLD'S BEAUTY. AND I BELIEVE YOU ARE FATED TO MEET HIM.
WHY WOULD YOU WISH FOR ME TO MEET YOUR SAVIOUR? SO I CAN KILL HIM?
KILL? NO, NEVER.
THAT IS THE TASK RICHARD SAYS I AM FATED FOR.
PROPHESY CAN BE READ MANY WAYS, HAMLET. WE PRODIGALS SEE THEE AS THE ONE TO RETURN SHAKESPEARE TO HIS PEOPLE. TO SAVE OUR FATHER, OUR PROTECTOR.
YOU ARE MAD. THIS WHOLE WORLD IS MAD.
YOU FOLLOWED ME?
I CAN PROMISE YOU THEY WERE EVEN LESS SO AFTER RICHARD LEFT, AFTER HE HAD BUTCHERED THE SONS OF EVERY FAMILY.
IF I CHOOSE?
I WILL NOT FORCE YOU. BUT I SHALL JOURNEY WITH YOU TO THE VERY END IF YOU SO DESIRE.
GODS, I NEED A DRINK.
AH, NOW ON THAT QUEST YOU HAVE NO CHOICE ABOUT MY COMPANY.

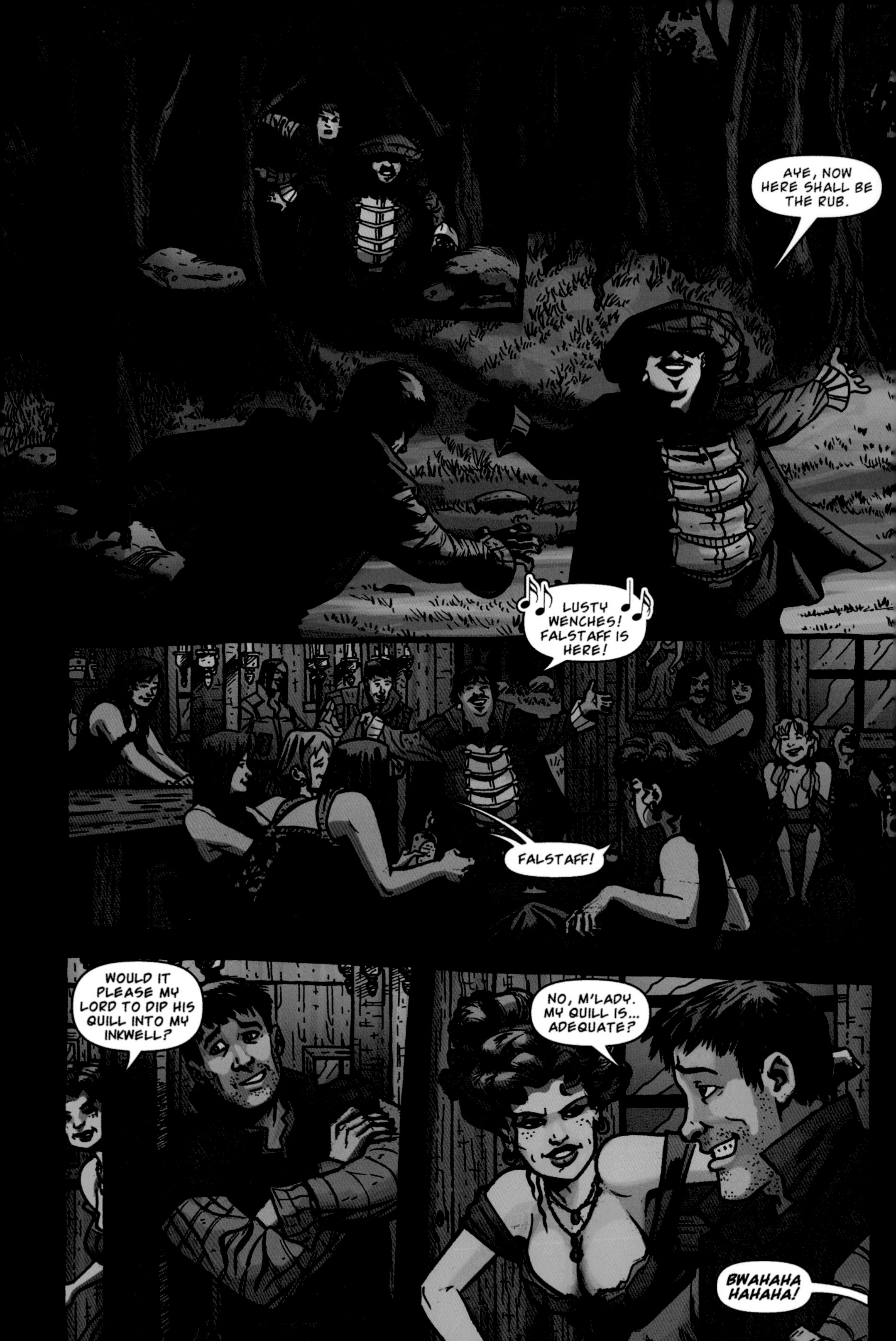
AYE, NOW HERE SHALL BE THE RUB.
LUSTY WENCHES! FALSTAFF IS HERE!
FALSTAFF!
WOULD IT PLEASE MY LORD TO DIP HIS QUILL INTO MY INKWELL?
NO, M'LADY. MY QUILL IS... ADEQUATE?
BWAHAHA HAHAHA!

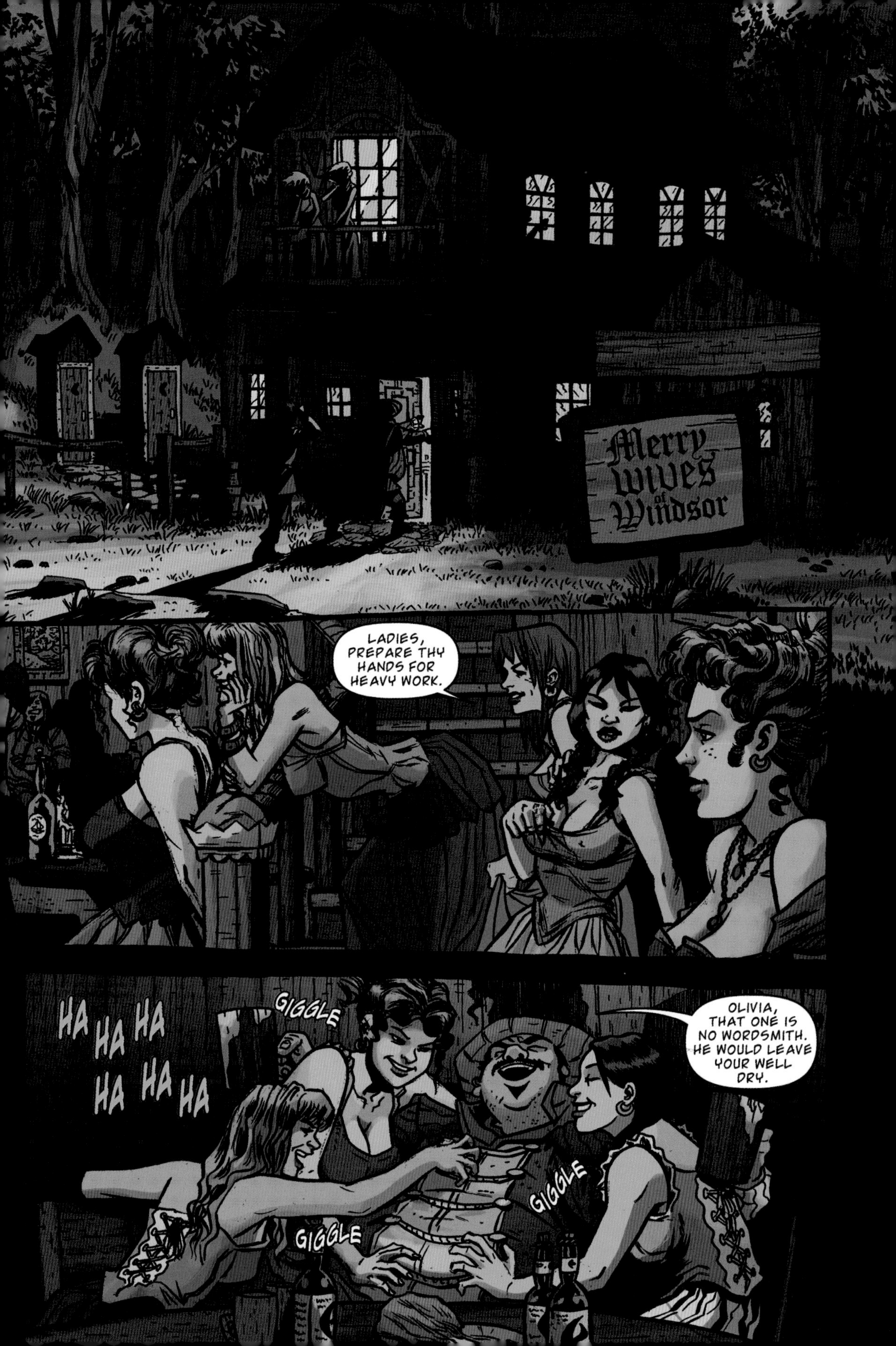
Merry Wives of Windsor
LADIES, PREPARE THY HANDS FOR HEAVY WORK.
HA HA HA HA HA HA
GIGGLE
OLIVIA, THAT ONE IS NO WORDSMITH. HE WOULD LEAVE YOUR WELL DRY.
GIGGLE
GIGGLE

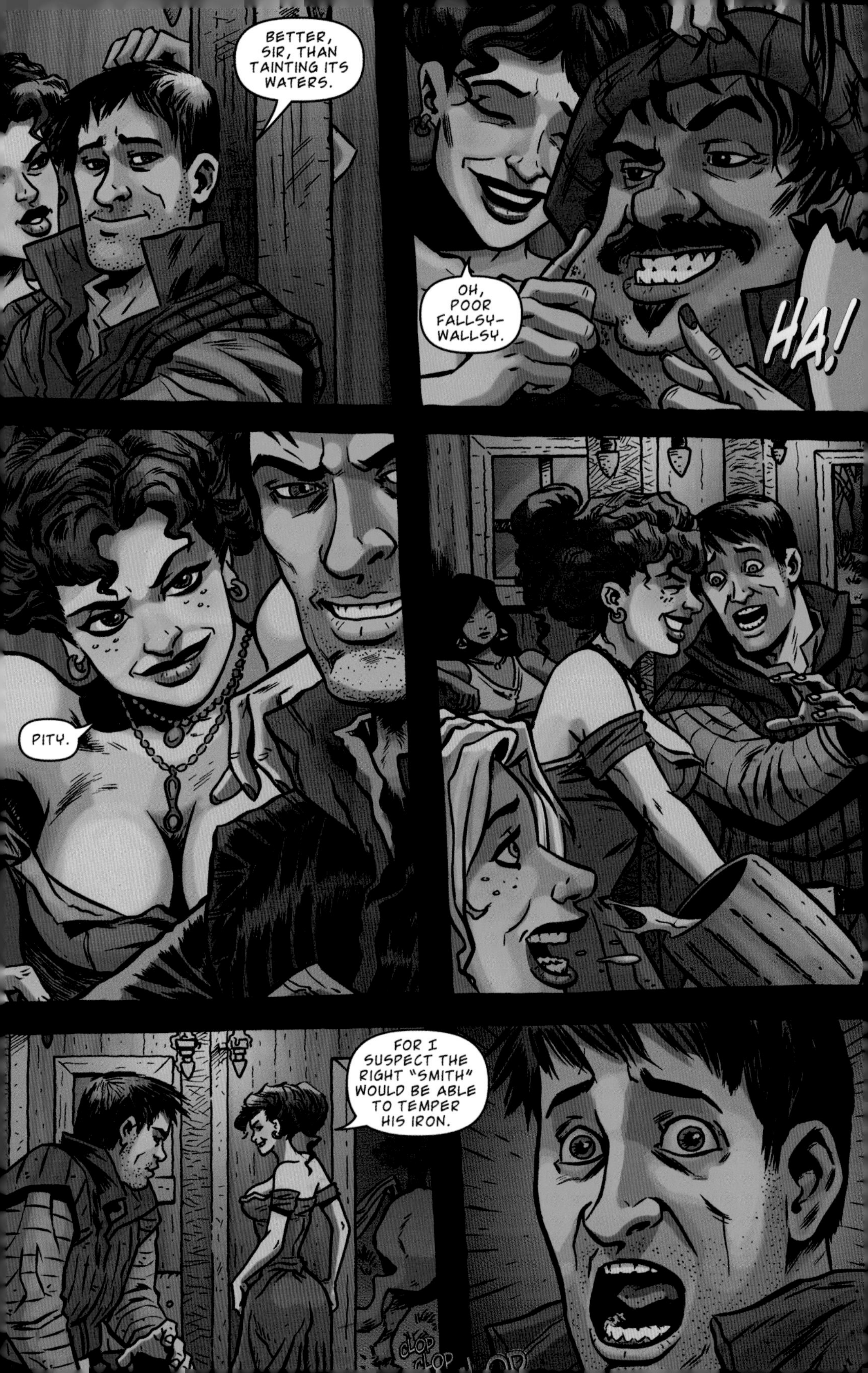
BETTER, SIR, THAN TAINTING ITS WATERS.
OH, POOR FALLSY-WALLSY.
HA!
PITY.
FOR I SUSPECT THE RIGHT "SMITH" WOULD BE ABLE TO TEMPER HIS IRON.
CLOP CLOP

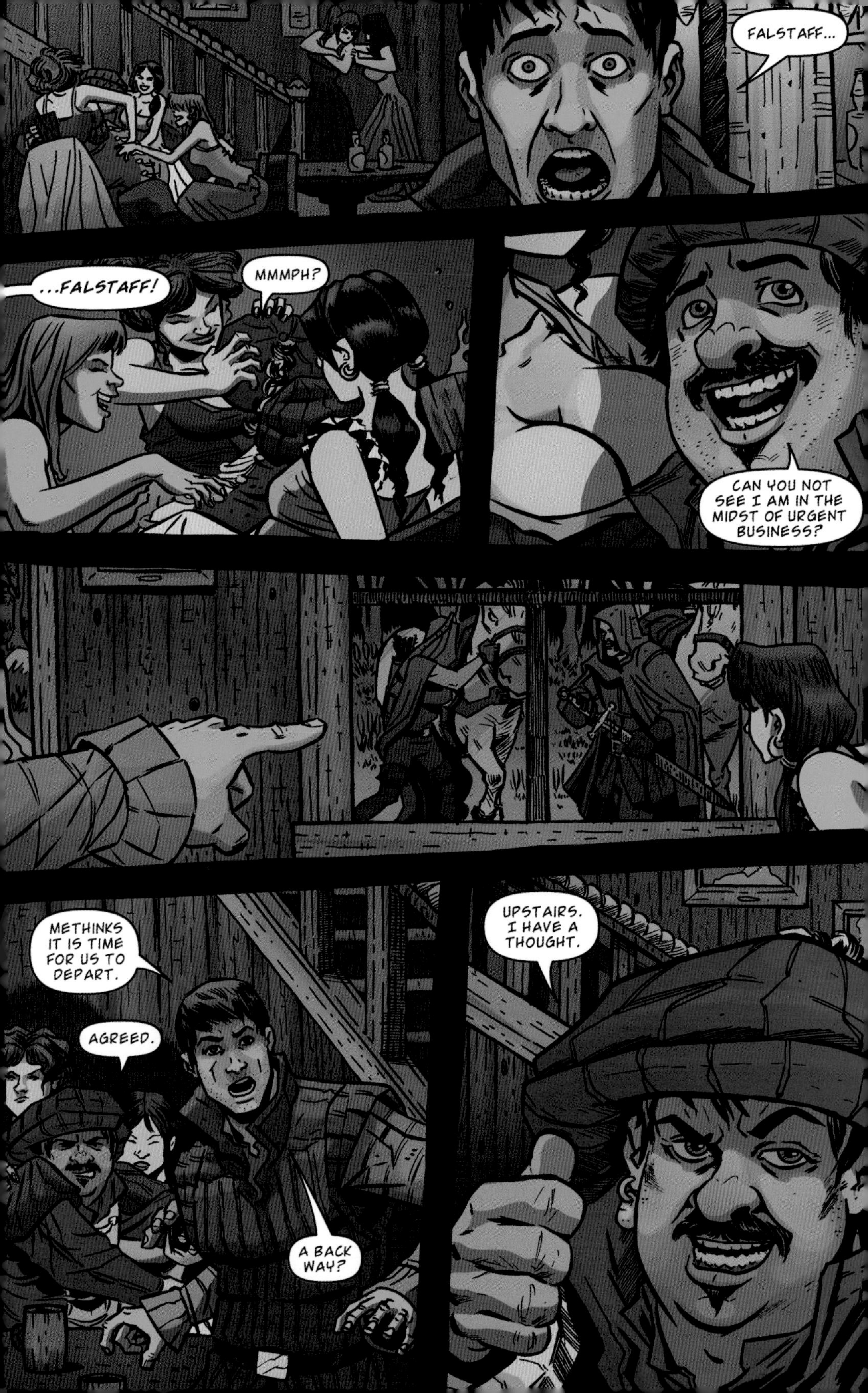
FALSTAFF...
...FALSTAFF!
MMMPH?
CAN YOU NOT SEE I AM IN THE MIDST OF URGENT BUSINESS?
METHINKS IT IS TIME FOR US TO DEPART.
AGREED.
A BACK WAY?
UPSTAIRS. I HAVE A THOUGHT.

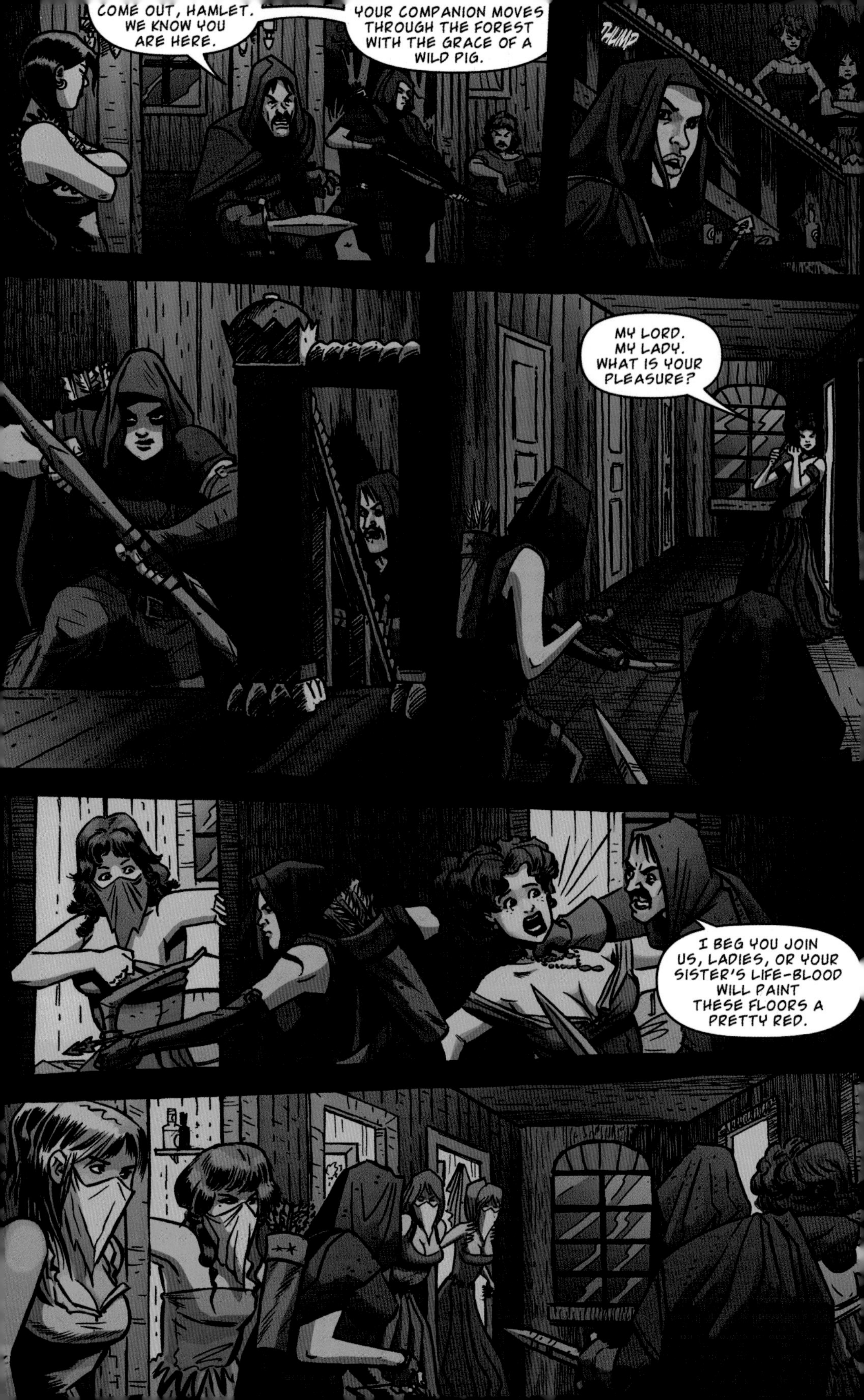
COME OUT, HAMLET. WE KNOW YOU ARE HERE.
YOUR COMPANION MOVES THROUGH THE FOREST WITH THE GRACE OF A WILD PIG.
THUMP
MY LORD. MY LADY. WHAT IS YOUR PLEASURE?
I BEG YOU JOIN US, LADIES, OR YOUR SISTER'S LIFE-BLOOD WILL PAINT THESE FLOORS A PRETTY RED.

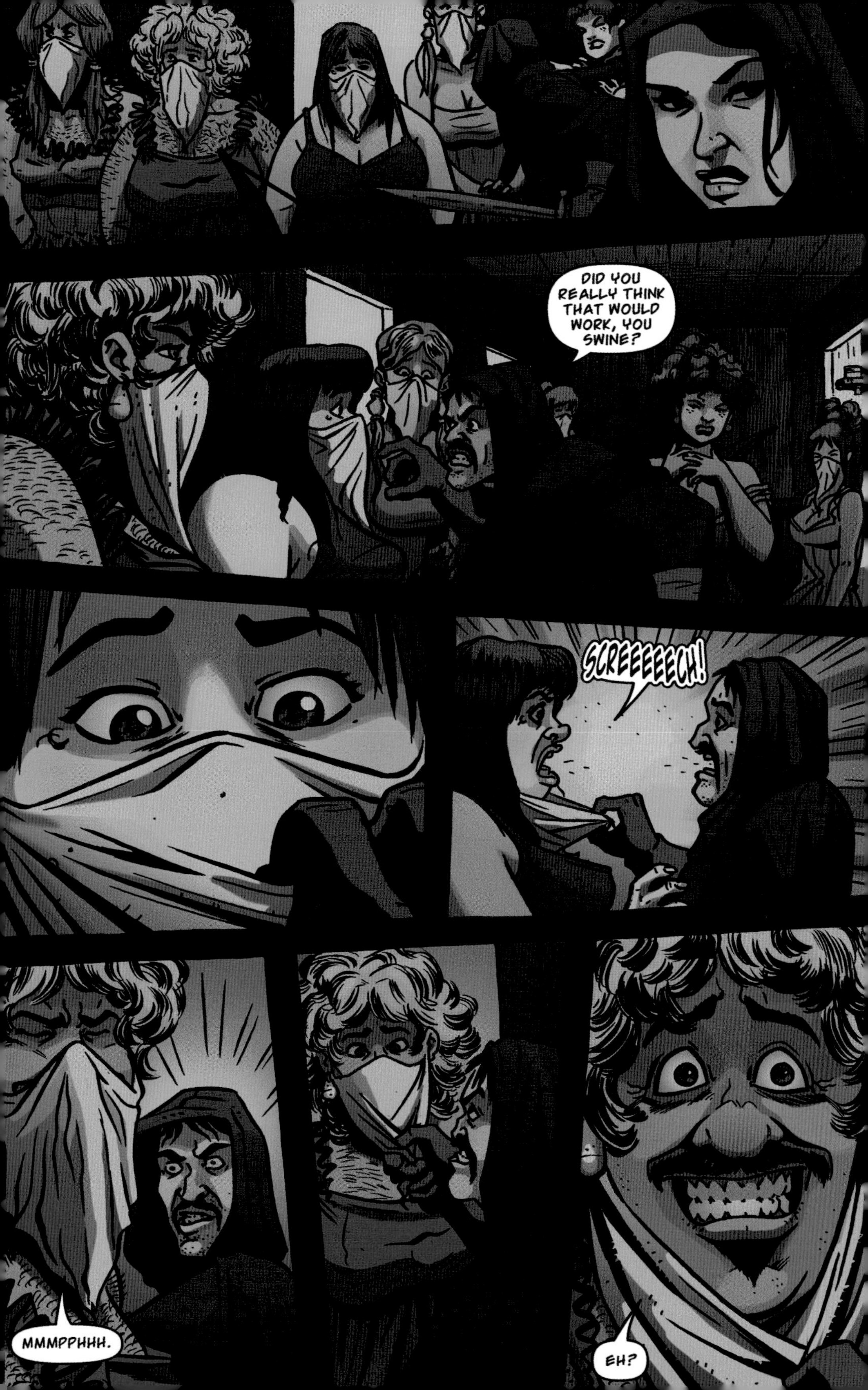
DID YOU REALLY THINK THAT WOULD WORK, YOU SWINE?
SCREEEEEECH!
MMMPPHHH.
EH?

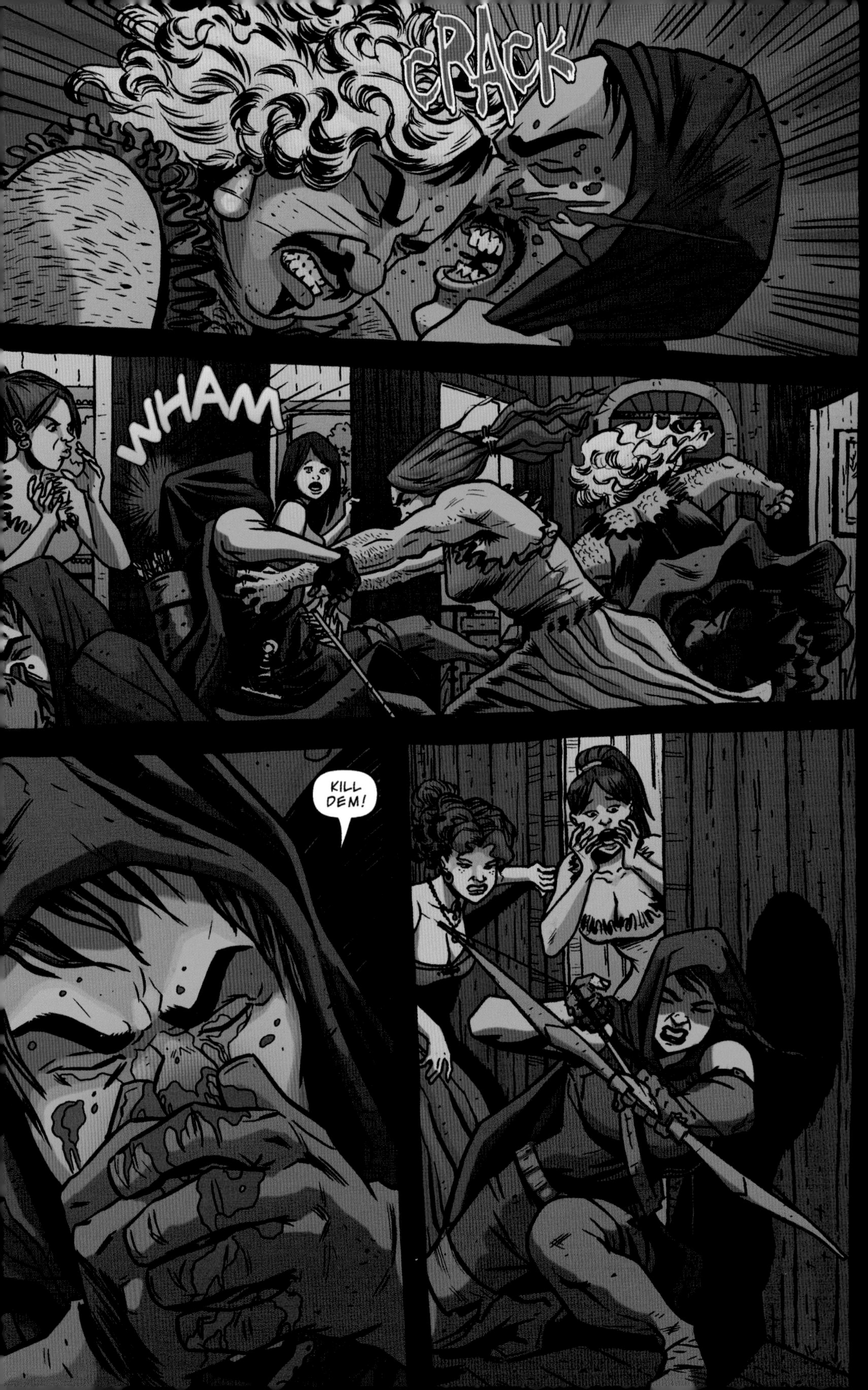
CRACK
WHAM
KILL DEM!

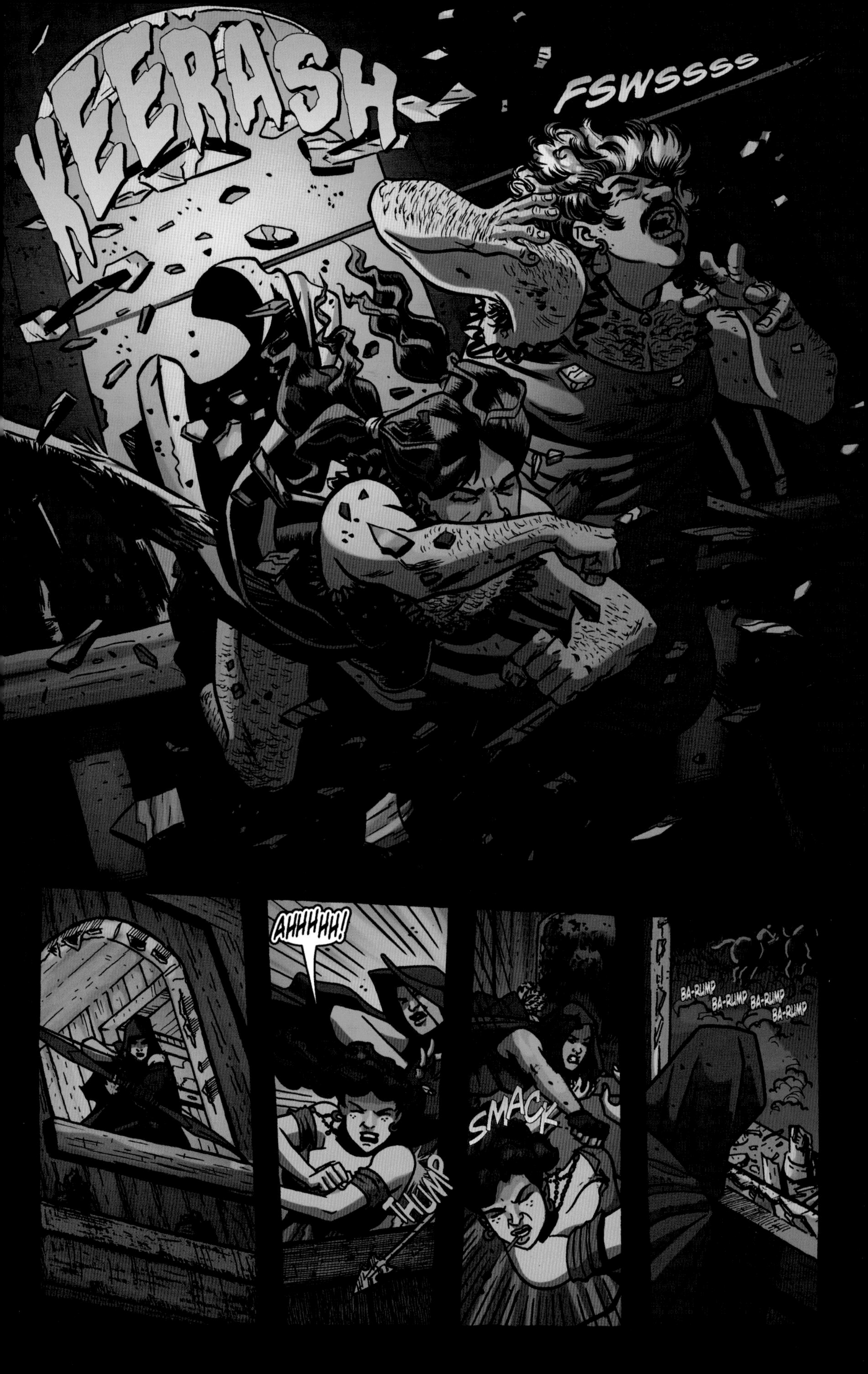
KEERASH
FSWSSSS
AHHHHH!
THUMP
SMACK
BA-RUMP
BA-RUMP
BA-RUMP
BA-RUMP

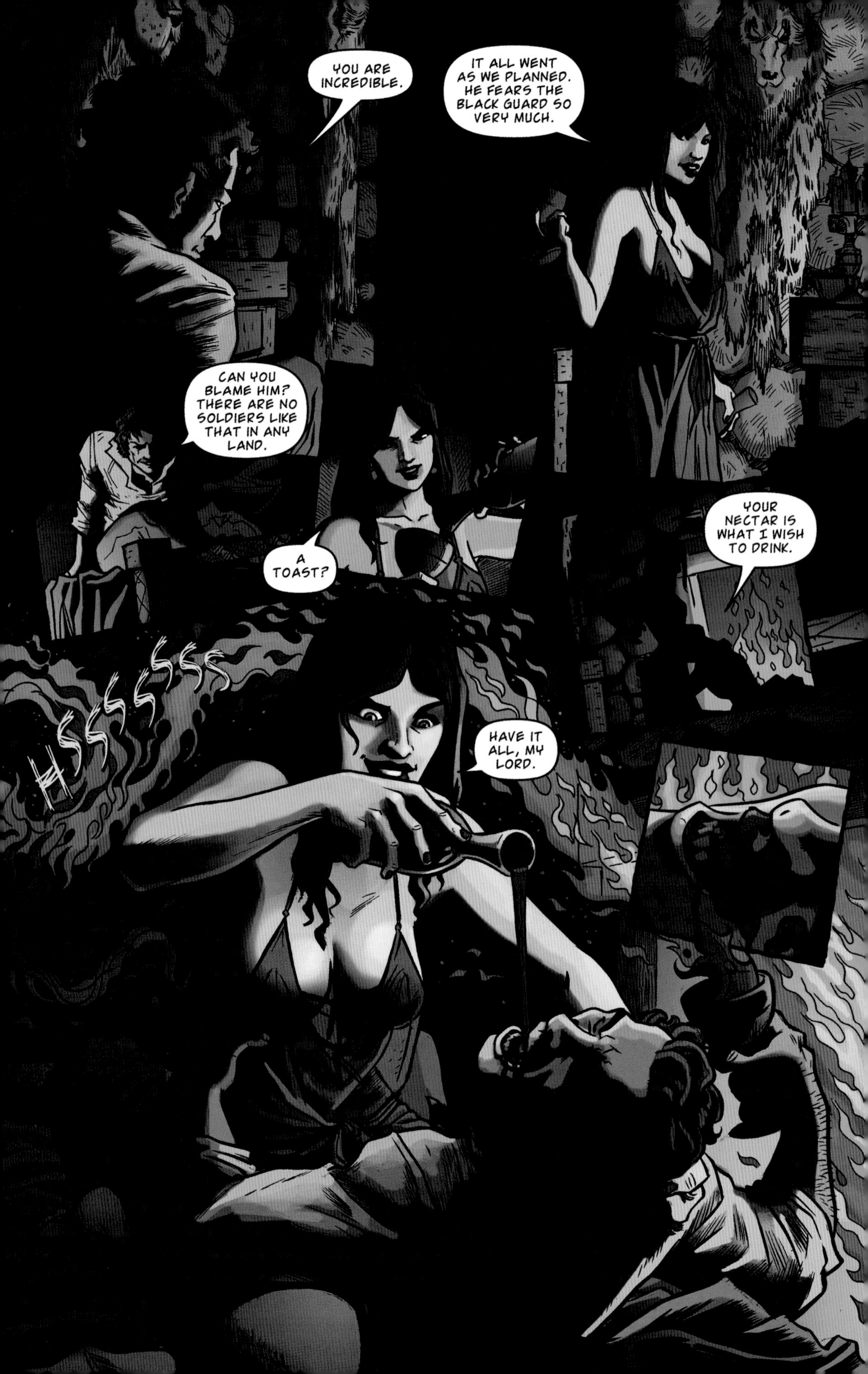
YOU ARE INCREDIBLE.
IT ALL WENT AS WE PLANNED. HE FEARS THE BLACK GUARD SO VERY MUCH.
CAN YOU BLAME HIM? THERE ARE NO SOLDIERS LIKE THAT IN ANY LAND.
A TOAST?
YOUR NECTAR IS WHAT I WISH TO DRINK.
HSSSSSS
HAVE IT ALL, MY LORD.

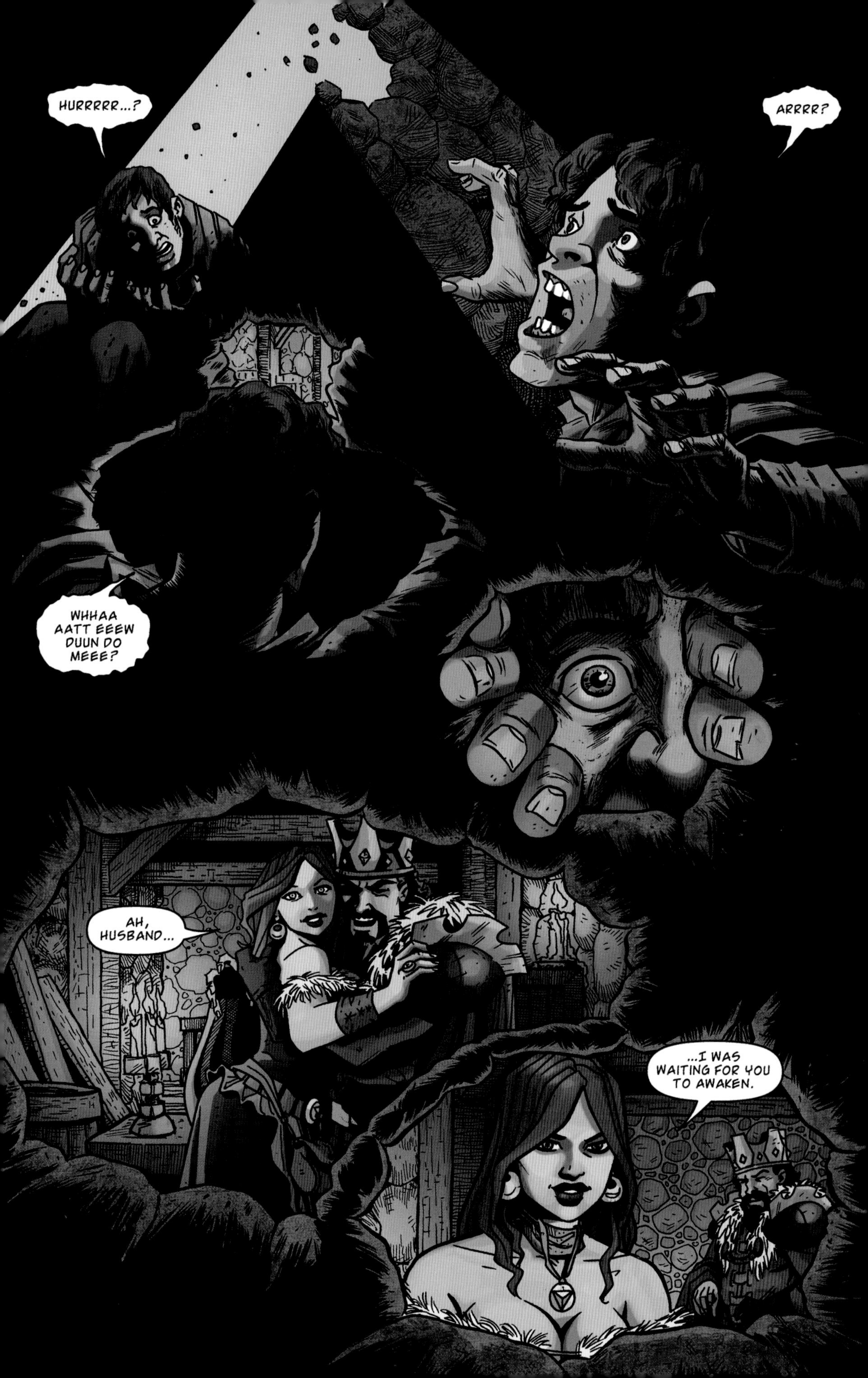
HURRRRR...?
ARRRR?
WHHAA AATT EEEW DUUN DO MEEE?
AH, HUSBAND...
...I WAS WAITING FOR YOU TO AWAKEN.

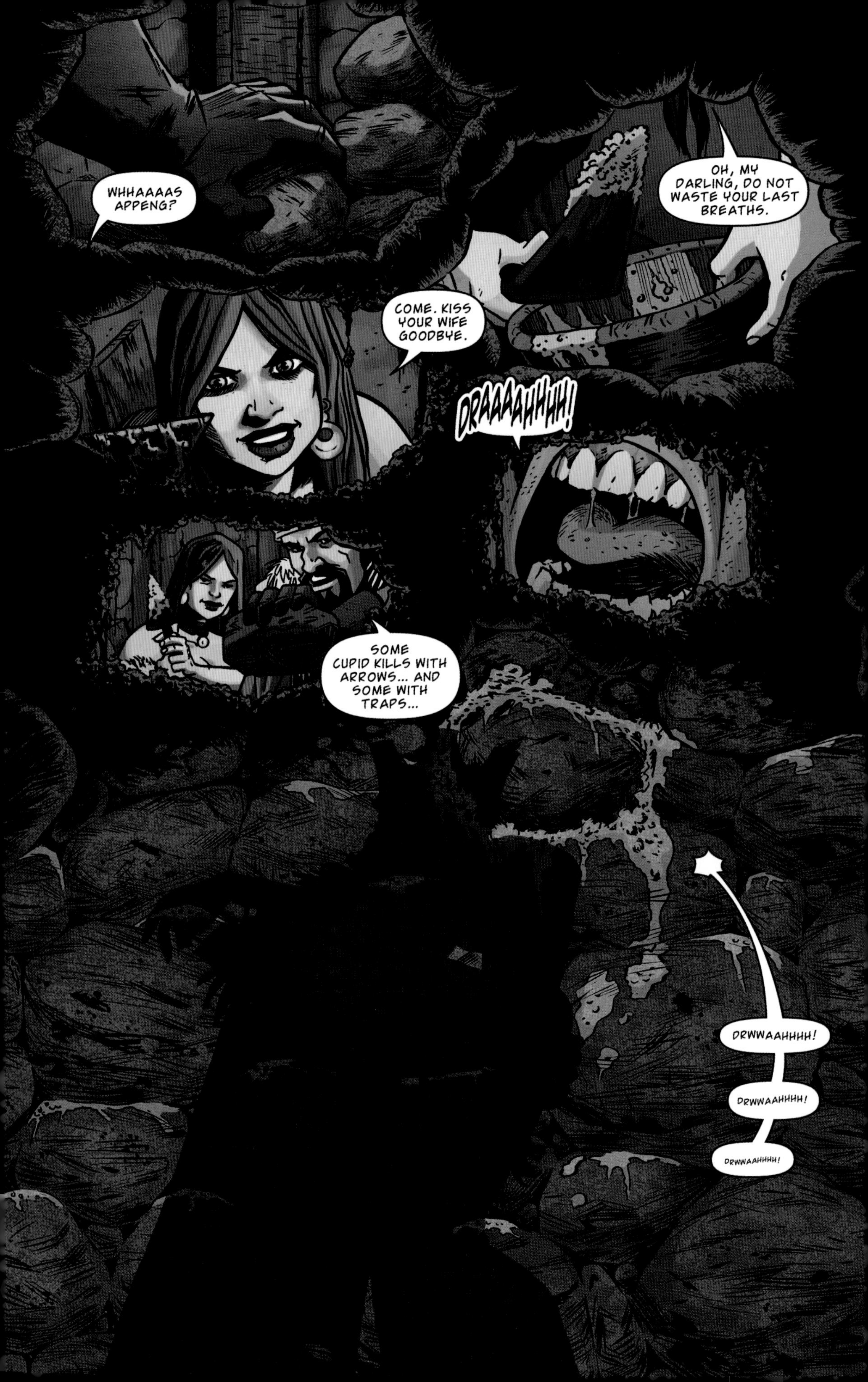
WHHAAAAS APPENG?
OH, MY DARLING, DO NOT WASTE YOUR LAST BREATHS.
COME. KISS YOUR WIFE GOODBYE.
DRAAAAHHHH!
SOME CUPID KILLS WITH ARROWS... AND SOME WITH TRAPS...
DRWWAAHHHH!
DRWWAAHHHH!
DRWWAAHHHH!

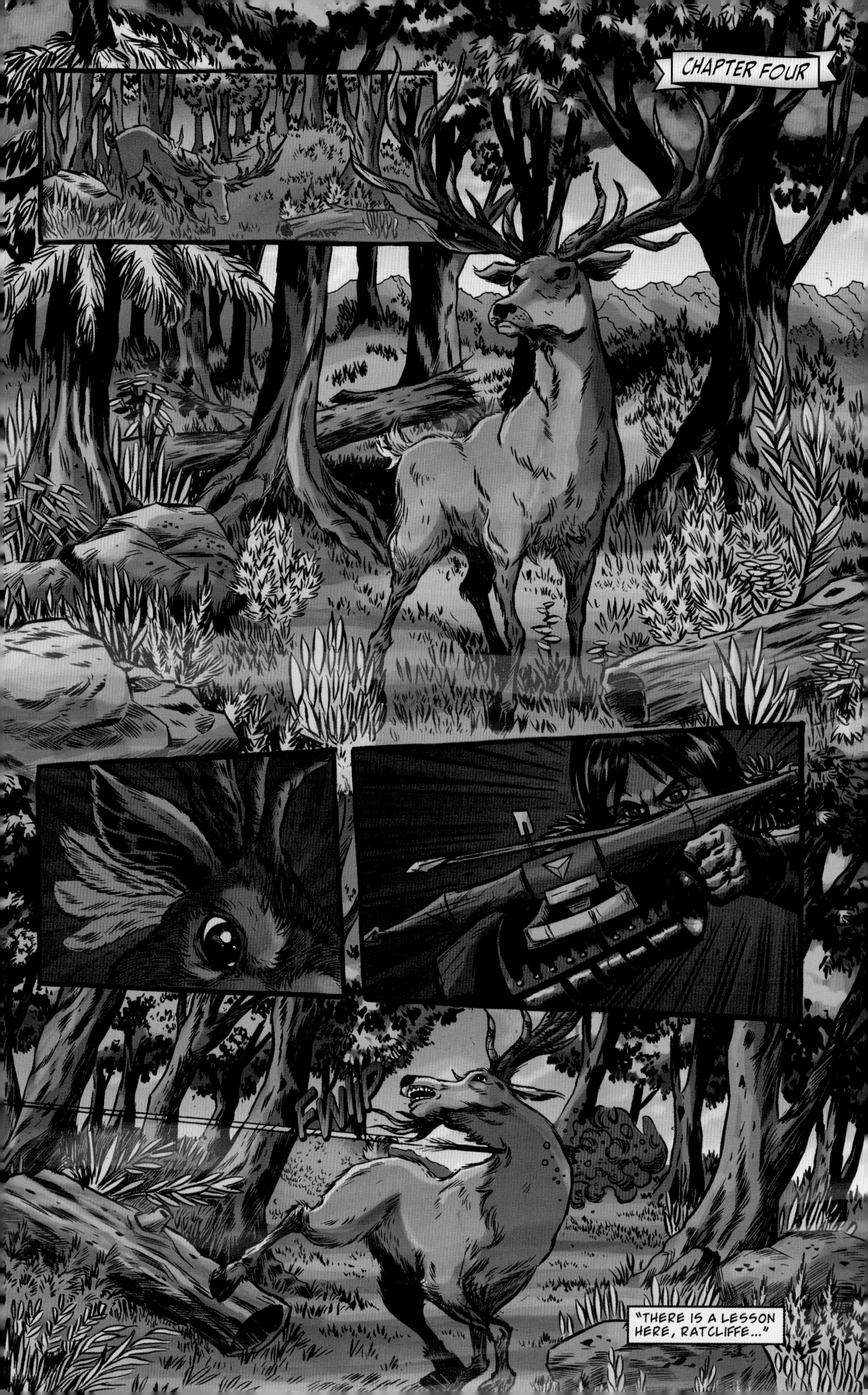
CHAPTER FOUR
FWIP
"THERE IS A LESSON HERE, RATCLIFFE..."

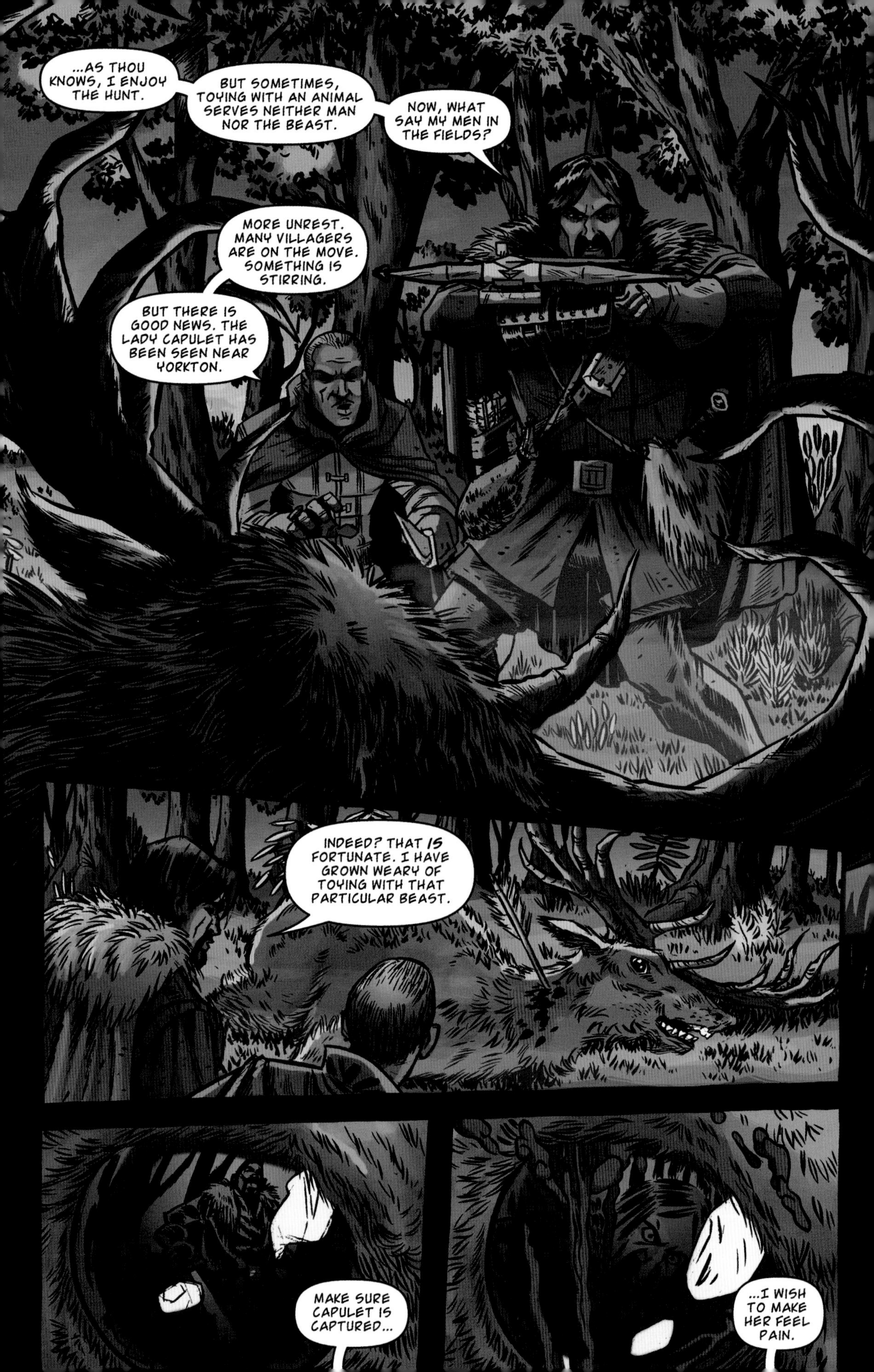
...AS THOU KNOWS, I ENJOY THE HUNT.
BUT SOMETIMES, TOYING WITH AN ANIMAL SERVES NEITHER MAN NOR THE BEAST.
NOW, WHAT SAY MY MEN IN THE FIELDS?
MORE UNREST. MANY VILLAGERS ARE ON THE MOVE. SOMETHING IS STIRRING.
BUT THERE IS GOOD NEWS. THE LADY CAPULET HAS BEEN SEEN NEAR YORKTON.
INDEED? THAT IS FORTUNATE. I HAVE GROWN WEARY OF TOYING WITH THAT PARTICULAR BEAST.
MAKE SURE CAPULET IS CAPTURED...
...I WISH TO MAKE HER FEEL PAIN.

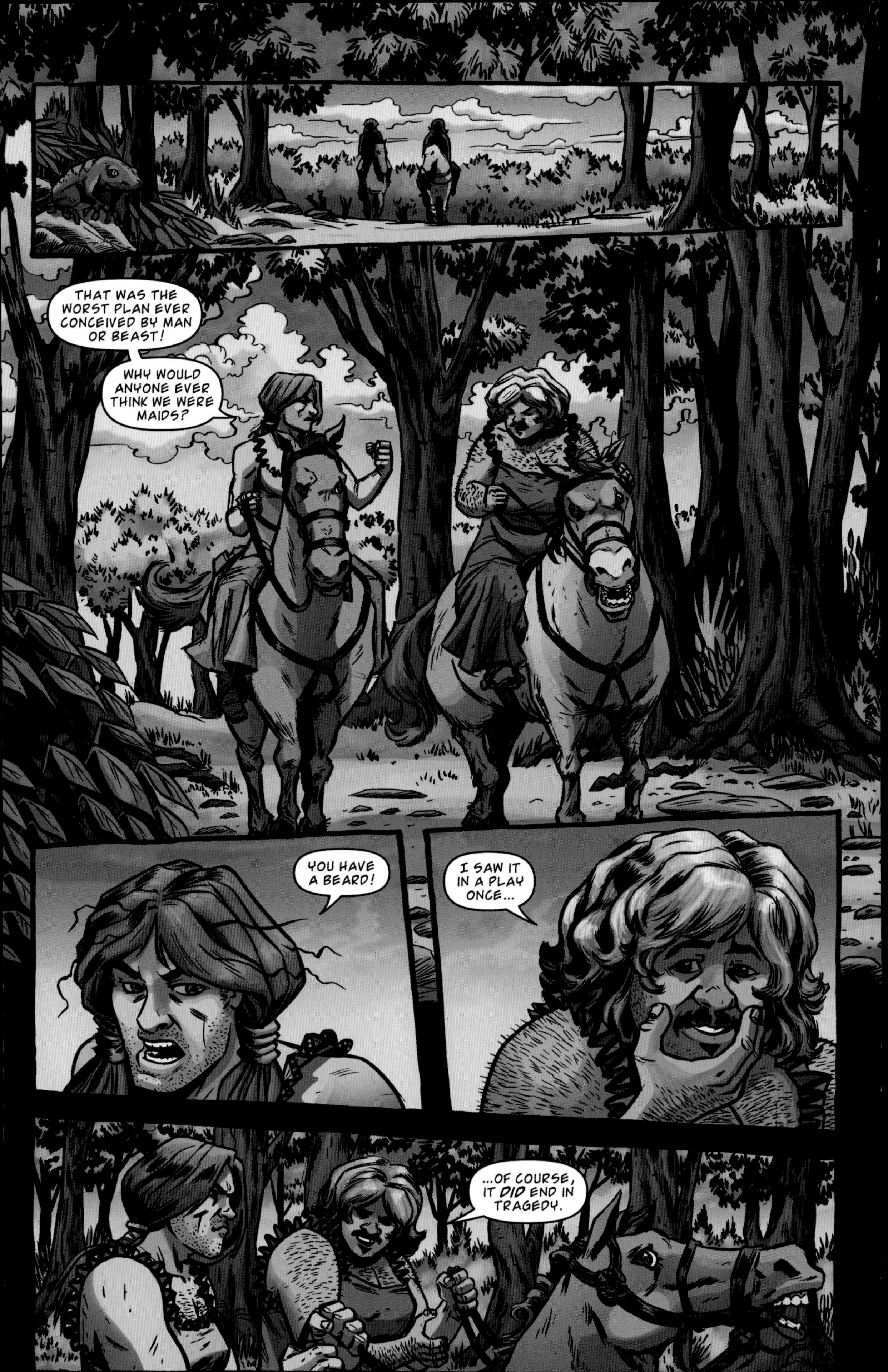
THAT WAS THE WORST PLAN EVER CONCEIVED BY MAN OR BEAST!
WHY WOULD ANYONE EVER THINK WE WERE MAIDS?
YOU HAVE A BEARD!
I SAW IT IN A PLAY ONCE...
...OF COURSE, IT *DID* END IN TRAGEDY.

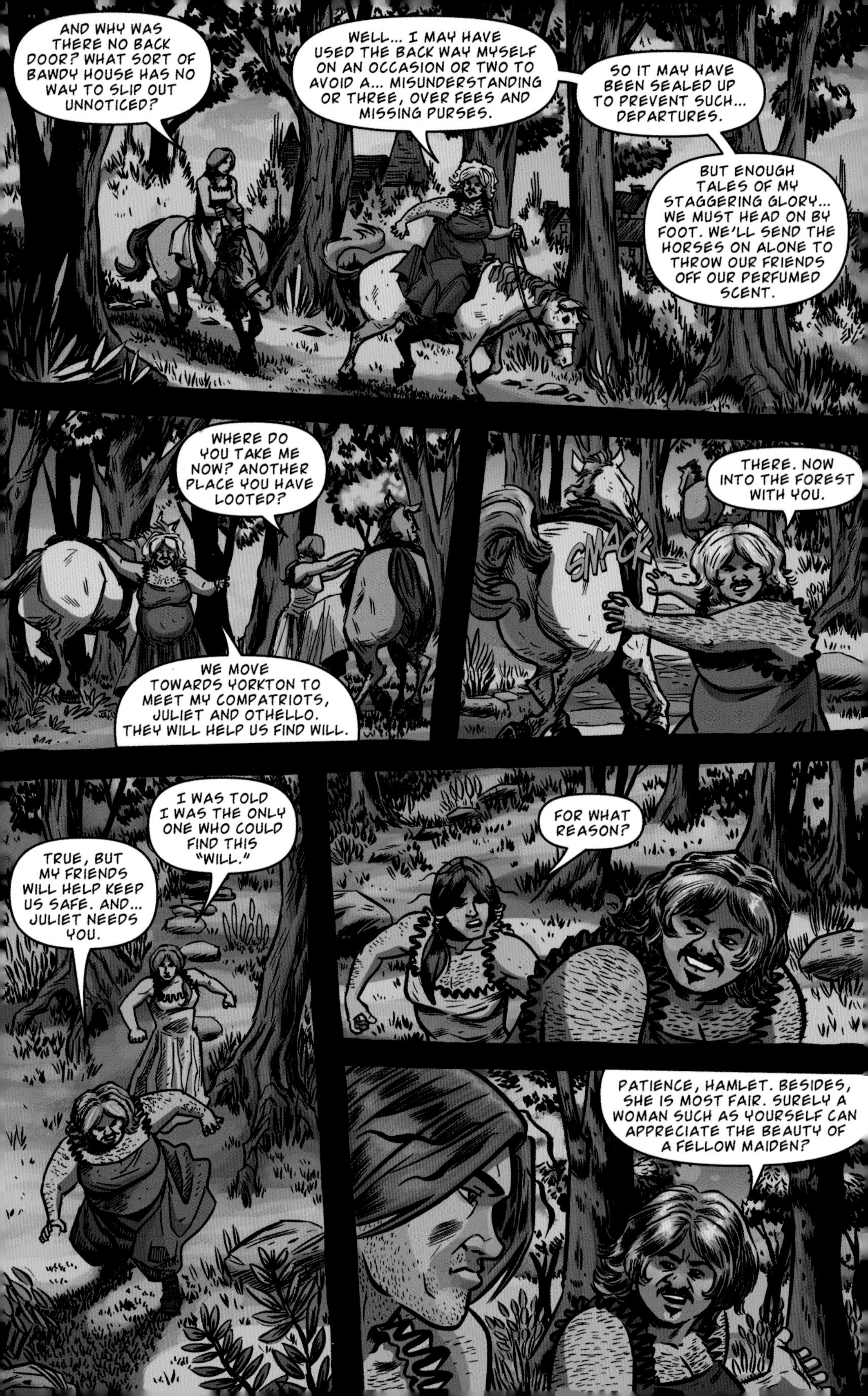
AND WHY WAS THERE NO BACK DOOR? WHAT SORT OF BAWDY HOUSE HAS NO WAY TO SLIP OUT UNNOTICED?
WELL... I MAY HAVE USED THE BACK WAY MYSELF ON AN OCCASION OR TWO TO AVOID A... MISUNDERSTANDING OR THREE, OVER FEES AND MISSING PURSES.
SO IT MAY HAVE BEEN SEALED UP TO PREVENT SUCH... DEPARTURES.
BUT ENOUGH TALES OF MY STAGGERING GLORY... WE MUST HEAD ON BY FOOT. WE'LL SEND THE HORSES ON ALONE TO THROW OUR FRIENDS OFF OUR PERFUMED SCENT.
WHERE DO YOU TAKE ME NOW? ANOTHER PLACE YOU HAVE LOOTED?
WE MOVE TOWARDS YORKTON TO MEET MY COMPATRIOTS, JULIET AND OTHELLO. THEY WILL HELP US FIND WILL.
SMACK
THERE. NOW INTO THE FOREST WITH YOU.
I WAS TOLD I WAS THE ONLY ONE WHO COULD FIND THIS "WILL."
TRUE, BUT MY FRIENDS WILL HELP KEEP US SAFE. AND... JULIET NEEDS YOU.
FOR WHAT REASON?
PATIENCE, HAMLET. BESIDES, SHE IS MOST FAIR. SURELY A WOMAN SUCH AS YOURSELF CAN APPRECIATE THE BEAUTY OF A FELLOW MAIDEN?

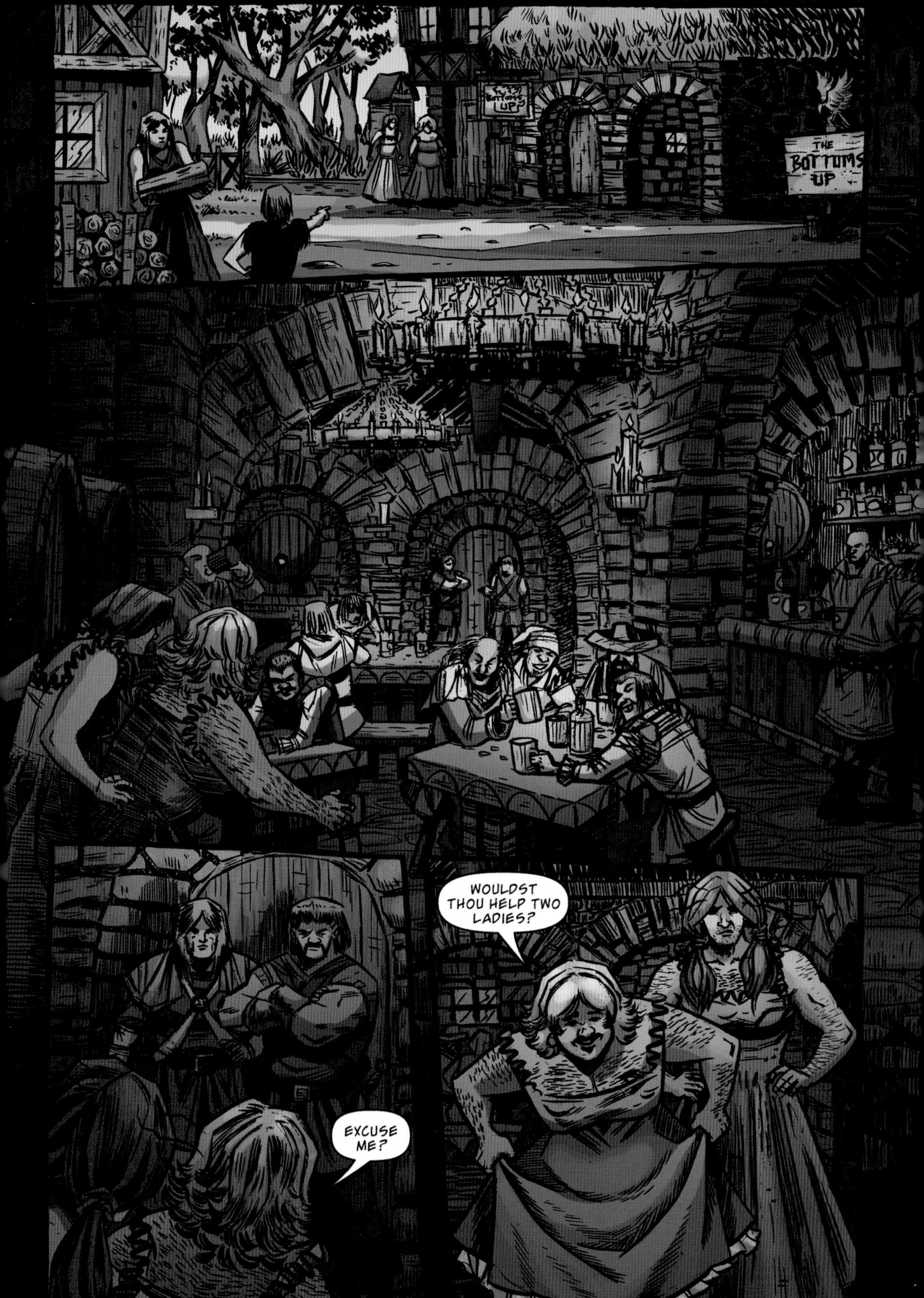
THE BOTTOMS UP
EXCUSE ME?
WOULDST THOU HELP TWO LADIES?

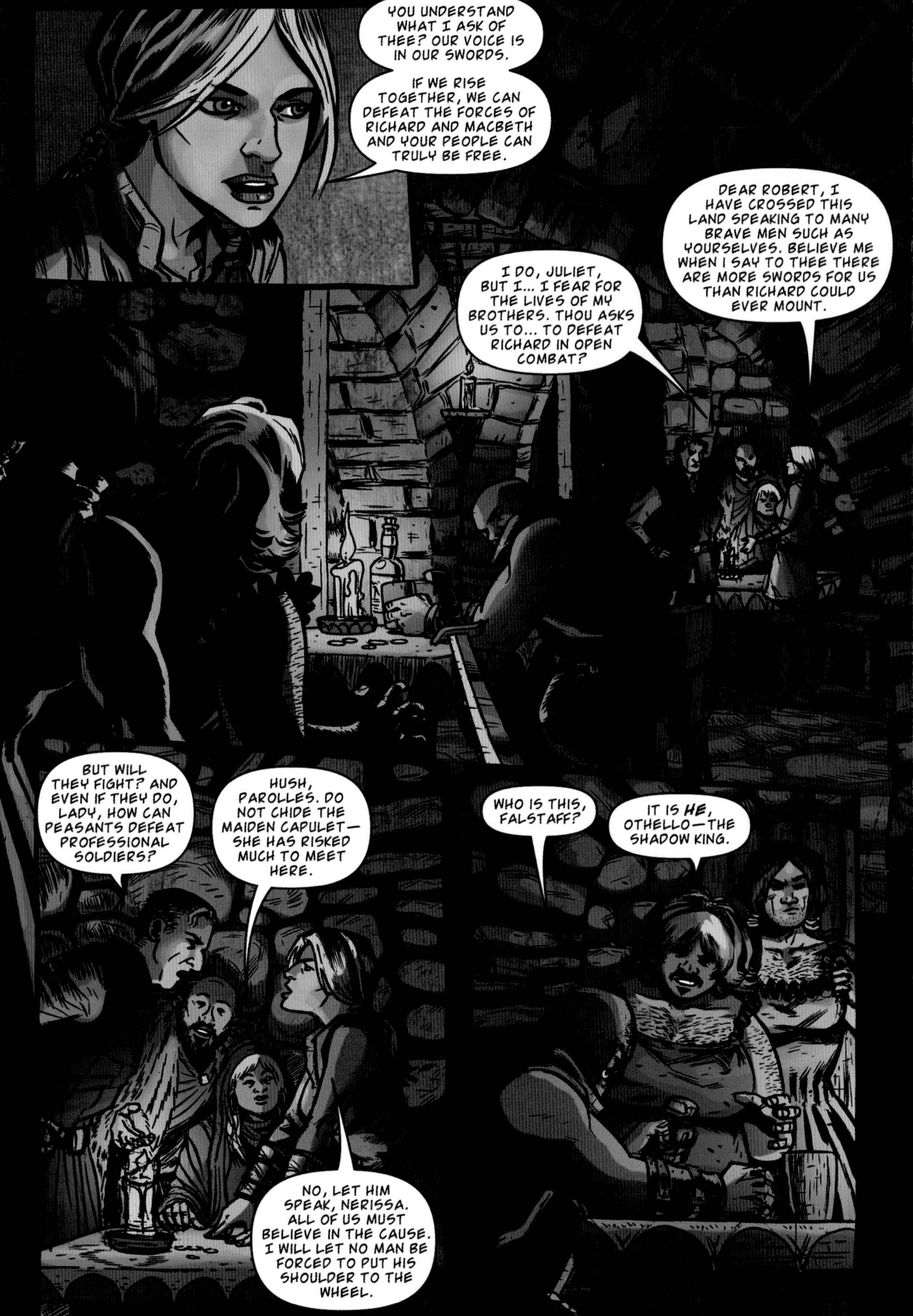
YOU UNDERSTAND WHAT I ASK OF THEE? OUR VOICE IS IN OUR SWORDS.
IF WE RISE TOGETHER, WE CAN DEFEAT THE FORCES OF RICHARD AND MACBETH AND YOUR PEOPLE CAN TRULY BE FREE.
I DO, JULIET, BUT I... I FEAR FOR THE LIVES OF MY BROTHERS. THOU ASKS US TO... TO DEFEAT RICHARD IN OPEN COMBAT?
DEAR ROBERT, I HAVE CROSSED THIS LAND SPEAKING TO MANY BRAVE MEN SUCH AS YOURSELVES. BELIEVE ME WHEN I SAY TO THEE THERE ARE MORE SWORDS FOR US THAN RICHARD COULD EVER MOUNT.
BUT WILL THEY FIGHT? AND EVEN IF THEY DO, LADY, HOW CAN PEASANTS DEFEAT PROFESSIONAL SOLDIERS?
HUSH, PAROLLES. DO NOT CHIDE THE MAIDEN CAPULET—SHE HAS RISKED MUCH TO MEET HERE.
NO, LET HIM SPEAK, NERISSA. ALL OF US MUST BELIEVE IN THE CAUSE. I WILL LET NO MAN BE FORCED TO PUT HIS SHOULDER TO THE WHEEL.
WHO IS THIS, FALSTAFF?
IT IS *HE*, OTHELLO—THE SHADOW KING.

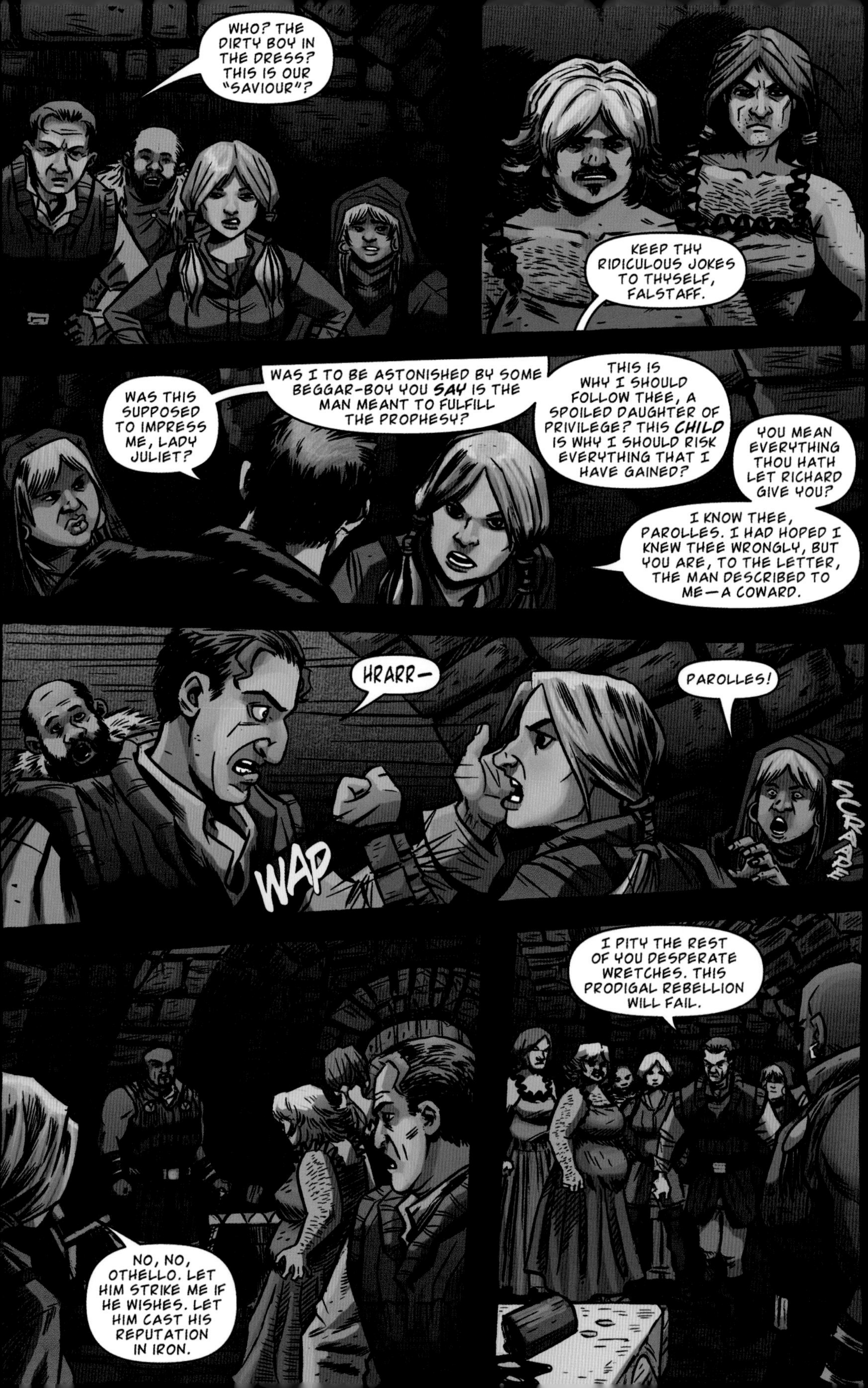
WHO? THE DIRTY BOY IN THE DRESS? THIS IS OUR "SAVIOUR"?
KEEP THY RIDICULOUS JOKES TO THYSELF, FALSTAFF.
WAS THIS SUPPOSED TO IMPRESS ME, LADY JULIET?
WAS I TO BE ASTONISHED BY SOME BEGGAR-BOY YOU *SAY* IS THE MAN MEANT TO FULFILL THE PROPHESY?
THIS IS WHY I SHOULD FOLLOW THEE, A SPOILED DAUGHTER OF PRIVILEGE? THIS *CHILD* IS WHY I SHOULD RISK EVERYTHING THAT I HAVE GAINED?
YOU MEAN EVERYTHING THOU HATH LET RICHARD GIVE YOU?
I KNOW THEE, PAROLLES. I HAD HOPED I KNEW THEE WRONGLY, BUT YOU ARE, TO THE LETTER, THE MAN DESCRIBED TO ME—A COWARD.
HRARR—
PAROLLES!
WAP
NO, NO, OTHELLO. LET HIM STRIKE ME IF HE WISHES. LET HIM CAST HIS REPUTATION IN IRON.
I PITY THE REST OF YOU DESPERATE WRETCHES. THIS PRODIGAL REBELLION WILL FAIL.

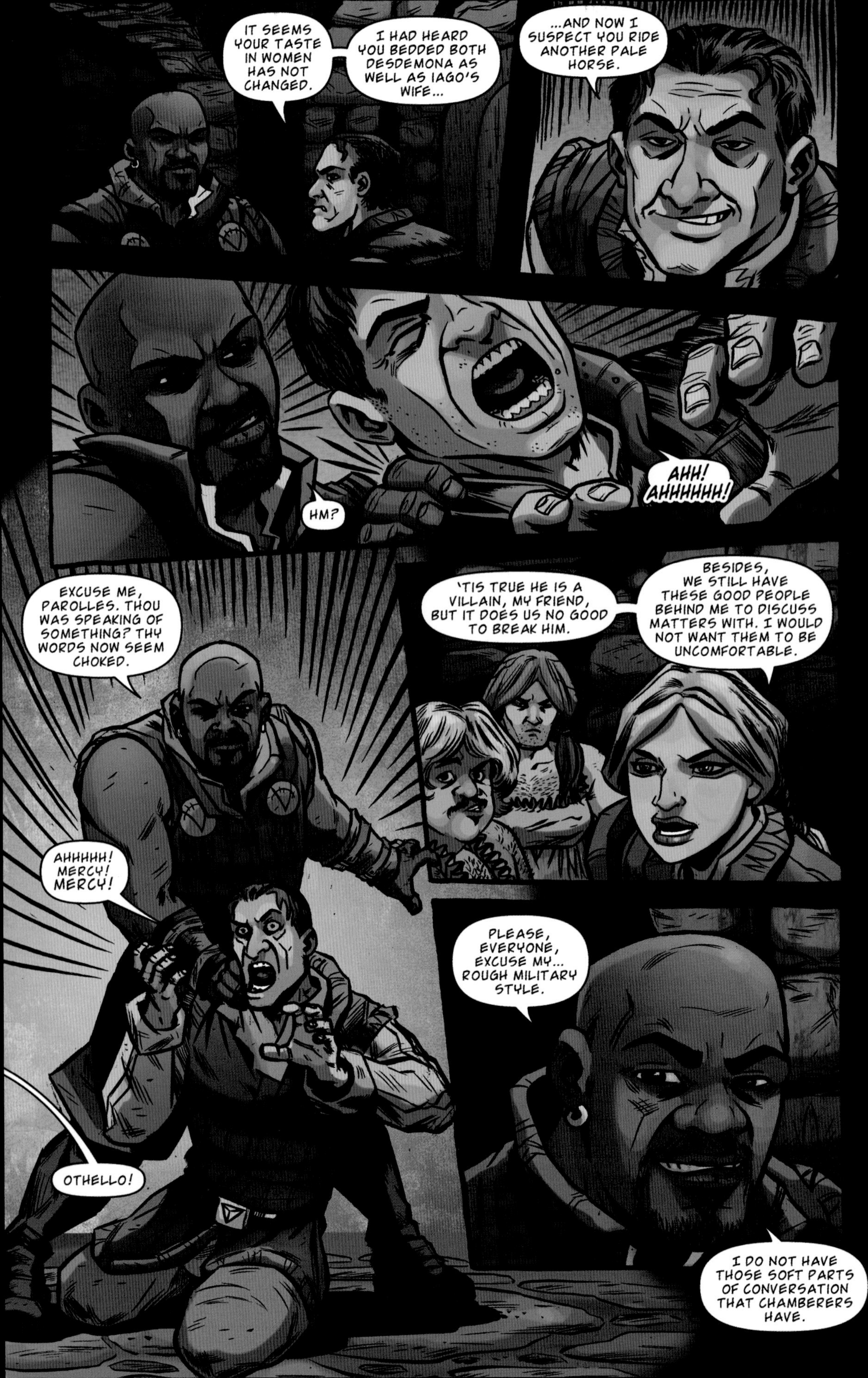
IT SEEMS YOUR TASTE IN WOMEN HAS NOT CHANGED.
I HAD HEARD YOU BEDDED BOTH DESDEMONA AS WELL AS IAGO'S WIFE...
...AND NOW I SUSPECT YOU RIDE ANOTHER PALE HORSE.
HM?
AHH! AHHHHHH!
EXCUSE ME, PAROLLES. THOU WAS SPEAKING OF SOMETHING? THY WORDS NOW SEEM CHOKED.
'TIS TRUE HE IS A VILLAIN, MY FRIEND, BUT IT DOES US NO GOOD TO BREAK HIM.
BESIDES, WE STILL HAVE THESE GOOD PEOPLE BEHIND ME TO DISCUSS MATTERS WITH. I WOULD NOT WANT THEM TO BE UNCOMFORTABLE.
AHHHHH! MERCY! MERCY!
PLEASE, EVERYONE, EXCUSE MY... ROUGH MILITARY STYLE.
OTHELLO!
I DO NOT HAVE THOSE SOFT PARTS OF CONVERSATION THAT CHAMBERERS HAVE.

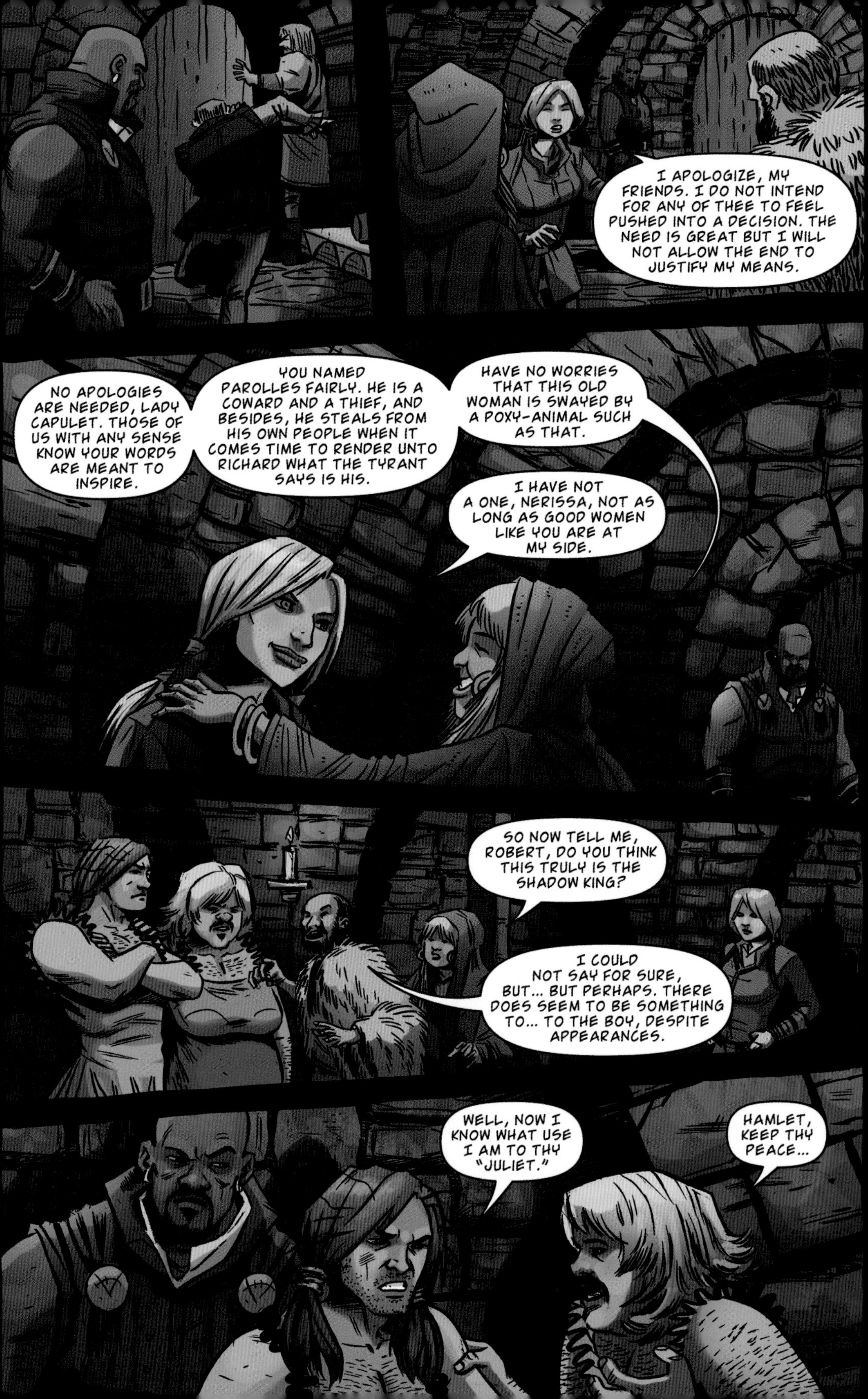
I APOLOGIZE, MY FRIENDS. I DO NOT INTEND FOR ANY OF THEE TO FEEL PUSHED INTO A DECISION. THE NEED IS GREAT BUT I WILL NOT ALLOW THE END TO JUSTIFY MY MEANS.
NO APOLOGIES ARE NEEDED, LADY CAPULET. THOSE OF US WITH ANY SENSE KNOW YOUR WORDS ARE MEANT TO INSPIRE.
YOU NAMED PAROLLES FAIRLY. HE IS A COWARD AND A THIEF, AND BESIDES, HE STEALS FROM HIS OWN PEOPLE WHEN IT COMES TIME TO RENDER UNTO RICHARD WHAT THE TYRANT SAYS IS HIS.
HAVE NO WORRIES THAT THIS OLD WOMAN IS SWAYED BY A POXY-ANIMAL SUCH AS THAT.
I HAVE NOT A ONE, NERISSA, NOT AS LONG AS GOOD WOMEN LIKE YOU ARE AT MY SIDE.
SO NOW TELL ME, ROBERT, DO YOU THINK THIS TRULY IS THE SHADOW KING?
I COULD NOT SAY FOR SURE, BUT... BUT PERHAPS. THERE DOES SEEM TO BE SOMETHING TO... TO THE BOY, DESPITE APPEARANCES.
WELL, NOW I KNOW WHAT USE I AM TO THY "JULIET."
HAMLET, KEEP THY PEACE...

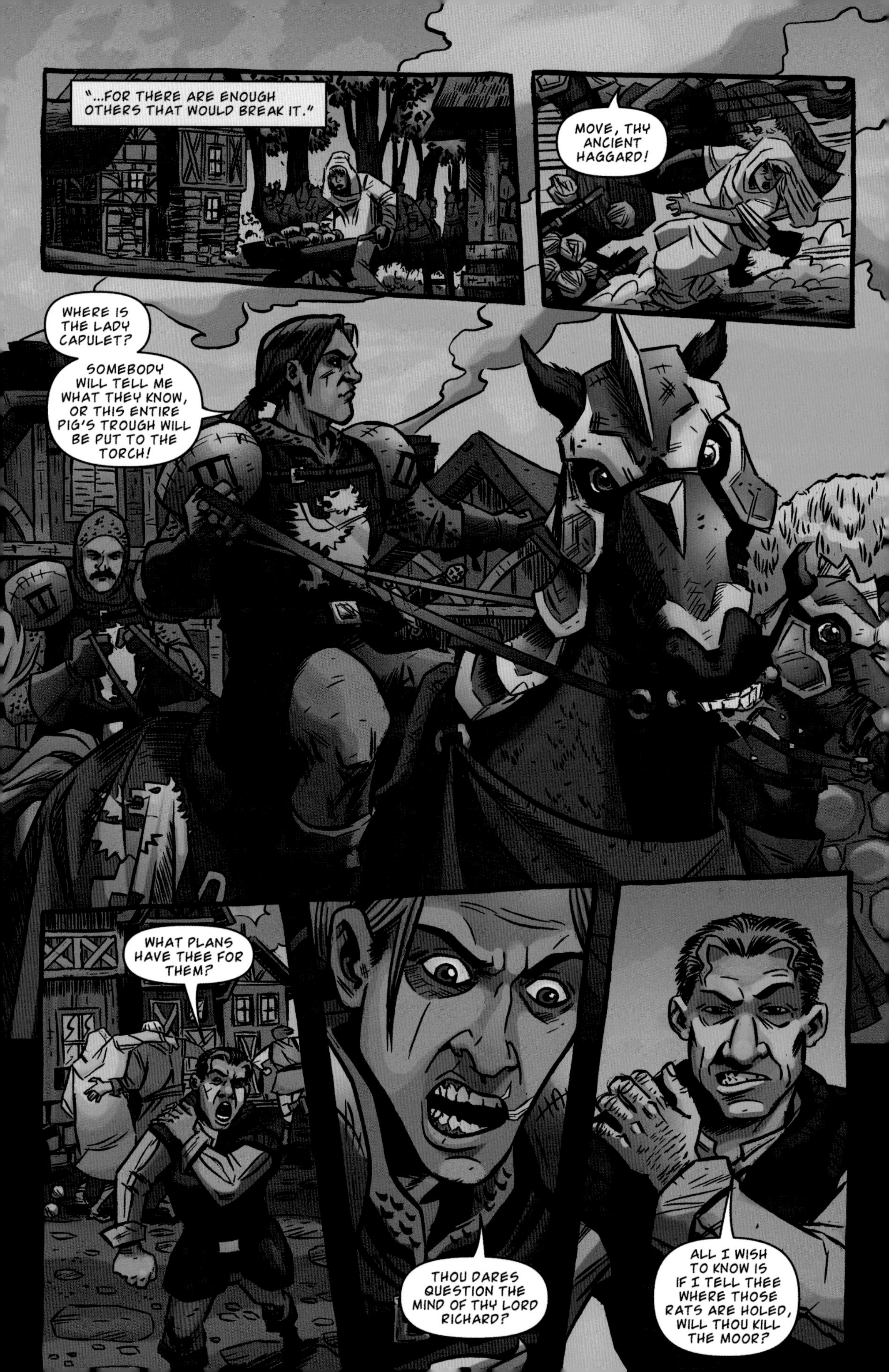
"...FOR THERE ARE ENOUGH OTHERS THAT WOULD BREAK IT."
MOVE, THY ANCIENT HAGGARD!
WHERE IS THE LADY CAPULET?
SOMEBODY WILL TELL ME WHAT THEY KNOW, OR THIS ENTIRE PIG'S TROUGH WILL BE PUT TO THE TORCH!
WHAT PLANS HAVE THEE FOR THEM?
THOU DARES QUESTION THE MIND OF THY LORD RICHARD?
ALL I WISH TO KNOW IS IF I TELL THEE WHERE THOSE RATS ARE HOLED, WILL THOU KILL THE MOOR?

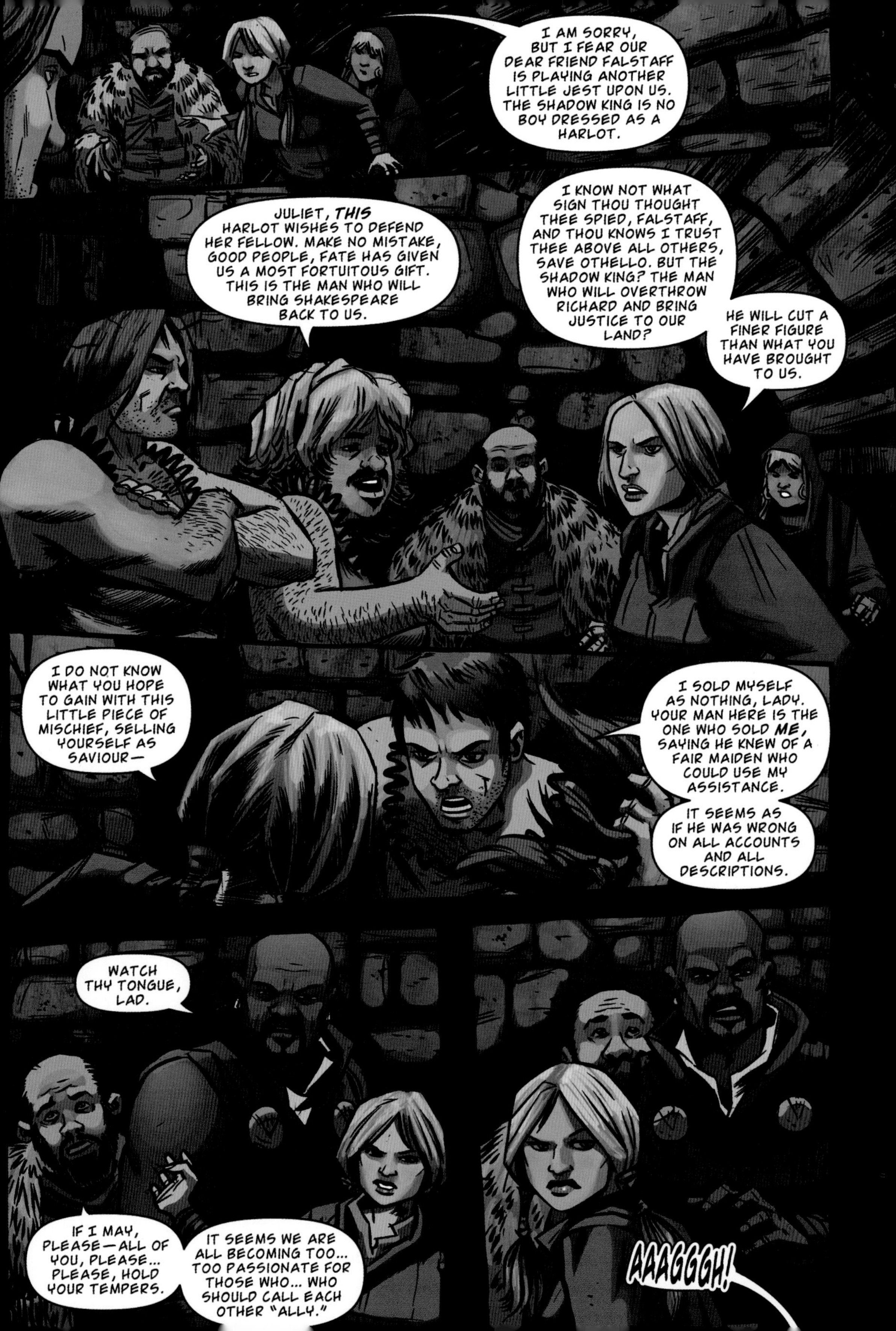
I AM SORRY, BUT I FEAR OUR DEAR FRIEND FALSTAFF IS PLAYING ANOTHER LITTLE JEST UPON US. THE SHADOW KING IS NO BOY DRESSED AS A HARLOT.
JULIET, THIS HARLOT WISHES TO DEFEND HER FELLOW. MAKE NO MISTAKE, GOOD PEOPLE, FATE HAS GIVEN US A MOST FORTUITOUS GIFT. THIS IS THE MAN WHO WILL BRING SHAKESPEARE BACK TO US.
I KNOW NOT WHAT SIGN THOU THOUGHT THEE SPIED, FALSTAFF, AND THOU KNOWS I TRUST THEE ABOVE ALL OTHERS, SAVE OTHELLO. BUT THE SHADOW KING? THE MAN WHO WILL OVERTHROW RICHARD AND BRING JUSTICE TO OUR LAND?
HE WILL CUT A FINER FIGURE THAN WHAT YOU HAVE BROUGHT TO US.
I DO NOT KNOW WHAT YOU HOPE TO GAIN WITH THIS LITTLE PIECE OF MISCHIEF, SELLING YOURSELF AS SAVIOUR—
I SOLD MYSELF AS NOTHING, LADY. YOUR MAN HERE IS THE ONE WHO SOLD ME, SAYING HE KNEW OF A FAIR MAIDEN WHO COULD USE MY ASSISTANCE.
IT SEEMS AS IF HE WAS WRONG ON ALL ACCOUNTS AND ALL DESCRIPTIONS.
WATCH THY TONGUE, LAD.
IF I MAY, PLEASE—ALL OF YOU, PLEASE... PLEASE, HOLD YOUR TEMPERS.
IT SEEMS WE ARE ALL BECOMING TOO... TOO PASSIONATE FOR THOSE WHO... WHO SHOULD CALL EACH OTHER "ALLY."
AAAGGGH!

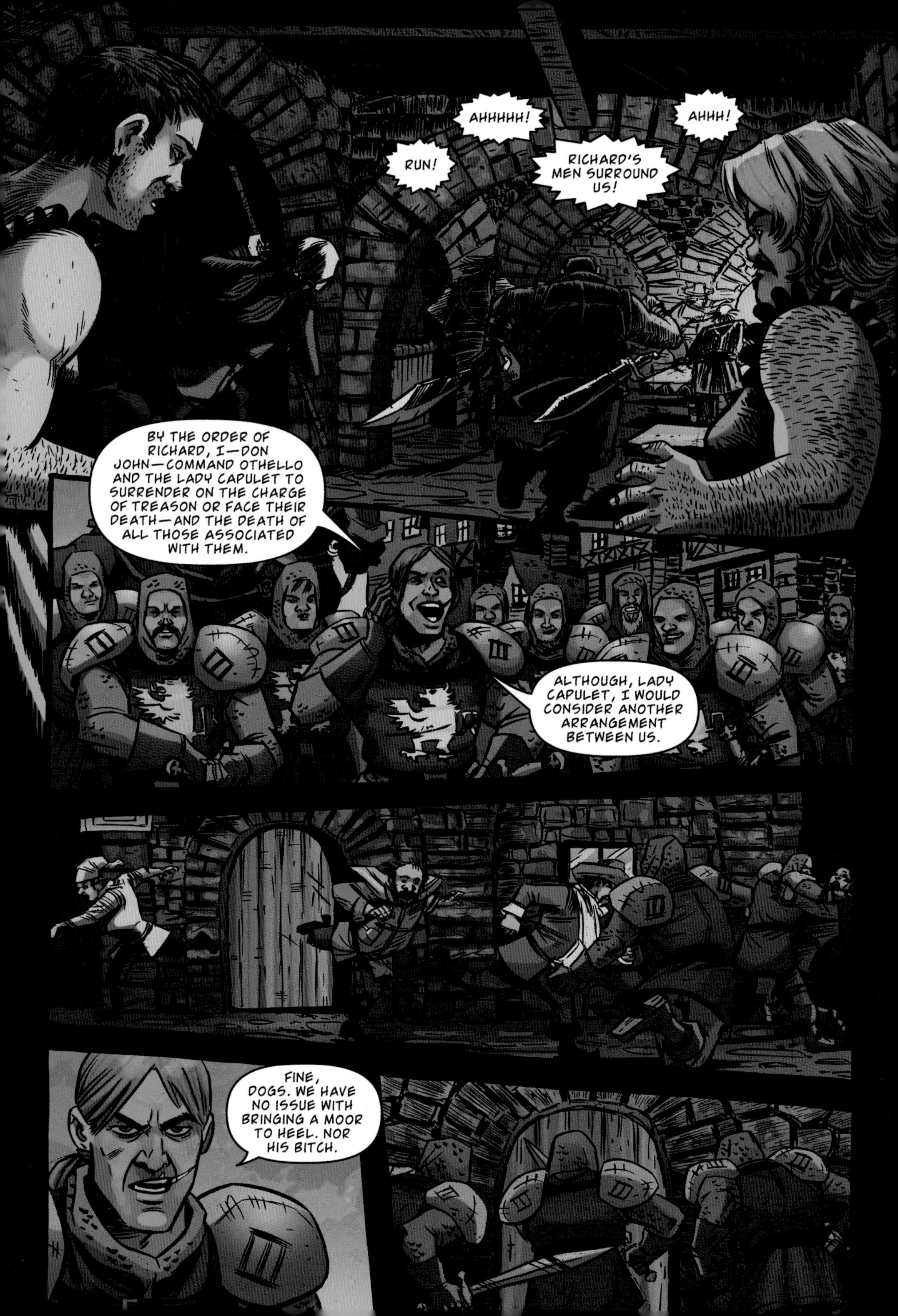
AHHHHH!
AHHH!
RUN!
RICHARD'S MEN SURROUND US!
BY THE ORDER OF RICHARD, I—DON JOHN—COMMAND OTHELLO AND THE LADY CAPULET TO SURRENDER ON THE CHARGE OF TREASON OR FACE THEIR DEATH—AND THE DEATH OF ALL THOSE ASSOCIATED WITH THEM.
ALTHOUGH, LADY CAPULET, I WOULD CONSIDER ANOTHER ARRANGEMENT BETWEEN US.
FINE, DOGS. WE HAVE NO ISSUE WITH BRINGING A MOOR TO HEEL. NOR HIS BITCH.

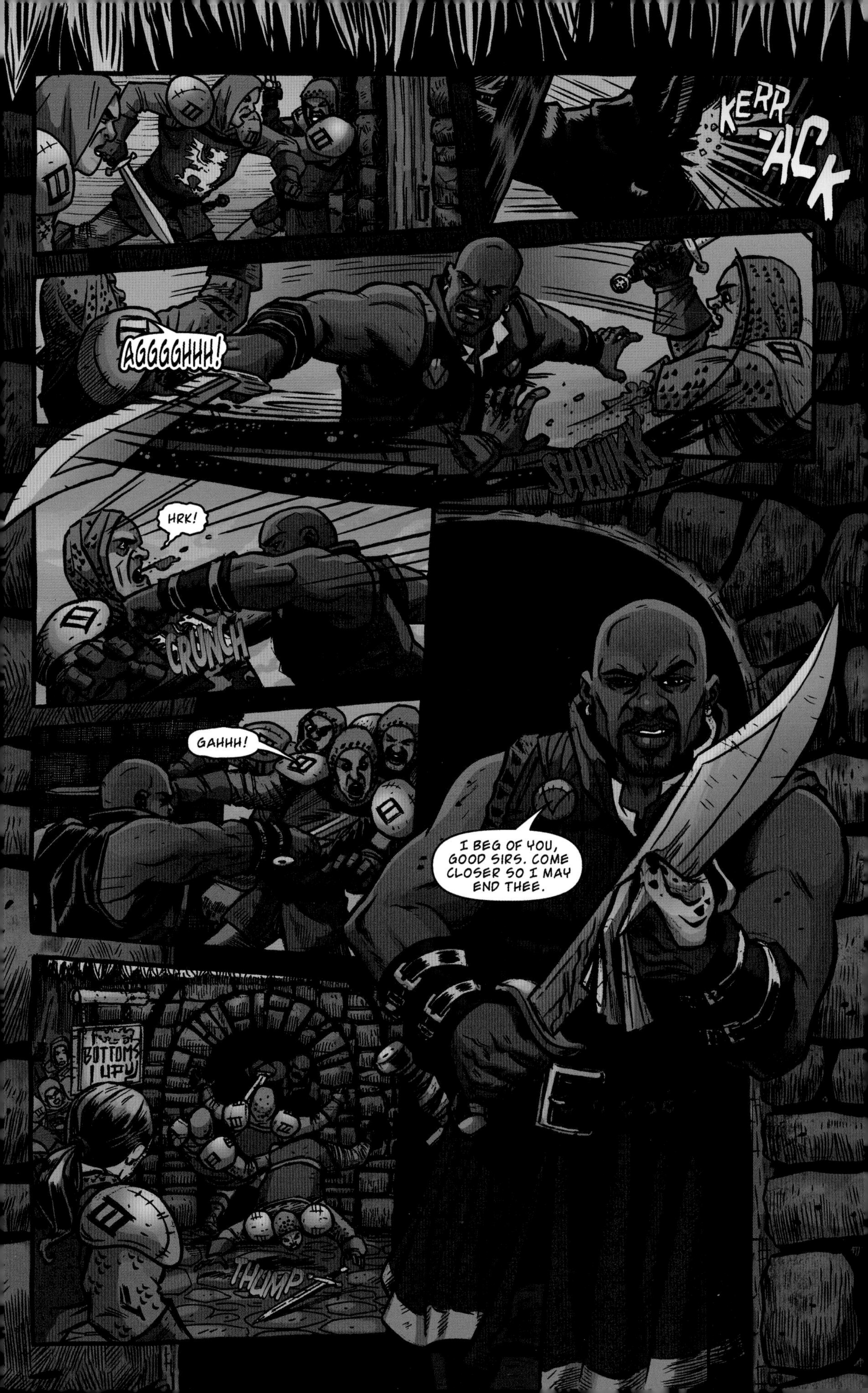
KERR-ACK
AGGGGHHH!
SHHIKK
HRK!
CRUNCH
GAHHH!
I BEG OF YOU, GOOD SIRS. COME CLOSER SO I MAY END THEE.
BOTTOMS UP
THUMP

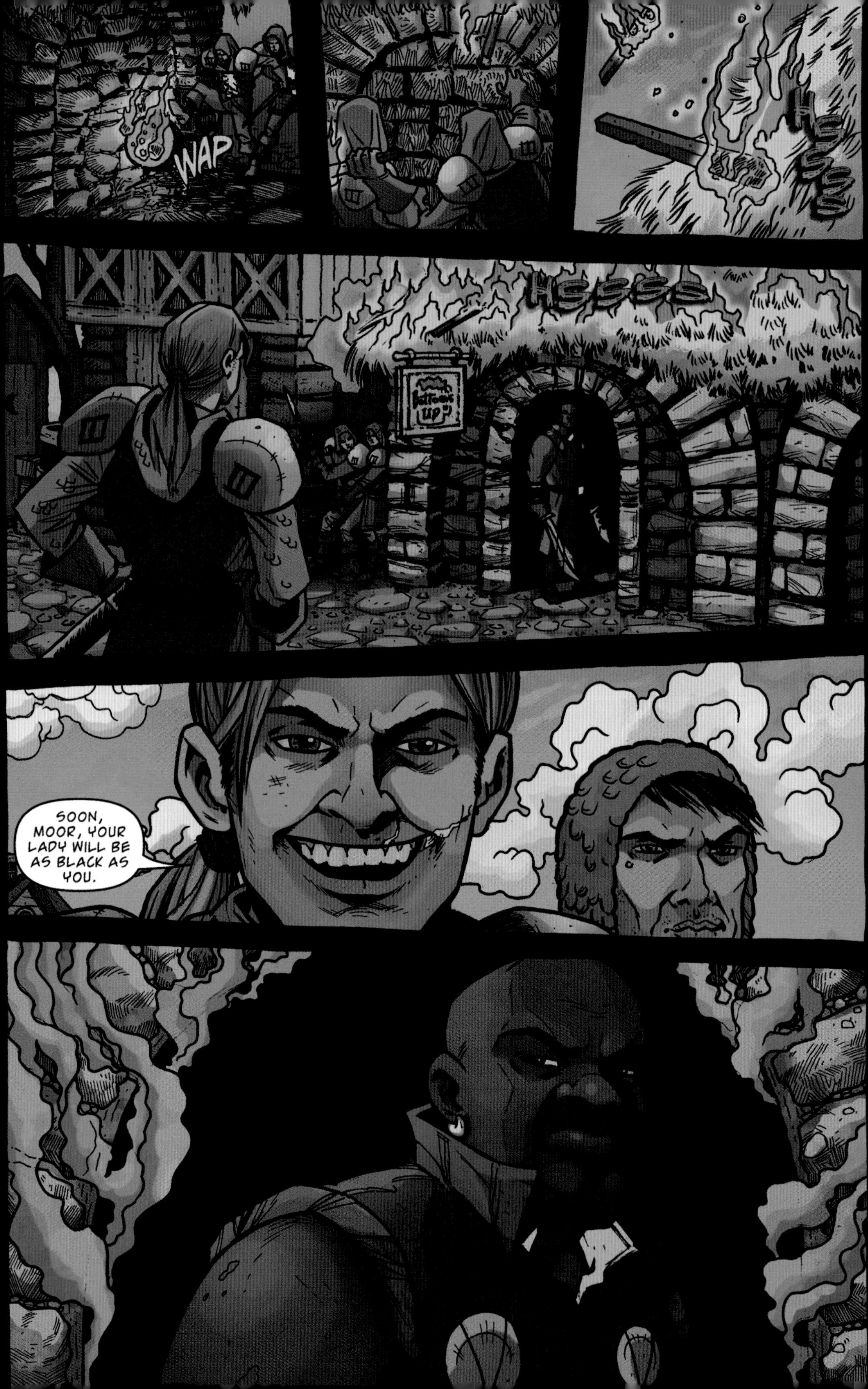
WAP
HSSSS
HSSSSS
SOON, MOOR, YOUR LADY WILL BE AS BLACK AS YOU.

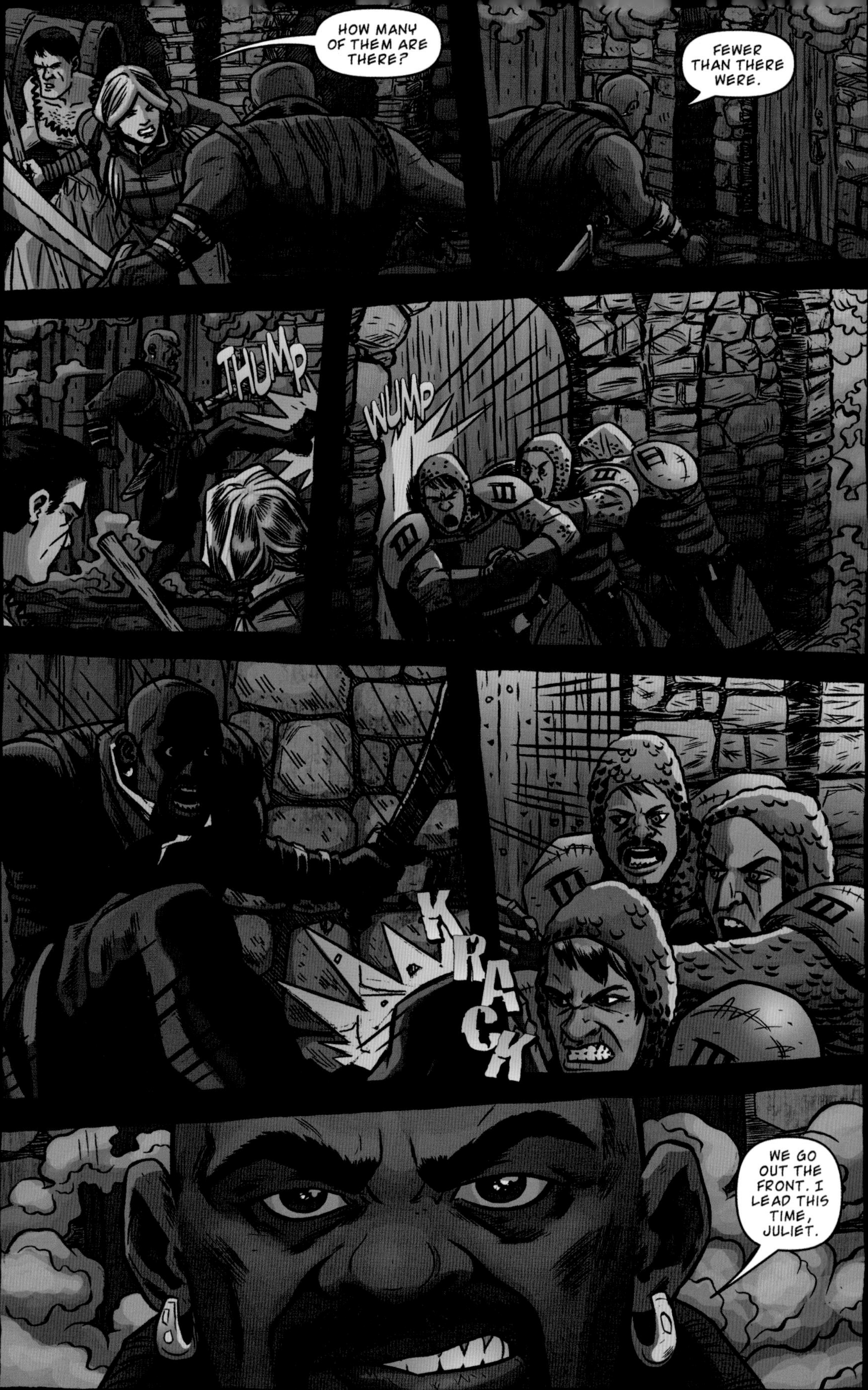
HOW MANY OF THEM ARE THERE?
FEWER THAN THERE WERE.
THUMP
WUMP
KRACK
WE GO OUT THE FRONT. I LEAD THIS TIME, JULIET.

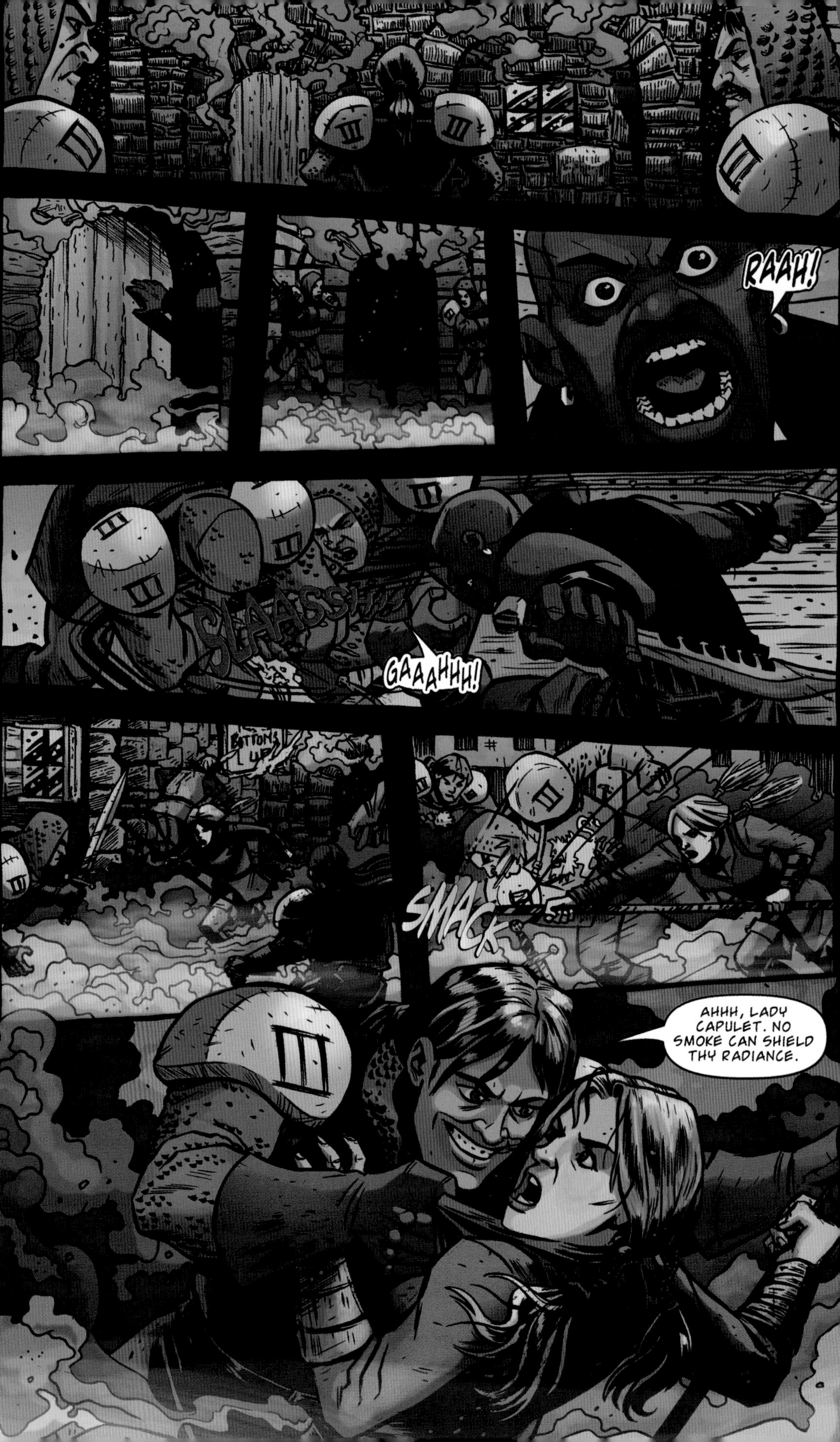
RAAH!
SLAASSH!
GAAAHHH!
BOTTOMS UP
SMACK
AHHH, LADY CAPULET. NO SMOKE CAN SHIELD THY RADIANCE.

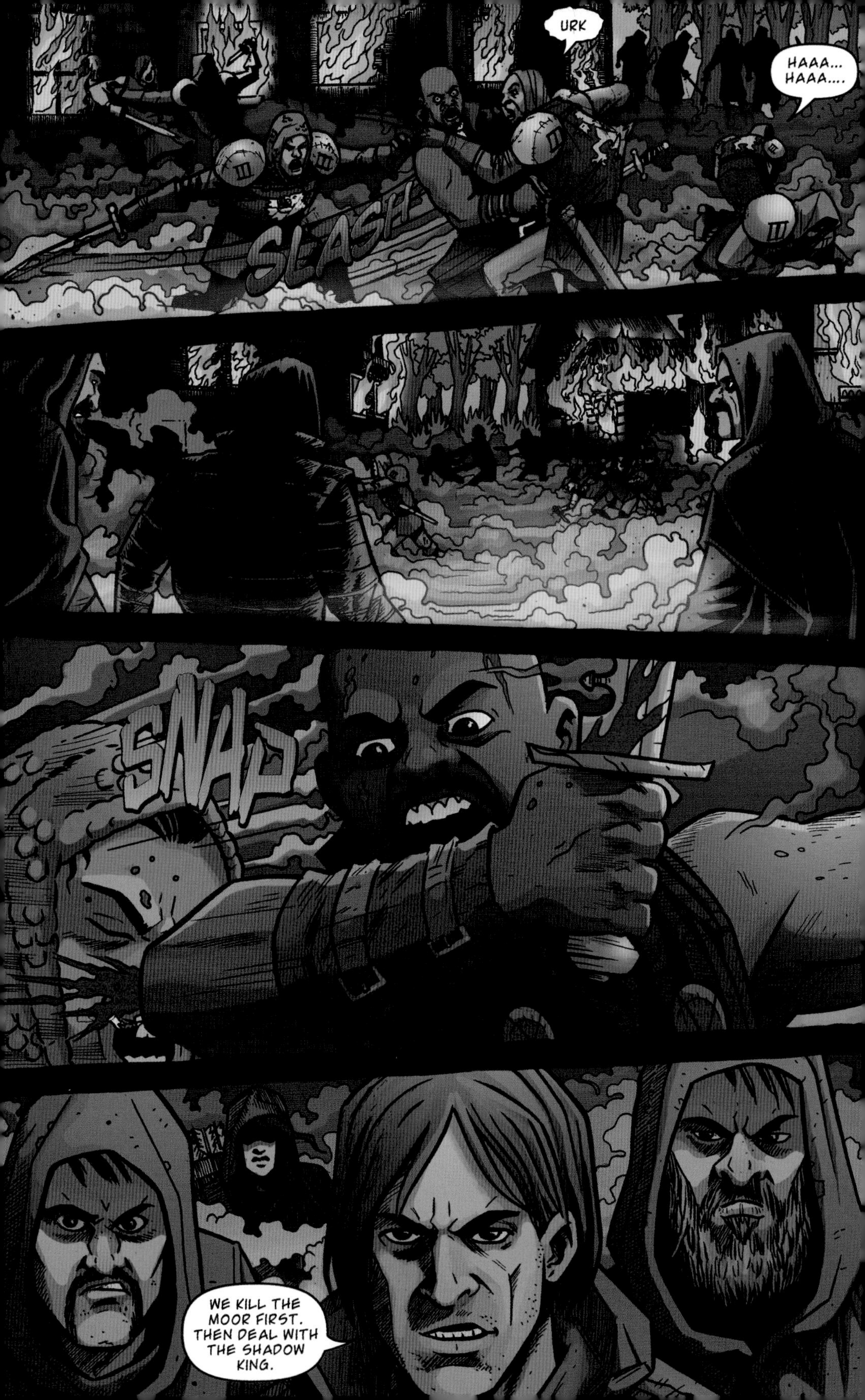
URK
HAAA... HAAA....
SLASH
SNAP
WE KILL THE MOOR FIRST. THEN DEAL WITH THE SHADOW KING.

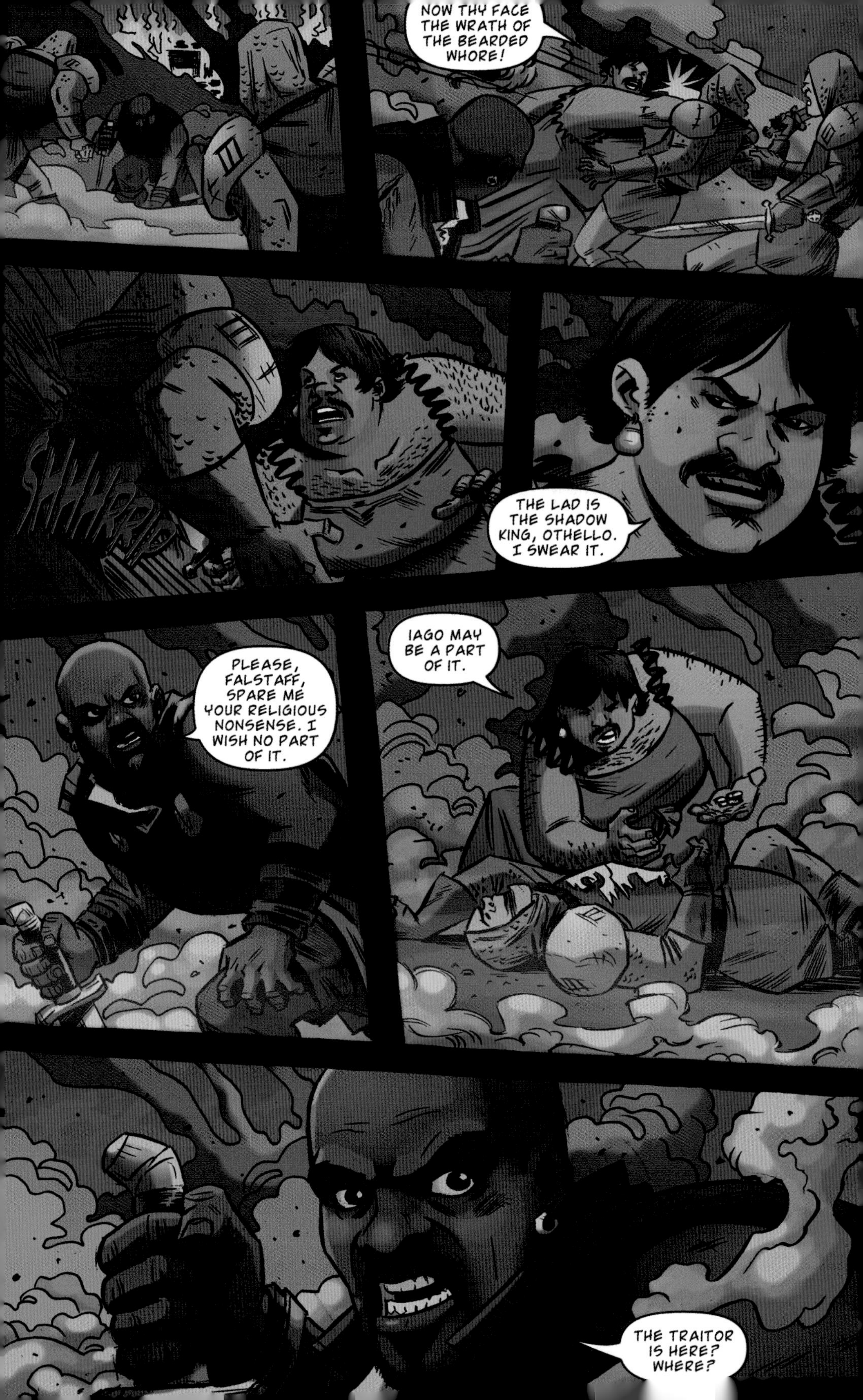

NOW THY FACE THE WRATH OF THE BEARDED WHORE!
SHHHRRRIP
THE LAD IS THE SHADOW KING, OTHELLO. I SWEAR IT.
PLEASE, FALSTAFF, SPARE ME YOUR RELIGIOUS NONSENSE. I WISH NO PART OF IT.
IAGO MAY BE A PART OF IT.
THE TRAITOR IS HERE? WHERE?

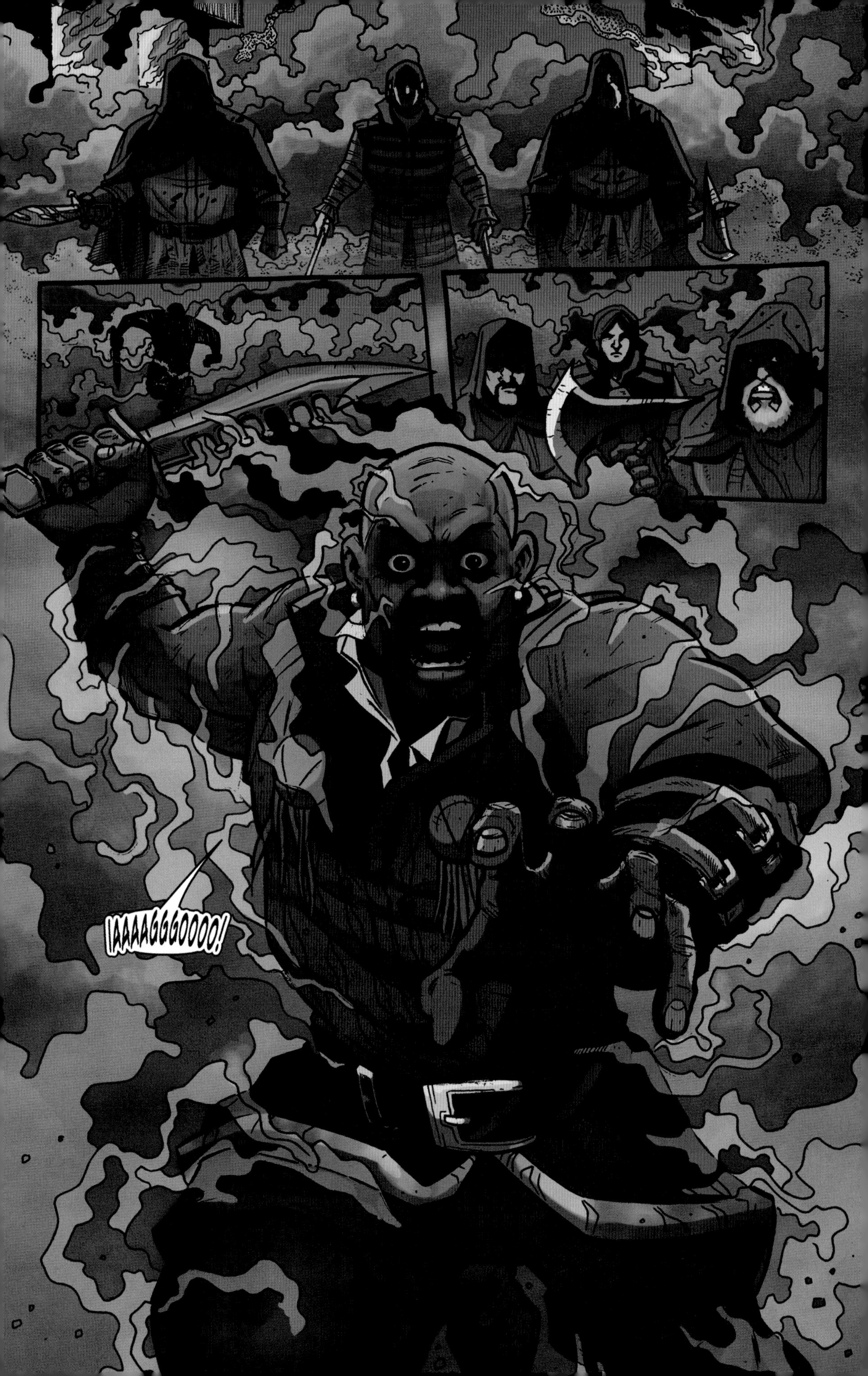
IAAAAGGGOOOO!

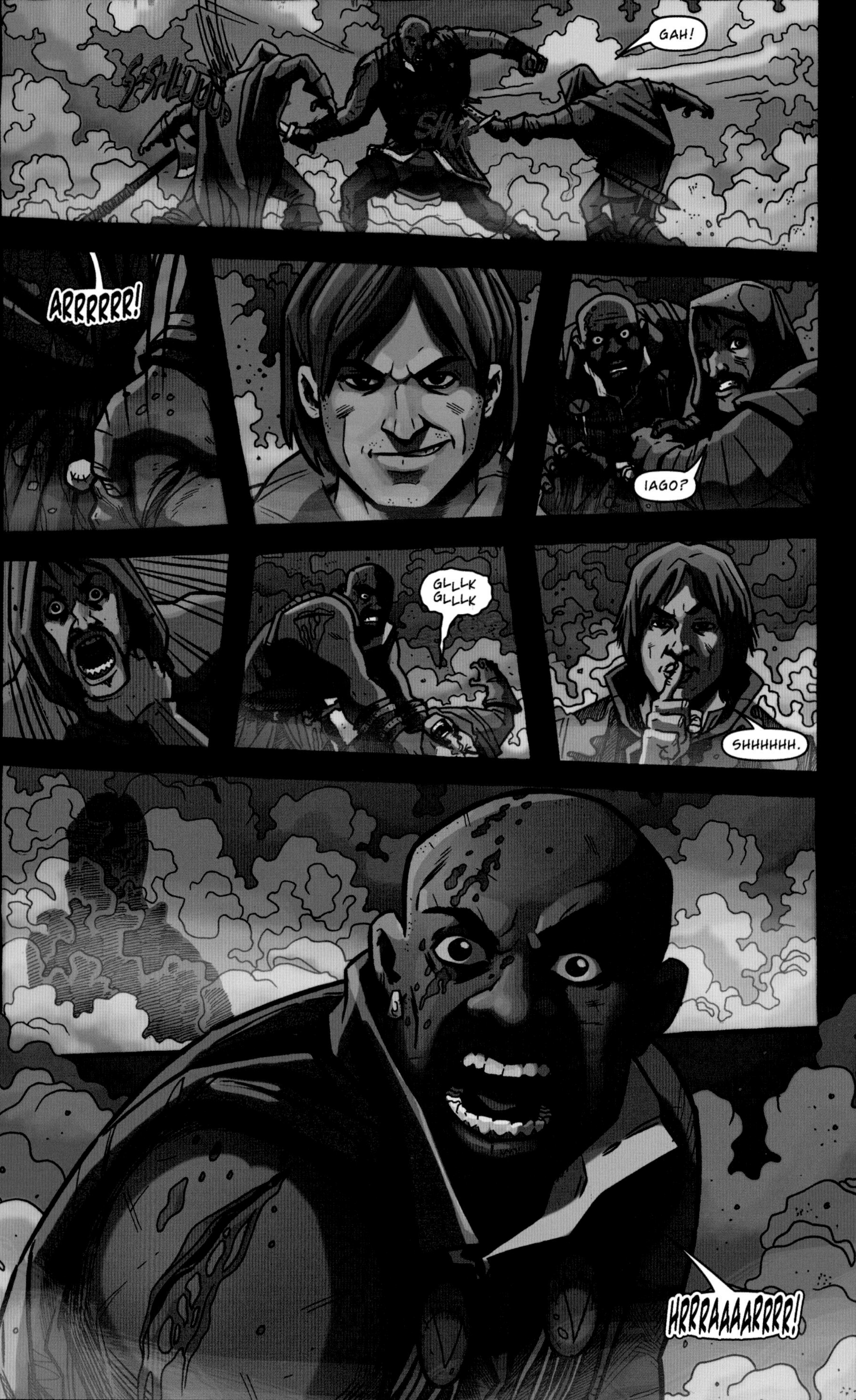
SSHLUUUP
SHK
GAH!
ARRRRRR!
IAGO?
GLLLK GLLLK
SHHHHHH.
HRRRAAAARRRR!

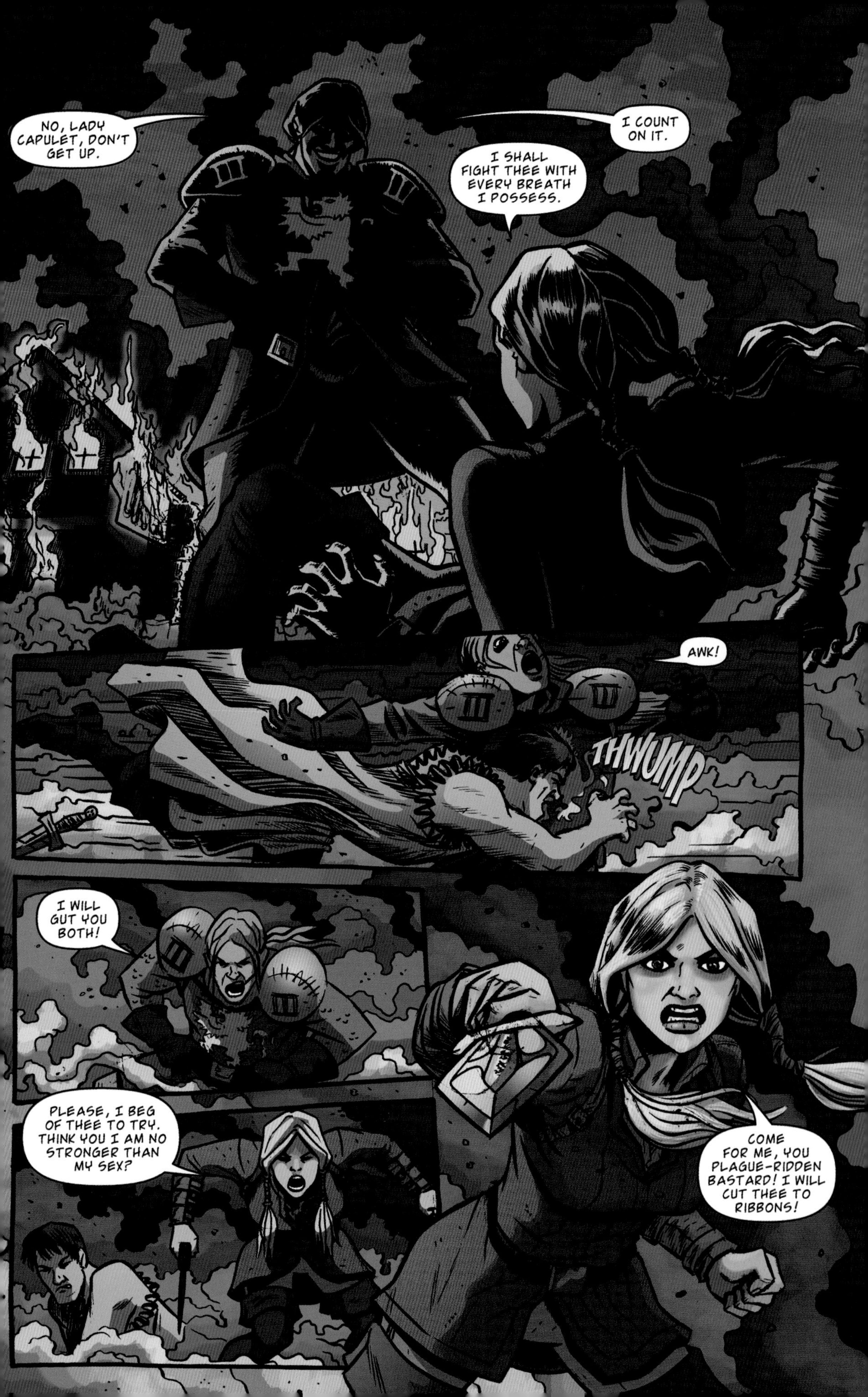
NO, LADY CAPULET, DON'T GET UP.
I COUNT ON IT.
I SHALL FIGHT THEE WITH EVERY BREATH I POSSESS.
AWK!
THWUMP
I WILL GUT YOU BOTH!
PLEASE, I BEG OF THEE TO TRY. THINK YOU I AM NO STRONGER THAN MY SEX?
COME FOR ME, YOU PLAGUE-RIDDEN BASTARD! I WILL CUT THEE TO RIBBONS!

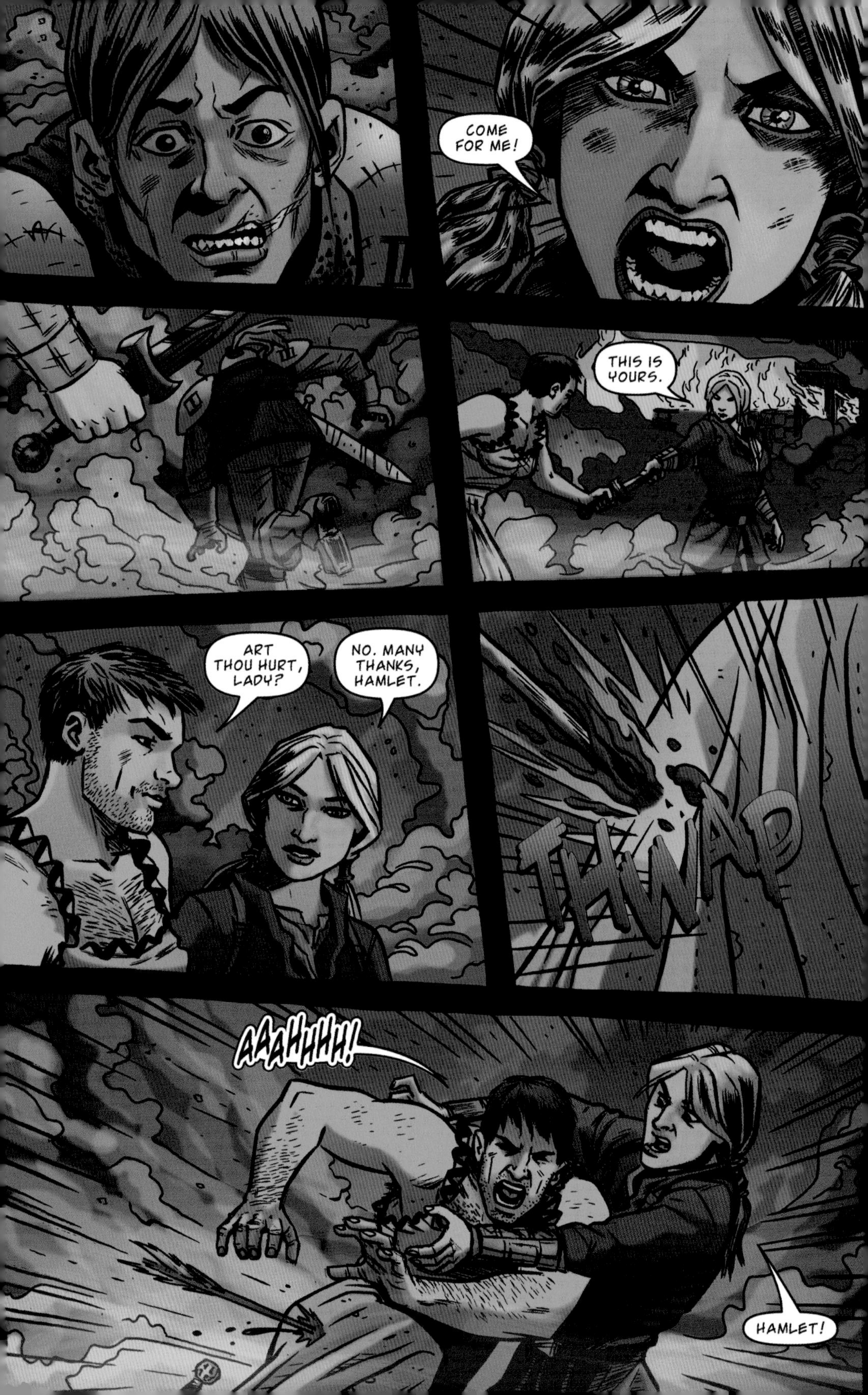
COME FOR ME!
THIS IS YOURS.
ART THOU HURT, LADY?
NO. MANY THANKS, HAMLET.
THWAP
AAAHHHH!
HAMLET!

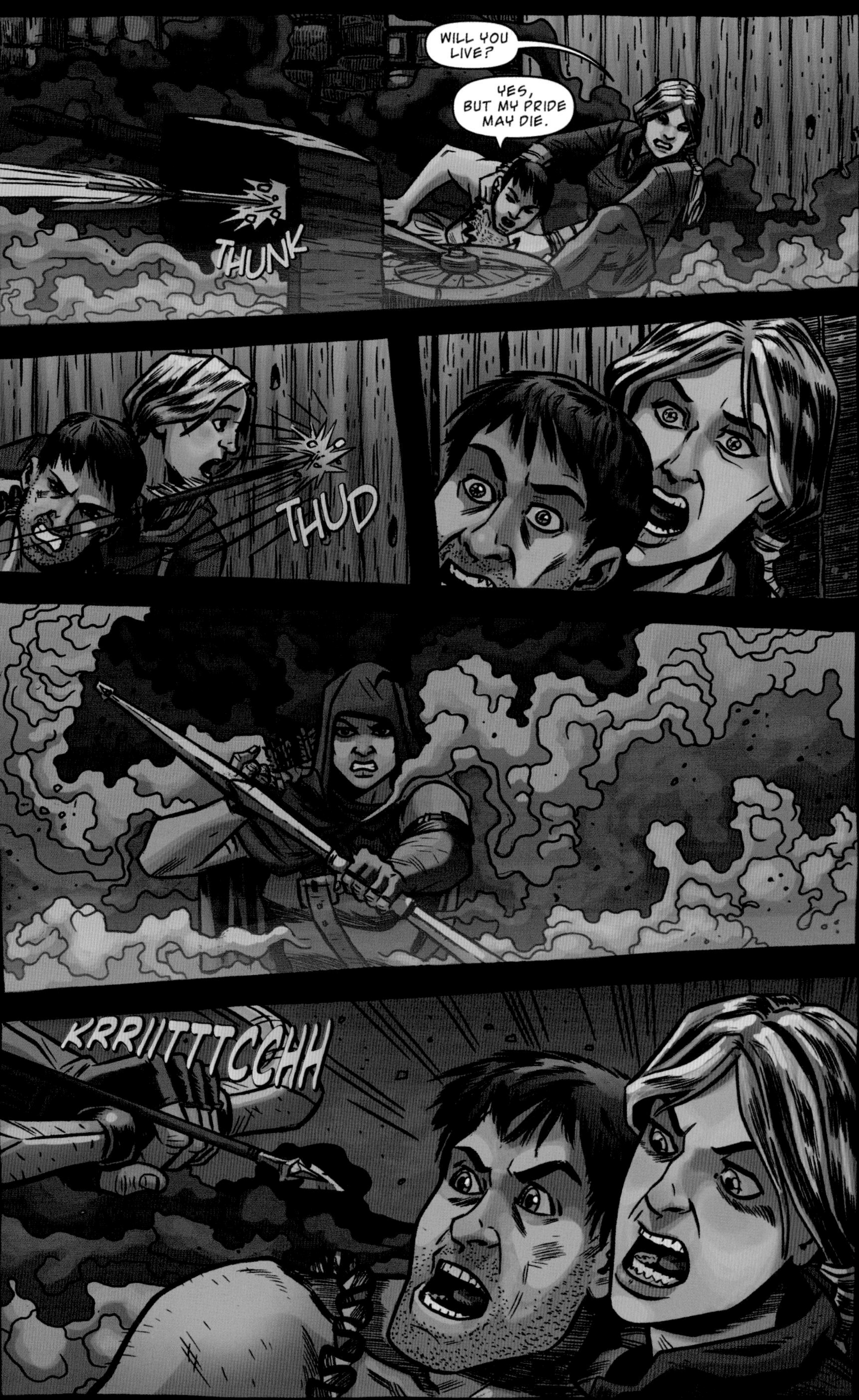
WILL YOU LIVE?
YES, BUT MY PRIDE MAY DIE.
THUNK
THUD
KRRIITTTCCHH

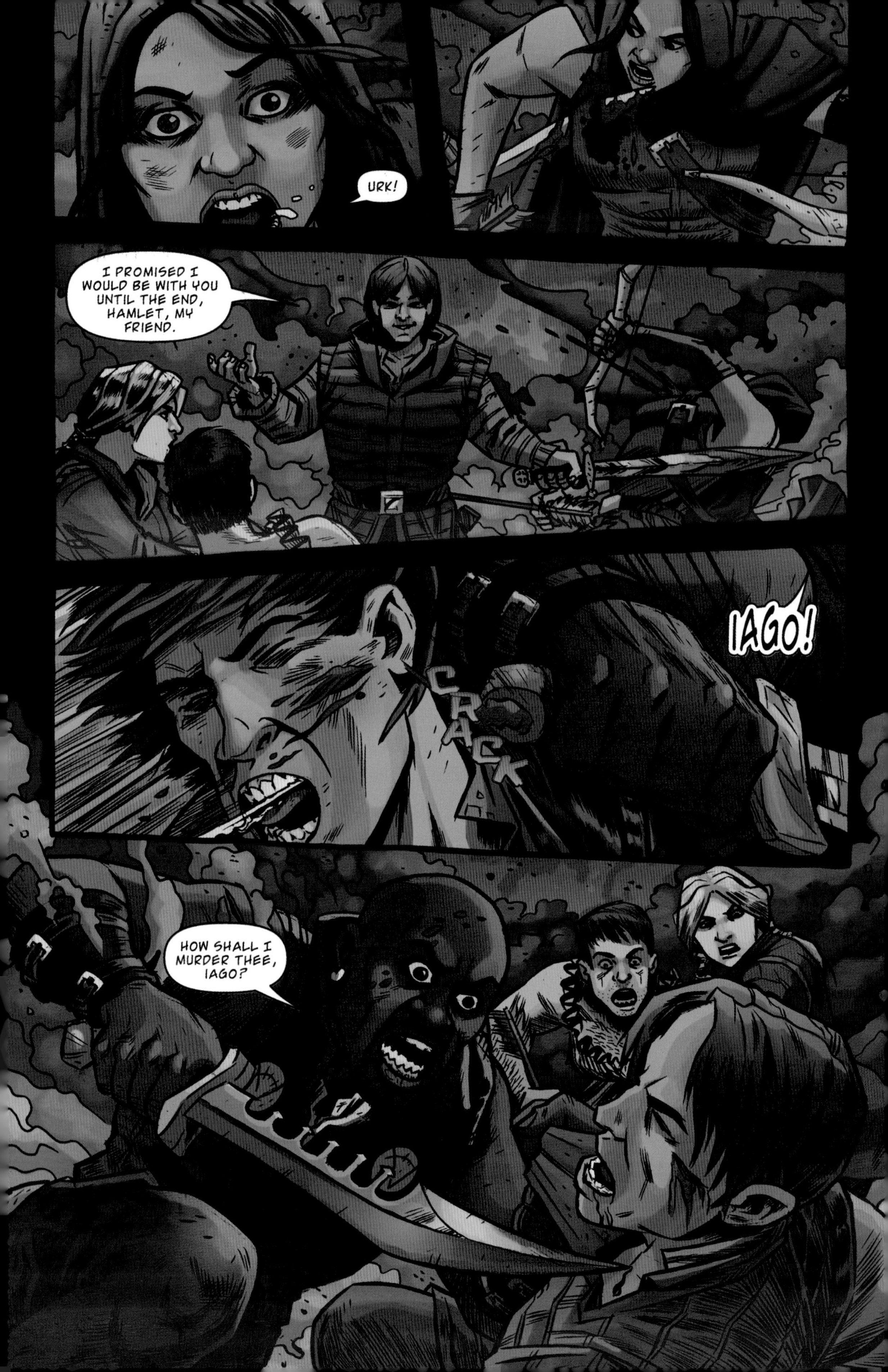
URK!
I PROMISED I WOULD BE WITH YOU UNTIL THE END, HAMLET, MY FRIEND.
IAGO!
CRACK
HOW SHALL I MURDER THEE, IAGO?

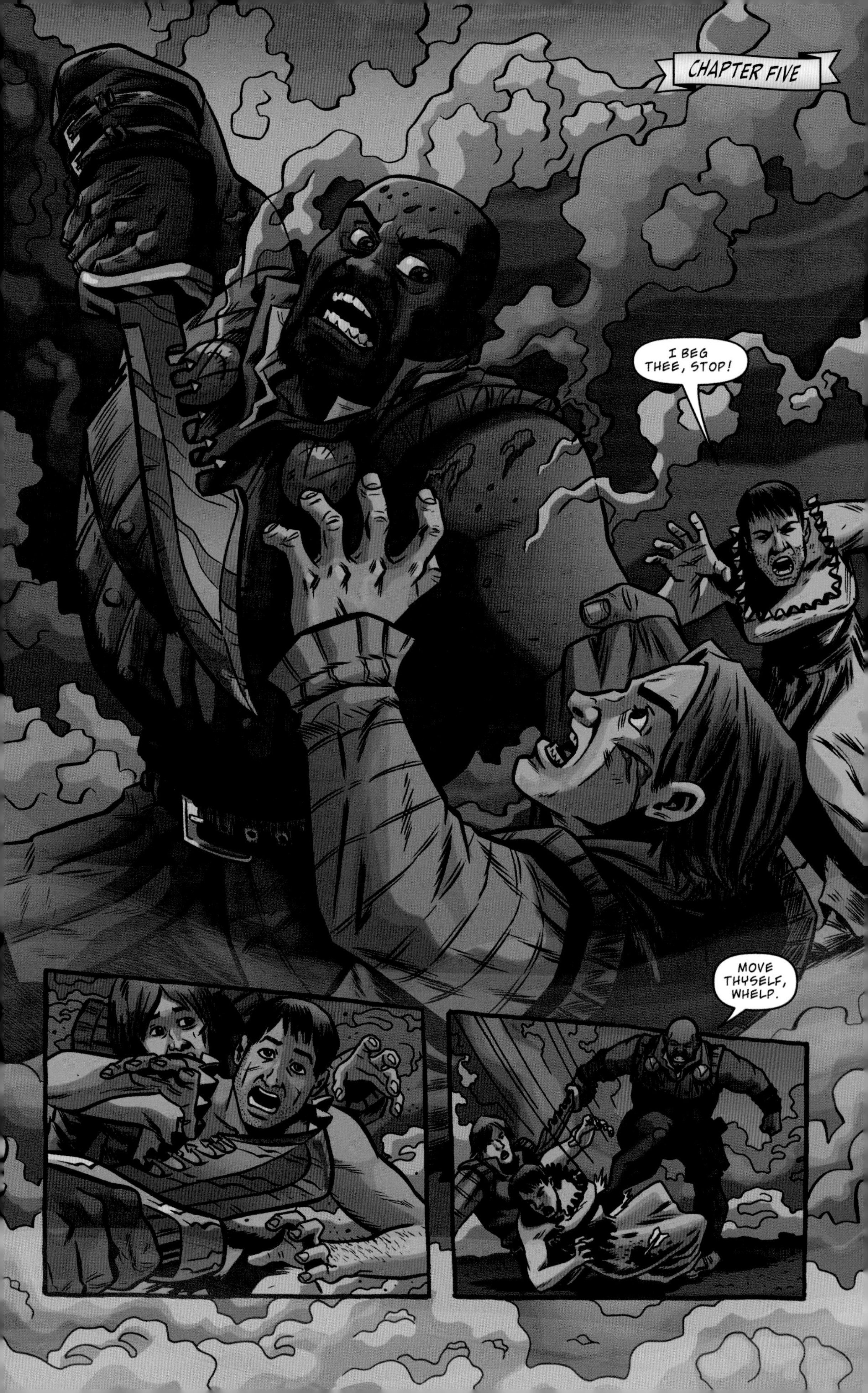
CHAPTER FIVE
I BEG THEE, STOP!
MOVE THYSELF, WHELP.

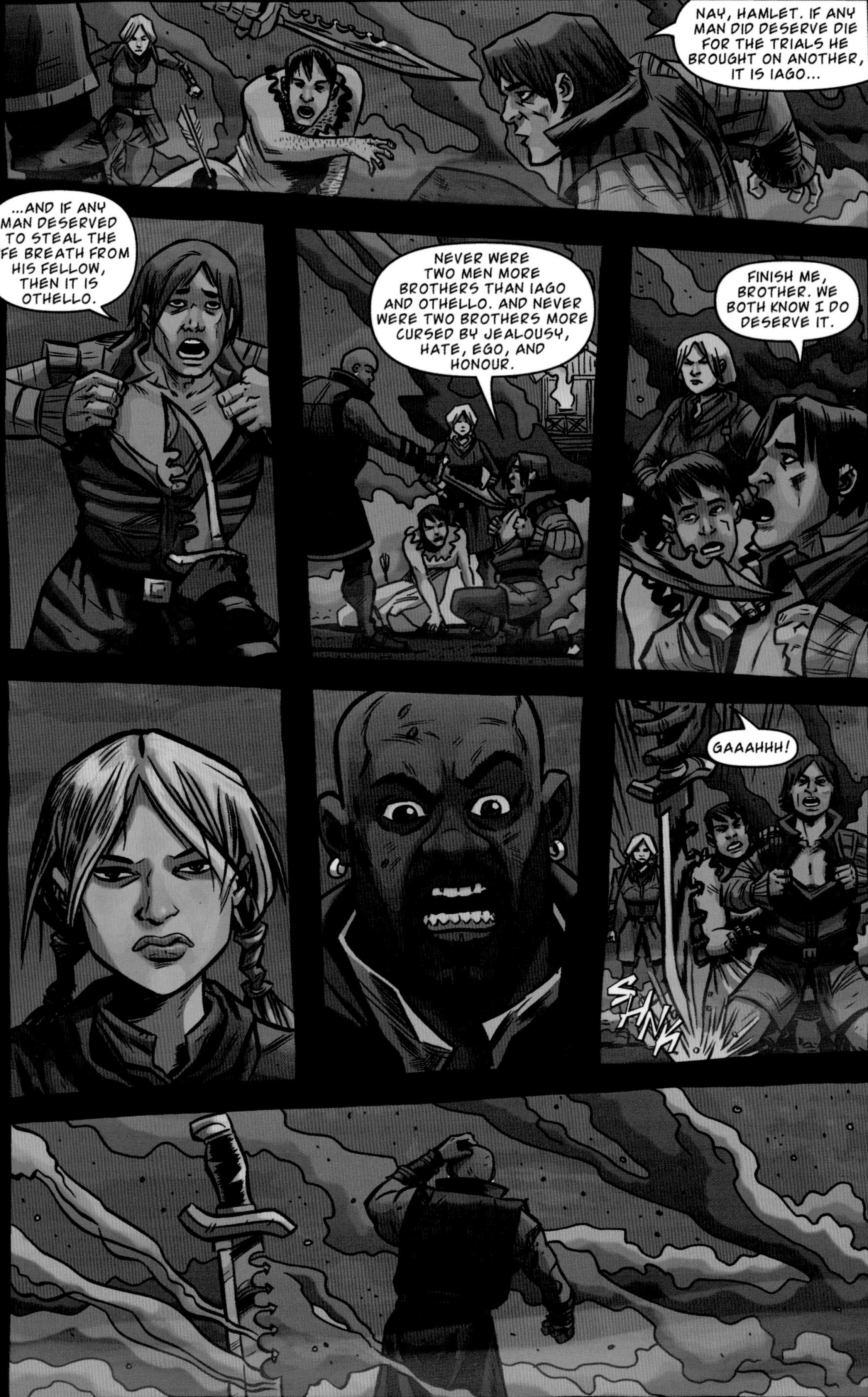
NAY, HAMLET. IF ANY MAN DID DESERVE DIE FOR THE TRIALS HE BROUGHT ON ANOTHER, IT IS IAGO...
...AND IF ANY MAN DESERVED TO STEAL THE LIFE BREATH FROM HIS FELLOW, THEN IT IS OTHELLO.
NEVER WERE TWO MEN MORE BROTHERS THAN IAGO AND OTHELLO. AND NEVER WERE TWO BROTHERS MORE CURSED BY JEALOUSY, HATE, EGO, AND HONOUR.
FINISH ME, BROTHER. WE BOTH KNOW I DO DESERVE IT.
GAAAHHH!
SHNK

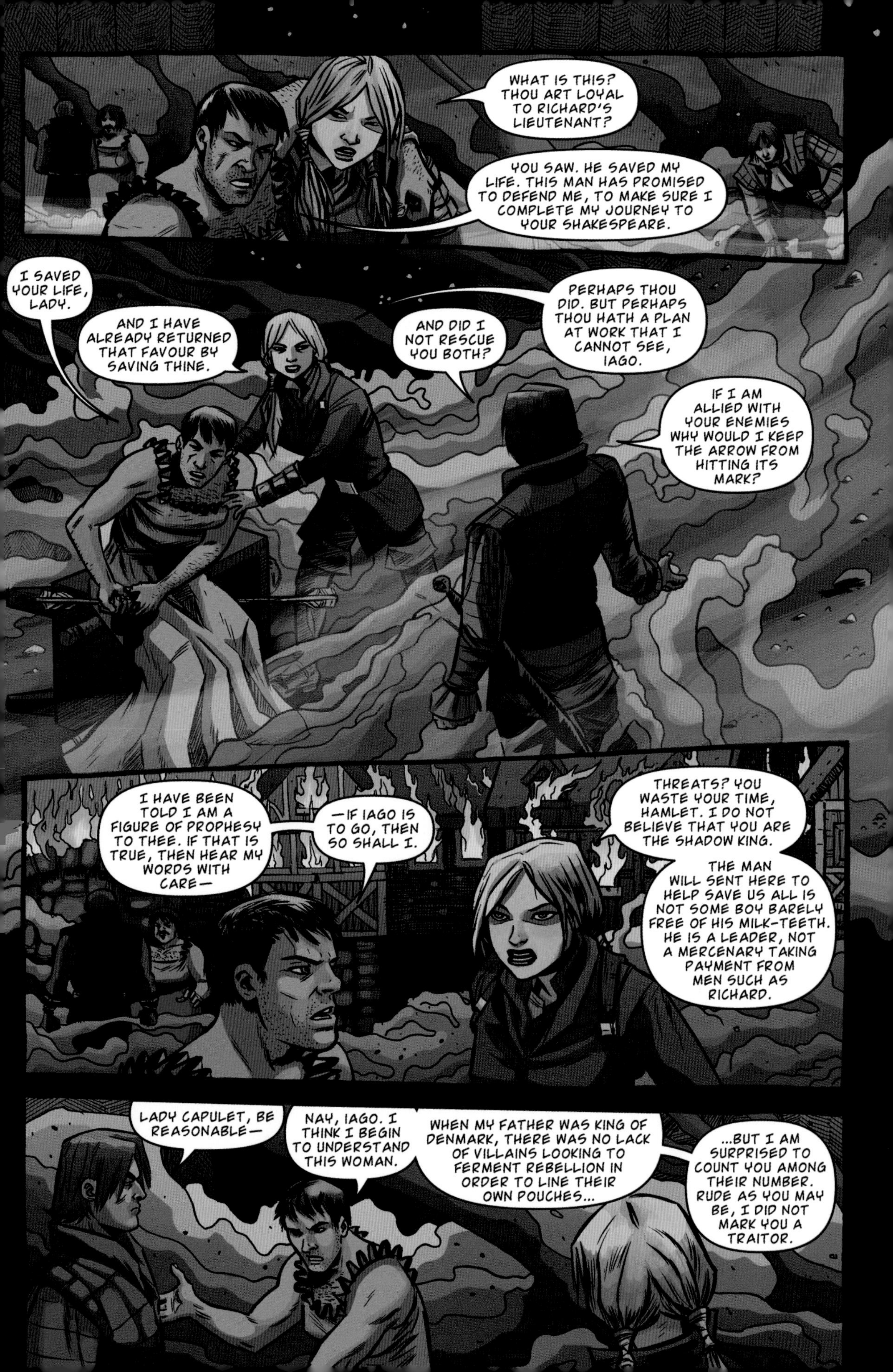
WHAT IS THIS? THOU ART LOYAL TO RICHARD'S LIEUTENANT?
YOU SAW. HE SAVED MY LIFE. THIS MAN HAS PROMISED TO DEFEND ME, TO MAKE SURE I COMPLETE MY JOURNEY TO YOUR SHAKESPEARE.
I SAVED YOUR LIFE, LADY.
AND I HAVE ALREADY RETURNED THAT FAVOUR BY SAVING THINE.
AND DID I NOT RESCUE YOU BOTH?
PERHAPS THOU DID. BUT PERHAPS THOU HATH A PLAN AT WORK THAT I CANNOT SEE, IAGO.
IF I AM ALLIED WITH YOUR ENEMIES WHY WOULD I KEEP THE ARROW FROM HITTING ITS MARK?
I HAVE BEEN TOLD I AM A FIGURE OF PROPHESY TO THEE. IF THAT IS TRUE, THEN HEAR MY WORDS WITH CARE—
—IF IAGO IS TO GO, THEN SO SHALL I.
THREATS? YOU WASTE YOUR TIME, HAMLET. I DO NOT BELIEVE THAT YOU ARE THE SHADOW KING.
THE MAN WILL SENT HERE TO HELP SAVE US ALL IS NOT SOME BOY BARELY FREE OF HIS MILK-TEETH. HE IS A LEADER, NOT A MERCENARY TAKING PAYMENT FROM MEN SUCH AS RICHARD.
LADY CAPULET, BE REASONABLE—
NAY, IAGO. I THINK I BEGIN TO UNDERSTAND THIS WOMAN.
WHEN MY FATHER WAS KING OF DENMARK, THERE WAS NO LACK OF VILLAINS LOOKING TO FERMENT REBELLION IN ORDER TO LINE THEIR OWN POUCHES...
...BUT I AM SURPRISED TO COUNT YOU AMONG THEIR NUMBER. RUDE AS YOU MAY BE, I DID NOT MARK YOU A TRAITOR.

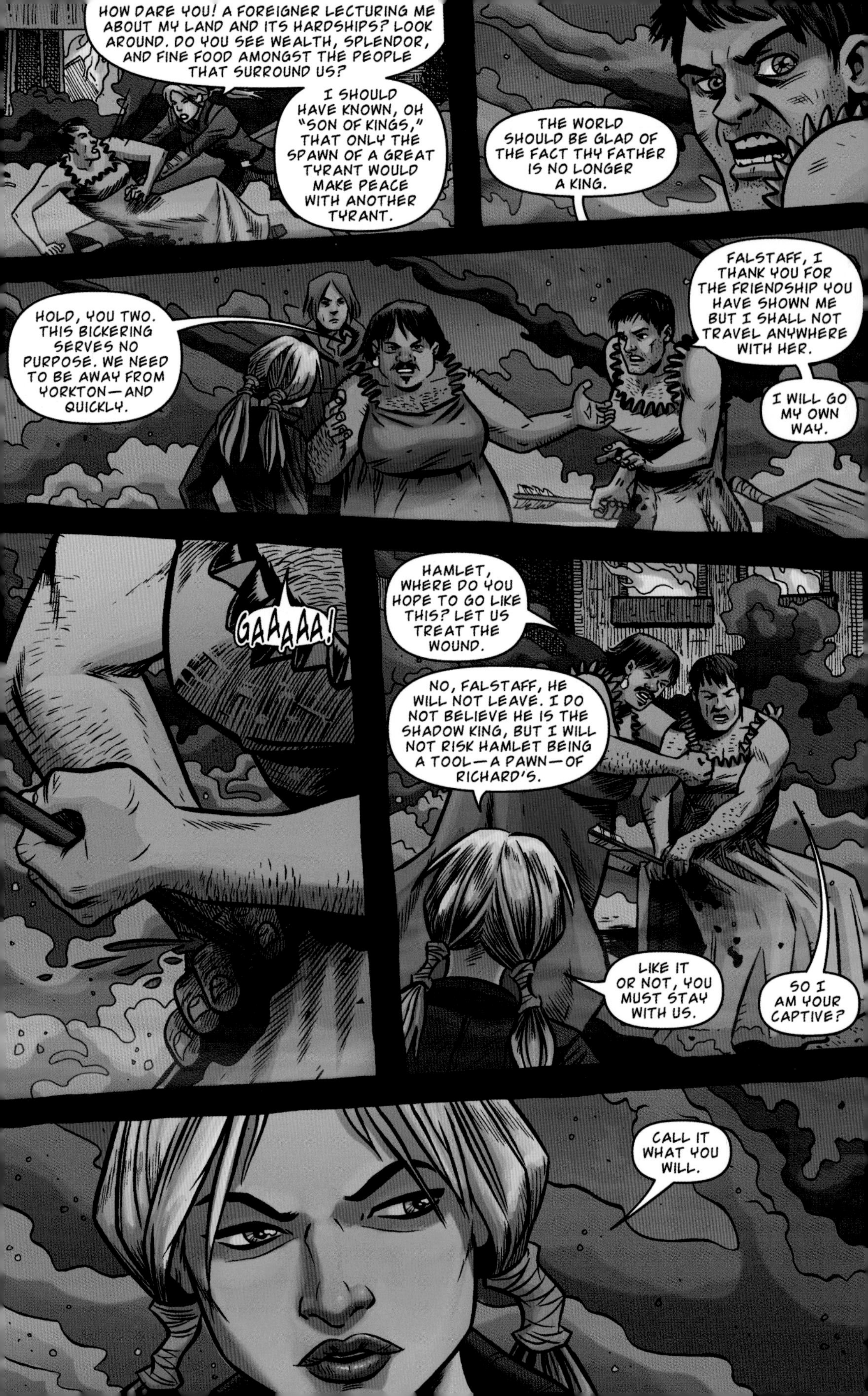
HOW DARE YOU! A FOREIGNER LECTURING ME ABOUT MY LAND AND ITS HARDSHIPS? LOOK AROUND. DO YOU SEE WEALTH, SPLENDOR, AND FINE FOOD AMONGST THE PEOPLE THAT SURROUND US?
I SHOULD HAVE KNOWN, OH "SON OF KINGS," THAT ONLY THE SPAWN OF A GREAT TYRANT WOULD MAKE PEACE WITH ANOTHER TYRANT.
THE WORLD SHOULD BE GLAD OF THE FACT THY FATHER IS NO LONGER A KING.
HOLD, YOU TWO. THIS BICKERING SERVES NO PURPOSE. WE NEED TO BE AWAY FROM YORKTON—AND QUICKLY.
FALSTAFF, I THANK YOU FOR THE FRIENDSHIP YOU HAVE SHOWN ME BUT I SHALL NOT TRAVEL ANYWHERE WITH HER.
I WILL GO MY OWN WAY.
GAAAAA!
HAMLET, WHERE DO YOU HOPE TO GO LIKE THIS? LET US TREAT THE WOUND.
NO, FALSTAFF, HE WILL NOT LEAVE. I DO NOT BELIEVE HE IS THE SHADOW KING, BUT I WILL NOT RISK HAMLET BEING A TOOL—A PAWN—OF RICHARD'S.
LIKE IT OR NOT, YOU MUST STAY WITH US.
SO I AM YOUR CAPTIVE?
CALL IT WHAT YOU WILL.

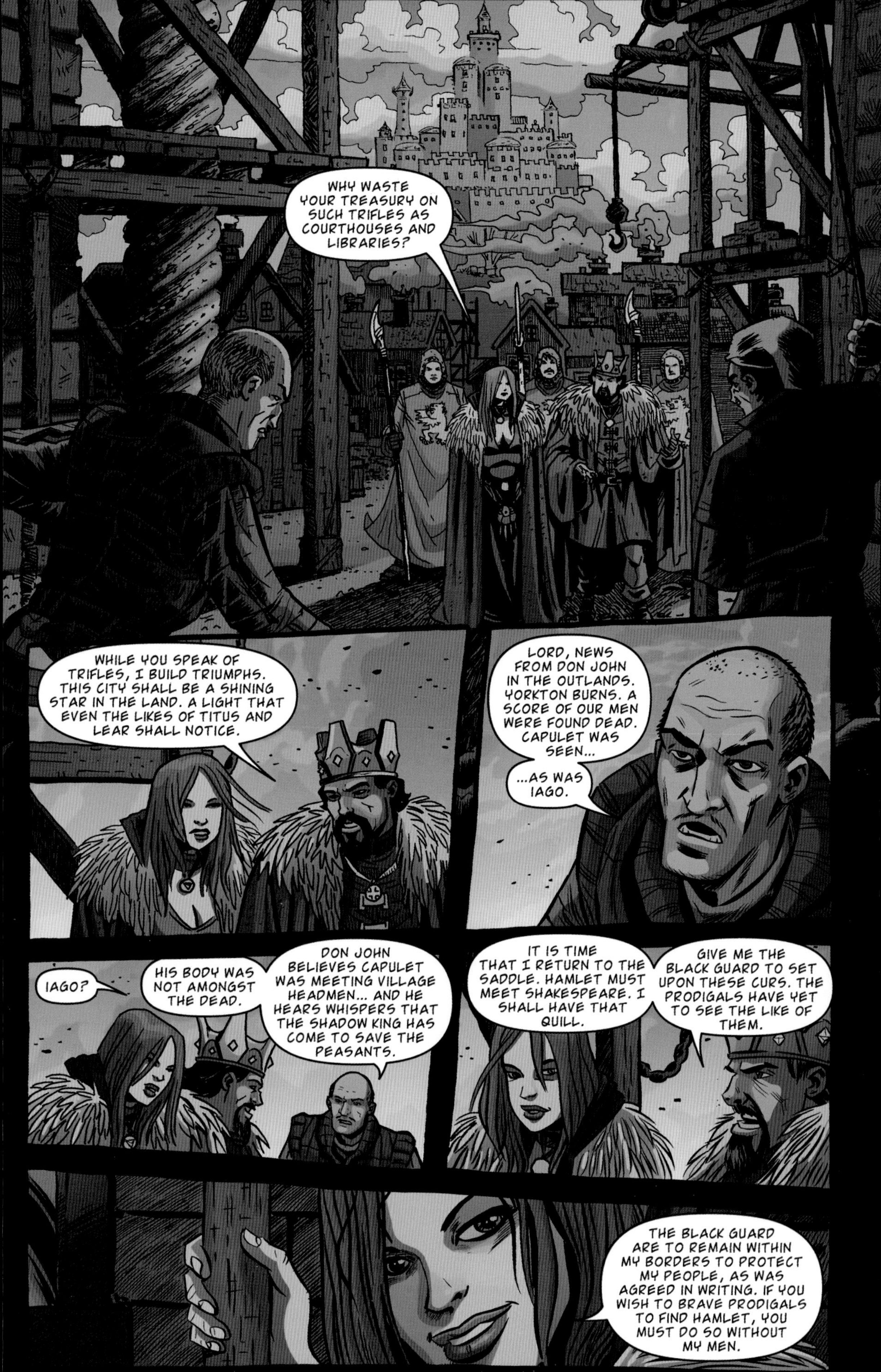
WHY WASTE YOUR TREASURY ON SUCH TRIFLES AS COURTHOUSES AND LIBRARIES?
WHILE YOU SPEAK OF TRIFLES, I BUILD TRIUMPHS. THIS CITY SHALL BE A SHINING STAR IN THE LAND. A LIGHT THAT EVEN THE LIKES OF TITUS AND LEAR SHALL NOTICE.
LORD, NEWS FROM DON JOHN IN THE OUTLANDS. YORKTON BURNS. A SCORE OF OUR MEN WERE FOUND DEAD. CAPULET WAS SEEN...
...AS WAS IAGO.
IAGO?
HIS BODY WAS NOT AMONGST THE DEAD.
DON JOHN BELIEVES CAPULET WAS MEETING VILLAGE HEADMEN... AND HE HEARS WHISPERS THAT THE SHADOW KING HAS COME TO SAVE THE PEASANTS.
IT IS TIME THAT I RETURN TO THE SADDLE. HAMLET MUST MEET SHAKESPEARE. I SHALL HAVE THAT QUILL.
GIVE ME THE BLACK GUARD TO SET UPON THESE CURS. THE PRODIGALS HAVE YET TO SEE THE LIKE OF THEM.
THE BLACK GUARD ARE TO REMAIN WITHIN MY BORDERS TO PROTECT MY PEOPLE, AS WAS AGREED IN WRITING. IF YOU WISH TO BRAVE PRODIGALS TO FIND HAMLET, YOU MUST DO SO WITHOUT MY MEN.

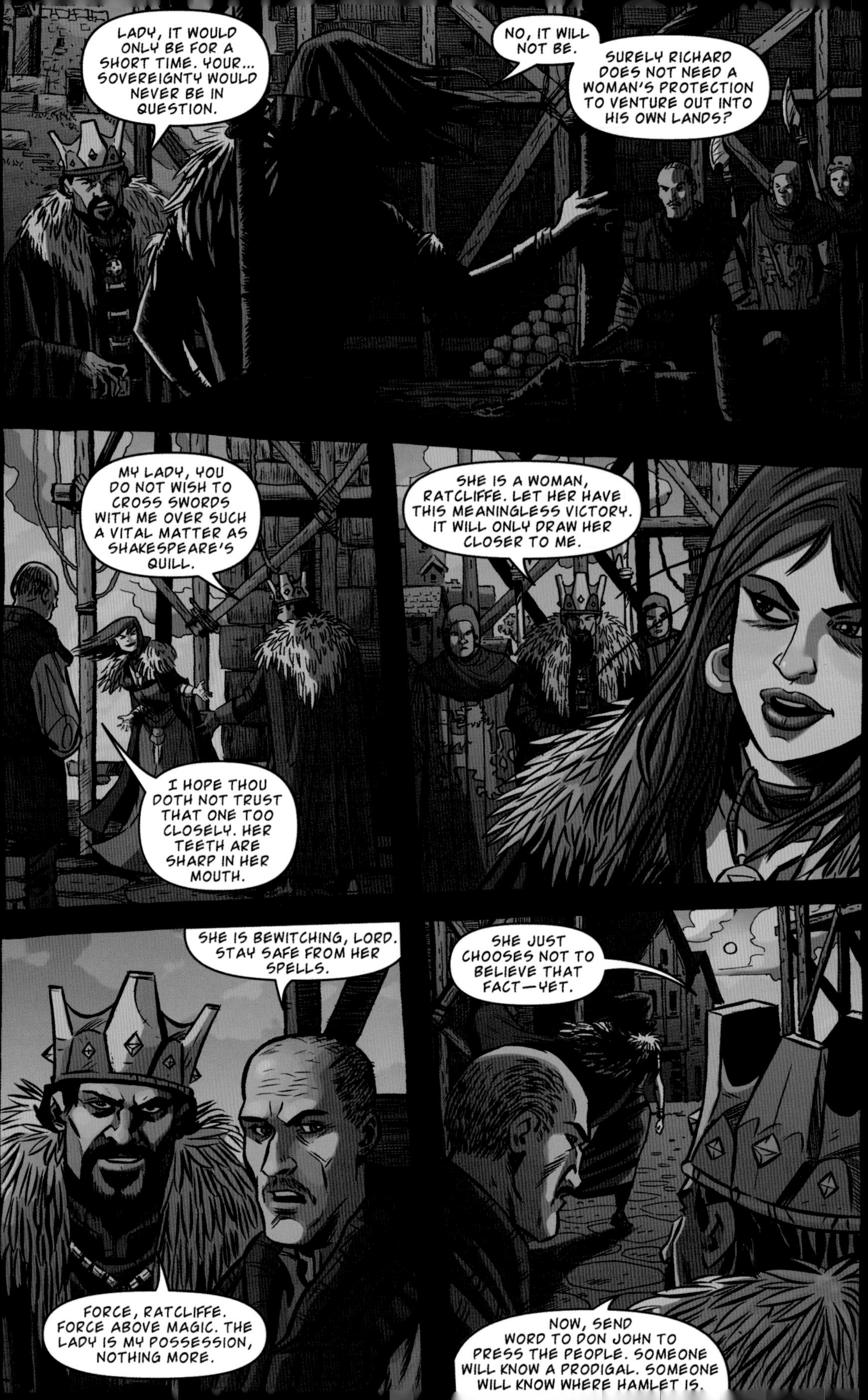
LADY, IT WOULD ONLY BE FOR A SHORT TIME. YOUR... SOVEREIGNTY WOULD NEVER BE IN QUESTION.
NO, IT WILL NOT BE.
SURELY RICHARD DOES NOT NEED A WOMAN'S PROTECTION TO VENTURE OUT INTO HIS OWN LANDS?
MY LADY, YOU DO NOT WISH TO CROSS SWORDS WITH ME OVER SUCH A VITAL MATTER AS SHAKESPEARE'S QUILL.
I HOPE THOU DOTH NOT TRUST THAT ONE TOO CLOSELY. HER TEETH ARE SHARP IN HER MOUTH.
SHE IS A WOMAN, RATCLIFFE. LET HER HAVE THIS MEANINGLESS VICTORY. IT WILL ONLY DRAW HER CLOSER TO ME.
SHE IS BEWITCHING, LORD. STAY SAFE FROM HER SPELLS.
FORCE, RATCLIFFE. FORCE ABOVE MAGIC. THE LADY IS MY POSSESSION, NOTHING MORE.
SHE JUST CHOOSES NOT TO BELIEVE THAT FACT—YET.
NOW, SEND WORD TO DON JOHN TO PRESS THE PEOPLE. SOMEONE WILL KNOW A PRODIGAL. SOMEONE WILL KNOW WHERE HAMLET IS.

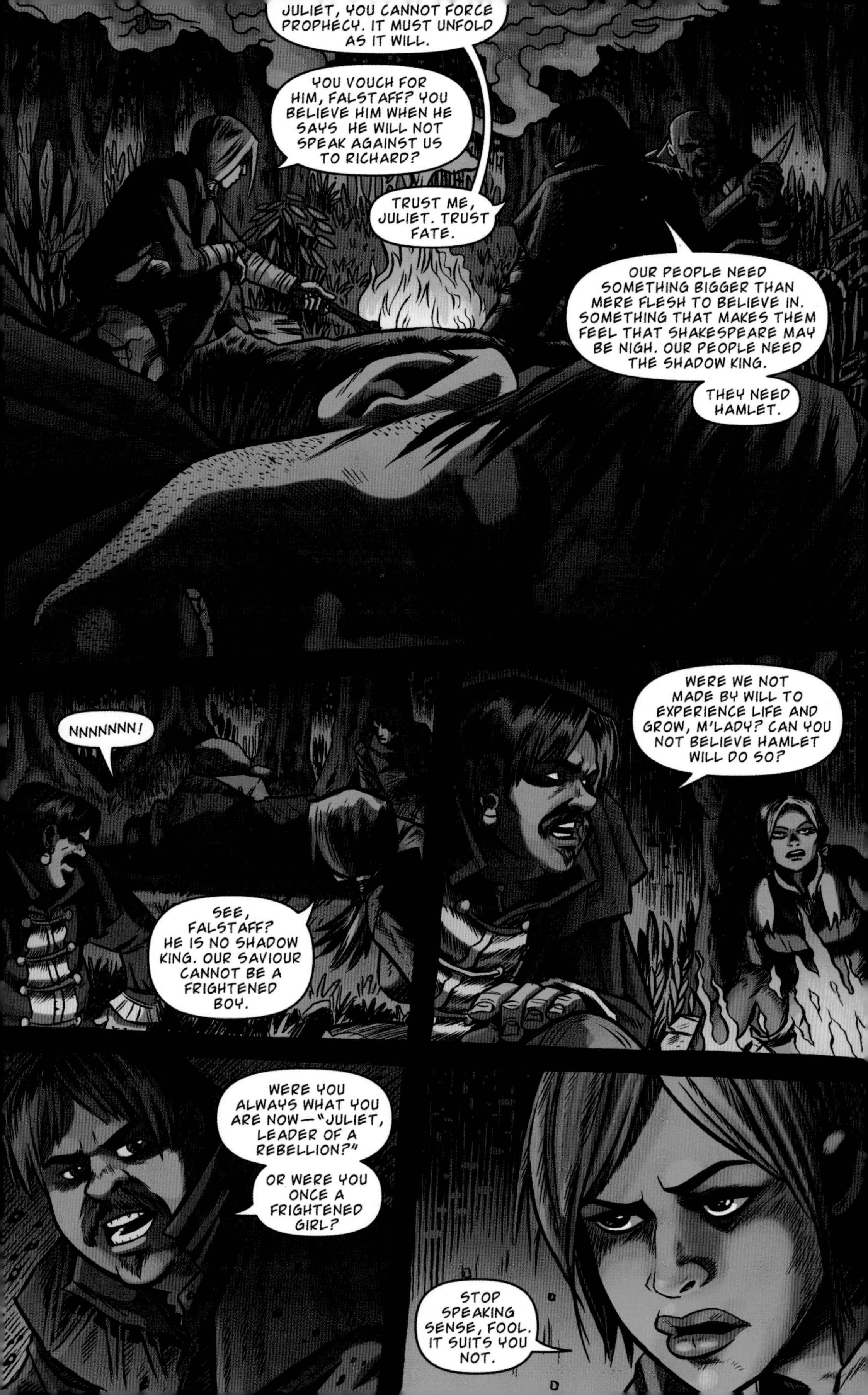
JULIET, YOU CANNOT FORCE PROPHECY. IT MUST UNFOLD AS IT WILL.
YOU VOUCH FOR HIM, FALSTAFF? YOU BELIEVE HIM WHEN HE SAYS HE WILL NOT SPEAK AGAINST US TO RICHARD?
TRUST ME, JULIET. TRUST FATE.
OUR PEOPLE NEED SOMETHING BIGGER THAN MERE FLESH TO BELIEVE IN. SOMETHING THAT MAKES THEM FEEL THAT SHAKESPEARE MAY BE NIGH. OUR PEOPLE NEED THE SHADOW KING.
THEY NEED HAMLET.
NNNNNNN!
SEE, FALSTAFF? HE IS NO SHADOW KING. OUR SAVIOUR CANNOT BE A FRIGHTENED BOY.
WERE WE NOT MADE BY WILL TO EXPERIENCE LIFE AND GROW, M'LADY? CAN YOU NOT BELIEVE HAMLET WILL DO SO?
WERE YOU ALWAYS WHAT YOU ARE NOW—"JULIET, LEADER OF A REBELLION?"
OR WERE YOU ONCE A FRIGHTENED GIRL?
STOP SPEAKING SENSE, FOOL. IT SUITS YOU NOT.

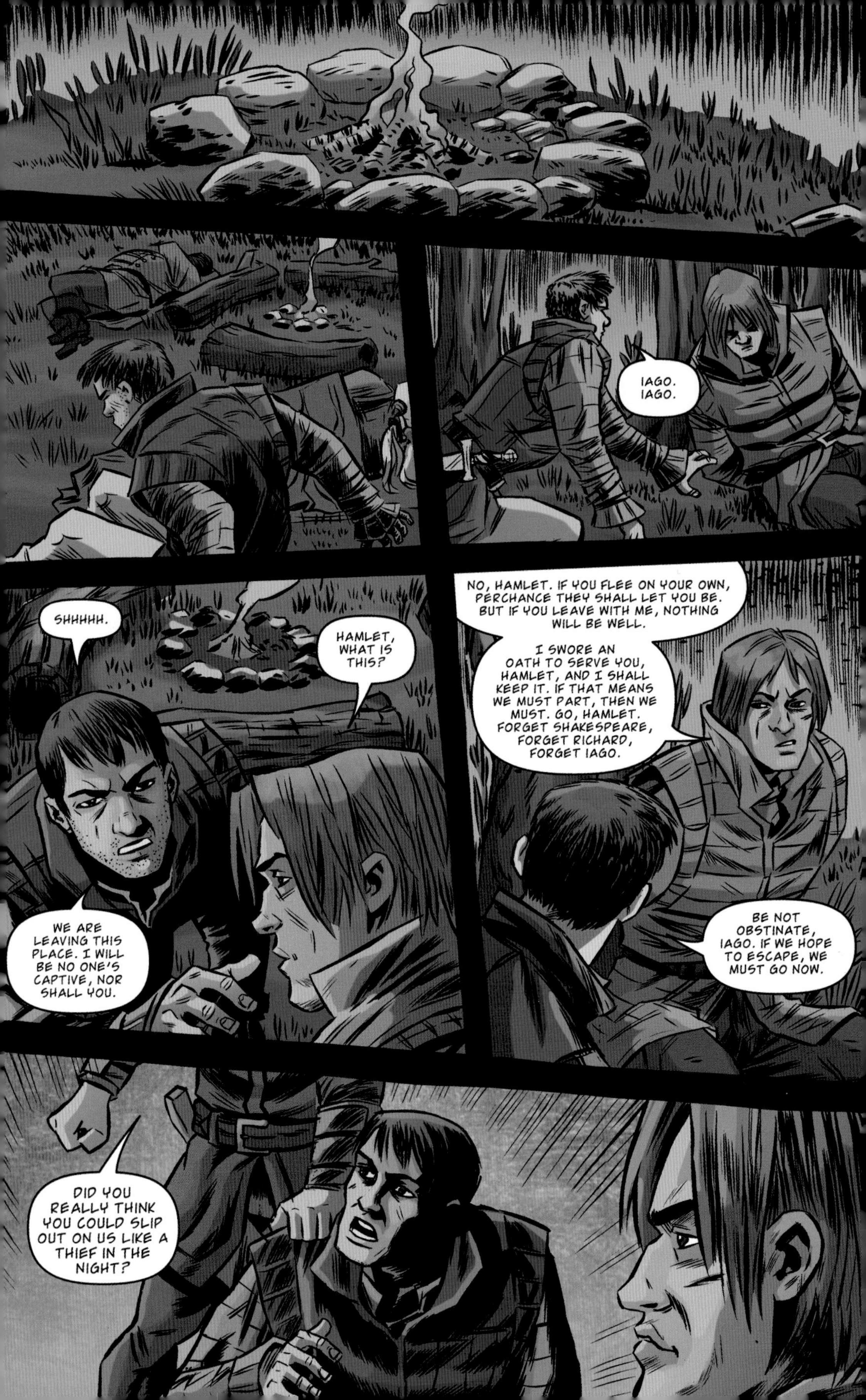
IAGO. IAGO.
SHHHHH.
HAMLET, WHAT IS THIS?
WE ARE LEAVING THIS PLACE. I WILL BE NO ONE'S CAPTIVE, NOR SHALL YOU.
NO, HAMLET. IF YOU FLEE ON YOUR OWN, PERCHANCE THEY SHALL LET YOU BE. BUT IF YOU LEAVE WITH ME, NOTHING WILL BE WELL.
I SWORE AN OATH TO SERVE YOU, HAMLET, AND I SHALL KEEP IT. IF THAT MEANS WE MUST PART, THEN WE MUST. GO, HAMLET. FORGET SHAKESPEARE, FORGET RICHARD, FORGET IAGO.
BE NOT OBSTINATE, IAGO. IF WE HOPE TO ESCAPE, WE MUST GO NOW.
DID YOU REALLY THINK YOU COULD SLIP OUT ON US LIKE A THIEF IN THE NIGHT?

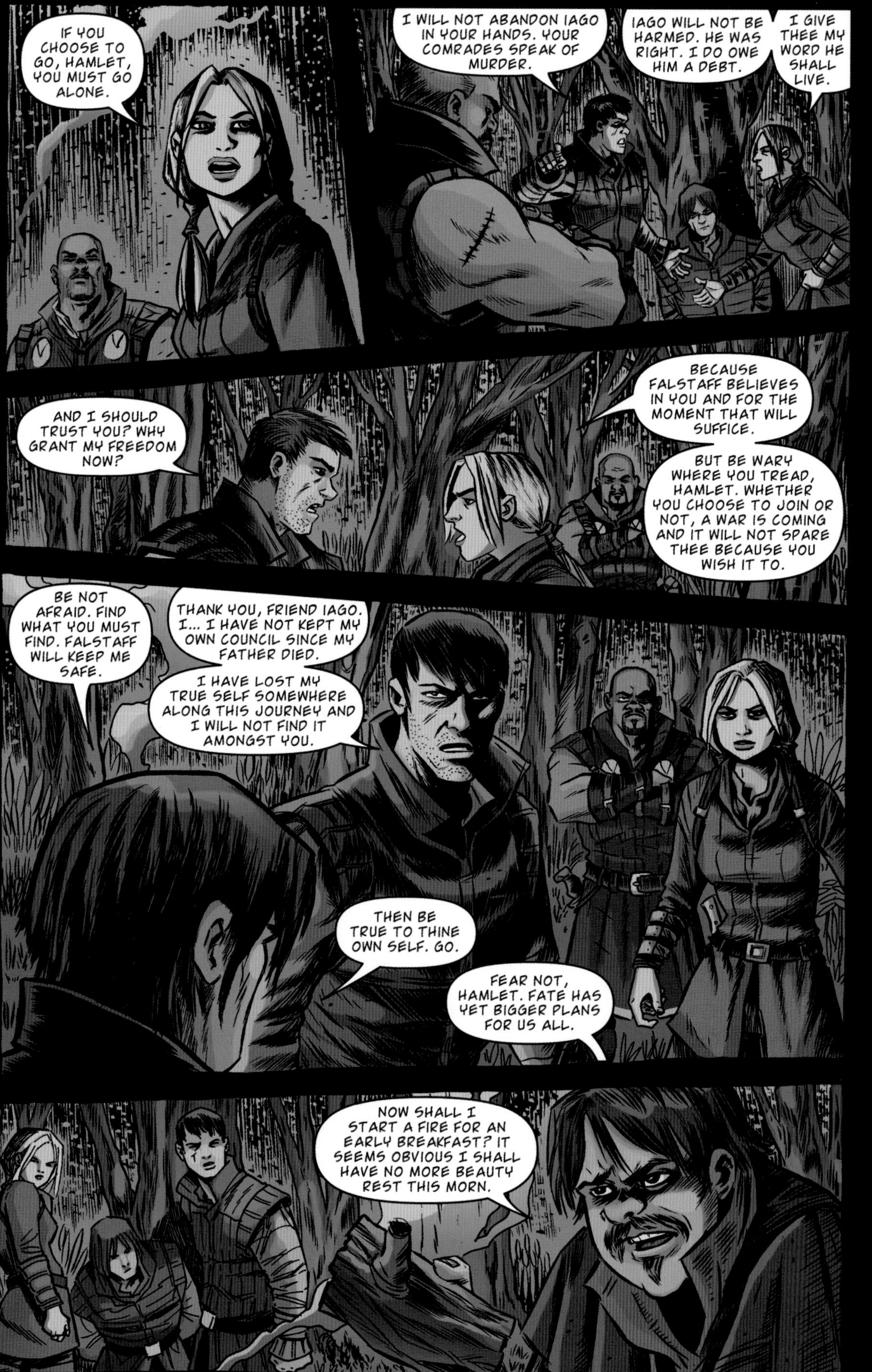
IF YOU CHOOSE TO GO, HAMLET, YOU MUST GO ALONE.
I WILL NOT ABANDON IAGO IN YOUR HANDS. YOUR COMRADES SPEAK OF MURDER.
IAGO WILL NOT BE HARMED. HE WAS RIGHT. I DO OWE HIM A DEBT.
I GIVE THEE MY WORD HE SHALL LIVE.
AND I SHOULD TRUST YOU? WHY GRANT MY FREEDOM NOW?
BECAUSE FALSTAFF BELIEVES IN YOU AND FOR THE MOMENT THAT WILL SUFFICE.
BUT BE WARY WHERE YOU TREAD, HAMLET. WHETHER YOU CHOOSE TO JOIN OR NOT, A WAR IS COMING AND IT WILL NOT SPARE THEE BECAUSE YOU WISH IT TO.
BE NOT AFRAID. FIND WHAT YOU MUST FIND. FALSTAFF WILL KEEP ME SAFE.
THANK YOU, FRIEND IAGO. I... I HAVE NOT KEPT MY OWN COUNCIL SINCE MY FATHER DIED.
I HAVE LOST MY TRUE SELF SOMEWHERE ALONG THIS JOURNEY AND I WILL NOT FIND IT AMONGST YOU.
THEN BE TRUE TO THINE OWN SELF. GO.
FEAR NOT, HAMLET. FATE HAS YET BIGGER PLANS FOR US ALL.
NOW SHALL I START A FIRE FOR AN EARLY BREAKFAST? IT SEEMS OBVIOUS I SHALL HAVE NO MORE BEAUTY REST THIS MORN.

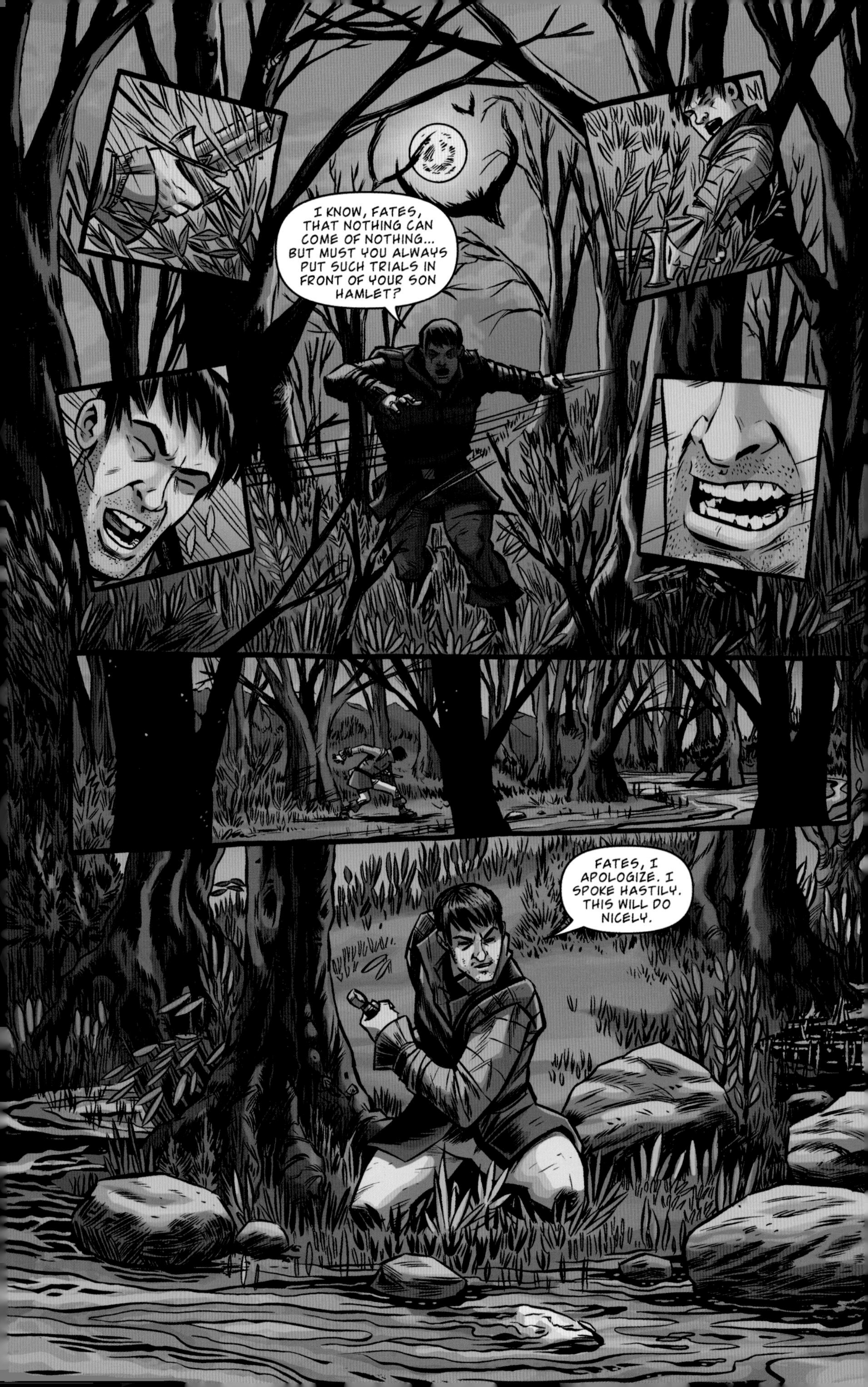
I KNOW, FATES, THAT NOTHING CAN COME OF NOTHING... BUT MUST YOU ALWAYS PUT SUCH TRIALS IN FRONT OF YOUR SON HAMLET?
FATES, I APOLOGIZE. I SPOKE HASTILY. THIS WILL DO NICELY.

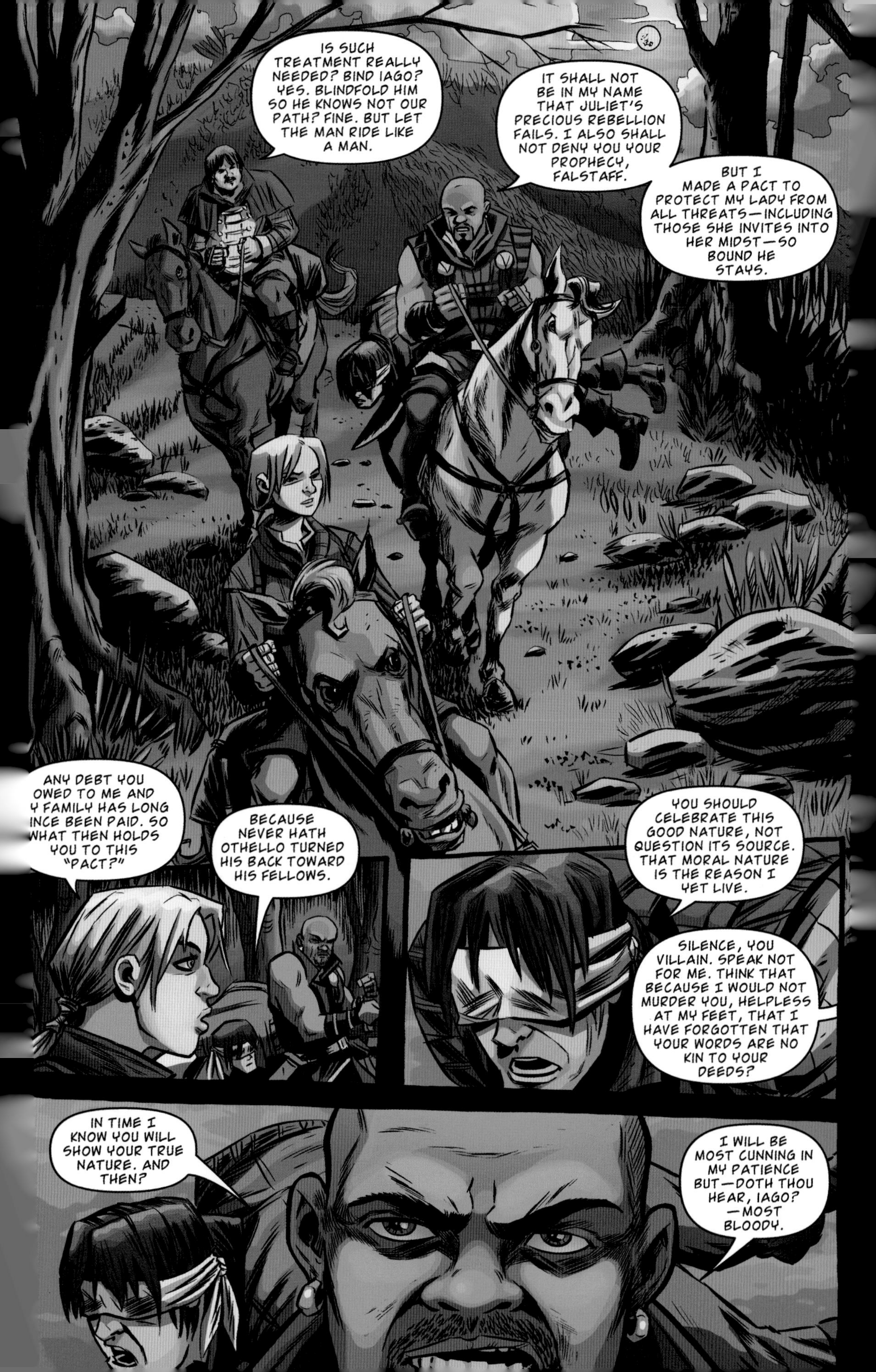
IS SUCH TREATMENT REALLY NEEDED? BIND IAGO? YES. BLINDFOLD HIM SO HE KNOWS NOT OUR PATH? FINE. BUT LET THE MAN RIDE LIKE A MAN.
IT SHALL NOT BE IN MY NAME THAT JULIET'S PRECIOUS REBELLION FAILS. I ALSO SHALL NOT DENY YOU YOUR PROPHECY, FALSTAFF.
BUT I MADE A PACT TO PROTECT MY LADY FROM ALL THREATS—INCLUDING THOSE SHE INVITES INTO HER MIDST—SO BOUND HE STAYS.
ANY DEBT YOU OWED TO ME AND Y FAMILY HAS LONG INCE BEEN PAID. SO WHAT THEN HOLDS YOU TO THIS "PACT?"
BECAUSE NEVER HATH OTHELLO TURNED HIS BACK TOWARD HIS FELLOWS.
YOU SHOULD CELEBRATE THIS GOOD NATURE, NOT QUESTION ITS SOURCE. THAT MORAL NATURE IS THE REASON I YET LIVE.
SILENCE, YOU VILLAIN. SPEAK NOT FOR ME. THINK THAT BECAUSE I WOULD NOT MURDER YOU, HELPLESS AT MY FEET, THAT I HAVE FORGOTTEN THAT YOUR WORDS ARE NO KIN TO YOUR DEEDS?
IN TIME I KNOW YOU WILL SHOW YOUR TRUE NATURE. AND THEN?
I WILL BE MOST CUNNING IN MY PATIENCE BUT—DOTH THOU HEAR, IAGO? —MOST BLOODY.

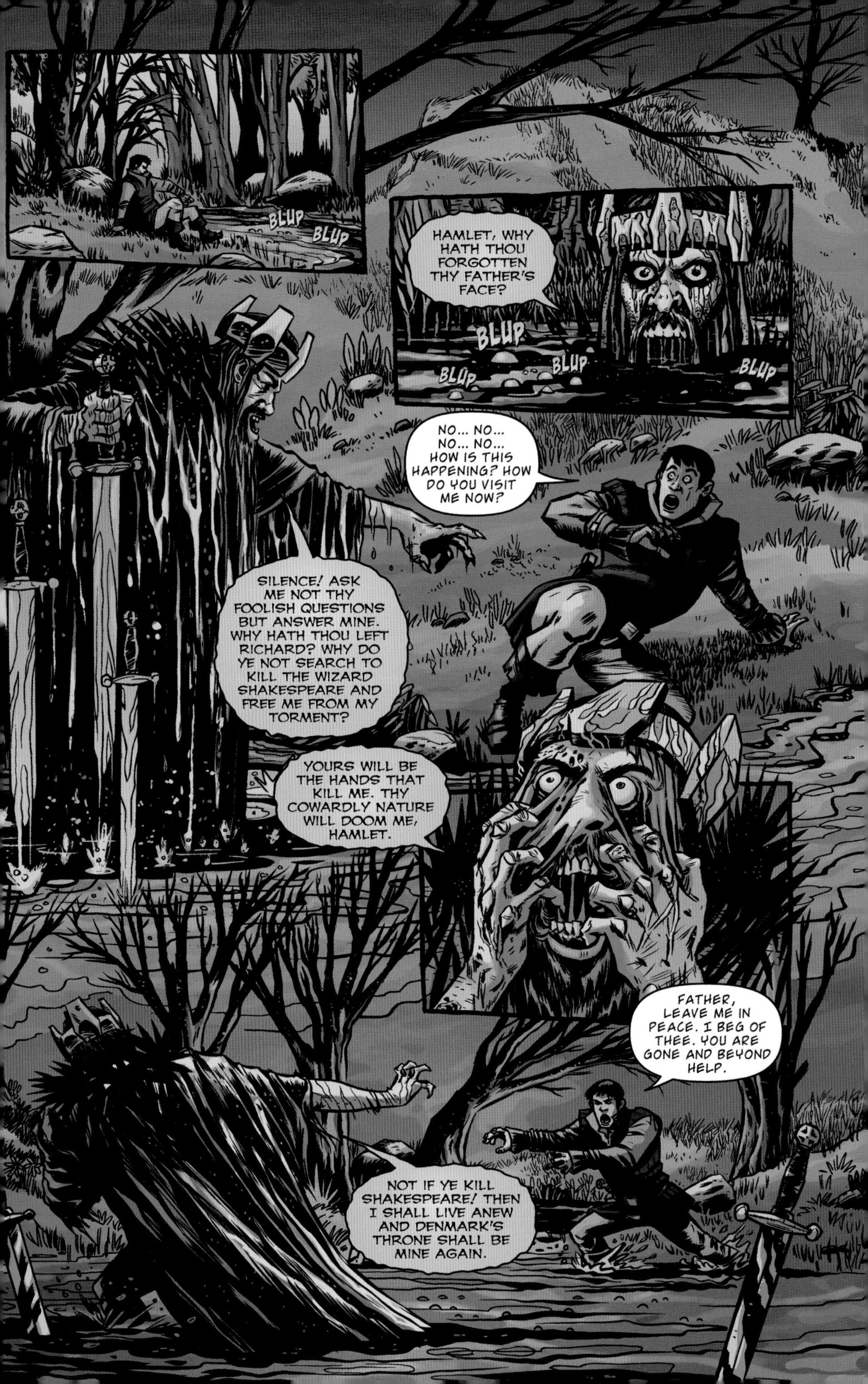
BLUP
BLUP
HAMLET, WHY HATH THOU FORGOTTEN THY FATHER'S FACE?
BLUP
BLUP
BLUP
BLUP
NO... NO... NO... NO... HOW IS THIS HAPPENING? HOW DO YOU VISIT ME NOW?
SILENCE! ASK ME NOT THY FOOLISH QUESTIONS BUT ANSWER MINE. WHY HATH THOU LEFT RICHARD? WHY DO YE NOT SEARCH TO KILL THE WIZARD SHAKESPEARE AND FREE ME FROM MY TORMENT?
YOURS WILL BE THE HANDS THAT KILL ME. THY COWARDLY NATURE WILL DOOM ME, HAMLET.
FATHER, LEAVE ME IN PEACE. I BEG OF THEE. YOU ARE GONE AND BEYOND HELP.
NOT IF YE KILL SHAKESPEARE! THEN I SHALL LIVE ANEW AND DENMARK'S THRONE SHALL BE MINE AGAIN.

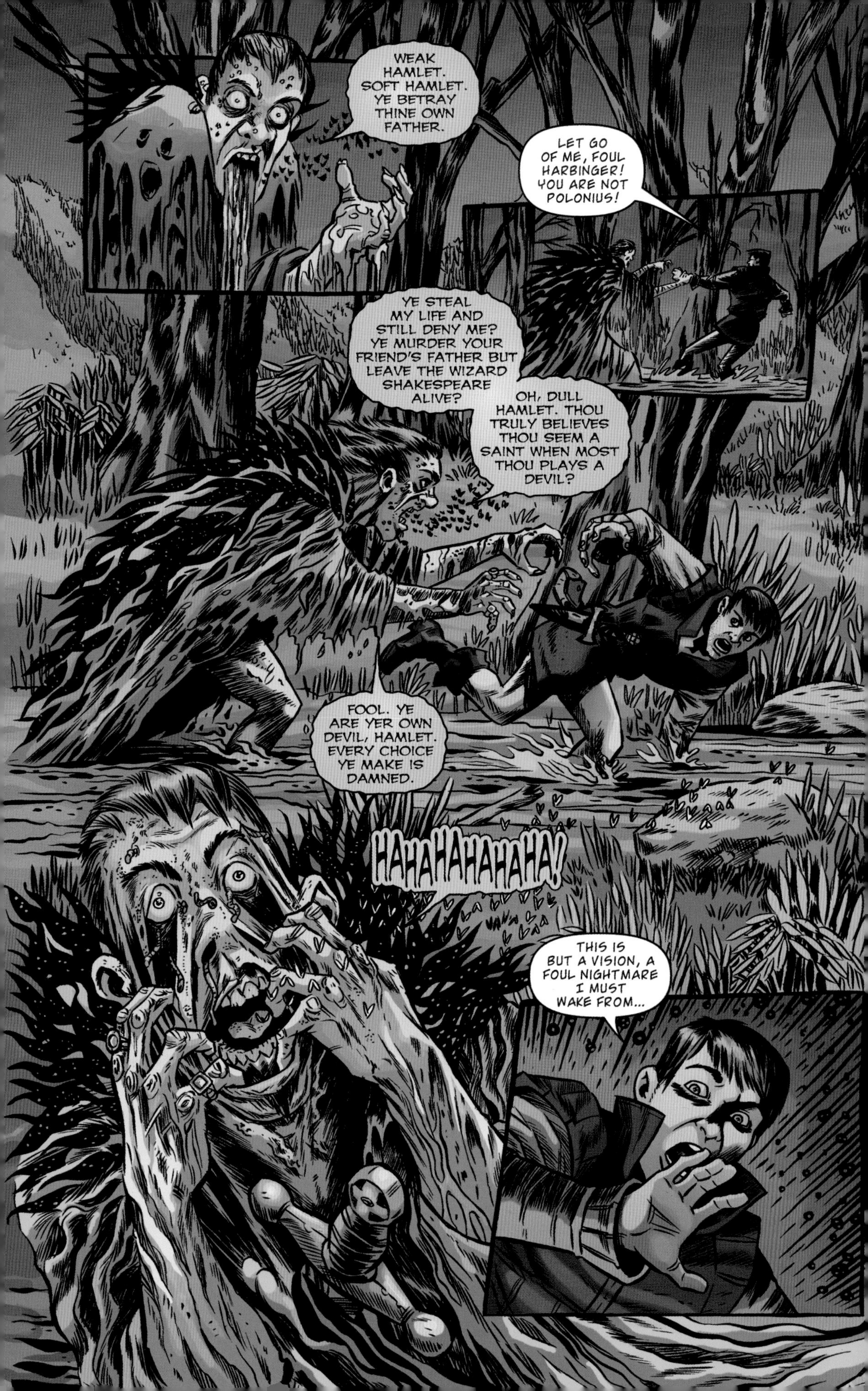
WEAK HAMLET. SOFT HAMLET. YE BETRAY THINE OWN FATHER.
LET GO OF ME, FOUL HARBINGER! YOU ARE NOT POLONIUS!
YE STEAL MY LIFE AND STILL DENY ME? YE MURDER YOUR FRIEND'S FATHER BUT LEAVE THE WIZARD SHAKESPEARE ALIVE?
OH, DULL HAMLET. THOU TRULY BELIEVES THOU SEEM A SAINT WHEN MOST THOU PLAYS A DEVIL?
FOOL. YE ARE YER OWN DEVIL, HAMLET. EVERY CHOICE YE MAKE IS DAMNED.
HAHAHAHAHAHA!
THIS IS BUT A VISION, A FOUL NIGHTMARE I MUST WAKE FROM...

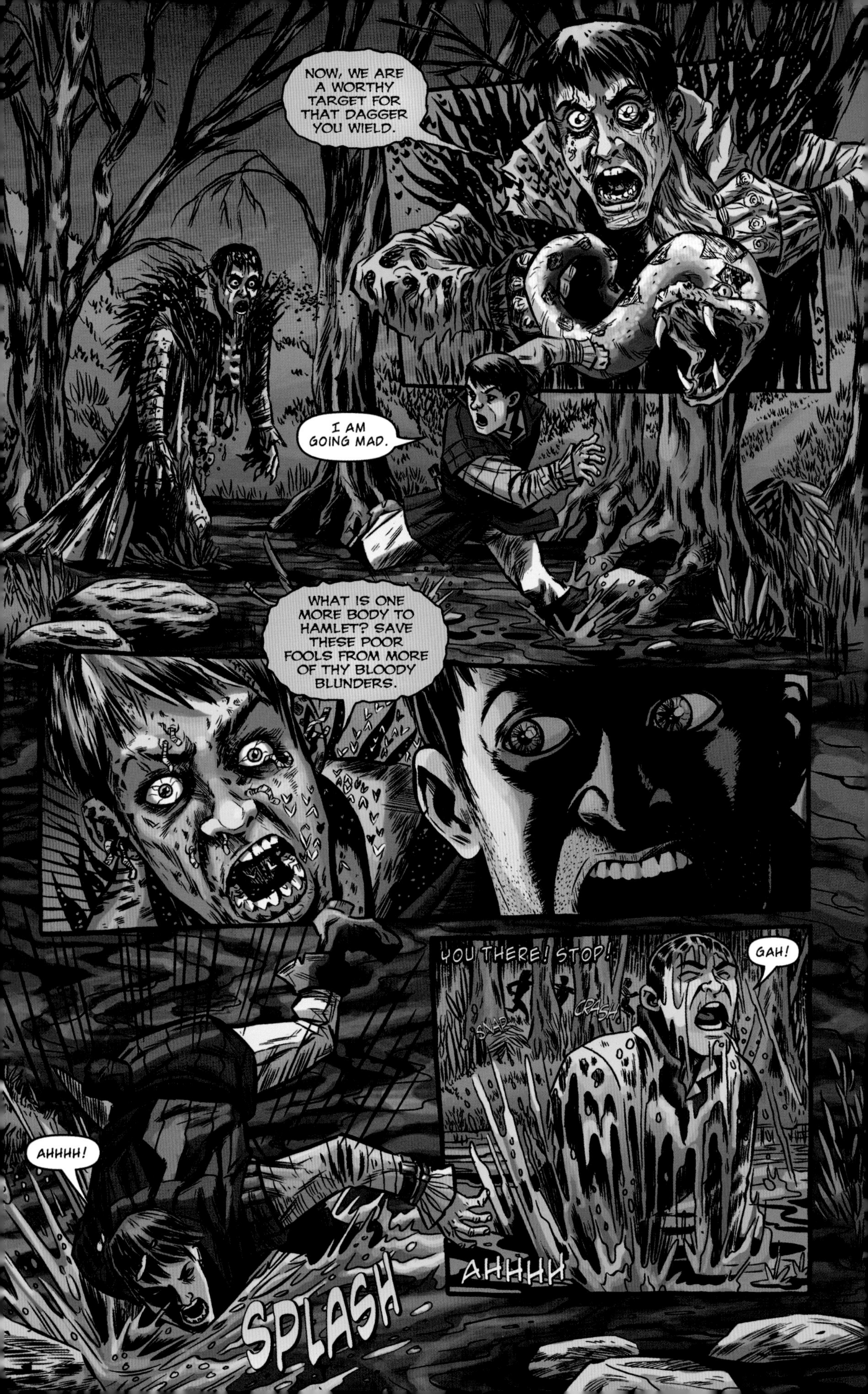
NOW, WE ARE A WORTHY TARGET FOR THAT DAGGER YOU WIELD.
I AM GOING MAD.
WHAT IS ONE MORE BODY TO HAMLET? SAVE THESE POOR FOOLS FROM MORE OF THY BLOODY BLUNDERS.
AHHHH!
SPLASH
YOU THERE! STOP!
SNAP
CRASH
GAH!
AHHHH

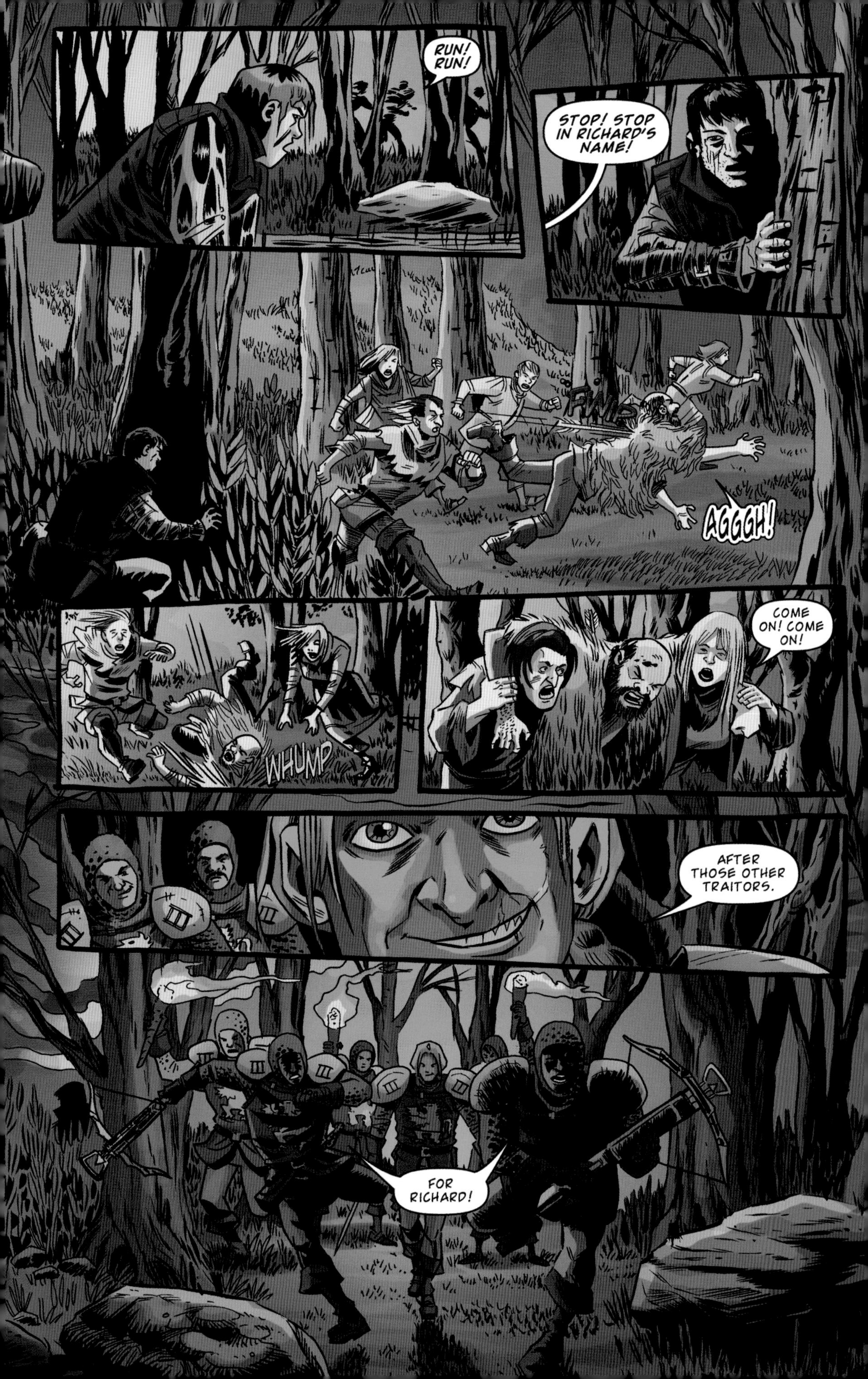
RUN! RUN!
STOP! STOP IN RICHARD'S NAME!
FWIP
AGGGH!
WHUMP
COME ON! COME ON!
AFTER THOSE OTHER TRAITORS.
FOR RICHARD!

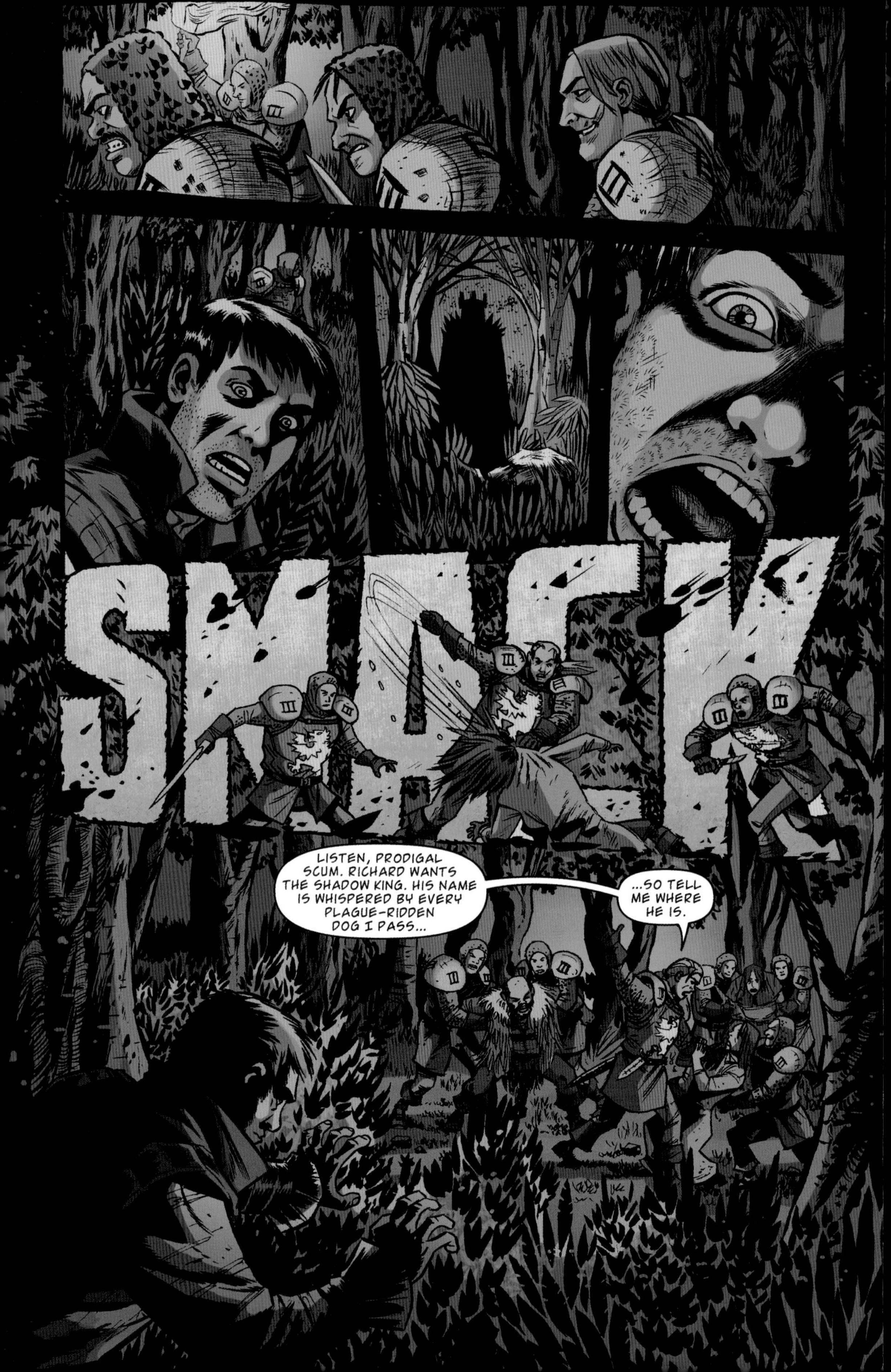
SMACK
LISTEN, PRODIGAL SCUM. RICHARD WANTS THE SHADOW KING. HIS NAME IS WHISPERED BY EVERY PLAGUE-RIDDEN DOG I PASS...
...SO TELL ME WHERE HE IS.

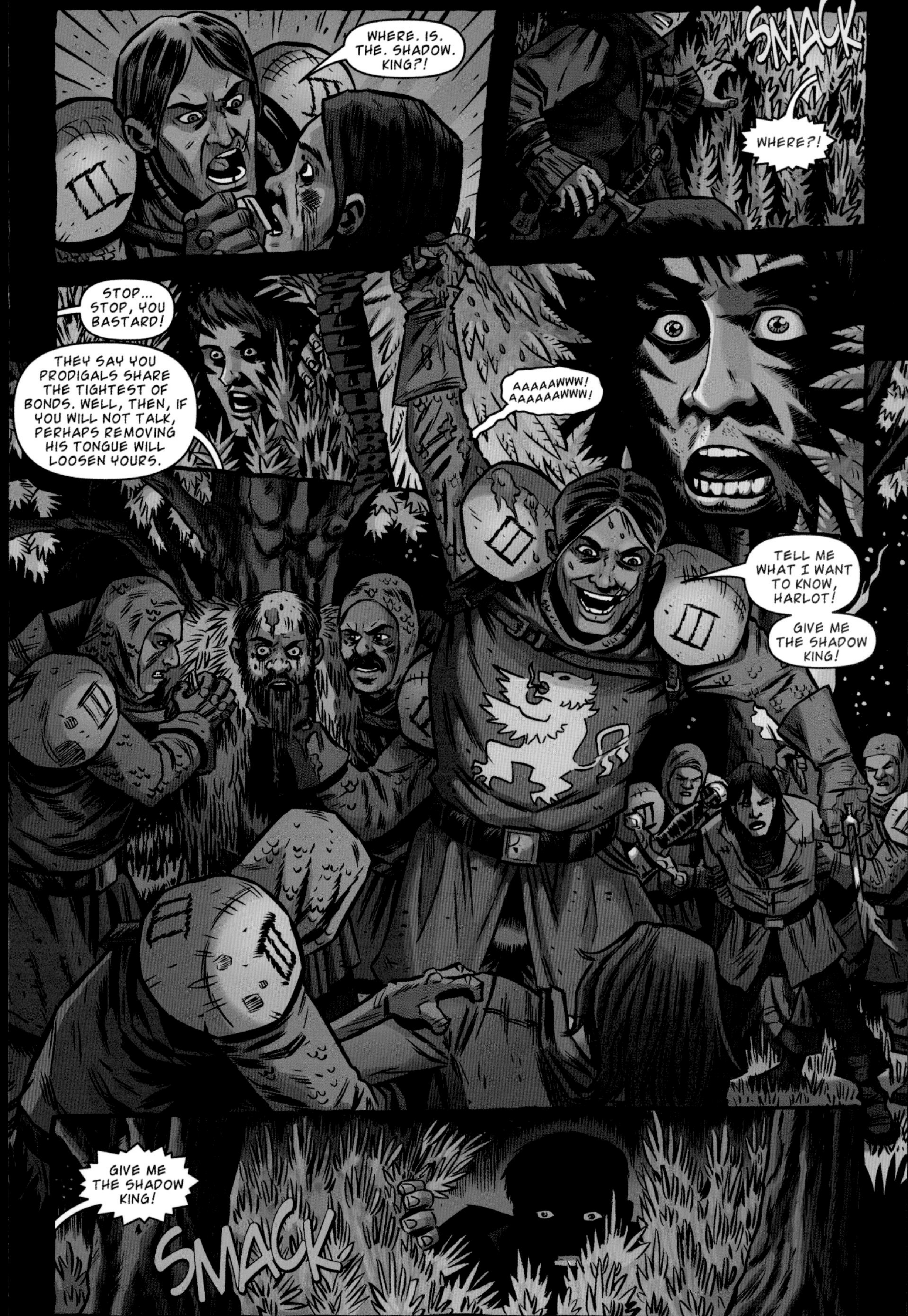
WHERE. IS. THE. SHADOW. KING?!
SMACK
WHERE?!
STOP... STOP, YOU BASTARD!
THEY SAY YOU PRODIGALS SHARE THE TIGHTEST OF BONDS. WELL, THEN, IF YOU WILL NOT TALK, PERHAPS REMOVING HIS TONGUE WILL LOOSEN YOURS.
AAAAAWWW! AAAAAAWWW!
TELL ME WHAT I WANT TO KNOW, HARLOT!
GIVE ME THE SHADOW KING!
GIVE ME THE SHADOW KING!
SMACK

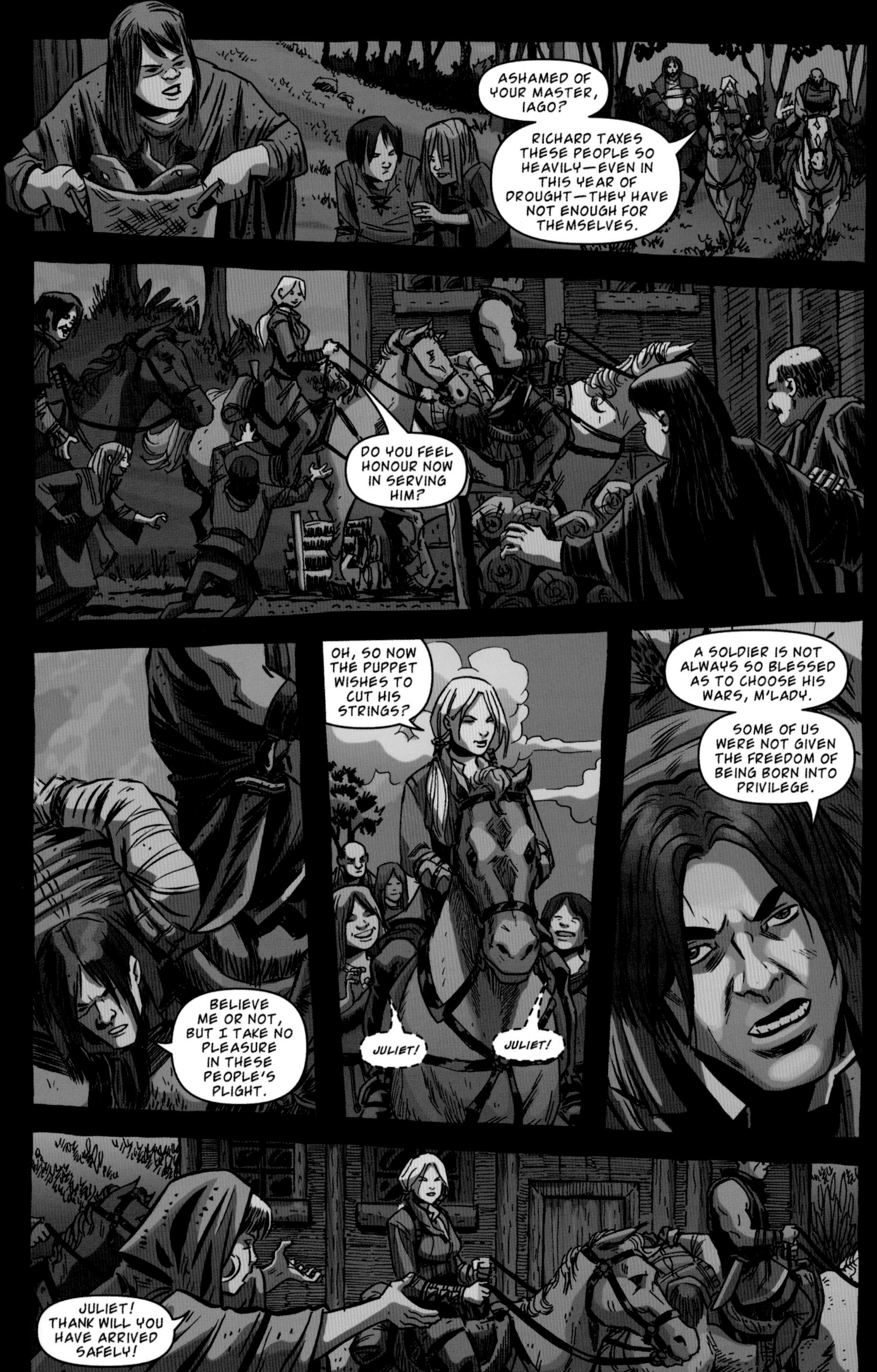
ASHAMED OF YOUR MASTER, IAGO?
RICHARD TAXES THESE PEOPLE SO HEAVILY—EVEN IN THIS YEAR OF DROUGHT—THEY HAVE NOT ENOUGH FOR THEMSELVES.
DO YOU FEEL HONOUR NOW IN SERVING HIM?
BELIEVE ME OR NOT, BUT I TAKE NO PLEASURE IN THESE PEOPLE'S PLIGHT.
OH, SO NOW THE PUPPET WISHES TO CUT HIS STRINGS?
JULIET!
JULIET!
A SOLDIER IS NOT ALWAYS SO BLESSED AS TO CHOOSE HIS WARS, M'LADY.
SOME OF US WERE NOT GIVEN THE FREEDOM OF BEING BORN INTO PRIVILEGE.
JULIET! THANK WILL YOU HAVE ARRIVED SAFELY!

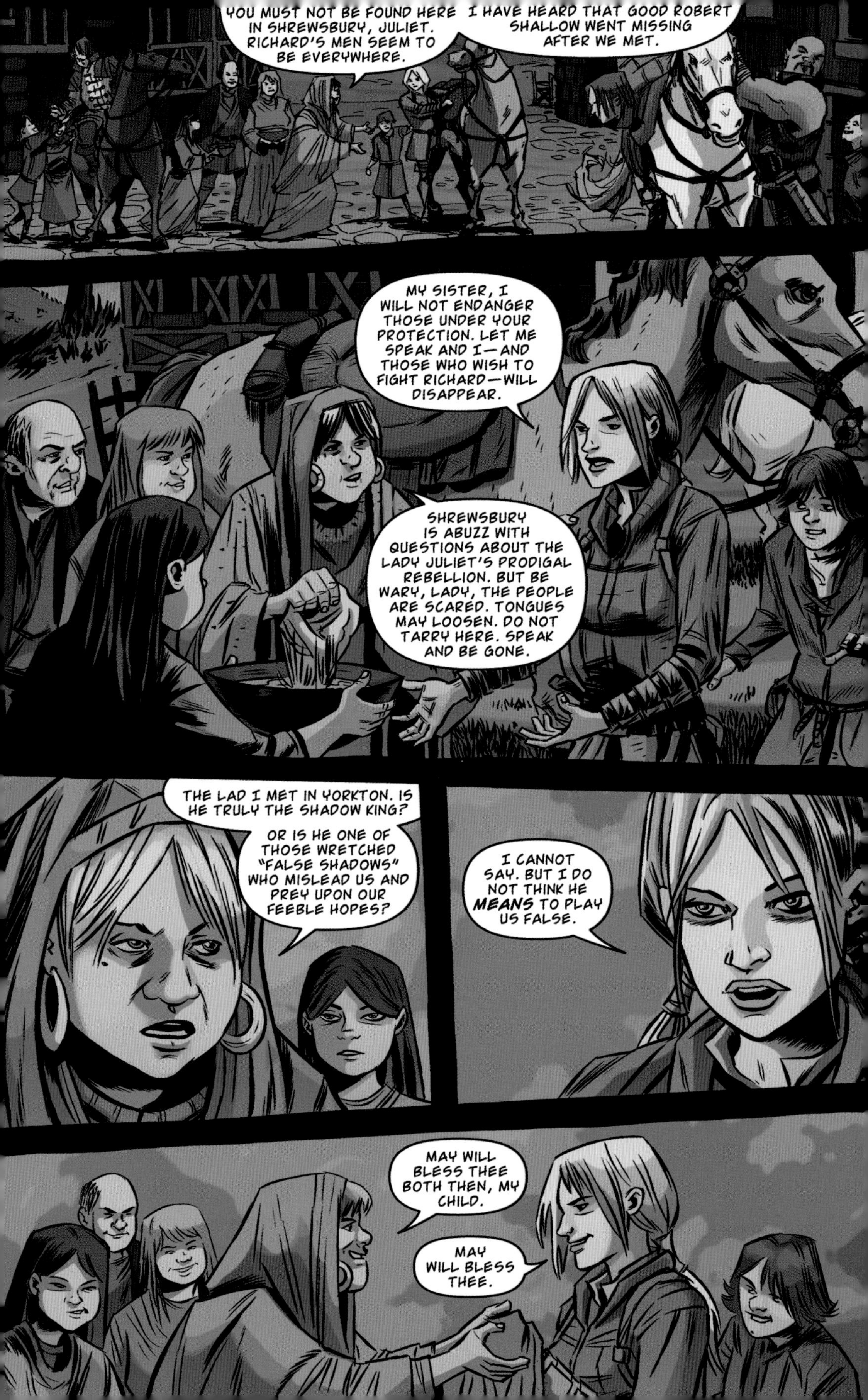
YOU MUST NOT BE FOUND HERE IN SHREWSBURY, JULIET. RICHARD'S MEN SEEM TO BE EVERYWHERE.
I HAVE HEARD THAT GOOD ROBERT SHALLOW WENT MISSING AFTER WE MET.
MY SISTER, I WILL NOT ENDANGER THOSE UNDER YOUR PROTECTION. LET ME SPEAK AND I—AND THOSE WHO WISH TO FIGHT RICHARD—WILL DISAPPEAR.
SHREWSBURY IS ABUZZ WITH QUESTIONS ABOUT THE LADY JULIET'S PRODIGAL REBELLION. BUT BE WARY, LADY, THE PEOPLE ARE SCARED. TONGUES MAY LOOSEN. DO NOT TARRY HERE. SPEAK AND BE GONE.
THE LAD I MET IN YORKTON. IS HE TRULY THE SHADOW KING?
OR IS HE ONE OF THOSE WRETCHED "FALSE SHADOWS" WHO MISLEAD US AND PREY UPON OUR FEEBLE HOPES?
I CANNOT SAY. BUT I DO NOT THINK HE ***MEANS*** TO PLAY US FALSE.
MAY WILL BLESS THEE BOTH THEN, MY CHILD.
MAY WILL BLESS THEE.

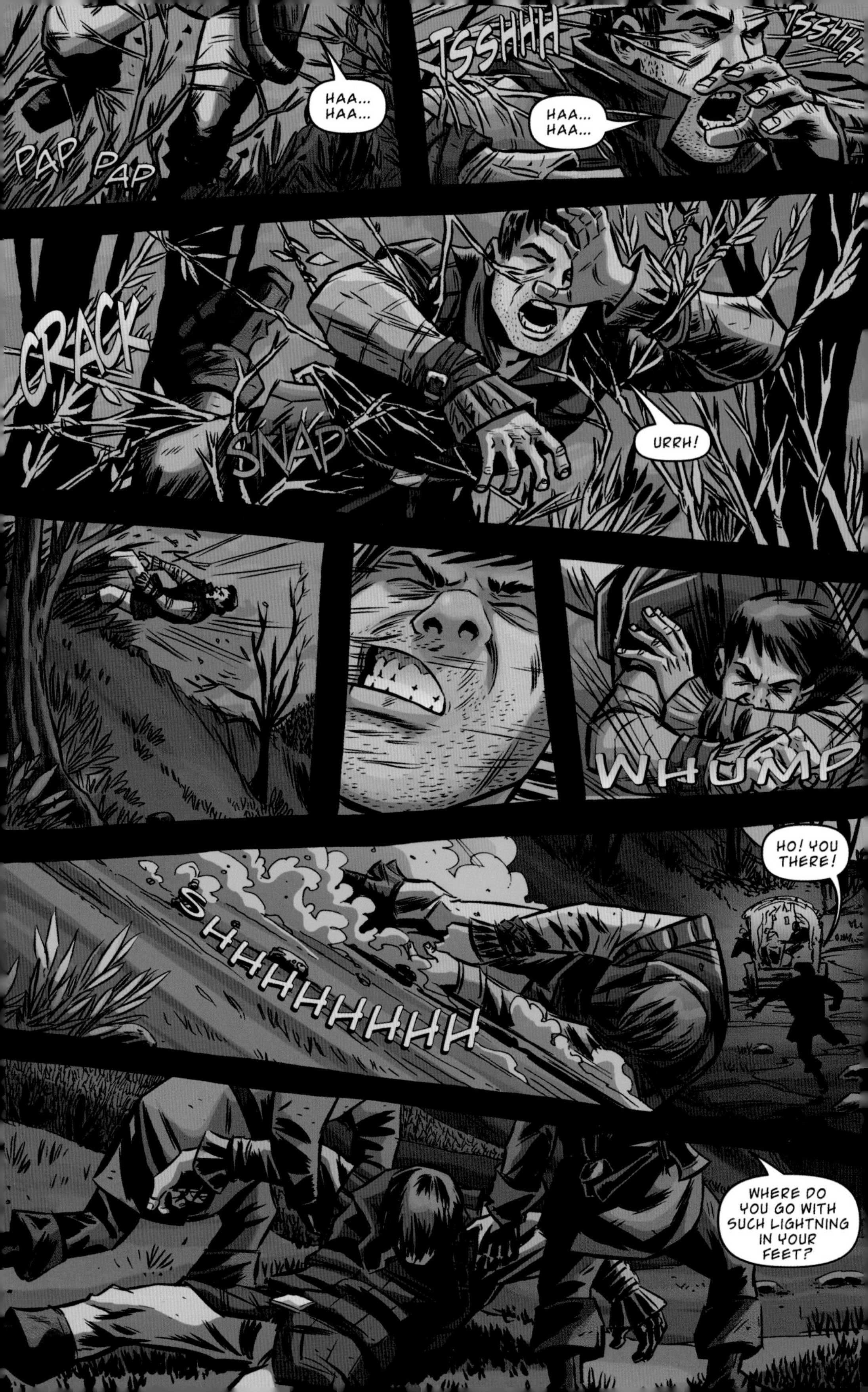
PAP PAP
HAA... HAA...
TSSHHH
HAA... HAA...
TSSHHH
CRACK
SNAP
URRH!
WHUMP
SHHHHHHHHH
HO! YOU THERE!
WHERE DO YOU GO WITH SUCH LIGHTNING IN YOUR FEET?

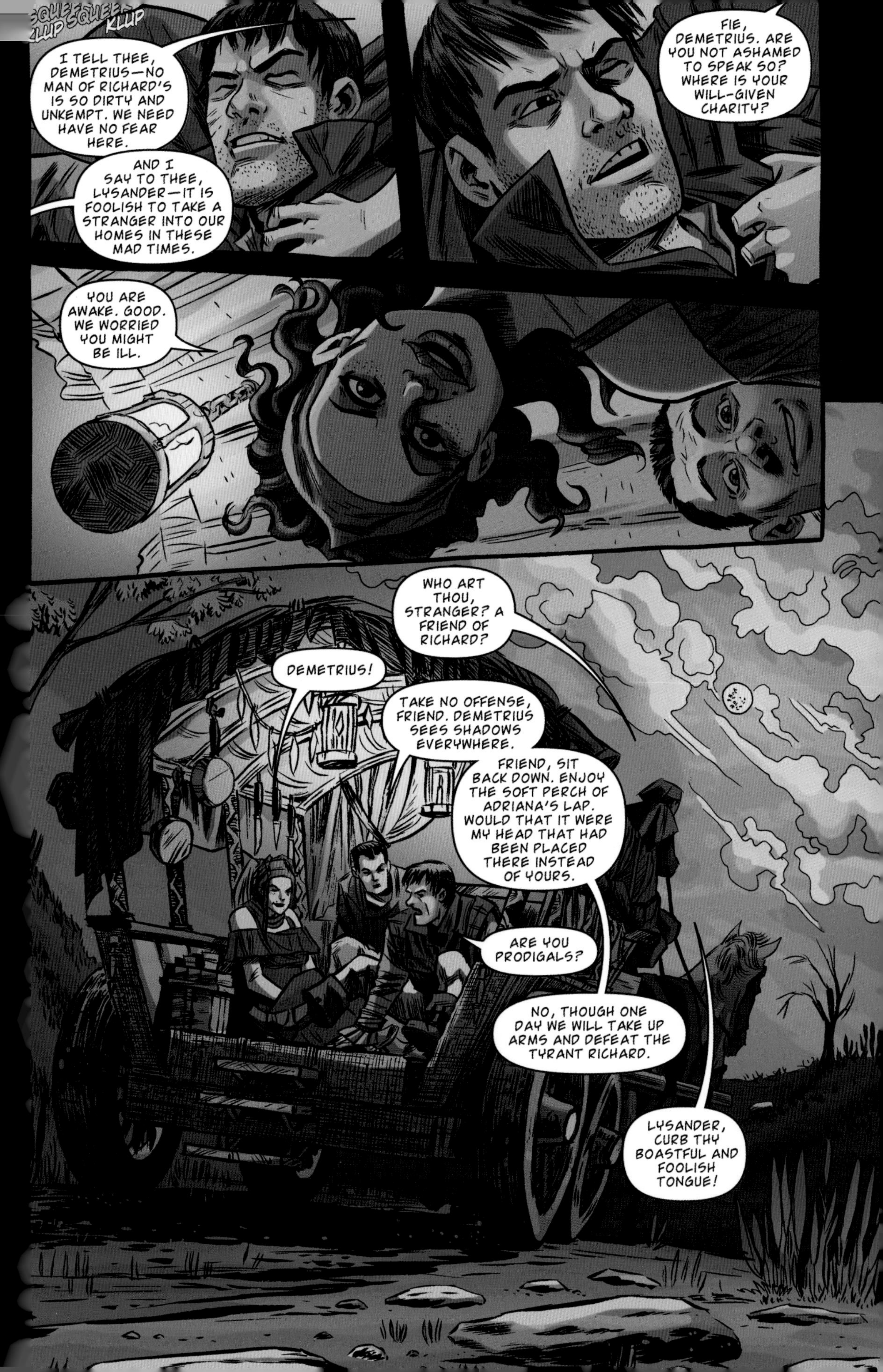
I TELL THEE, DEMETRIUS—NO MAN OF RICHARD'S IS SO DIRTY AND UNKEMPT. WE NEED HAVE NO FEAR HERE.
AND I SAY TO THEE, LYSANDER—IT IS FOOLISH TO TAKE A STRANGER INTO OUR HOMES IN THESE MAD TIMES.
FIE, DEMETRIUS. ARE YOU NOT ASHAMED TO SPEAK SO? WHERE IS YOUR WILL-GIVEN CHARITY?
YOU ARE AWAKE. GOOD. WE WORRIED YOU MIGHT BE ILL.
WHO ART THOU, STRANGER? A FRIEND OF RICHARD?
DEMETRIUS!
TAKE NO OFFENSE, FRIEND. DEMETRIUS SEES SHADOWS EVERYWHERE.
FRIEND, SIT BACK DOWN. ENJOY THE SOFT PERCH OF ADRIANA'S LAP. WOULD THAT IT WERE MY HEAD THAT HAD BEEN PLACED THERE INSTEAD OF YOURS.
ARE YOU PRODIGALS?
NO, THOUGH ONE DAY WE WILL TAKE UP ARMS AND DEFEAT THE TYRANT RICHARD.
LYSANDER, CURB THY BOASTFUL AND FOOLISH TONGUE!

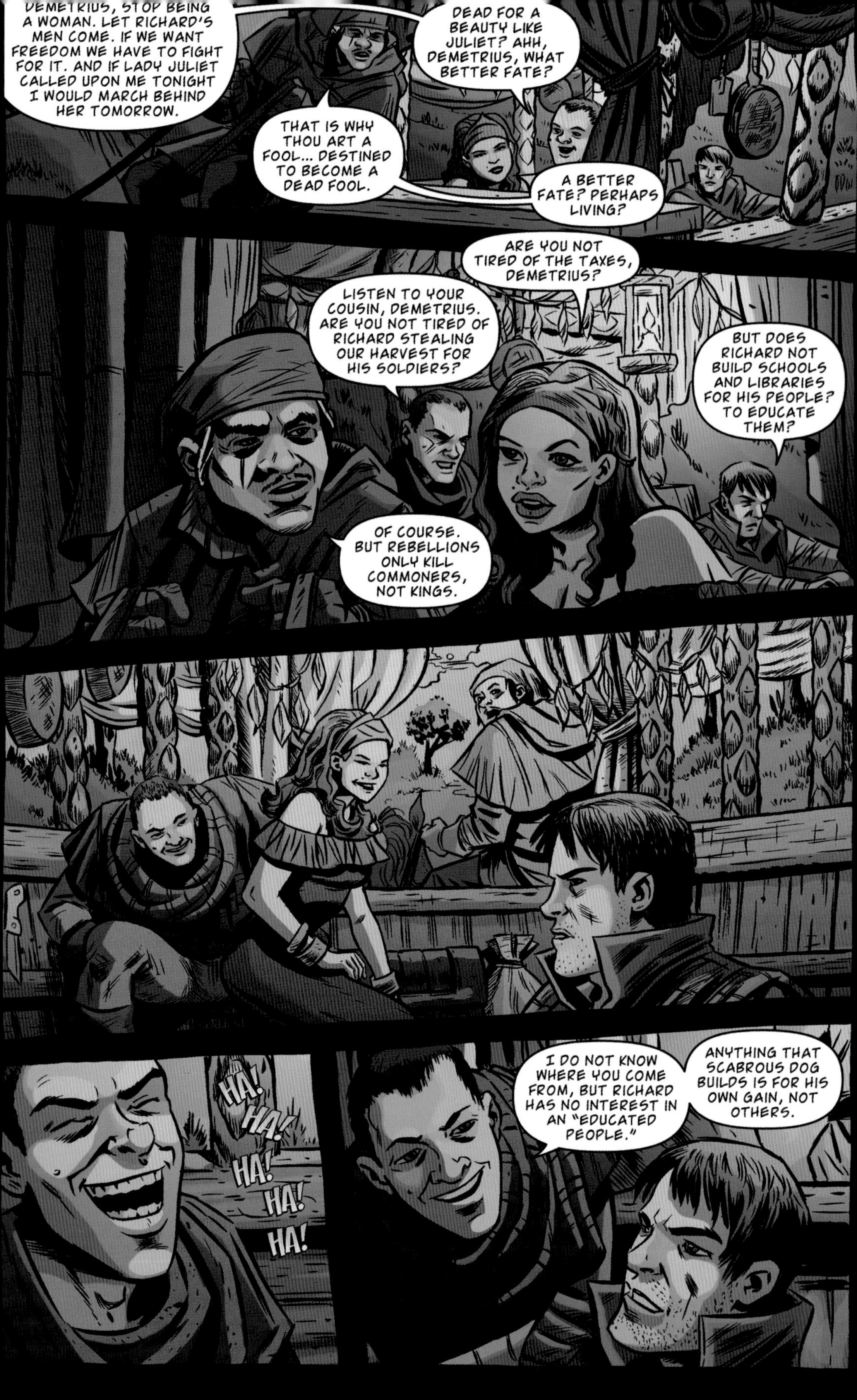
DEMETRIUS, STOP BEING A WOMAN. LET RICHARD'S MEN COME. IF WE WANT FREEDOM WE HAVE TO FIGHT FOR IT. AND IF LADY JULIET CALLED UPON ME TONIGHT I WOULD MARCH BEHIND HER TOMORROW.
DEAD FOR A BEAUTY LIKE JULIET? AHH, DEMETRIUS, WHAT BETTER FATE?
THAT IS WHY THOU ART A FOOL... DESTINED TO BECOME A DEAD FOOL.
A BETTER FATE? PERHAPS LIVING?
ARE YOU NOT TIRED OF THE TAXES, DEMETRIUS?
LISTEN TO YOUR COUSIN, DEMETRIUS. ARE YOU NOT TIRED OF RICHARD STEALING OUR HARVEST FOR HIS SOLDIERS?
BUT DOES RICHARD NOT BUILD SCHOOLS AND LIBRARIES FOR HIS PEOPLE? TO EDUCATE THEM?
OF COURSE. BUT REBELLIONS ONLY KILL COMMONERS, NOT KINGS.
HA! HA! HA! HA! HA!
I DO NOT KNOW WHERE YOU COME FROM, BUT RICHARD HAS NO INTEREST IN AN "EDUCATED PEOPLE."
ANYTHING THAT SCABROUS DOG BUILDS IS FOR HIS OWN GAIN, NOT OTHERS.

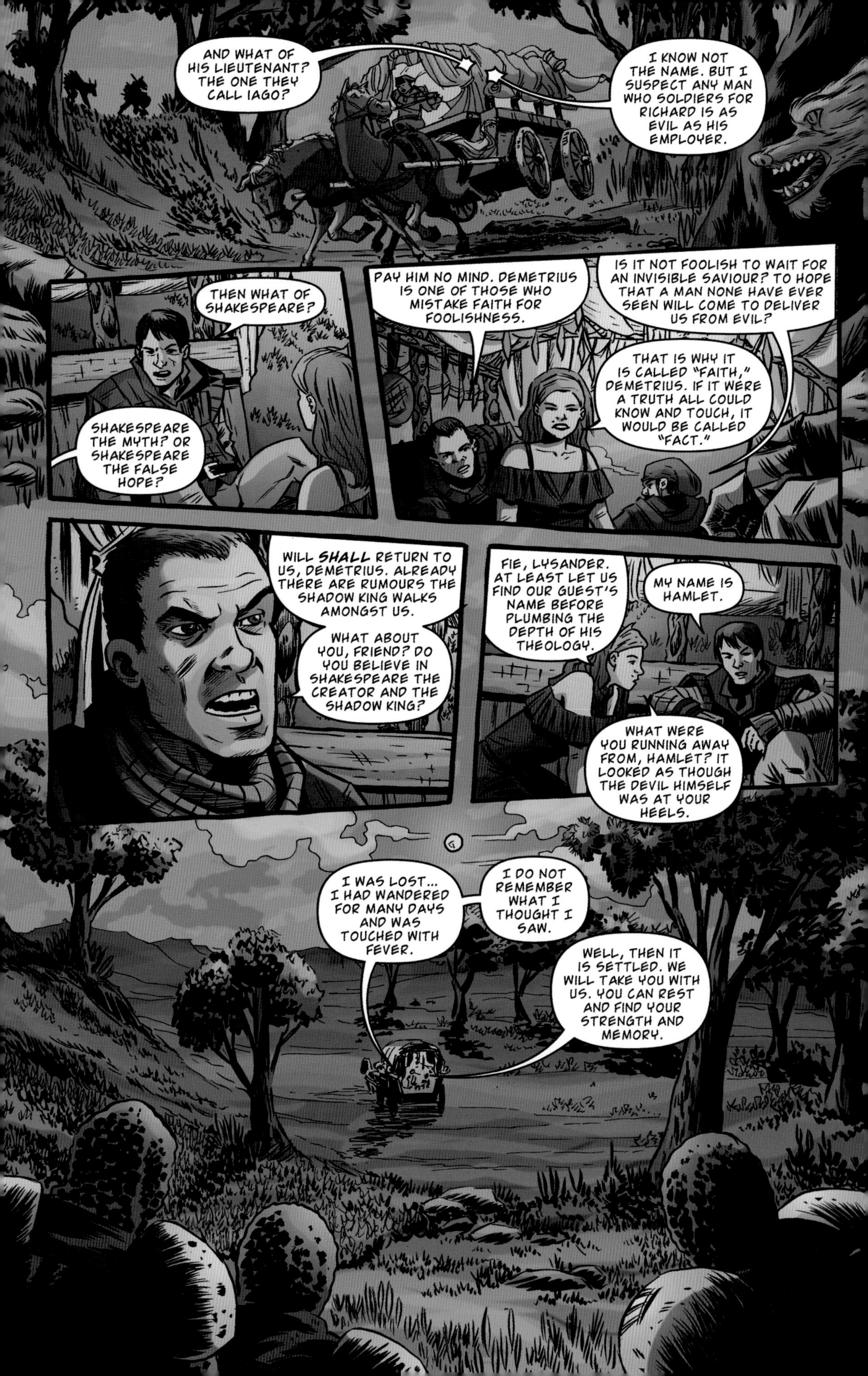
AND WHAT OF HIS LIEUTENANT? THE ONE THEY CALL IAGO?
I KNOW NOT THE NAME. BUT I SUSPECT ANY MAN WHO SOLDIERS FOR RICHARD IS AS EVIL AS HIS EMPLOYER.
THEN WHAT OF SHAKESPEARE?
SHAKESPEARE THE MYTH? OR SHAKESPEARE THE FALSE HOPE?
PAY HIM NO MIND. DEMETRIUS IS ONE OF THOSE WHO MISTAKE FAITH FOR FOOLISHNESS.
IS IT NOT FOOLISH TO WAIT FOR AN INVISIBLE SAVIOUR? TO HOPE THAT A MAN NONE HAVE EVER SEEN WILL COME TO DELIVER US FROM EVIL?
THAT IS WHY IT IS CALLED "FAITH," DEMETRIUS. IF IT WERE A TRUTH ALL COULD KNOW AND TOUCH, IT WOULD BE CALLED "FACT."
WILL SHALL RETURN TO US, DEMETRIUS. ALREADY THERE ARE RUMOURS THE SHADOW KING WALKS AMONGST US.
WHAT ABOUT YOU, FRIEND? DO YOU BELIEVE IN SHAKESPEARE THE CREATOR AND THE SHADOW KING?
FIE, LYSANDER. AT LEAST LET US FIND OUR GUEST'S NAME BEFORE PLUMBING THE DEPTH OF HIS THEOLOGY.
MY NAME IS HAMLET.
WHAT WERE YOU RUNNING AWAY FROM, HAMLET? IT LOOKED AS THOUGH THE DEVIL HIMSELF WAS AT YOUR HEELS.
I WAS LOST... I HAD WANDERED FOR MANY DAYS AND WAS TOUCHED WITH FEVER.
I DO NOT REMEMBER WHAT I THOUGHT I SAW.
WELL, THEN IT IS SETTLED. WE WILL TAKE YOU WITH US. YOU CAN REST AND FIND YOUR STRENGTH AND MEMORY.

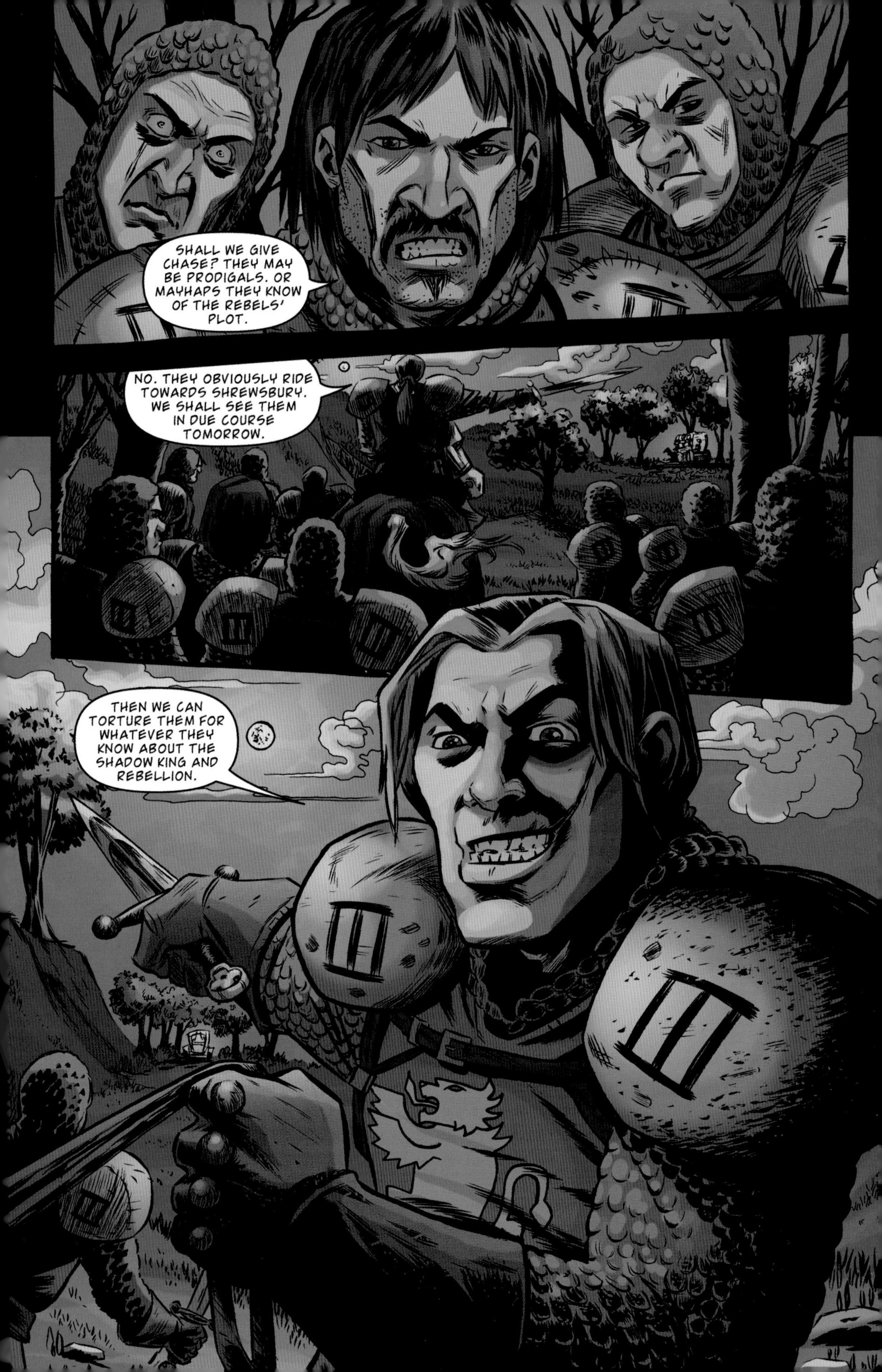
SHALL WE GIVE CHASE? THEY MAY BE PRODIGALS. OR MAYHAPS THEY KNOW OF THE REBELS' PLOT.
NO. THEY OBVIOUSLY RIDE TOWARDS SHREWSBURY. WE SHALL SEE THEM IN DUE COURSE TOMORROW.
THEN WE CAN TORTURE THEM FOR WHATEVER THEY KNOW ABOUT THE SHADOW KING AND REBELLION.

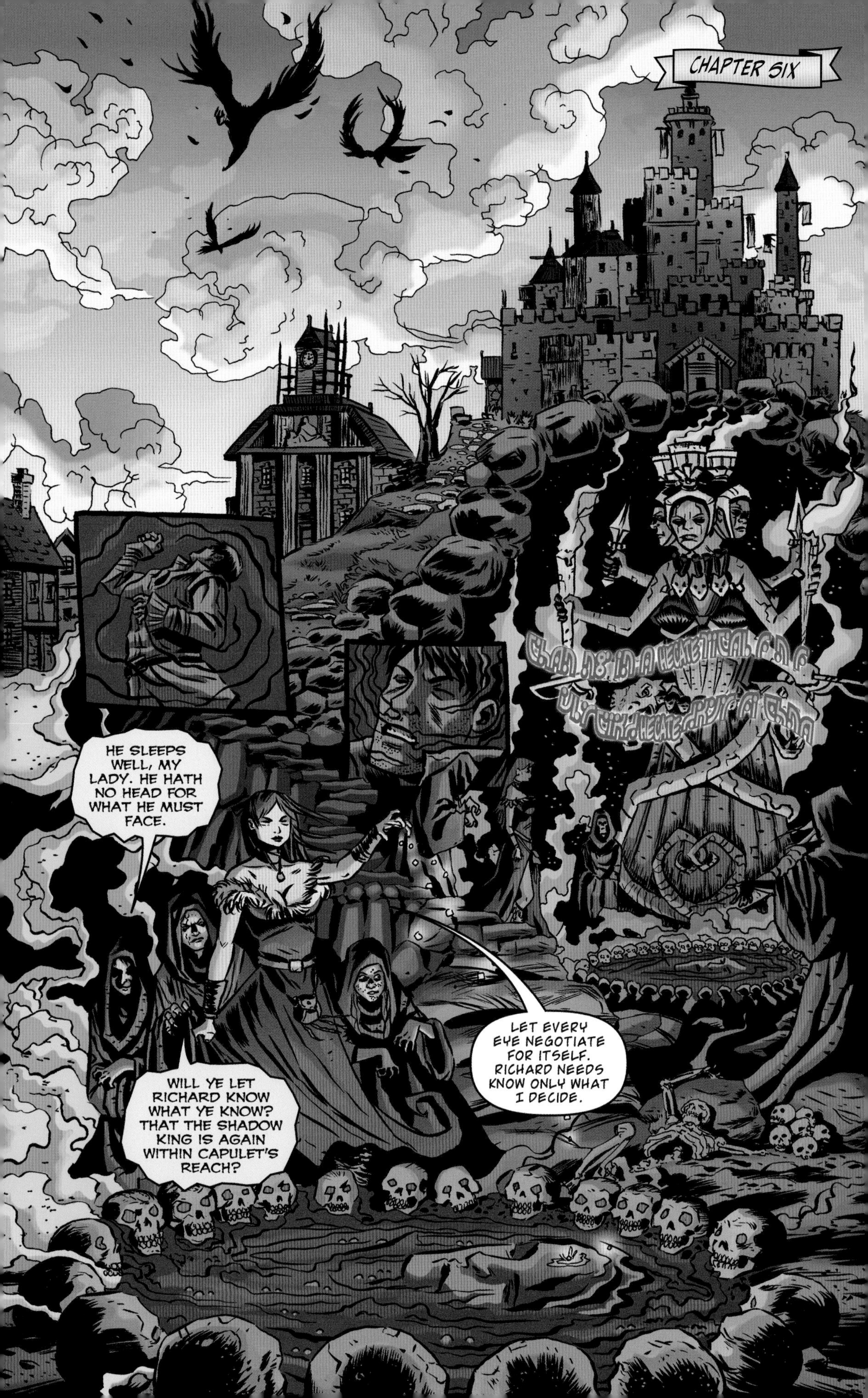
CHAPTER SIX
HE SLEEPS WELL, MY LADY. HE HATH NO HEAD FOR WHAT HE MUST FACE.
WILL YE LET RICHARD KNOW WHAT YE KNOW? THAT THE SHADOW KING IS AGAIN WITHIN CAPULET'S REACH?
LET EVERY EYE NEGOTIATE FOR ITSELF. RICHARD NEEDS KNOW ONLY WHAT I DECIDE.

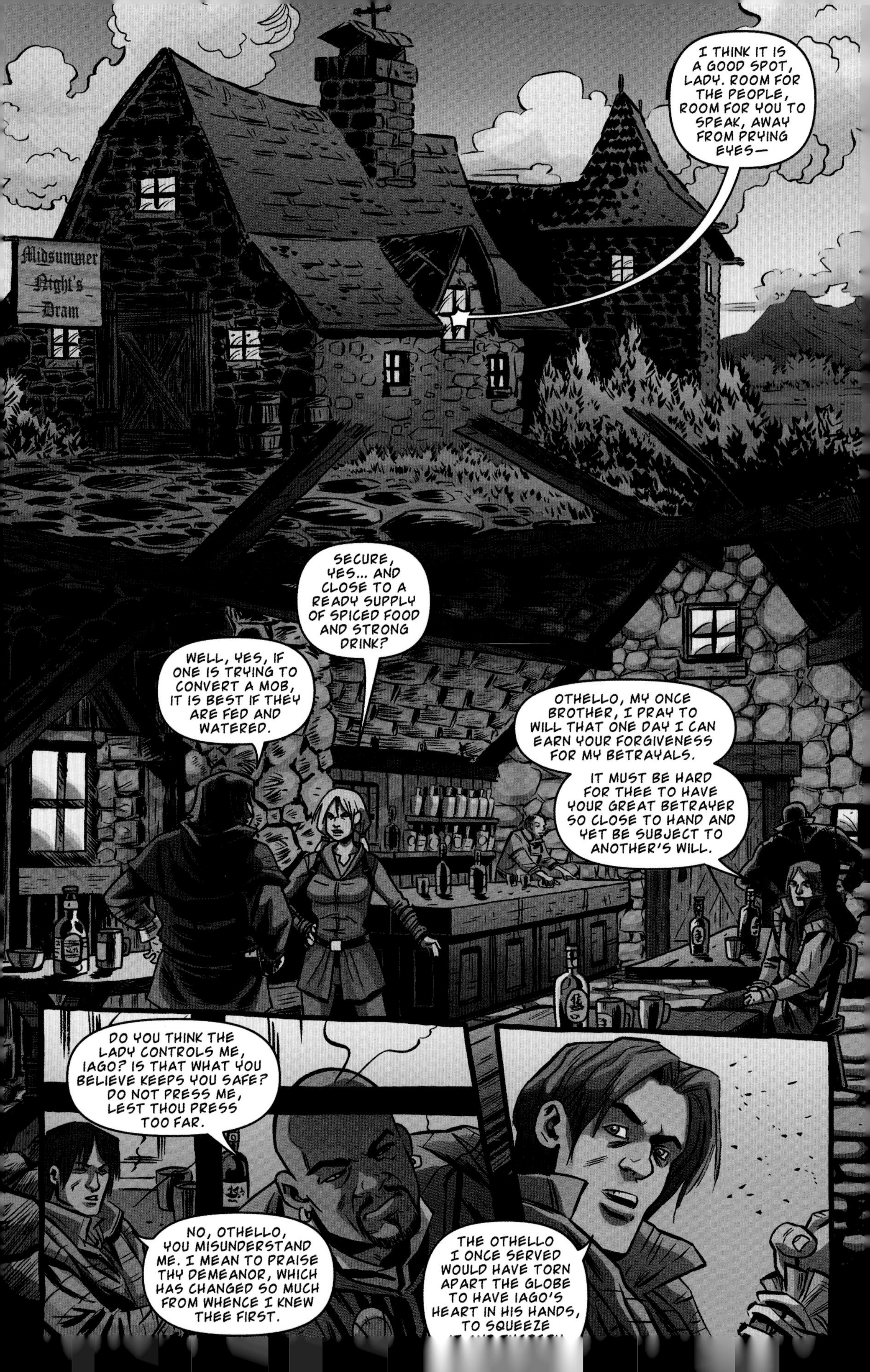
Midsummer Night's Dram
I THINK IT IS A GOOD SPOT, LADY. ROOM FOR THE PEOPLE, ROOM FOR YOU TO SPEAK, AWAY FROM PRYING EYES—
SECURE, YES... AND CLOSE TO A READY SUPPLY OF SPICED FOOD AND STRONG DRINK?
WELL, YES, IF ONE IS TRYING TO CONVERT A MOB, IT IS BEST IF THEY ARE FED AND WATERED.
OTHELLO, MY ONCE BROTHER, I PRAY TO WILL THAT ONE DAY I CAN EARN YOUR FORGIVENESS FOR MY BETRAYALS.
IT MUST BE HARD FOR THEE TO HAVE YOUR GREAT BETRAYER SO CLOSE TO HAND AND YET BE SUBJECT TO ANOTHER'S WILL.
DO YOU THINK THE LADY CONTROLS ME, IAGO? IS THAT WHAT YOU BELIEVE KEEPS YOU SAFE? DO NOT PRESS ME, LEST THOU PRESS TOO FAR.
NO, OTHELLO, YOU MISUNDERSTAND ME. I MEAN TO PRAISE THY DEMEANOR, WHICH HAS CHANGED SO MUCH FROM WHENCE I KNEW THEE FIRST.
THE OTHELLO I ONCE SERVED WOULD HAVE TORN APART THE GLOBE TO HAVE IAGO'S HEART IN HIS HANDS, TO SQUEEZE

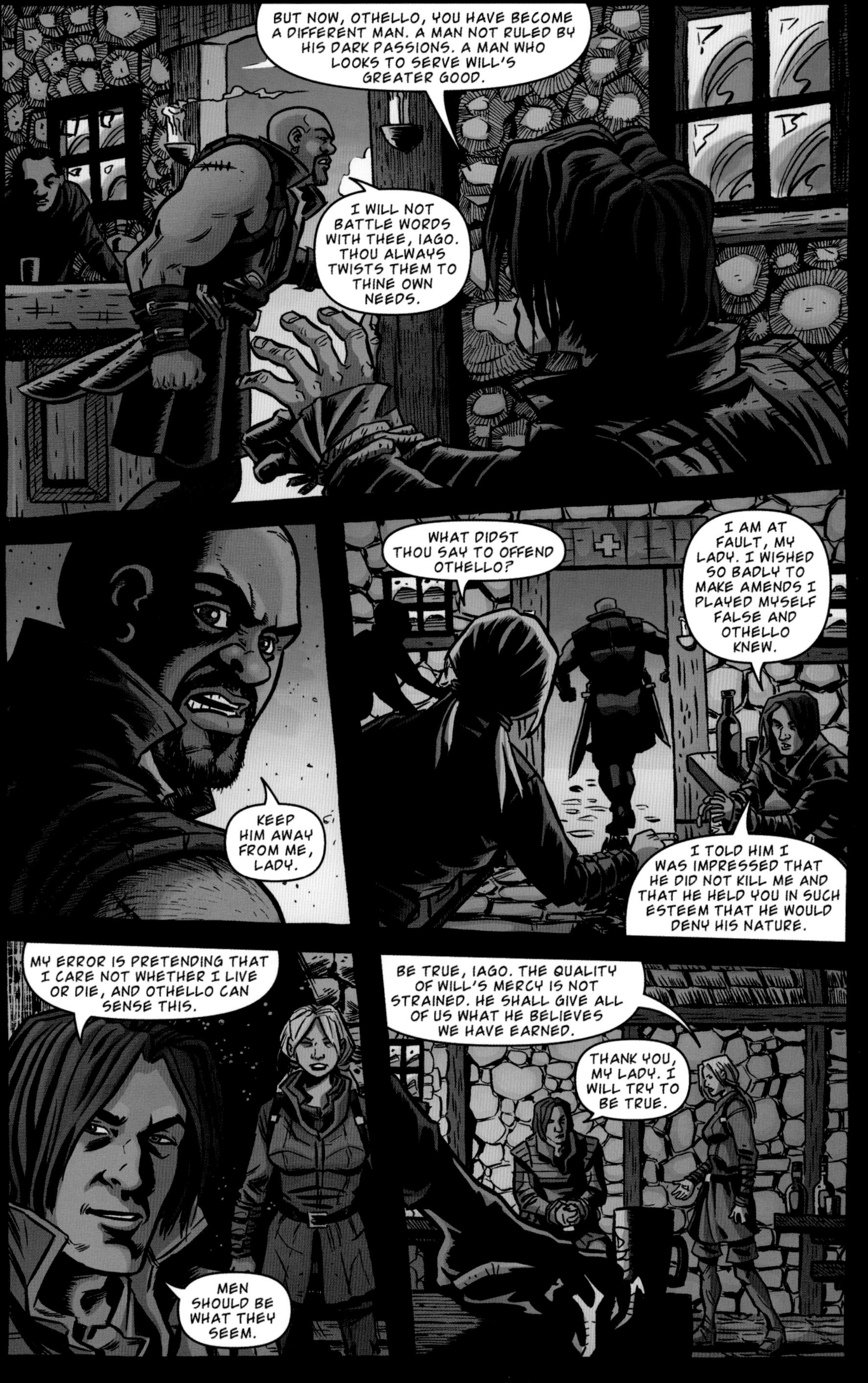
BUT NOW, OTHELLO, YOU HAVE BECOME A DIFFERENT MAN. A MAN NOT RULED BY HIS DARK PASSIONS. A MAN WHO LOOKS TO SERVE WILL'S GREATER GOOD.
I WILL NOT BATTLE WORDS WITH THEE, IAGO. THOU ALWAYS TWISTS THEM TO THINE OWN NEEDS.
KEEP HIM AWAY FROM ME, LADY.
WHAT DIDST THOU SAY TO OFFEND OTHELLO?
I AM AT FAULT, MY LADY. I WISHED SO BADLY TO MAKE AMENDS I PLAYED MYSELF FALSE AND OTHELLO KNEW.
I TOLD HIM I WAS IMPRESSED THAT HE DID NOT KILL ME AND THAT HE HELD YOU IN SUCH ESTEEM THAT HE WOULD DENY HIS NATURE.
MY ERROR IS PRETENDING THAT I CARE NOT WHETHER I LIVE OR DIE, AND OTHELLO CAN SENSE THIS.
MEN SHOULD BE WHAT THEY SEEM.
BE TRUE, IAGO. THE QUALITY OF WILL'S MERCY IS NOT STRAINED. HE SHALL GIVE ALL OF US WHAT HE BELIEVES WE HAVE EARNED.
THANK YOU, MY LADY. I WILL TRY TO BE TRUE.

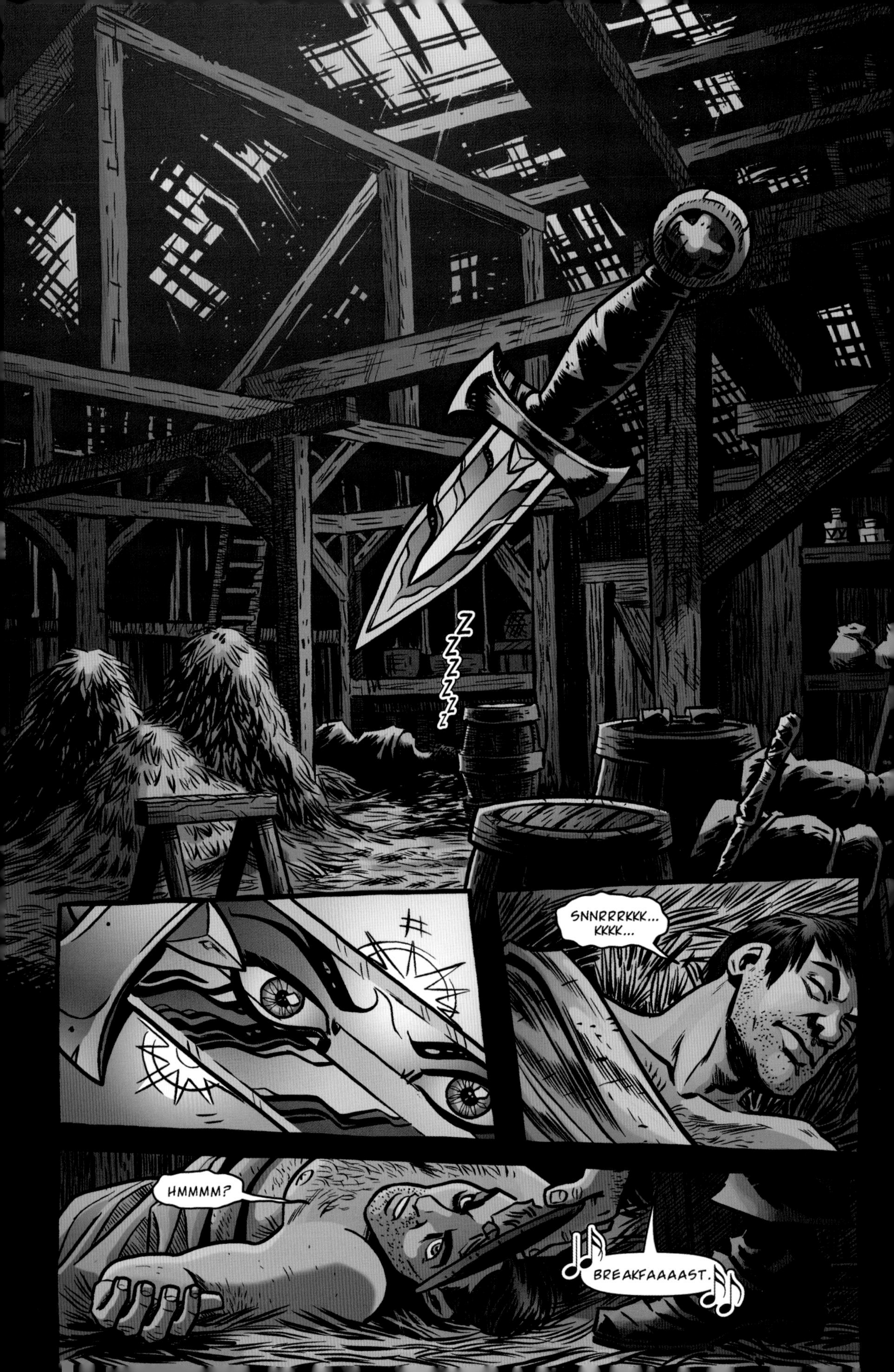
ZZZZZZ
SNNRRRKKK... KKKK...
HMMMM?
BREAKFAAAAST.

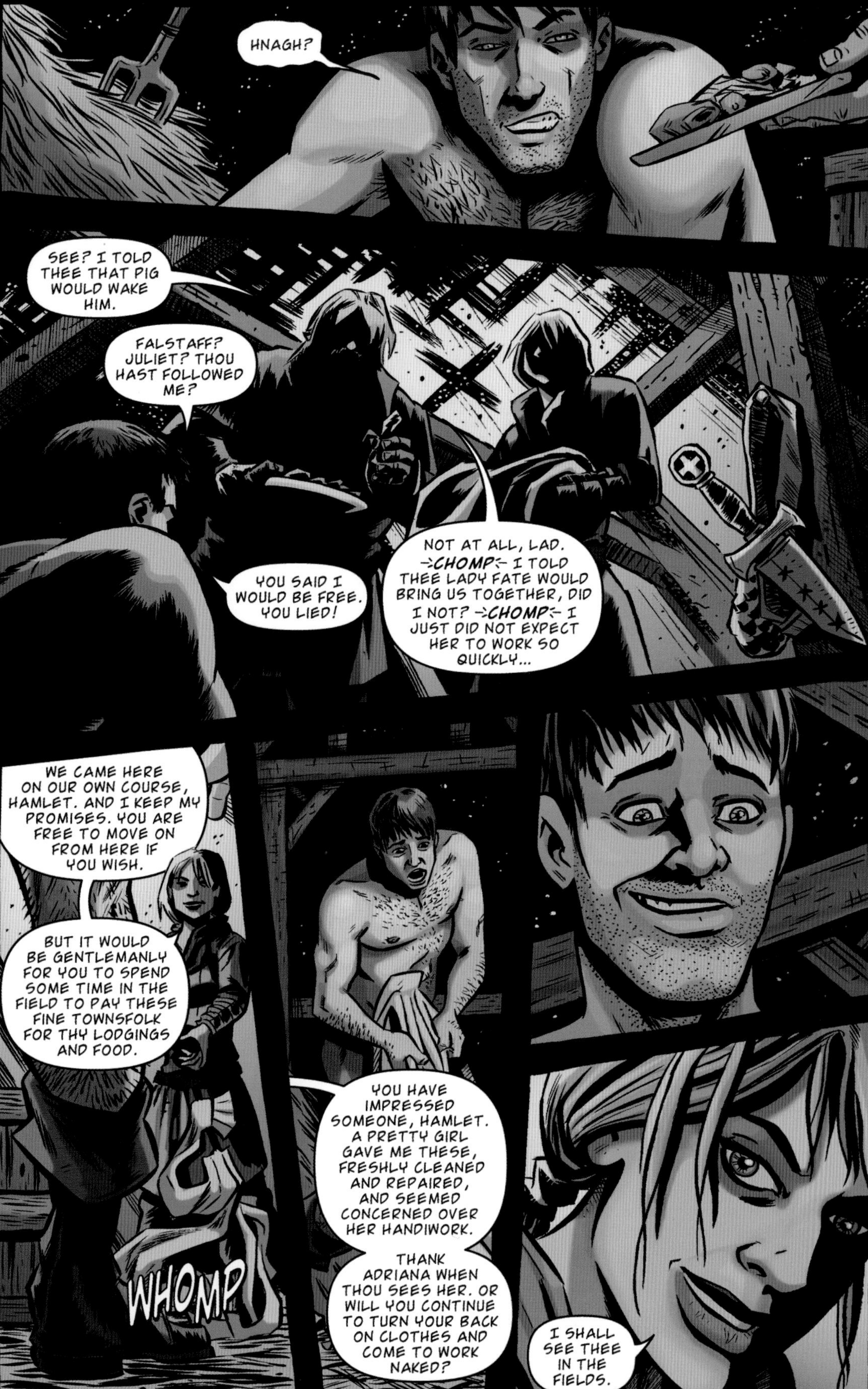
HNAGH?
SEE? I TOLD THEE THAT PIG WOULD WAKE HIM.
FALSTAFF? JULIET? THOU HAST FOLLOWED ME?
YOU SAID I WOULD BE FREE. YOU LIED!
NOT AT ALL, LAD. ⟹CHOMP⟸ I TOLD THEE LADY FATE WOULD BRING US TOGETHER, DID I NOT? ⟹CHOMP⟸ I JUST DID NOT EXPECT HER TO WORK SO QUICKLY...
WE CAME HERE ON OUR OWN COURSE, HAMLET. AND I KEEP MY PROMISES. YOU ARE FREE TO MOVE ON FROM HERE IF YOU WISH.
BUT IT WOULD BE GENTLEMANLY FOR YOU TO SPEND SOME TIME IN THE FIELD TO PAY THESE FINE TOWNSFOLK FOR THY LODGINGS AND FOOD.
WHOMP
YOU HAVE IMPRESSED SOMEONE, HAMLET. A PRETTY GIRL GAVE ME THESE, FRESHLY CLEANED AND REPAIRED, AND SEEMED CONCERNED OVER HER HANDIWORK.
THANK ADRIANA WHEN THOU SEES HER. OR WILL YOU CONTINUE TO TURN YOUR BACK ON CLOTHES AND COME TO WORK NAKED?
I SHALL SEE THEE IN THE FIELDS.

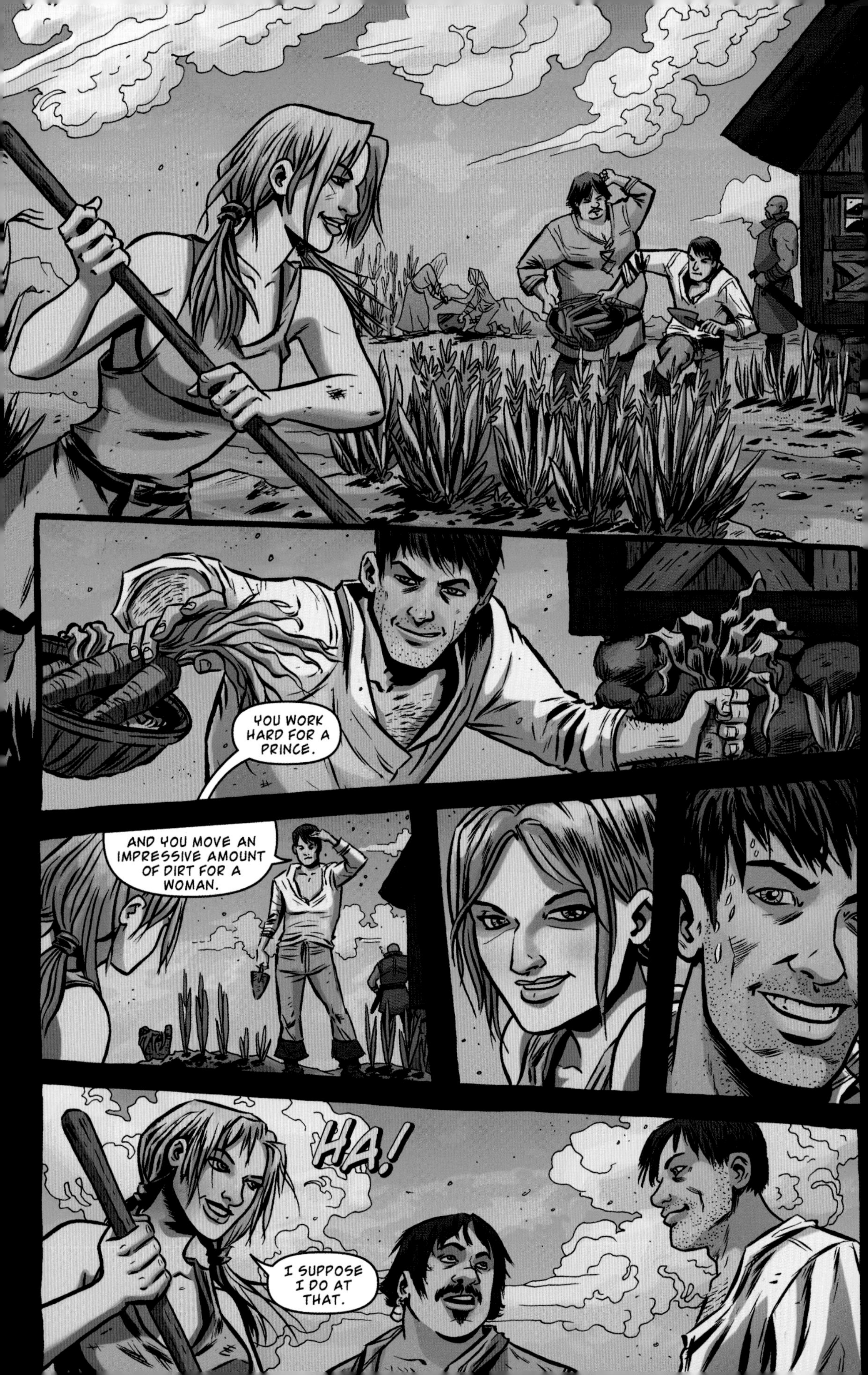
YOU WORK HARD FOR A PRINCE.
AND YOU MOVE AN IMPRESSIVE AMOUNT OF DIRT FOR A WOMAN.
HA!
I SUPPOSE I DO AT THAT.

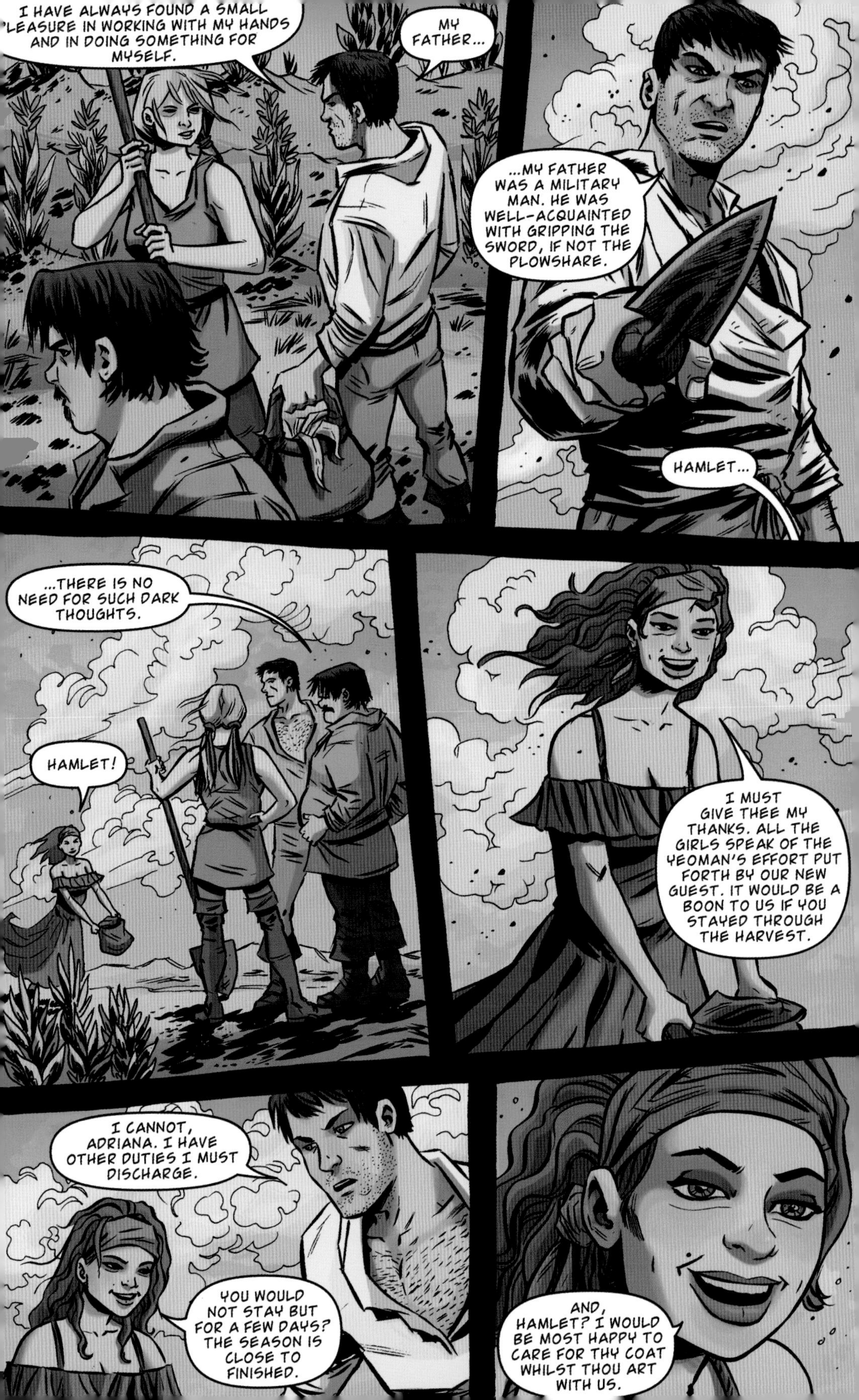

I HAVE ALWAYS FOUND A SMALL 'LEASURE IN WORKING WITH MY HANDS AND IN DOING SOMETHING FOR MYSELF.
MY FATHER...
...MY FATHER WAS A MILITARY MAN. HE WAS WELL-ACQUAINTED WITH GRIPPING THE SWORD, IF NOT THE PLOWSHARE.
HAMLET...
...THERE IS NO NEED FOR SUCH DARK THOUGHTS.
HAMLET!
I MUST GIVE THEE MY THANKS. ALL THE GIRLS SPEAK OF THE YEOMAN'S EFFORT PUT FORTH BY OUR NEW GUEST. IT WOULD BE A BOON TO US IF YOU STAYED THROUGH THE HARVEST.
I CANNOT, ADRIANA. I HAVE OTHER DUTIES I MUST DISCHARGE.
YOU WOULD NOT STAY BUT FOR A FEW DAYS? THE SEASON IS CLOSE TO FINISHED.
AND, HAMLET? I WOULD BE MOST HAPPY TO CARE FOR THY COAT WHILST THOU ART WITH US.

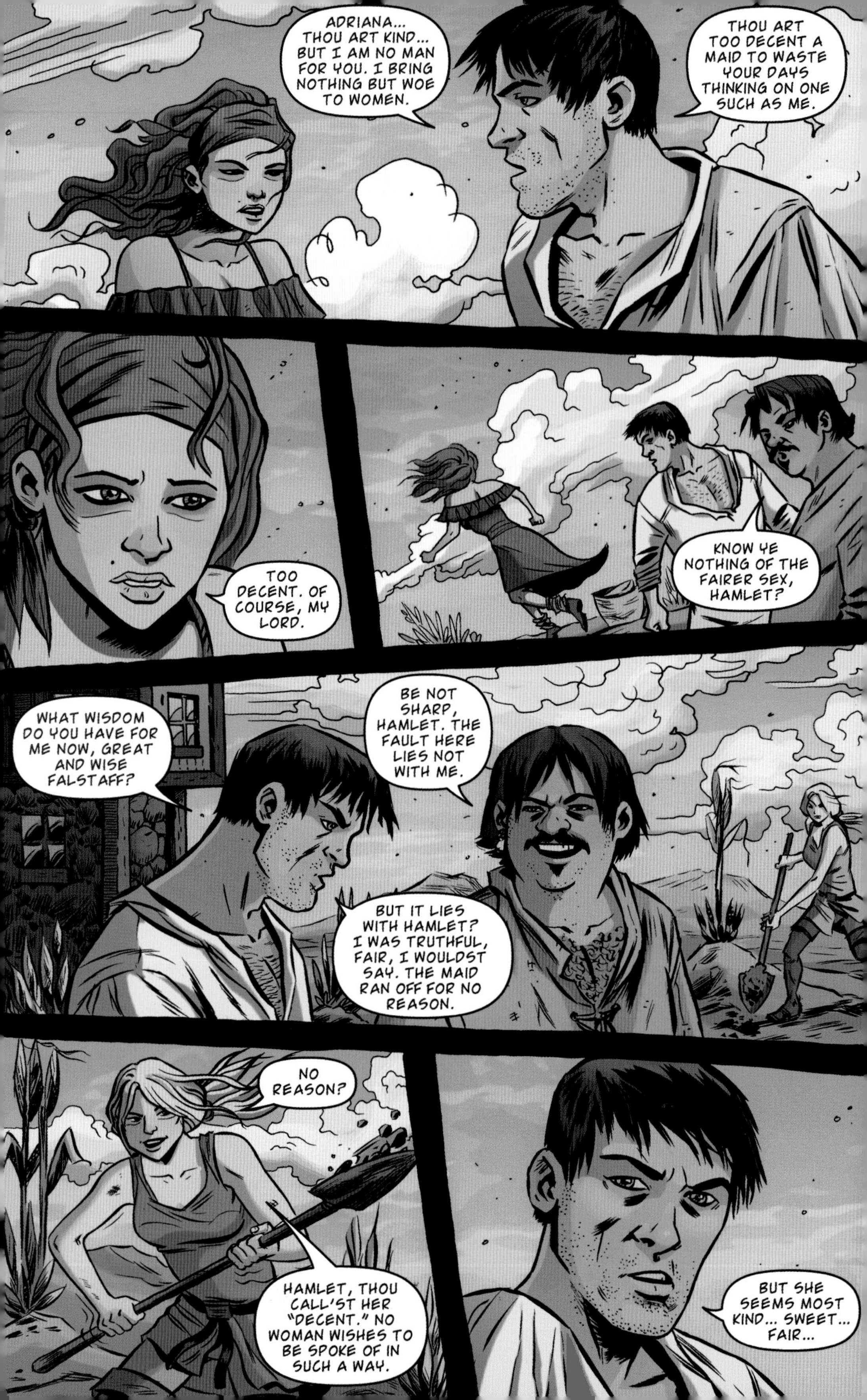
ADRIANA... THOU ART KIND... BUT I AM NO MAN FOR YOU. I BRING NOTHING BUT WOE TO WOMEN.
THOU ART TOO DECENT A MAID TO WASTE YOUR DAYS THINKING ON ONE SUCH AS ME.
TOO DECENT. OF COURSE, MY LORD.
KNOW YE NOTHING OF THE FAIRER SEX, HAMLET?
WHAT WISDOM DO YOU HAVE FOR ME NOW, GREAT AND WISE FALSTAFF?
BE NOT SHARP, HAMLET. THE FAULT HERE LIES NOT WITH ME.
BUT IT LIES WITH HAMLET? I WAS TRUTHFUL, FAIR, I WOULDST SAY. THE MAID RAN OFF FOR NO REASON.
NO REASON?
HAMLET, THOU CALL'ST HER "DECENT." NO WOMAN WISHES TO BE SPOKE OF IN SUCH A WAY.
BUT SHE SEEMS MOST KIND... SWEET... FAIR...

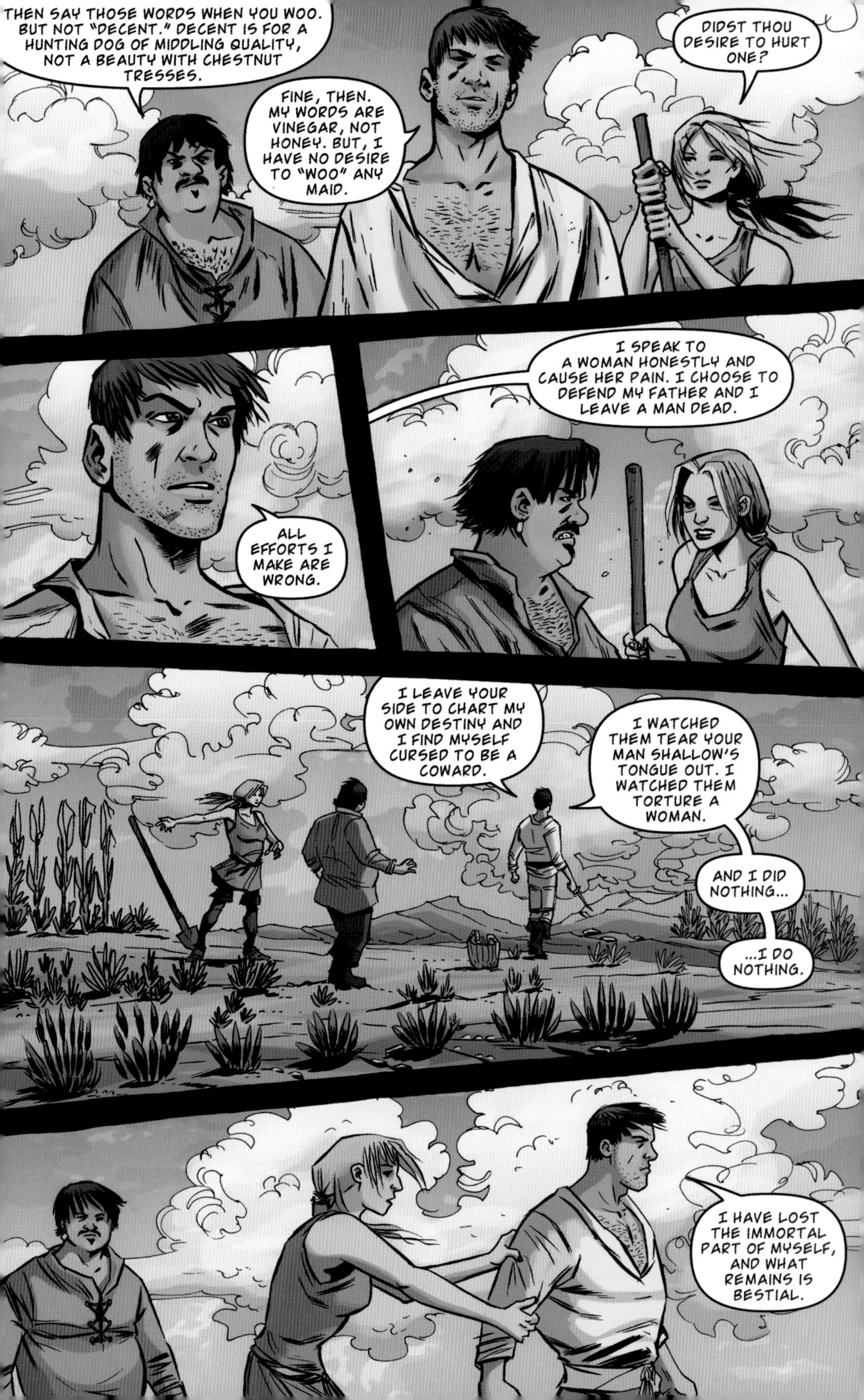
THEN SAY THOSE WORDS WHEN YOU WOO. BUT NOT "DECENT." DECENT IS FOR A HUNTING DOG OF MIDDLING QUALITY, NOT A BEAUTY WITH CHESTNUT TRESSES.
FINE, THEN. MY WORDS ARE VINEGAR, NOT HONEY. BUT, I HAVE NO DESIRE TO "WOO" ANY MAID.
DIDST THOU DESIRE TO HURT ONE?
ALL EFFORTS I MAKE ARE WRONG.
I SPEAK TO A WOMAN HONESTLY AND CAUSE HER PAIN. I CHOOSE TO DEFEND MY FATHER AND I LEAVE A MAN DEAD.
I LEAVE YOUR SIDE TO CHART MY OWN DESTINY AND I FIND MYSELF CURSED TO BE A COWARD.
I WATCHED THEM TEAR YOUR MAN SHALLOW'S TONGUE OUT. I WATCHED THEM TORTURE A WOMAN.
AND I DID NOTHING...
...I DO NOTHING.
I HAVE LOST THE IMMORTAL PART OF MYSELF, AND WHAT REMAINS IS BESTIAL.

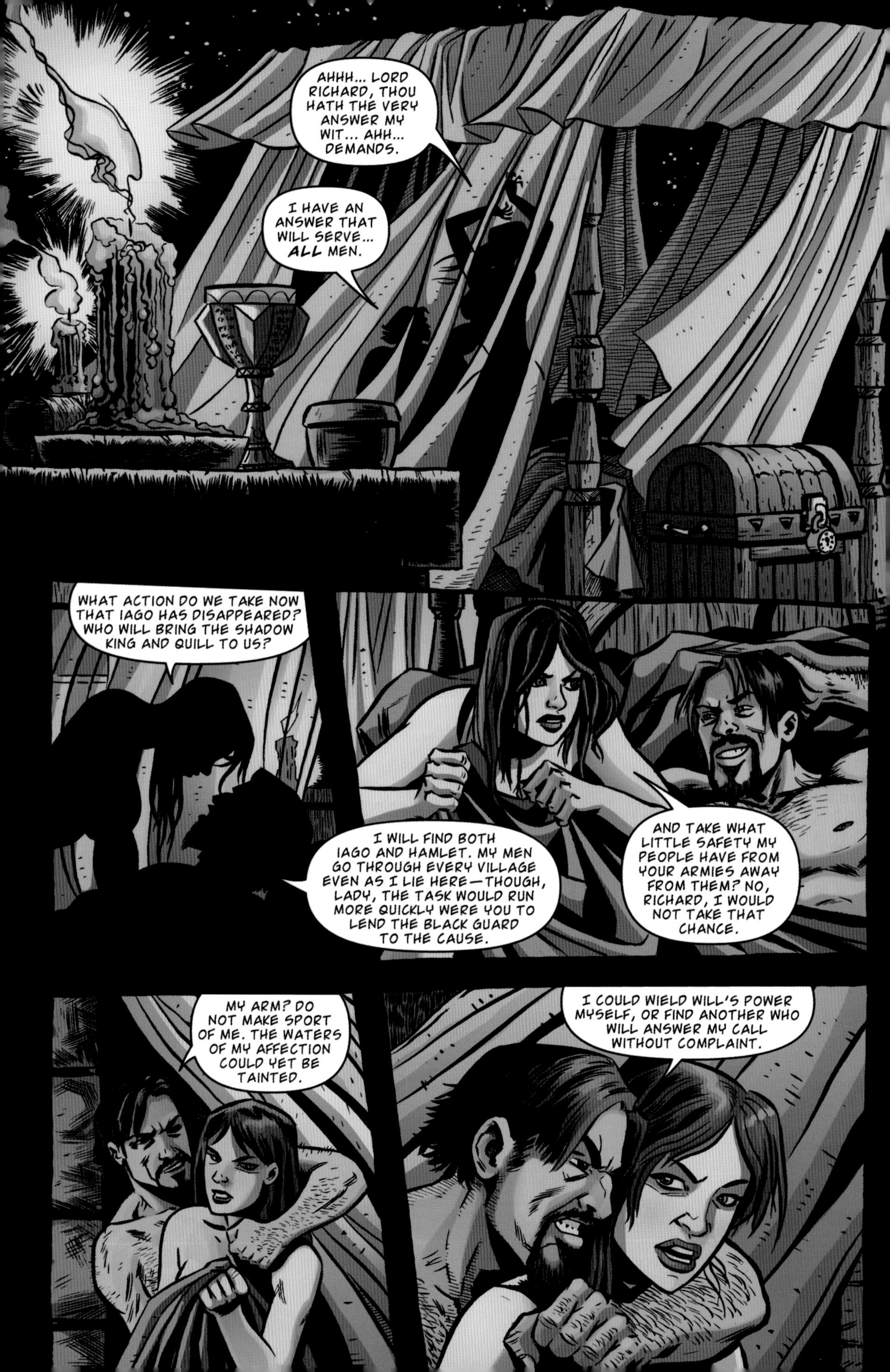
AHHH... LORD RICHARD, THOU HATH THE VERY ANSWER MY WIT... AHH... DEMANDS.
I HAVE AN ANSWER THAT WILL SERVE... ALL MEN.
WHAT ACTION DO WE TAKE NOW THAT IAGO HAS DISAPPEARED? WHO WILL BRING THE SHADOW KING AND QUILL TO US?
I WILL FIND BOTH IAGO AND HAMLET. MY MEN GO THROUGH EVERY VILLAGE EVEN AS I LIE HERE—THOUGH, LADY, THE TASK WOULD RUN MORE QUICKLY WERE YOU TO LEND THE BLACK GUARD TO THE CAUSE.
AND TAKE WHAT LITTLE SAFETY MY PEOPLE HAVE FROM YOUR ARMIES AWAY FROM THEM? NO, RICHARD, I WOULD NOT TAKE THAT CHANCE.
MY ARM? DO NOT MAKE SPORT OF ME. THE WATERS OF MY AFFECTION COULD YET BE TAINTED.
I COULD WIELD WILL'S POWER MYSELF, OR FIND ANOTHER WHO WILL ANSWER MY CALL WITHOUT COMPLAINT.

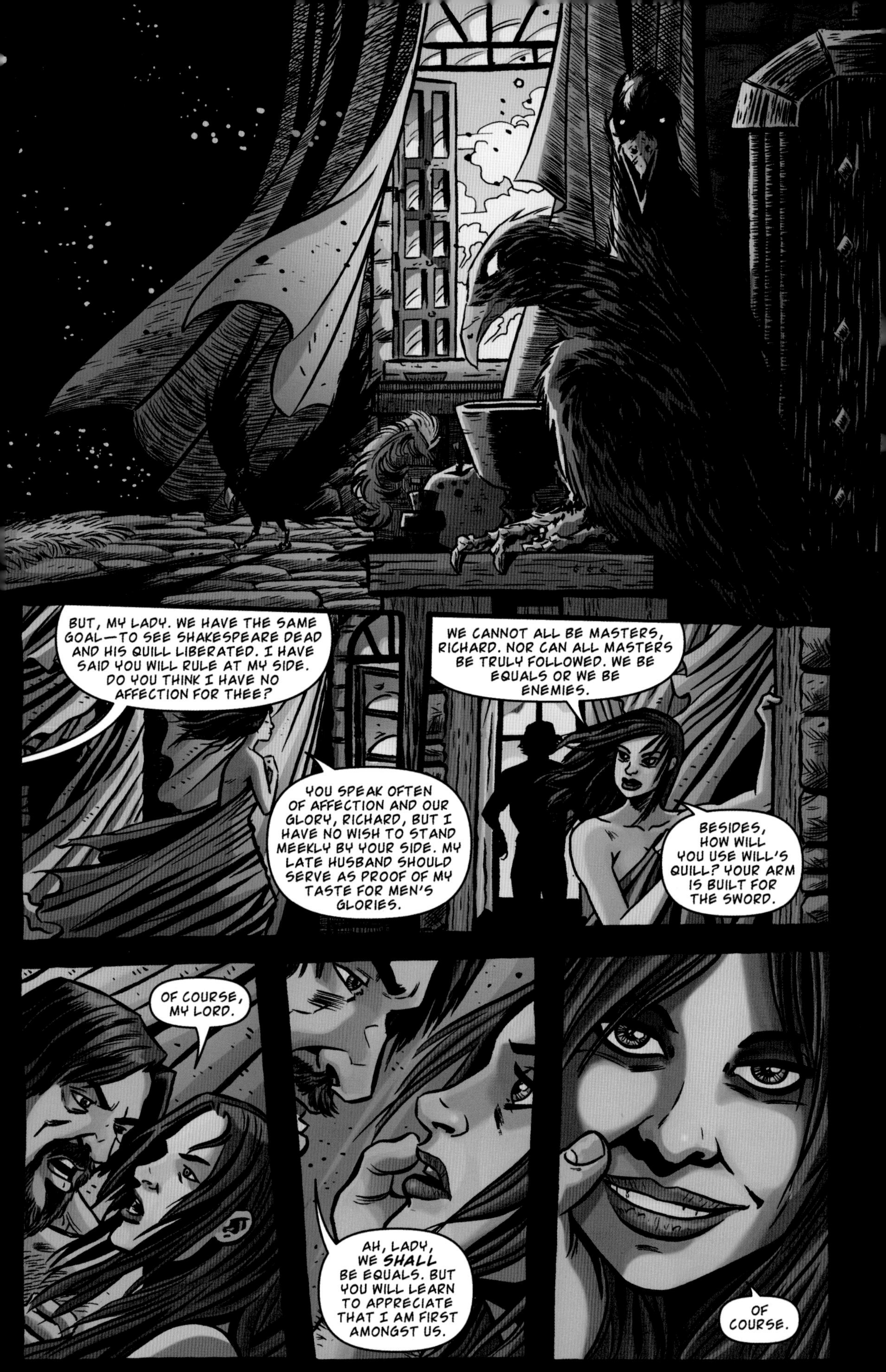
BUT, MY LADY. WE HAVE THE SAME GOAL—TO SEE SHAKESPEARE DEAD AND HIS QUILL LIBERATED. I HAVE SAID YOU WILL RULE AT MY SIDE. DO YOU THINK I HAVE NO AFFECTION FOR THEE?
YOU SPEAK OFTEN OF AFFECTION AND OUR GLORY, RICHARD, BUT I HAVE NO WISH TO STAND MEEKLY BY YOUR SIDE. MY LATE HUSBAND SHOULD SERVE AS PROOF OF MY TASTE FOR MEN'S GLORIES.
WE CANNOT ALL BE MASTERS, RICHARD. NOR CAN ALL MASTERS BE TRULY FOLLOWED. WE BE EQUALS OR WE BE ENEMIES.
BESIDES, HOW WILL YOU USE WILL'S QUILL? YOUR ARM IS BUILT FOR THE SWORD.
OF COURSE, MY LORD.
AH, LADY, WE SHALL BE EQUALS. BUT YOU WILL LEARN TO APPRECIATE THAT I AM FIRST AMONGST US.
OF COURSE.

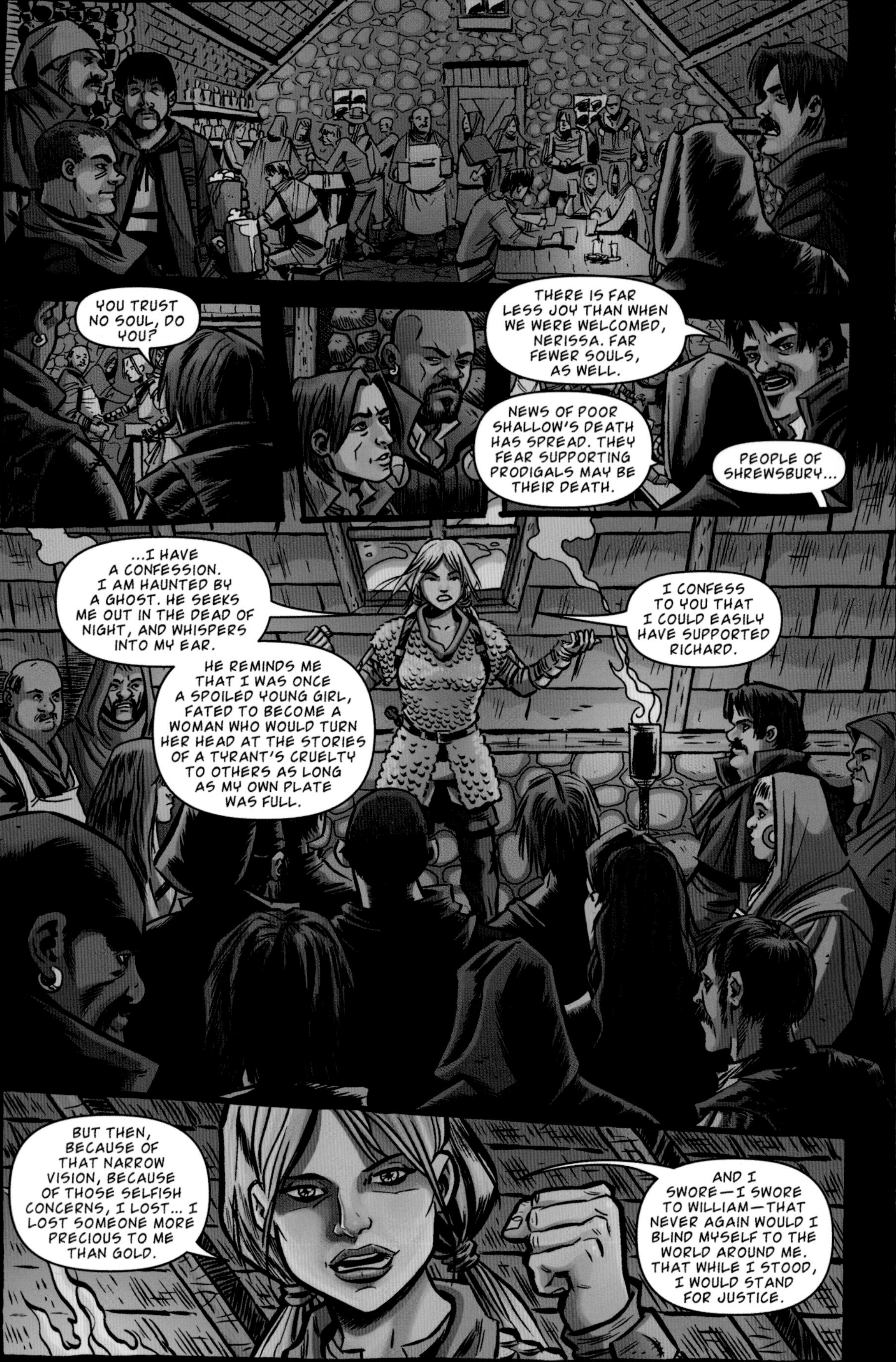
YOU TRUST NO SOUL, DO YOU?
THERE IS FAR LESS JOY THAN WHEN WE WERE WELCOMED, NERISSA. FAR FEWER SOULS, AS WELL.
NEWS OF POOR SHALLOW'S DEATH HAS SPREAD. THEY FEAR SUPPORTING PRODIGALS MAY BE THEIR DEATH.
PEOPLE OF SHREWSBURY...
...I HAVE A CONFESSION. I AM HAUNTED BY A GHOST. HE SEEKS ME OUT IN THE DEAD OF NIGHT, AND WHISPERS INTO MY EAR.
HE REMINDS ME THAT I WAS ONCE A SPOILED YOUNG GIRL, FATED TO BECOME A WOMAN WHO WOULD TURN HER HEAD AT THE STORIES OF A TYRANT'S CRUELTY TO OTHERS AS LONG AS MY OWN PLATE WAS FULL.
I CONFESS TO YOU THAT I COULD EASILY HAVE SUPPORTED RICHARD.
BUT THEN, BECAUSE OF THAT NARROW VISION, BECAUSE OF THOSE SELFISH CONCERNS, I LOST... I LOST SOMEONE MORE PRECIOUS TO ME THAN GOLD.
AND I SWORE—I SWORE TO WILLIAM—THAT NEVER AGAIN WOULD I BLIND MYSELF TO THE WORLD AROUND ME. THAT WHILE I STOOD, I WOULD STAND FOR JUSTICE.

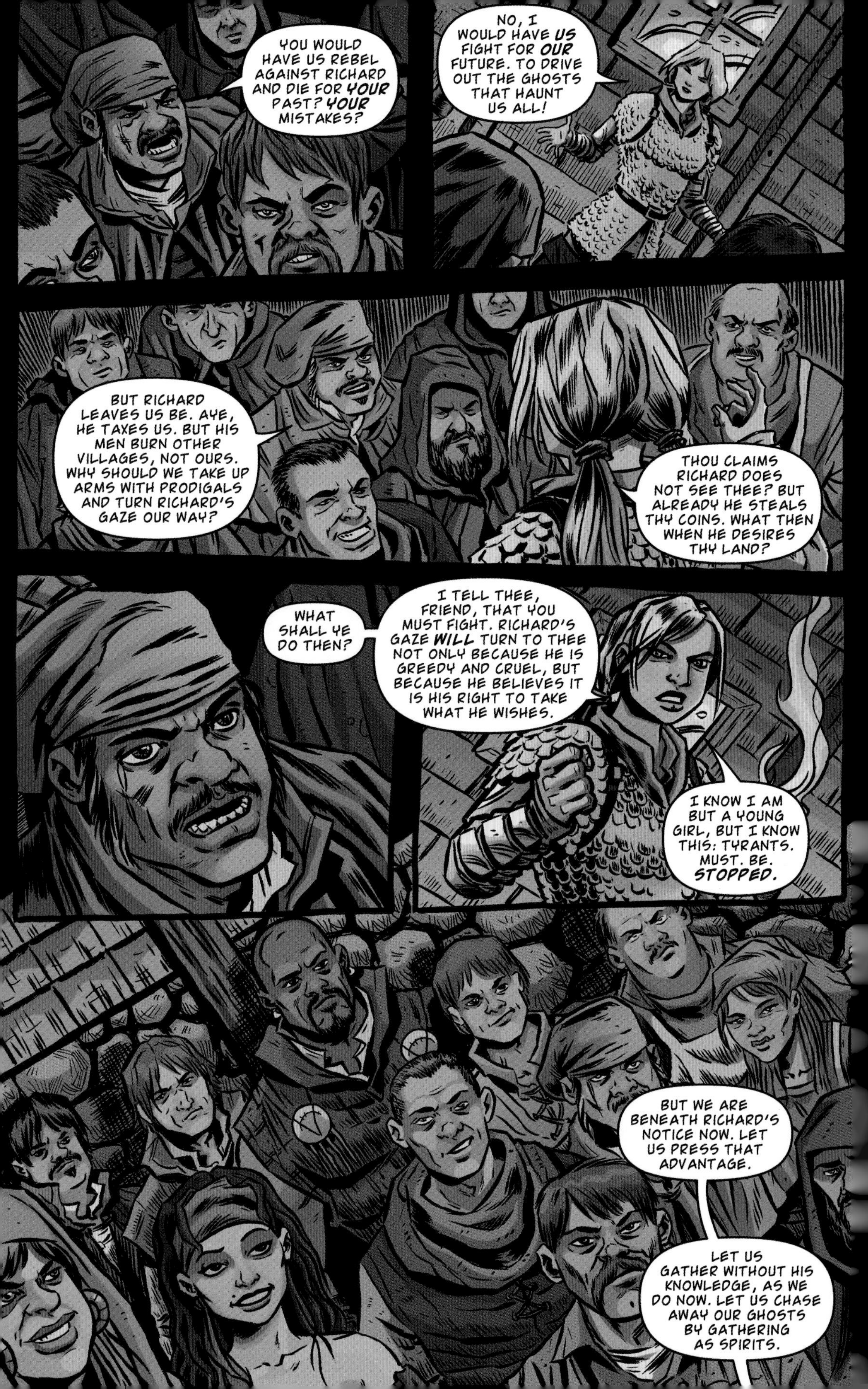
YOU WOULD HAVE US REBEL AGAINST RICHARD AND DIE FOR YOUR PAST? YOUR MISTAKES?
NO, I WOULD HAVE US FIGHT FOR OUR FUTURE. TO DRIVE OUT THE GHOSTS THAT HAUNT US ALL!
BUT RICHARD LEAVES US BE. AYE, HE TAXES US. BUT HIS MEN BURN OTHER VILLAGES, NOT OURS. WHY SHOULD WE TAKE UP ARMS WITH PRODIGALS AND TURN RICHARD'S GAZE OUR WAY?
THOU CLAIMS RICHARD DOES NOT SEE THEE? BUT ALREADY HE STEALS THY COINS. WHAT THEN WHEN HE DESIRES THY LAND?
WHAT SHALL YE DO THEN?
I TELL THEE, FRIEND, THAT YOU MUST FIGHT. RICHARD'S GAZE WILL TURN TO THEE NOT ONLY BECAUSE HE IS GREEDY AND CRUEL, BUT BECAUSE HE BELIEVES IT IS HIS RIGHT TO TAKE WHAT HE WISHES.
I KNOW I AM BUT A YOUNG GIRL, BUT I KNOW THIS: TYRANTS. MUST. BE. STOPPED.
BUT WE ARE BENEATH RICHARD'S NOTICE NOW. LET US PRESS THAT ADVANTAGE.
LET US GATHER WITHOUT HIS KNOWLEDGE, AS WE DO NOW. LET US CHASE AWAY OUR GHOSTS BY GATHERING AS SPIRITS.

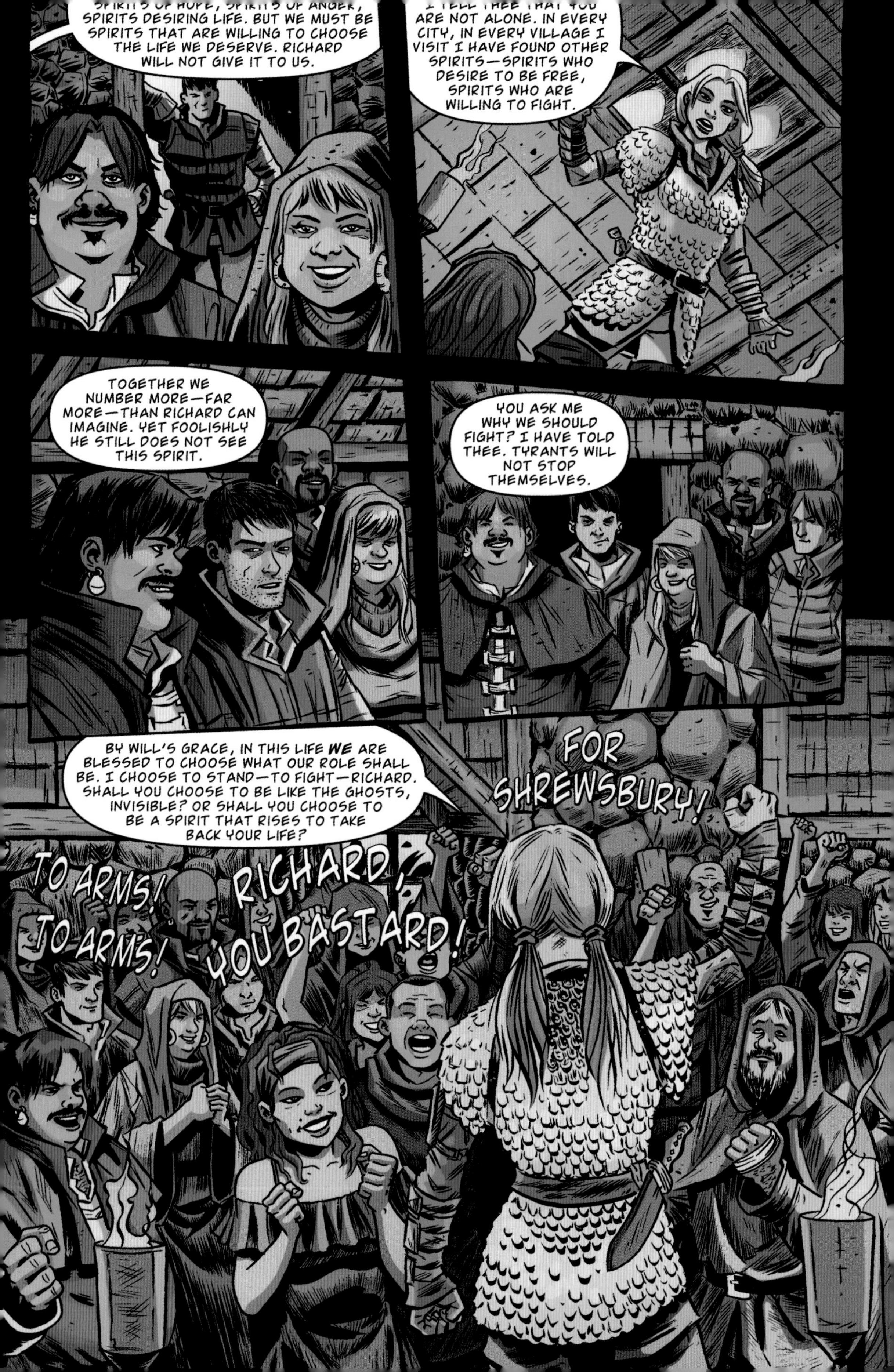
SPIRITS DESIRING LIFE. BUT WE MUST BE SPIRITS THAT ARE WILLING TO CHOOSE THE LIFE WE DESERVE. RICHARD WILL NOT GIVE IT TO US.
ARE NOT ALONE. IN EVERY CITY, IN EVERY VILLAGE I VISIT I HAVE FOUND OTHER SPIRITS—SPIRITS WHO DESIRE TO BE FREE, SPIRITS WHO ARE WILLING TO FIGHT.
TOGETHER WE NUMBER MORE—FAR MORE—THAN RICHARD CAN IMAGINE. YET FOOLISHLY HE STILL DOES NOT SEE THIS SPIRIT.
YOU ASK ME WHY WE SHOULD FIGHT? I HAVE TOLD THEE. TYRANTS WILL NOT STOP THEMSELVES.
BY WILL'S GRACE, IN THIS LIFE *WE* ARE BLESSED TO CHOOSE WHAT OUR ROLE SHALL BE. I CHOOSE TO STAND—TO FIGHT—RICHARD. SHALL YOU CHOOSE TO BE LIKE THE GHOSTS, INVISIBLE? OR SHALL YOU CHOOSE TO BE A SPIRIT THAT RISES TO TAKE BACK YOUR LIFE?
FOR SHREWSBURY!
TO ARMS! TO ARMS!
RICHARD, YOU BASTARD!

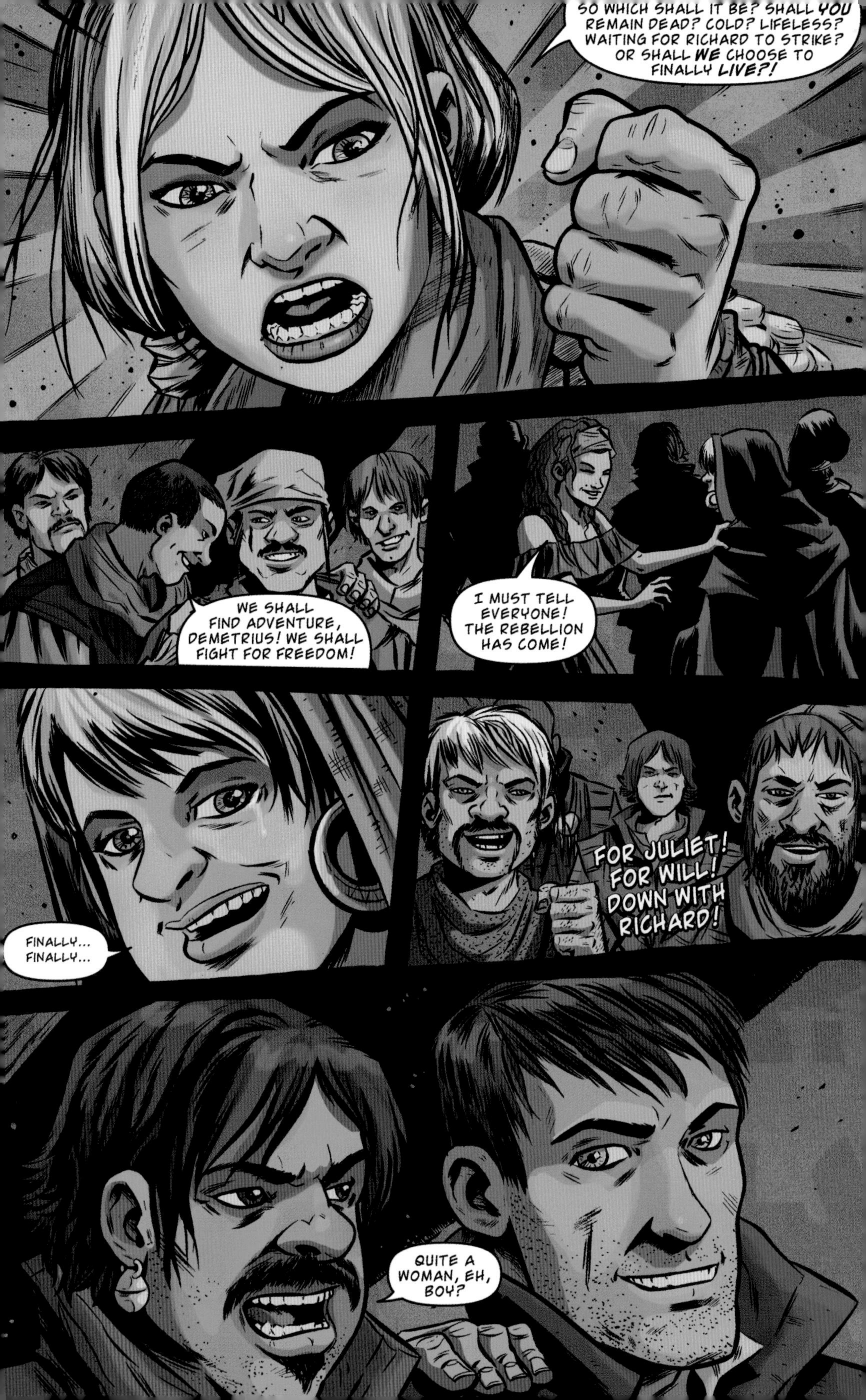
SO WHICH SHALL IT BE? SHALL YOU REMAIN DEAD? COLD? LIFELESS? WAITING FOR RICHARD TO STRIKE? OR SHALL WE CHOOSE TO FINALLY LIVE?!
WE SHALL FIND ADVENTURE, DEMETRIUS! WE SHALL FIGHT FOR FREEDOM!
I MUST TELL EVERYONE! THE REBELLION HAS COME!
FINALLY... FINALLY...
FOR JULIET! FOR WILL! DOWN WITH RICHARD!
QUITE A WOMAN, EH, BOY?

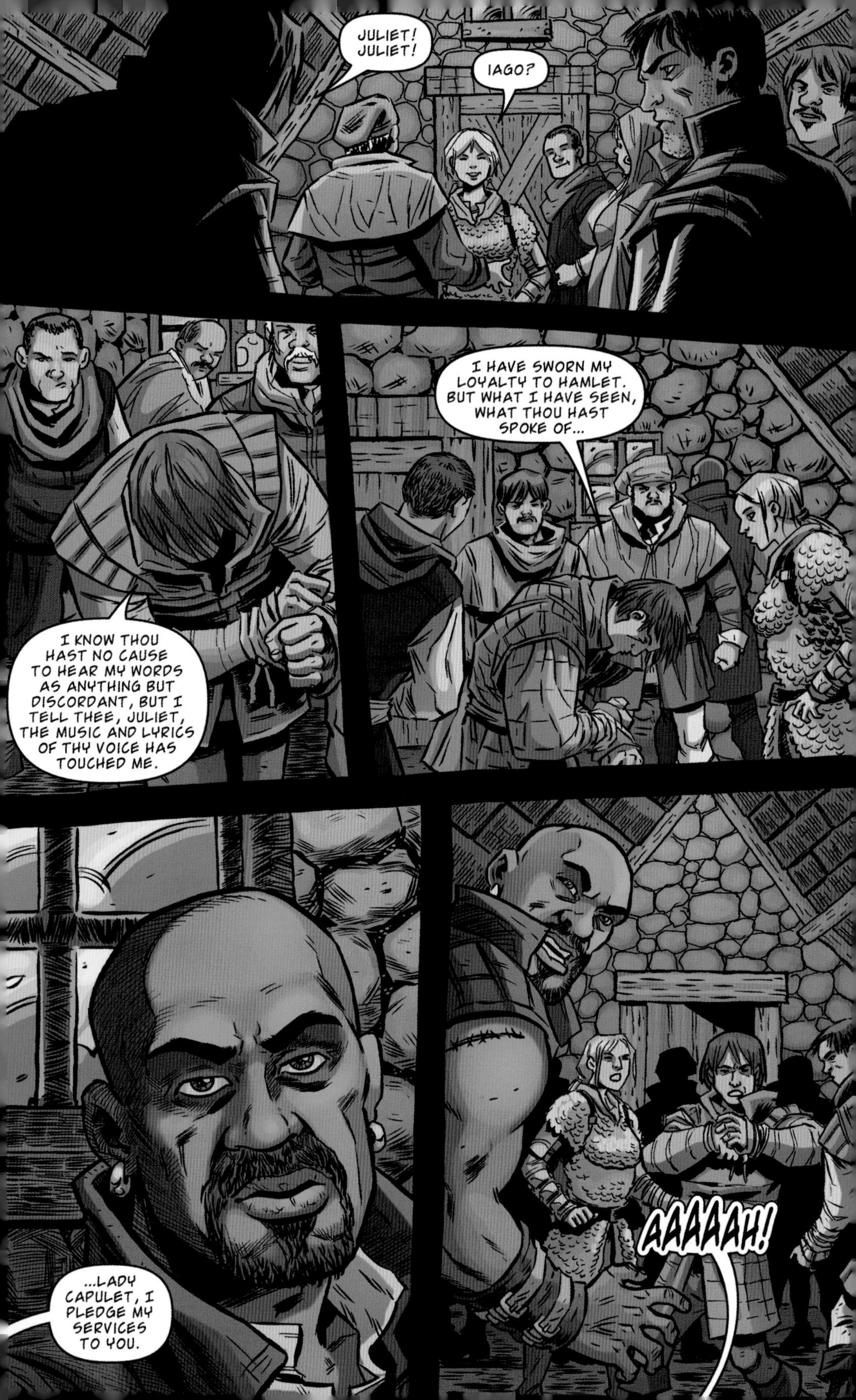
JULIET! JULIET!
IAGO?
I KNOW THOU HAST NO CAUSE TO HEAR MY WORDS AS ANYTHING BUT DISCORDANT, BUT I TELL THEE, JULIET, THE MUSIC AND LYRICS OF THY VOICE HAS TOUCHED ME.
I HAVE SWORN MY LOYALTY TO HAMLET. BUT WHAT I HAVE SEEN, WHAT THOU HAST SPOKE OF...
...LADY CAPULET, I PLEDGE MY SERVICES TO YOU.
AAAAAH!

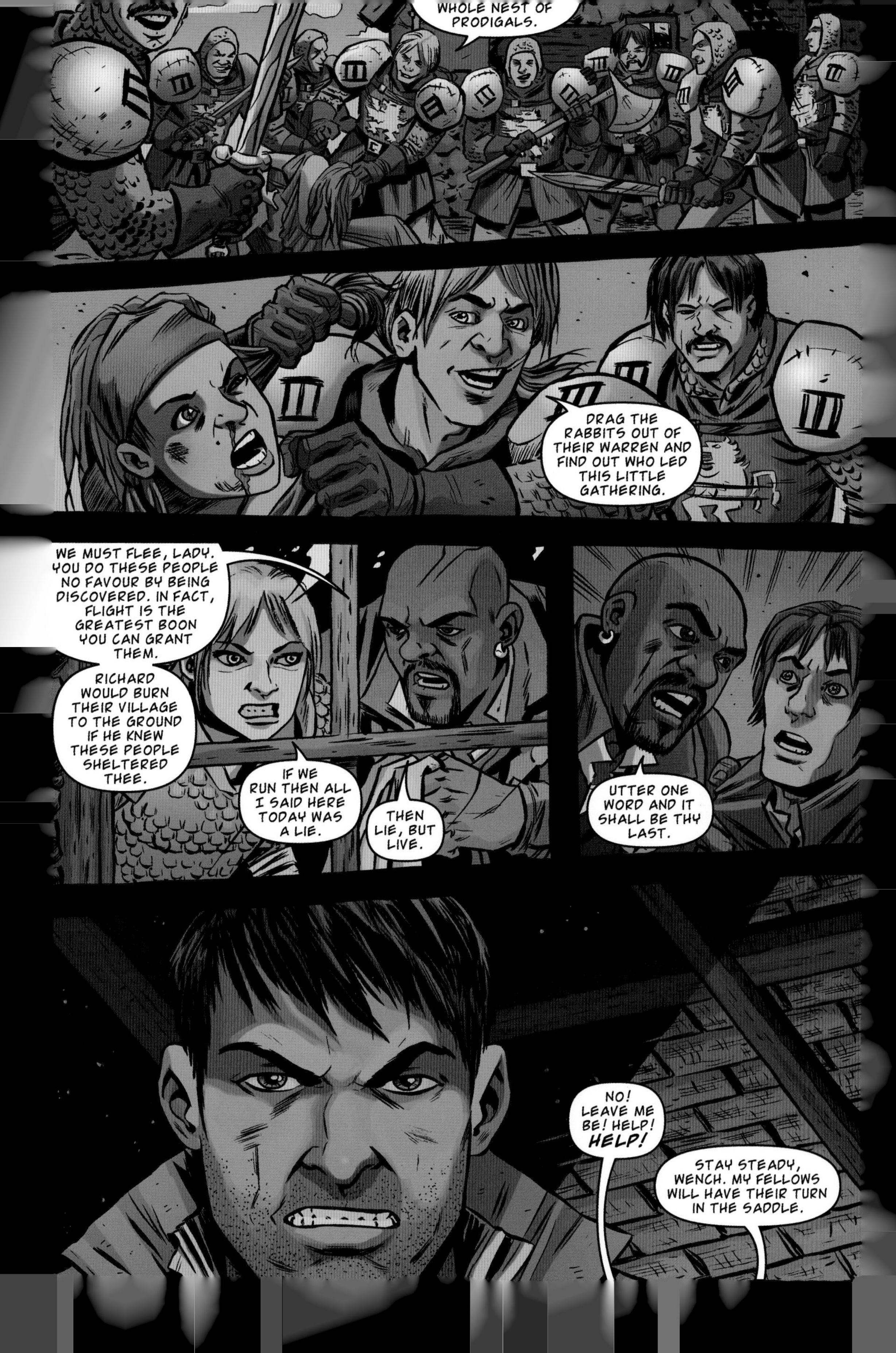
WHOLE NEST OF PRODIGALS.
DRAG THE RABBITS OUT OF THEIR WARREN AND FIND OUT WHO LED THIS LITTLE GATHERING.
WE MUST FLEE, LADY. YOU DO THESE PEOPLE NO FAVOUR BY BEING DISCOVERED. IN FACT, FLIGHT IS THE GREATEST BOON YOU CAN GRANT THEM.
RICHARD WOULD BURN THEIR VILLAGE TO THE GROUND IF HE KNEW THESE PEOPLE SHELTERED THEE.
IF WE RUN THEN ALL I SAID HERE TODAY WAS A LIE.
THEN LIE, BUT LIVE.
UTTER ONE WORD AND IT SHALL BE THY LAST.
NO! LEAVE ME BE! HELP! HELP!
STAY STEADY, WENCH. MY FELLOWS WILL HAVE THEIR TURN IN THE SADDLE.

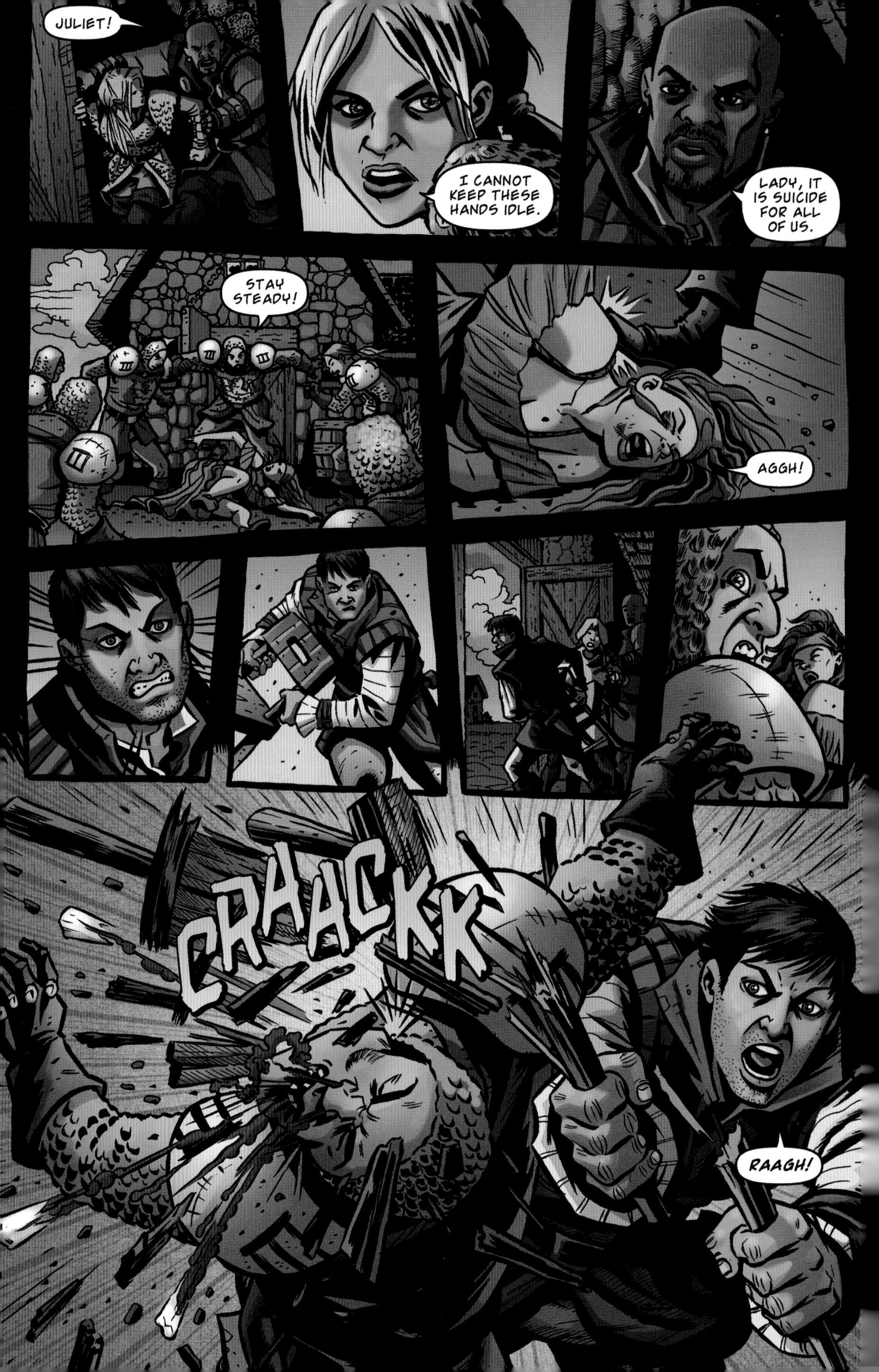
JULIET!
I CANNOT KEEP THESE HANDS IDLE.
LADY, IT IS SUICIDE FOR ALL OF US.
STAY STEADY!
AGGH!
CRAACKK
RAAGH!

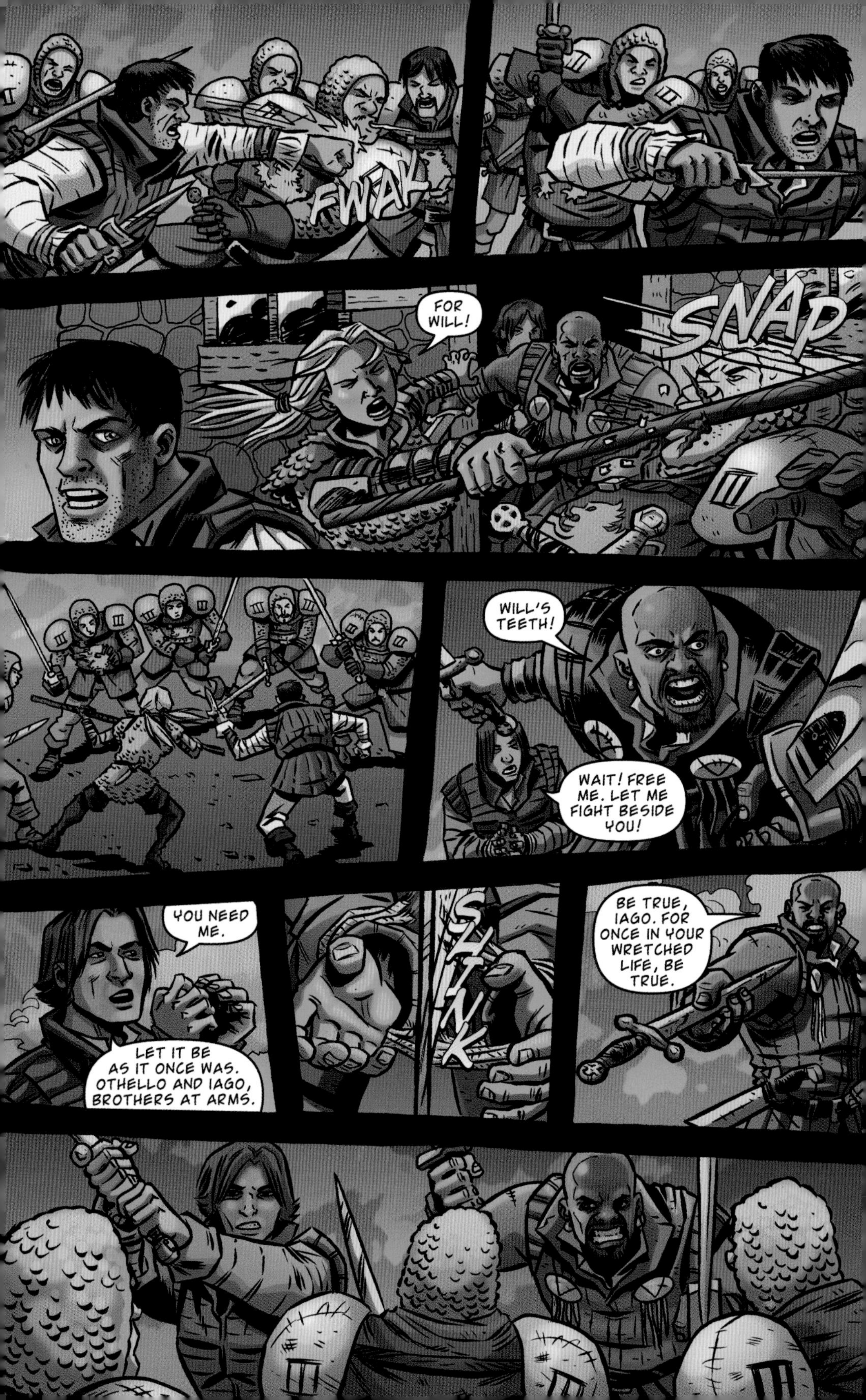
FWAK
FOR WILL!
SNAP
WILL'S TEETH!
WAIT! FREE ME. LET ME FIGHT BESIDE YOU!
YOU NEED ME.
LET IT BE AS IT ONCE WAS. OTHELLO AND IAGO, BROTHERS AT ARMS.
SHINK
BE TRUE, IAGO. FOR ONCE IN YOUR WRETCHED LIFE, BE TRUE.

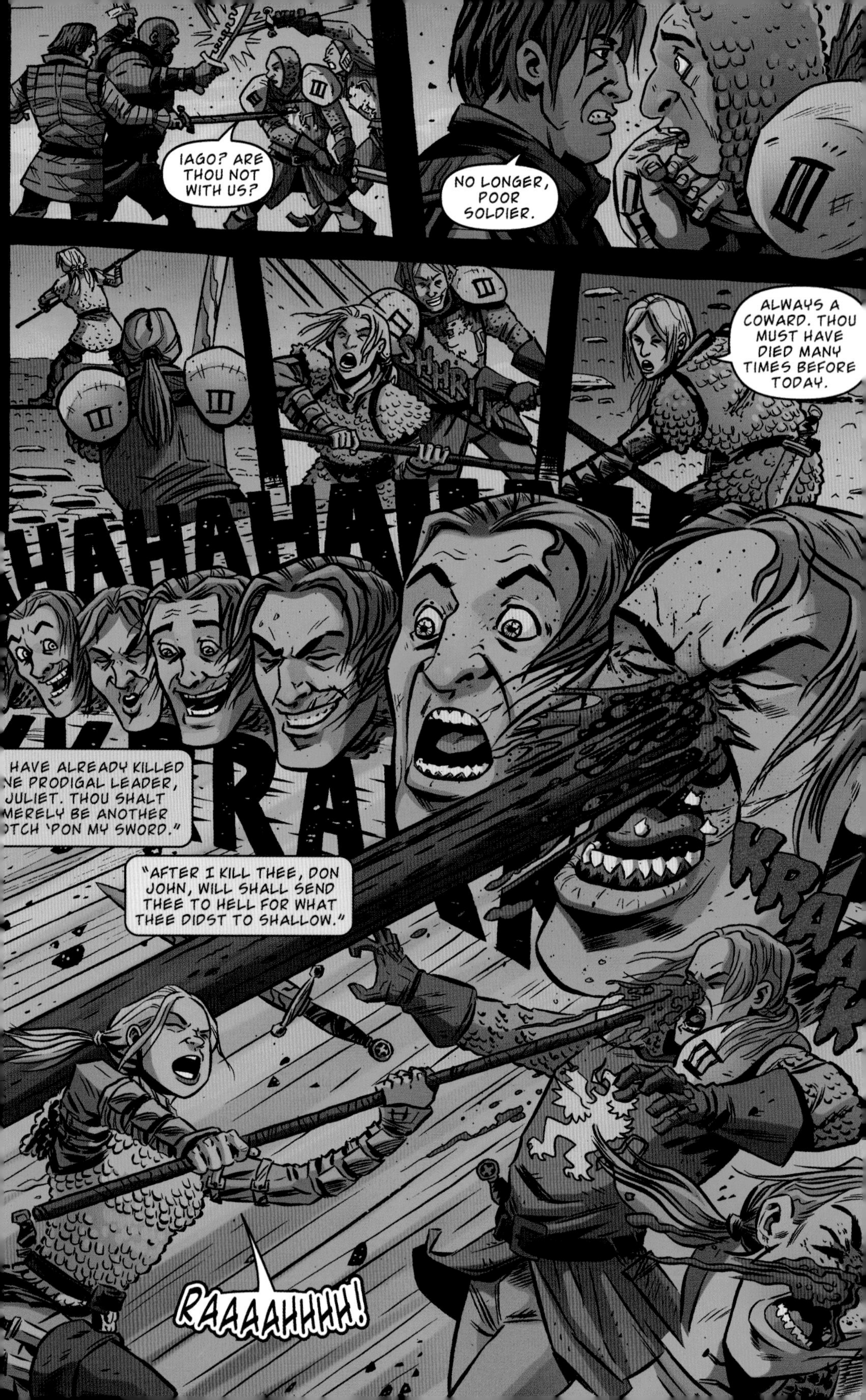
IAGO? ARE THOU NOT WITH US?
NO LONGER, POOR SOLDIER.
SHHRIK
ALWAYS A COWARD. THOU MUST HAVE DIED MANY TIMES BEFORE TODAY.
HAVE ALREADY KILLED NE PRODIGAL LEADER, JULIET. THOU SHALT MERELY BE ANOTHER OTCH 'PON MY SWORD."
"AFTER I KILL THEE, DON JOHN, WILL SHALL SEND THEE TO HELL FOR WHAT THEE DIDST TO SHALLOW."
RAAAAHHHH!

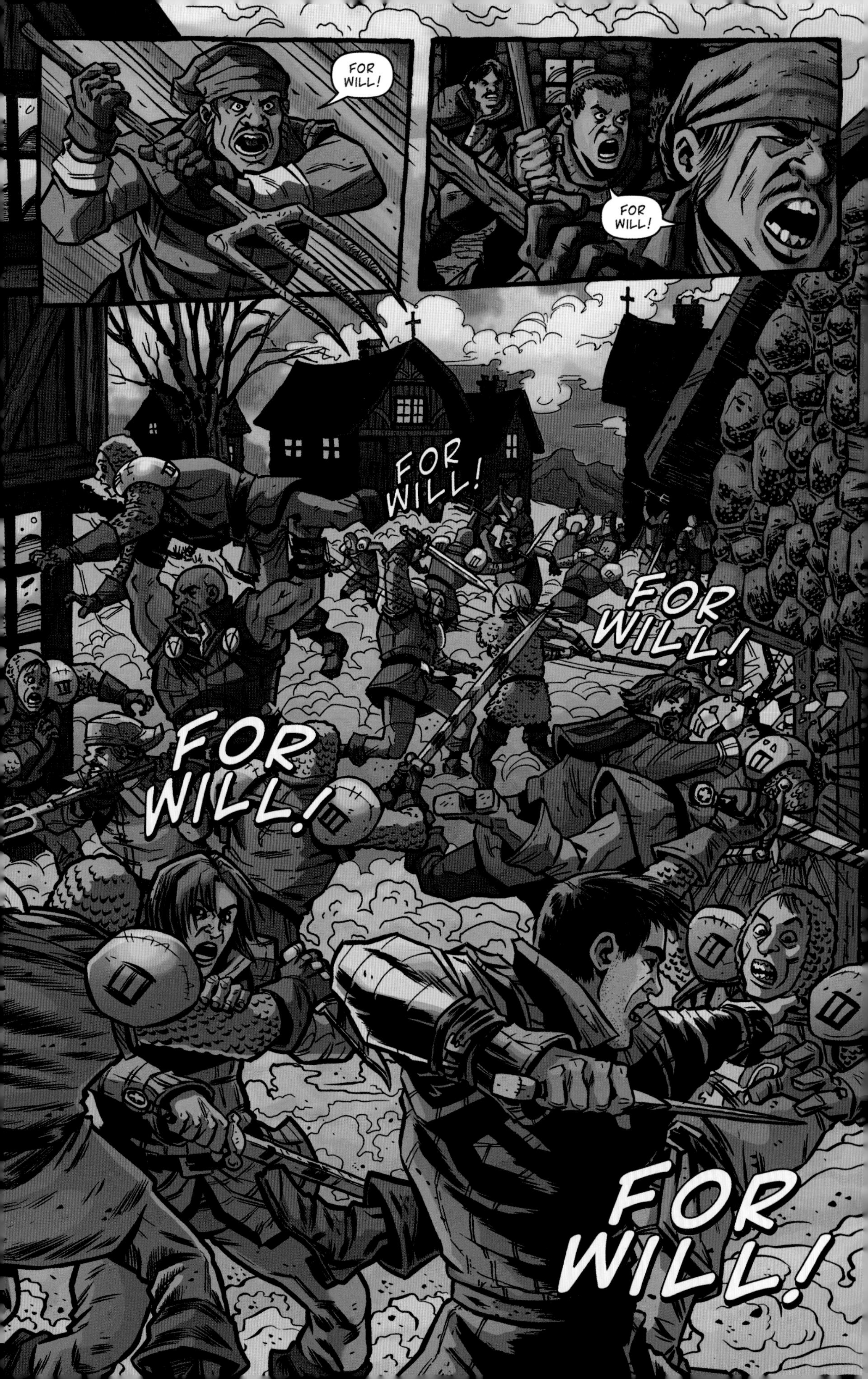
FOR WILL!
FOR WILL!
FOR WILL!
FOR WILL!
FOR WILL!
FOR WILL!

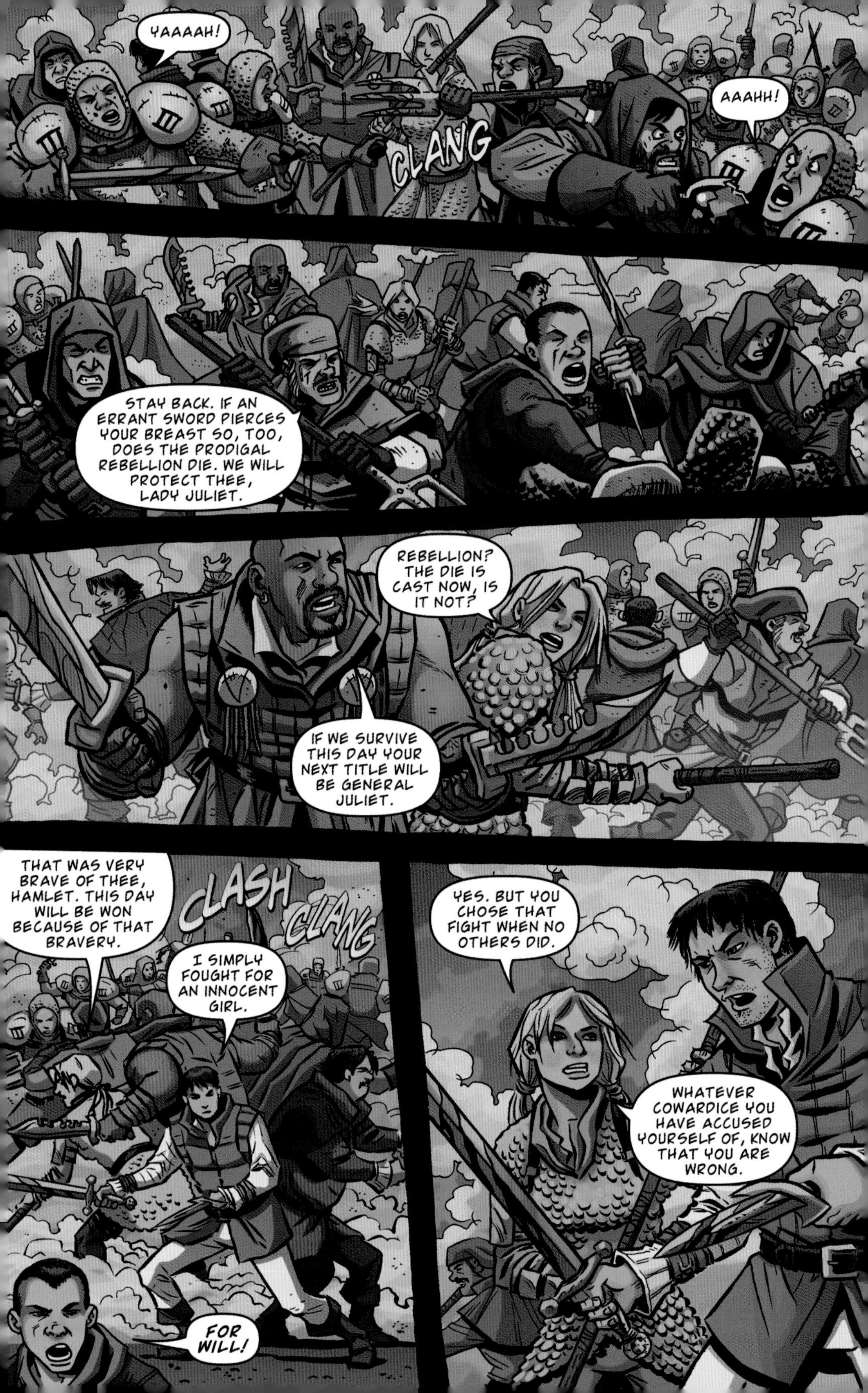
YAAAAH!
CLANG
AAAHH!
STAY BACK. IF AN ERRANT SWORD PIERCES YOUR BREAST SO, TOO, DOES THE PRODIGAL REBELLION DIE. WE WILL PROTECT THEE, LADY JULIET.
REBELLION? THE DIE IS CAST NOW, IS IT NOT?
IF WE SURVIVE THIS DAY YOUR NEXT TITLE WILL BE GENERAL JULIET.
THAT WAS VERY BRAVE OF THEE, HAMLET. THIS DAY WILL BE WON BECAUSE OF THAT BRAVERY.
CLASH
CLANG
I SIMPLY FOUGHT FOR AN INNOCENT GIRL.
FOR WILL!
YES. BUT YOU CHOSE THAT FIGHT WHEN NO OTHERS DID.
WHATEVER COWARDICE YOU HAVE ACCUSED YOURSELF OF, KNOW THAT YOU ARE WRONG.

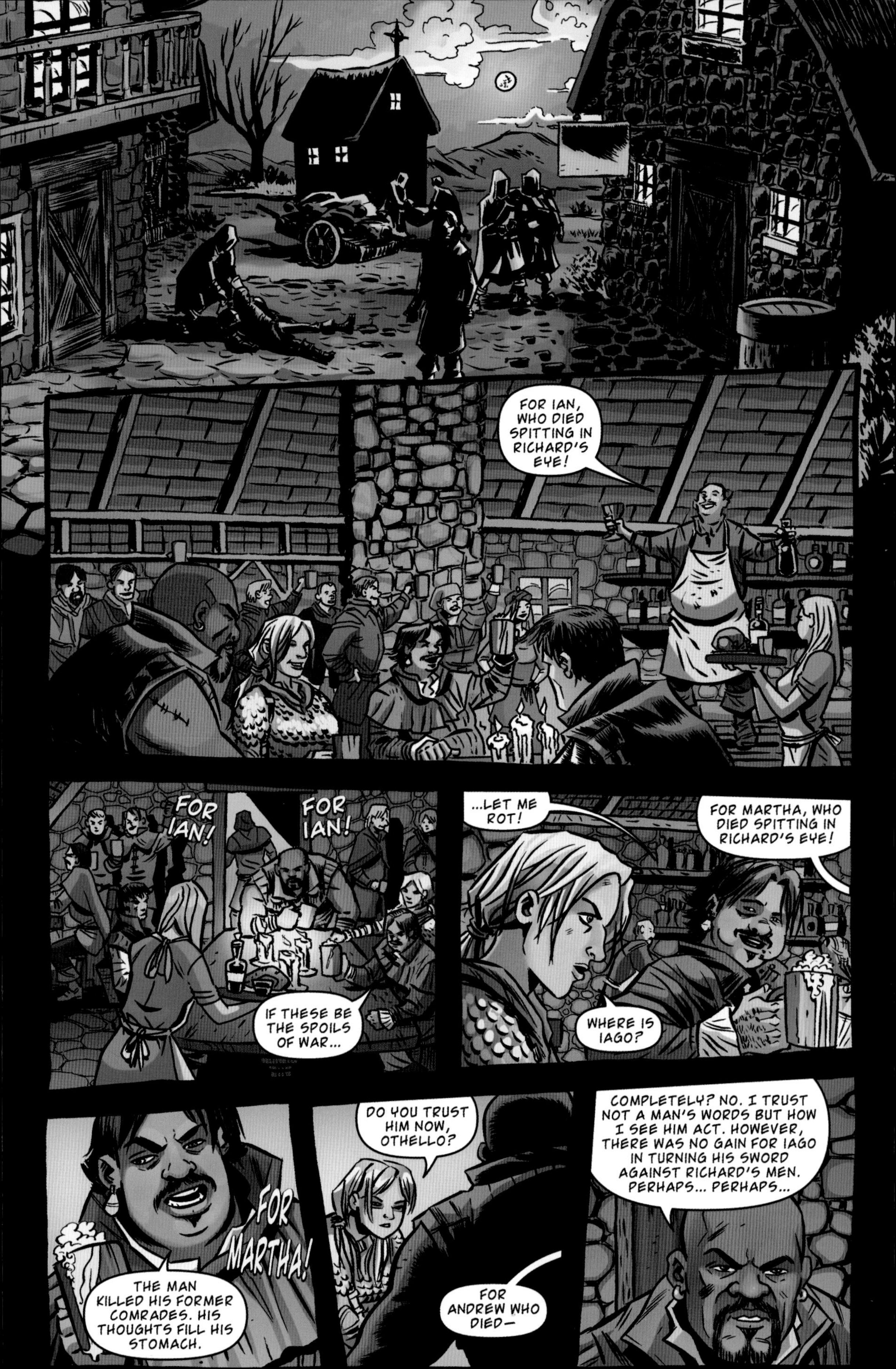
FOR IAN, WHO DIED SPITTING IN RICHARD'S EYE!
FOR IAN!
FOR IAN!
IF THESE BE THE SPOILS OF WAR...
...LET ME ROT!
FOR MARTHA, WHO DIED SPITTING IN RICHARD'S EYE!
WHERE IS IAGO?
FOR MARTHA!
THE MAN KILLED HIS FORMER COMRADES. HIS THOUGHTS FILL HIS STOMACH.
DO YOU TRUST HIM NOW, OTHELLO?
FOR ANDREW WHO DIED—
COMPLETELY? NO. I TRUST NOT A MAN'S WORDS BUT HOW I SEE HIM ACT. HOWEVER, THERE WAS NO GAIN FOR IAGO IN TURNING HIS SWORD AGAINST RICHARD'S MEN. PERHAPS... PERHAPS...

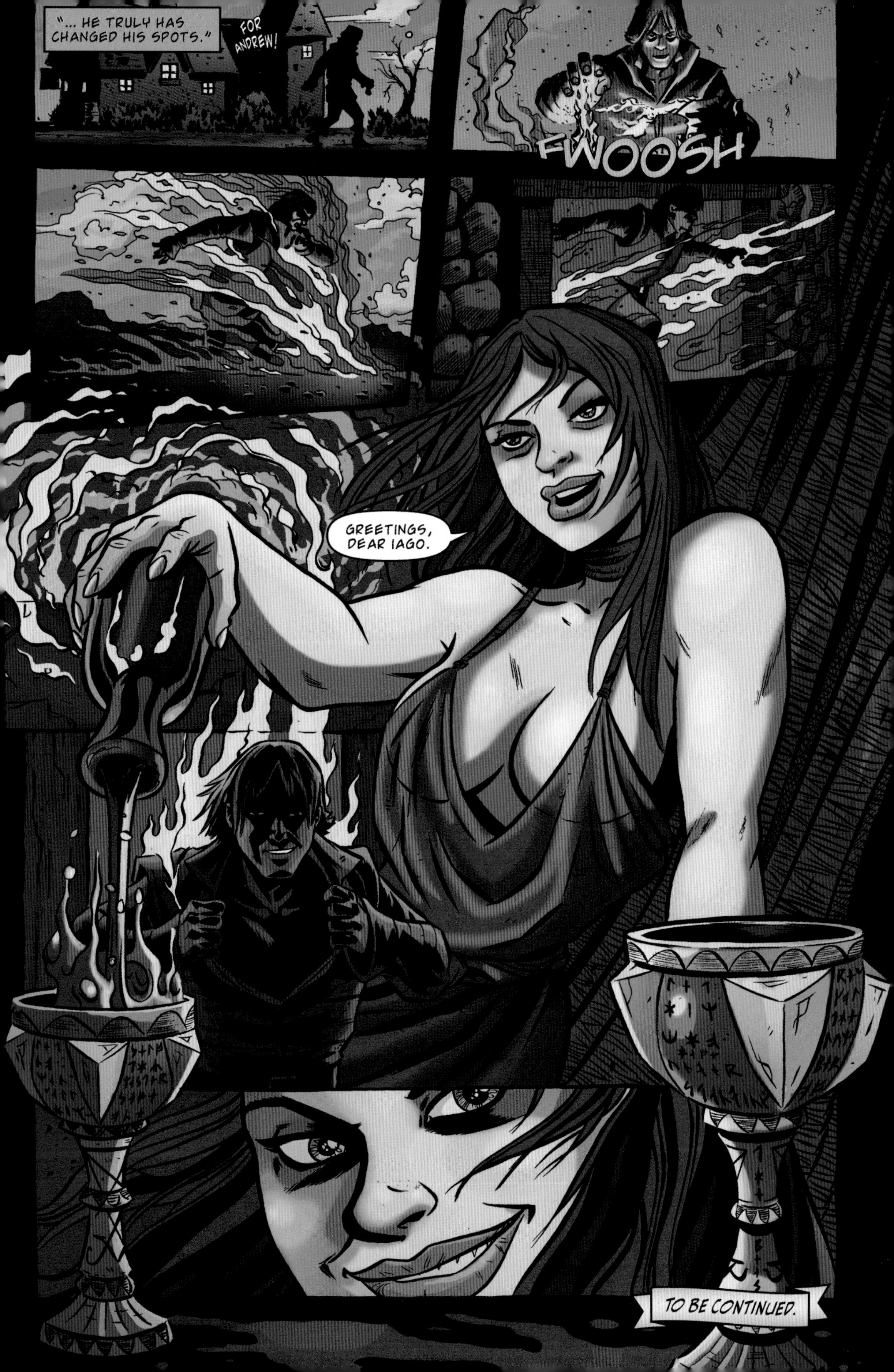
"... HE TRULY HAS CHANGED HIS SPOTS."
FOR ANDREW!
FWOOSH
GREETINGS, DEAR IAGO.
TO BE CONTINUED.

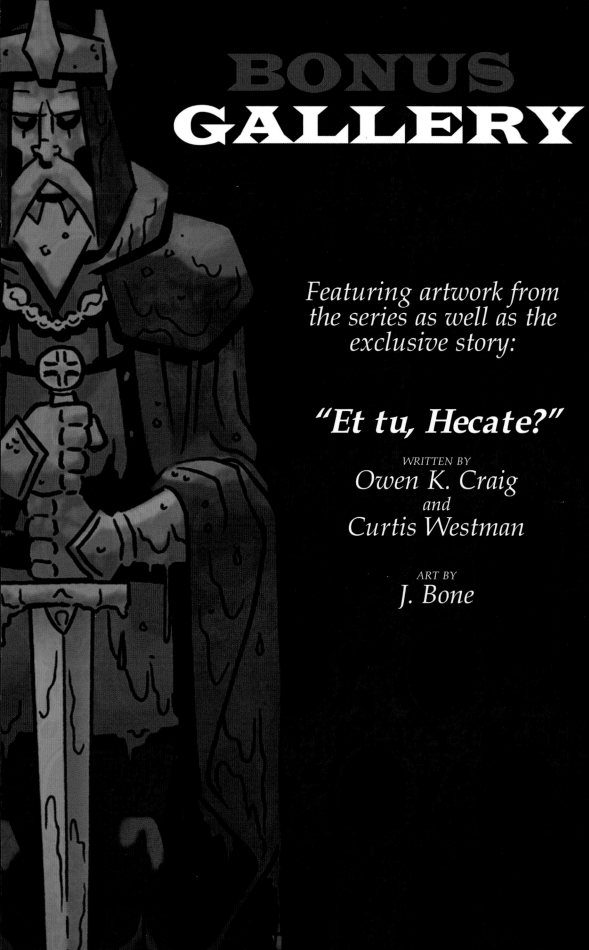

BONUS
GALLERY

Featuring artwork from the series as well as the exclusive story:

"Et tu, Hecate?"

WRITTEN BY
Owen K. Craig
and
Curtis Westman

ART BY
J. Bone

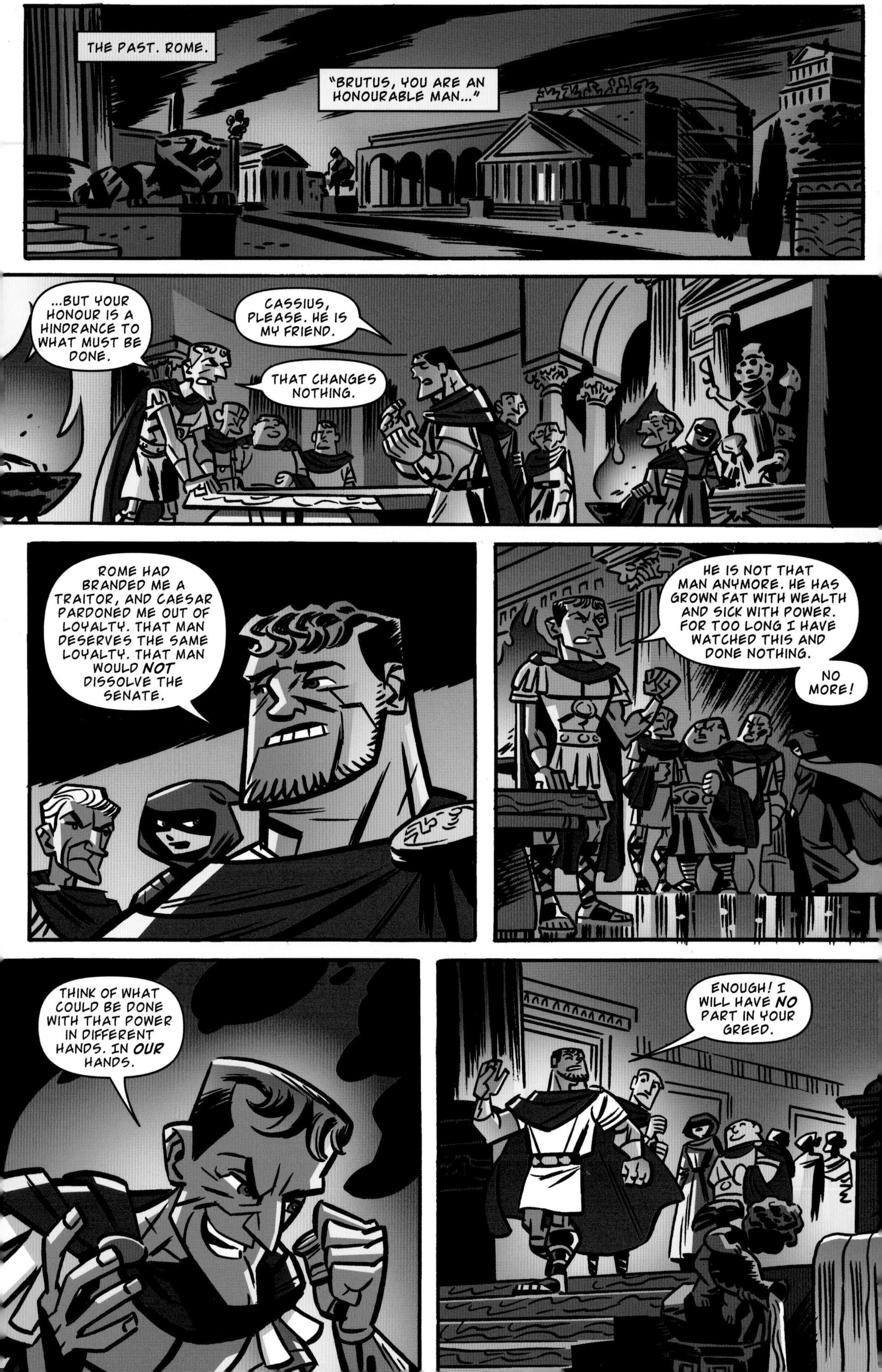
THE PAST. ROME.
"BRUTUS, YOU ARE AN HONOURABLE MAN..."
...BUT YOUR HONOUR IS A HINDRANCE TO WHAT MUST BE DONE.
CASSIUS, PLEASE. HE IS MY FRIEND.
THAT CHANGES NOTHING.
ROME HAD BRANDED ME A TRAITOR, AND CAESAR PARDONED ME OUT OF LOYALTY. THAT MAN DESERVES THE SAME LOYALTY. THAT MAN WOULD NOT DISSOLVE THE SENATE.
HE IS NOT THAT MAN ANYMORE. HE HAS GROWN FAT WITH WEALTH AND SICK WITH POWER. FOR TOO LONG I HAVE WATCHED THIS AND DONE NOTHING.
NO MORE!
THINK OF WHAT COULD BE DONE WITH THAT POWER IN DIFFERENT HANDS. IN OUR HANDS.
ENOUGH! I WILL HAVE NO PART IN YOUR GREED.

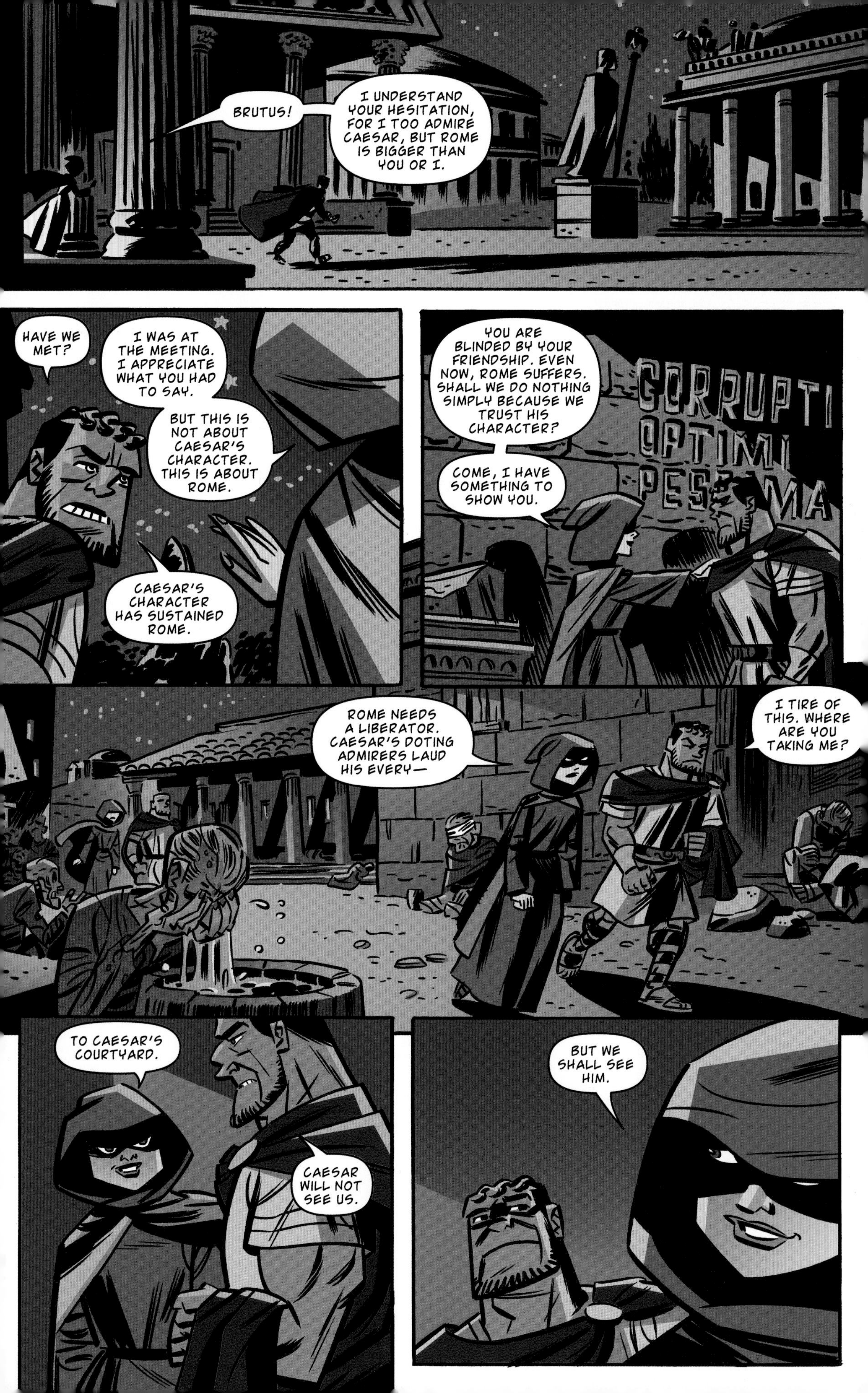
BRUTUS!
I UNDERSTAND YOUR HESITATION, FOR I TOO ADMIRE CAESAR, BUT ROME IS BIGGER THAN YOU OR I.
HAVE WE MET?
I WAS AT THE MEETING. I APPRECIATE WHAT YOU HAD TO SAY.
BUT THIS IS NOT ABOUT CAESAR'S CHARACTER. THIS IS ABOUT ROME.
CAESAR'S CHARACTER HAS SUSTAINED ROME.
YOU ARE BLINDED BY YOUR FRIENDSHIP. EVEN NOW, ROME SUFFERS. SHALL WE DO NOTHING SIMPLY BECAUSE WE TRUST HIS CHARACTER?
COME, I HAVE SOMETHING TO SHOW YOU.
ROME NEEDS A LIBERATOR. CAESAR'S DOTING ADMIRERS LAUD HIS EVERY—
I TIRE OF THIS. WHERE ARE YOU TAKING ME?
TO CAESAR'S COURTYARD.
CAESAR WILL NOT SEE US.
BUT WE SHALL SEE HIM.

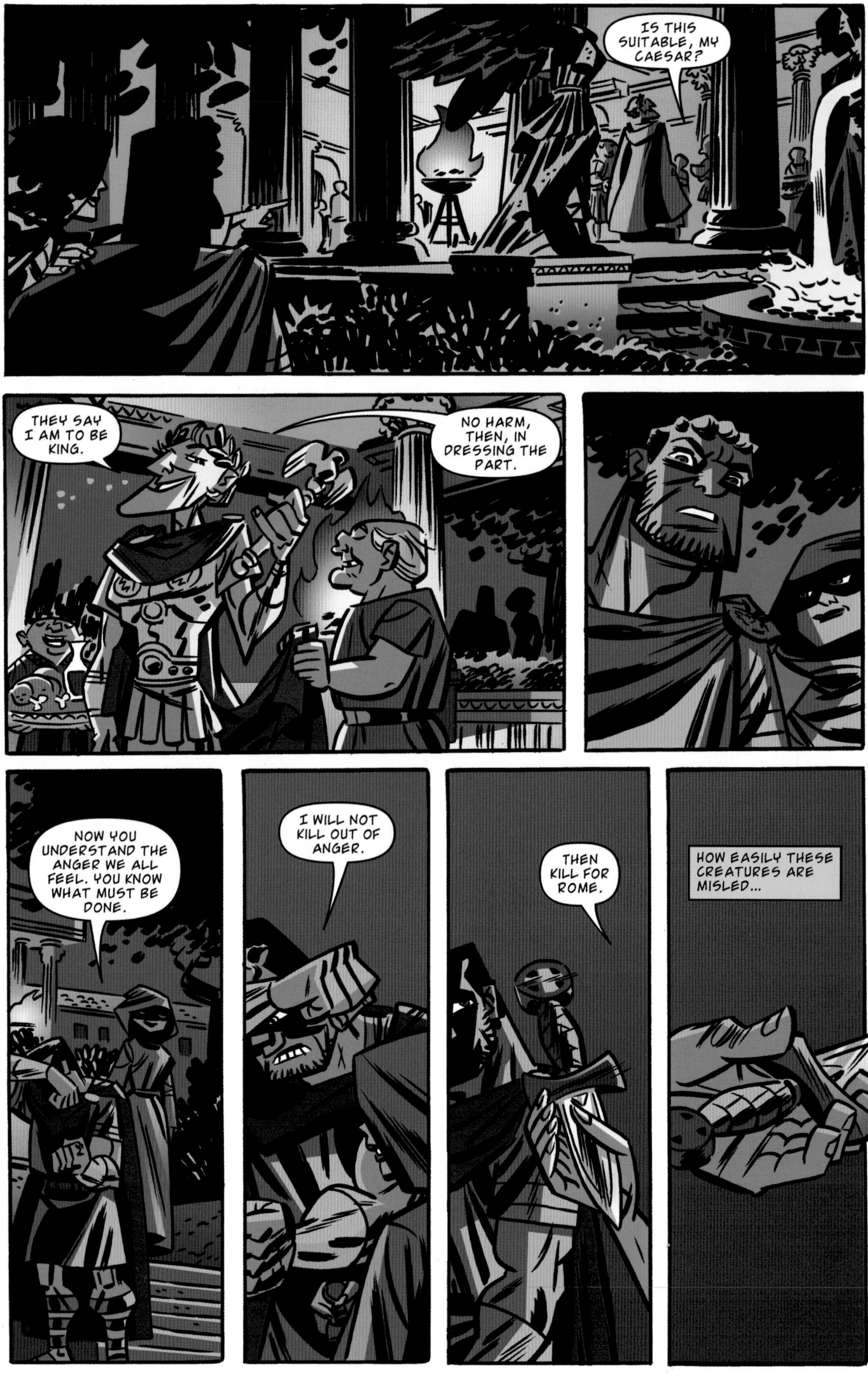
IS THIS SUITABLE, MY CAESAR?
THEY SAY I AM TO BE KING.
NO HARM, THEN, IN DRESSING THE PART.
NOW YOU UNDERSTAND THE ANGER WE ALL FEEL. YOU KNOW WHAT MUST BE DONE.
I WILL NOT KILL OUT OF ANGER.
THEN KILL FOR ROME.
HOW EASILY THESE CREATURES ARE MISLED...

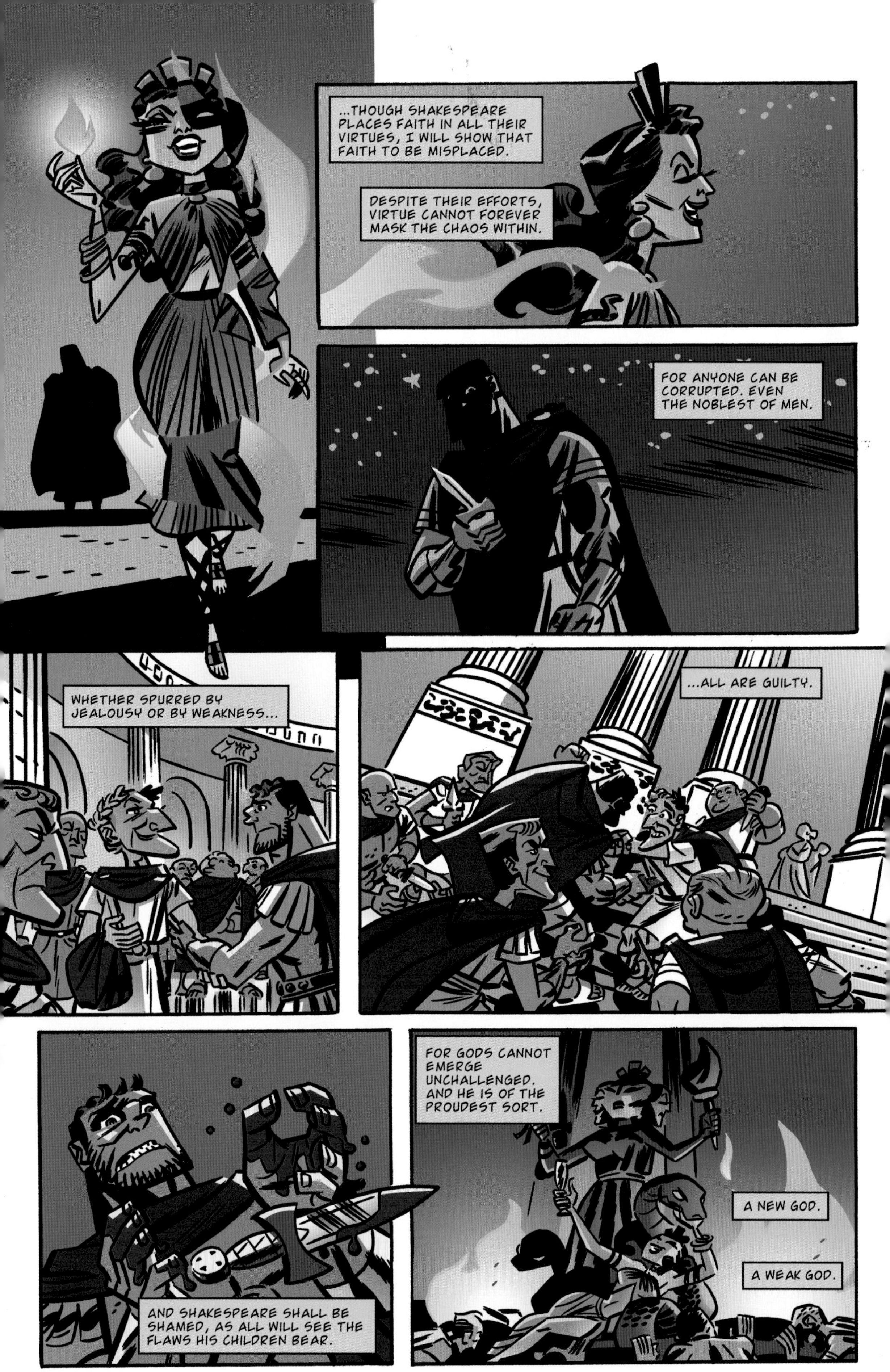
...THOUGH SHAKESPEARE PLACES FAITH IN ALL THEIR VIRTUES, I WILL SHOW THAT FAITH TO BE MISPLACED.
DESPITE THEIR EFFORTS, VIRTUE CANNOT FOREVER MASK THE CHAOS WITHIN.
FOR ANYONE CAN BE CORRUPTED. EVEN THE NOBLEST OF MEN.
WHETHER SPURRED BY JEALOUSY OR BY WEAKNESS...
...ALL ARE GUILTY.
AND SHAKESPEARE SHALL BE SHAMED, AS ALL WILL SEE THE FLAWS HIS CHILDREN BEAR.
FOR GODS CANNOT EMERGE UNCHALLENGED. AND HE IS OF THE PROUDEST SORT.
A NEW GOD.
A WEAK GOD.

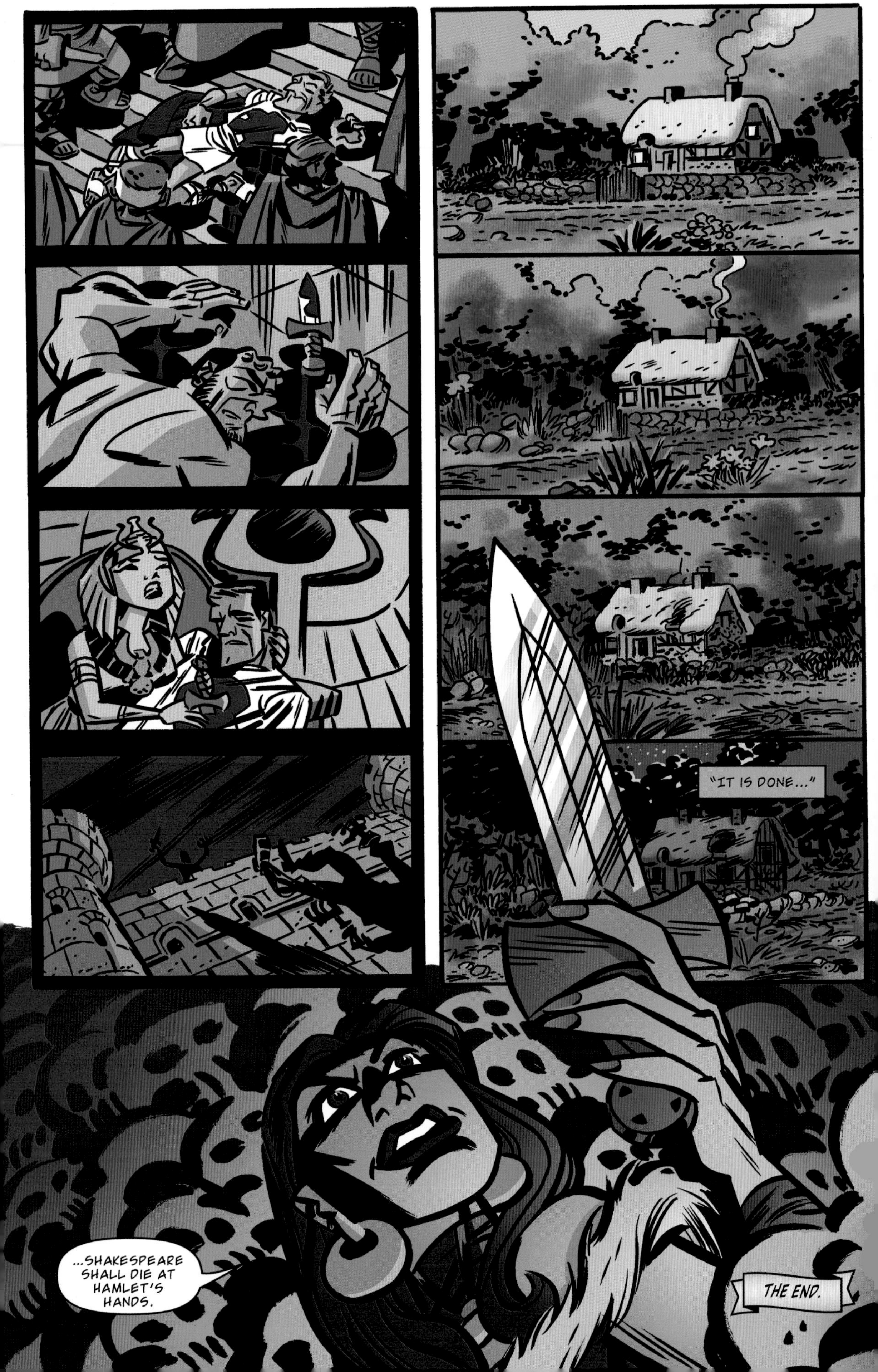
"IT IS DONE..."
...SHAKESPEARE SHALL DIE AT HAMLET'S HANDS.
THE END.

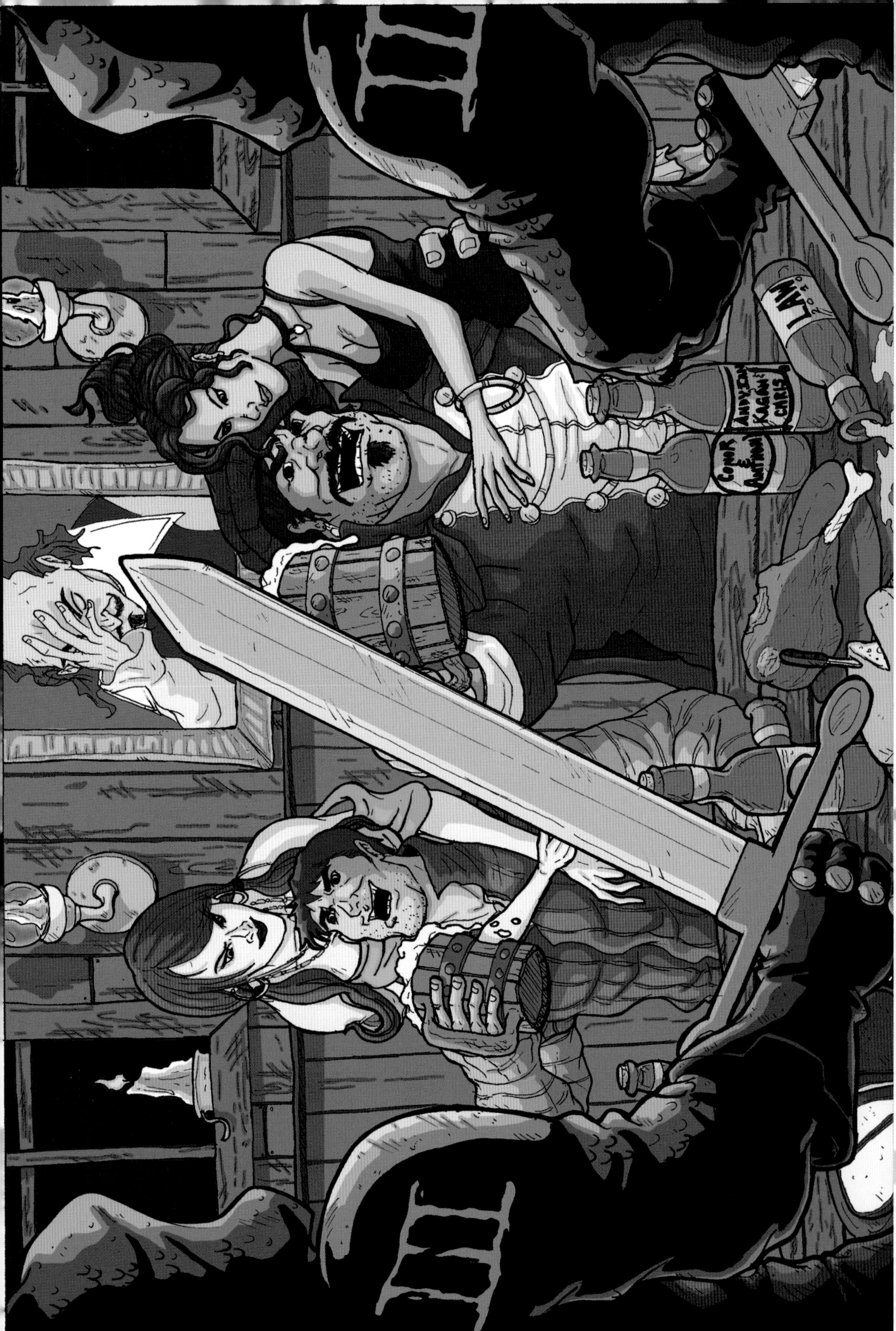

LAW
2010
ANDY, JOHN, KAGAN & CHRIS
CONOR & ANTHONY

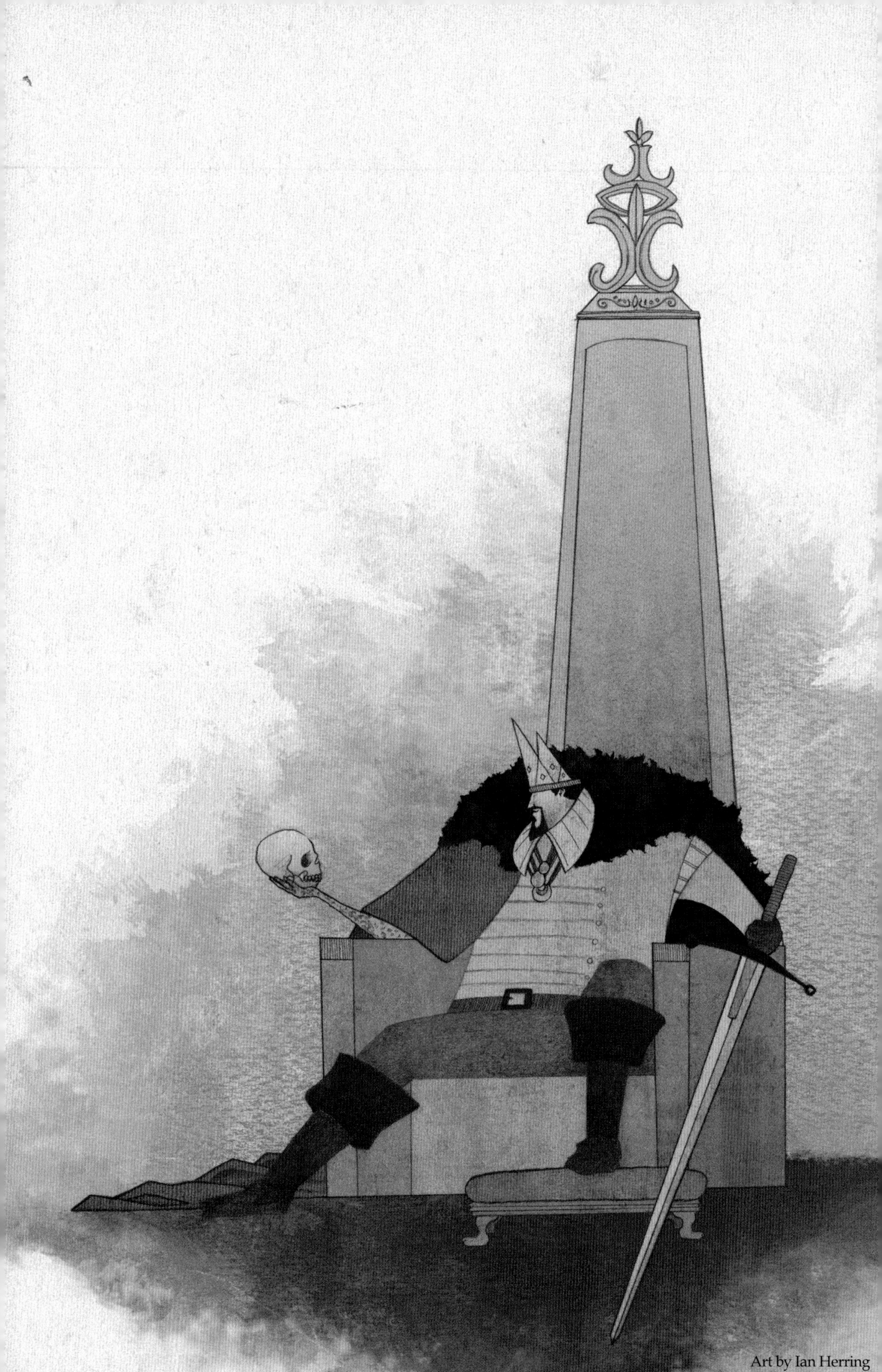

Art by Ian Herring

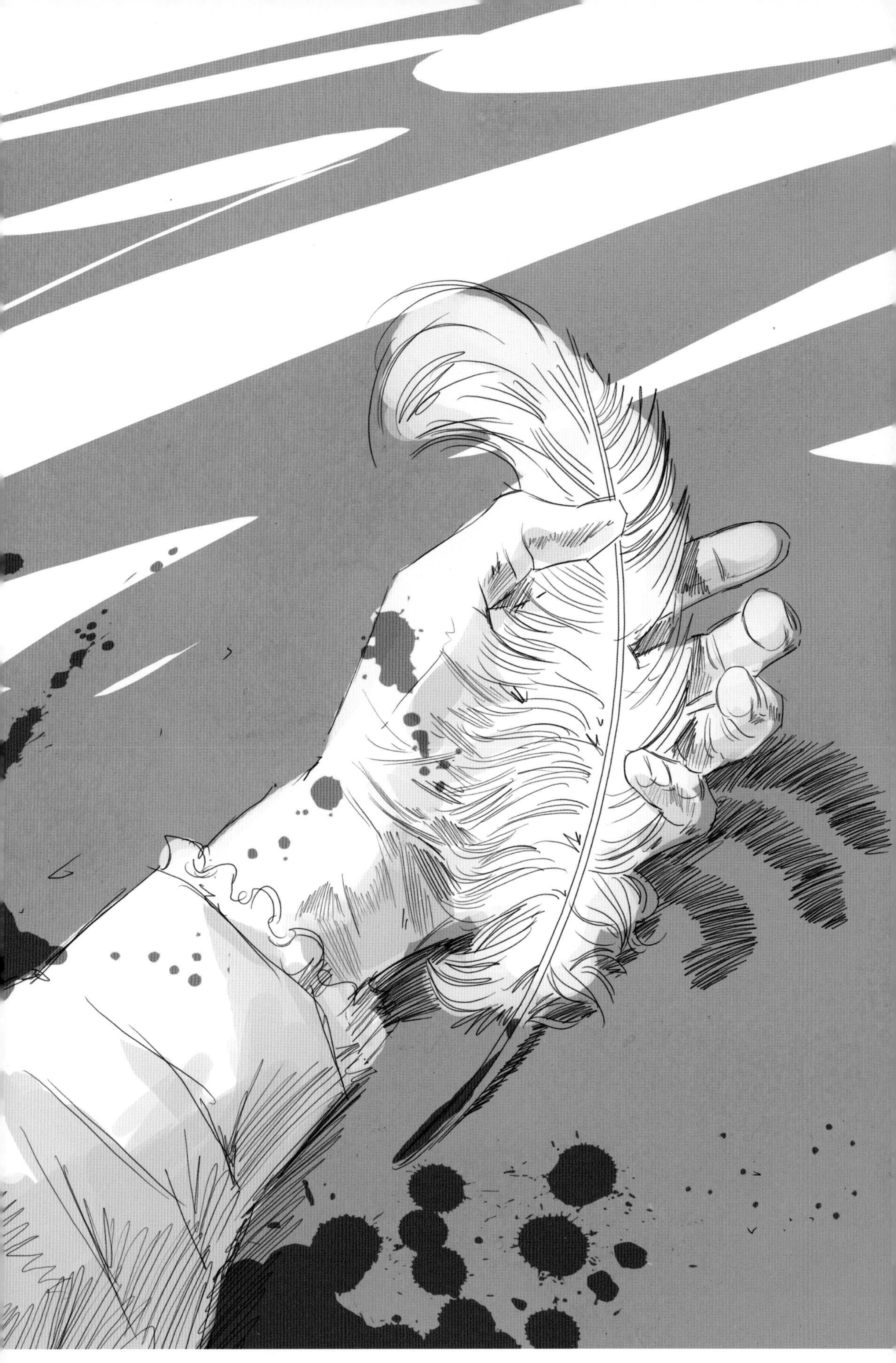

Cover #1 RI by Kagan McLeod

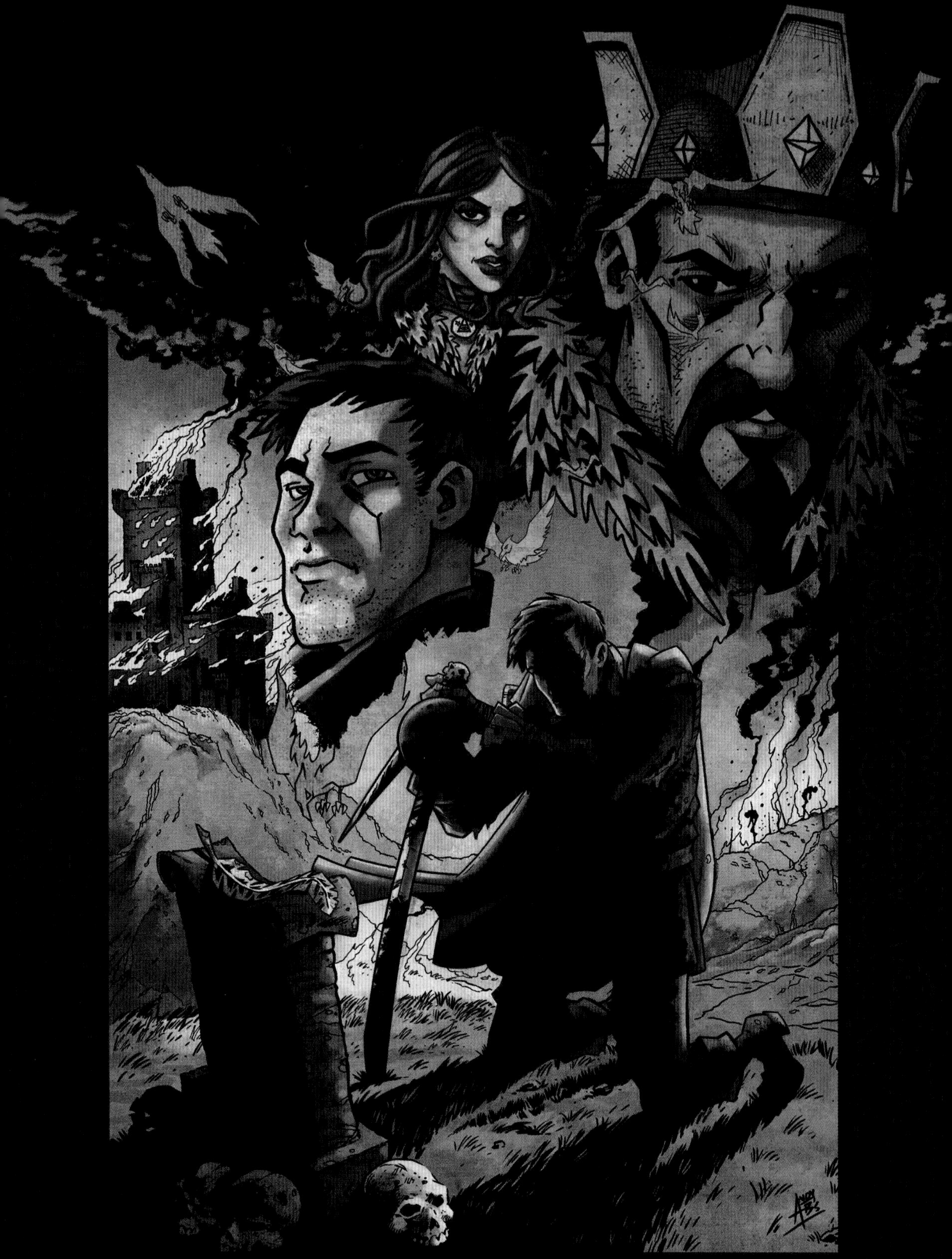

Cover #1B by Andy Belanger

Cover #2A by Kagan McLeod

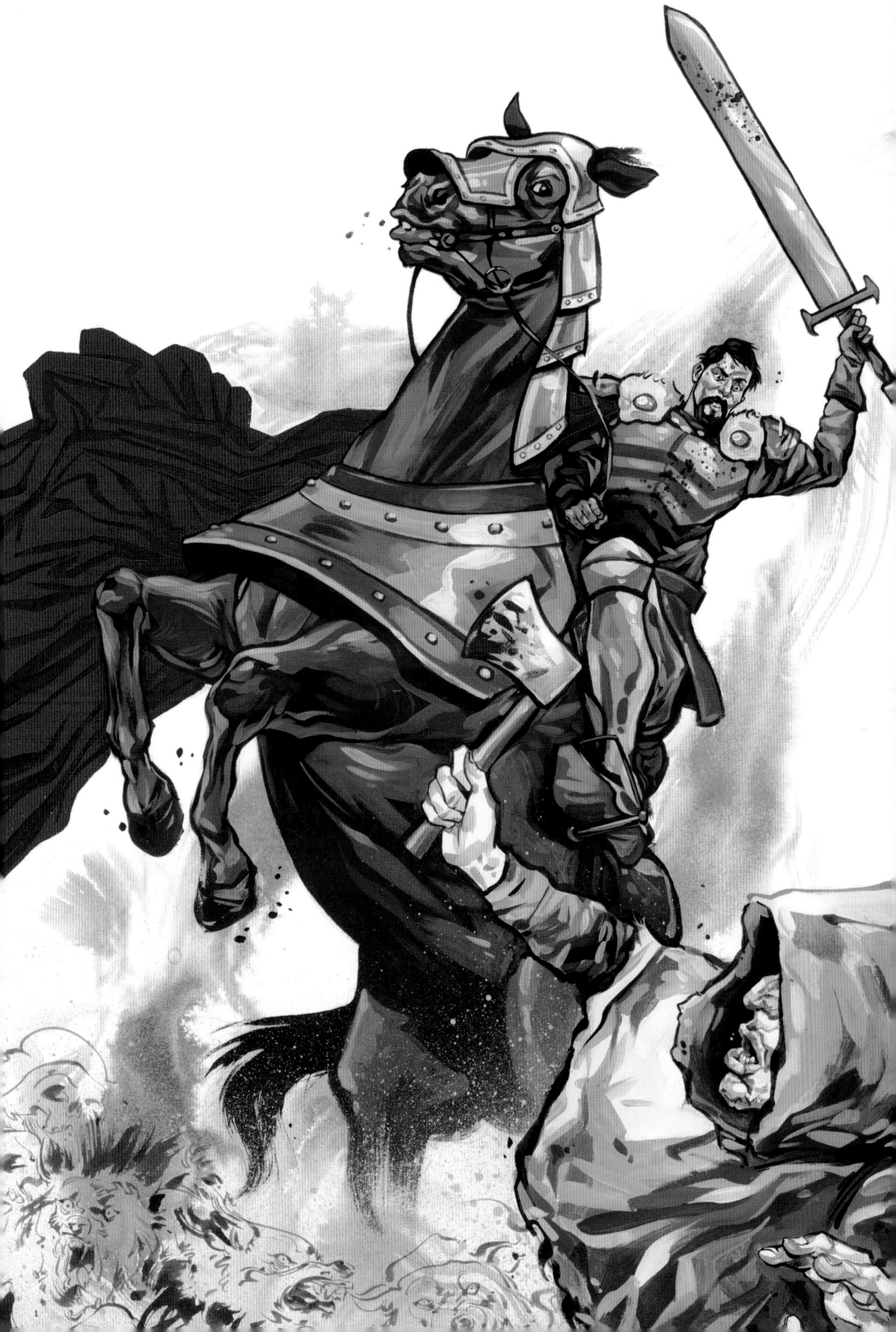

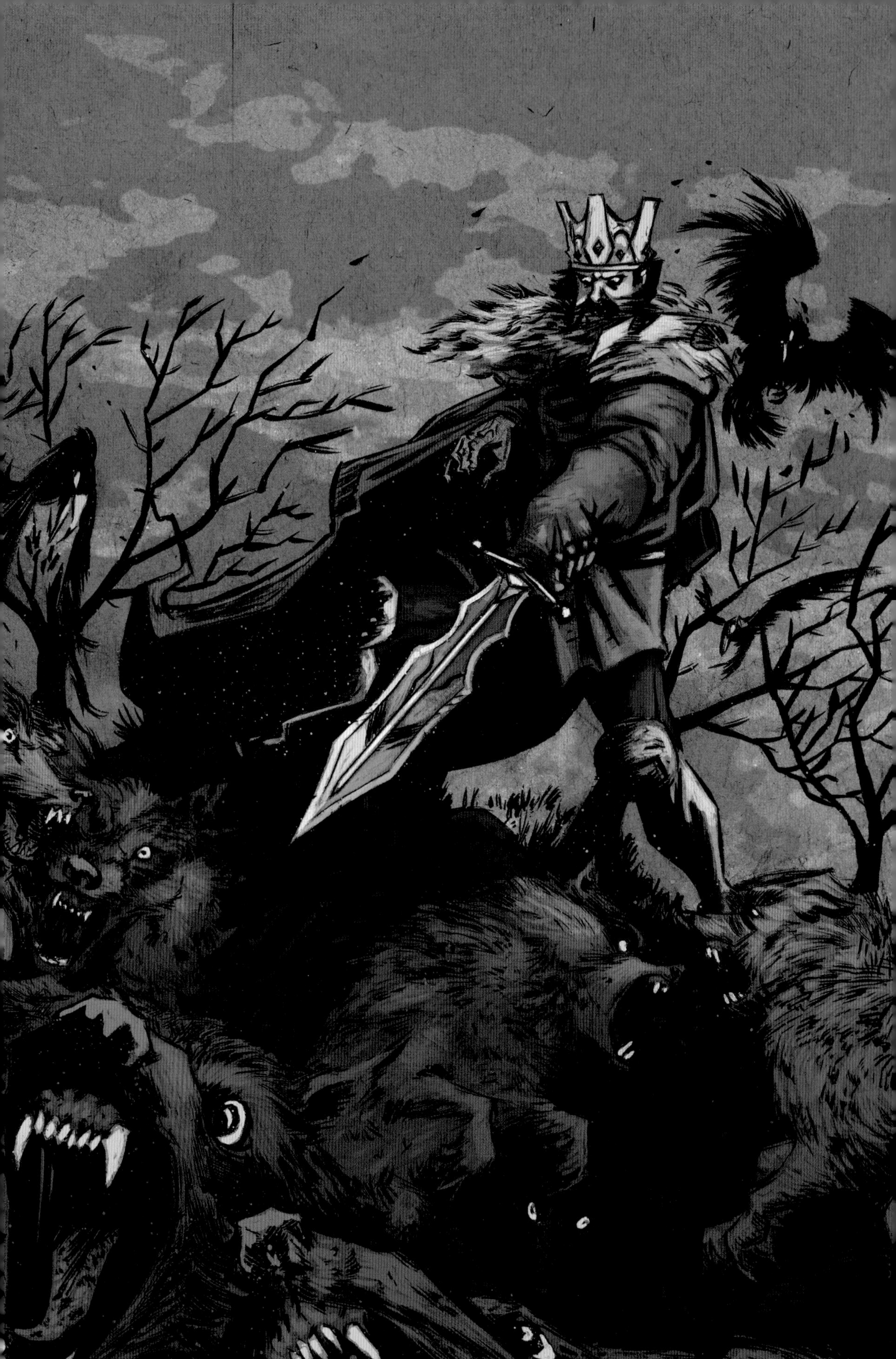

Cover #2B by Andy Belanger